Defending British India against Napoleon

WORLDS OF THE EAST INDIA COMPANY

ISSN 1752-5667

This series offers high-quality studies of the East India Company, drawn from across a broad chronological, geographical and thematic range. The rich history of the Company has long been of interest to those who engage in the study of Britain's commercial, imperial, maritime and military past, but in recent years it has also attracted considerable attention from those who explore art, cultural and social themes within an historical context. The series will thus provide a forum for scholars from different disciplinary backgrounds, and for those whose have interests in the history of Britain (London and the regions), India, China, Indonesia, as well as the seas and oceans.

The editors welcome submissions from both established scholars and those beginning their career; monographs are particularly encouraged but volumes of essays will also be considered. All submissions will receive rapid, informed attention. They should be sent in the first instance to:

Professor H. V. Bowen, Department of History and Classics, Swansea University, Swansea SA2 8PP

Previously published titles are listed at the back of this volume

DEFENDING BRITISH INDIA AGAINST NAPOLEON

The Foreign Policy of Governor-General
Lord Minto, 1807–13

Amita Das

Edited and updated by
Aditya Das

THE BOYDELL PRESS

First published 2016
The Boydell Press, Woodbridge

ISBN 978-1-78327-129-0

The Boydell Press is an imprint of Boydell & Brewer Ltd
PO Box 9, Woodbridge, Suffolk IP12 3DF, UK
and of Boydell & Brewer Inc.
668 Mt Hope Avenue, Rochester, NY 14620–2731, USA
website: www.boydellandbrewer.com

A CIP catalogue record for this title is available from the British Library

The publisher has no responsibility for the continued existence or accuracy of URLs for external or third-party internet websites referred to in this book, and does not guarantee that any content on such websites is, or will remain, accurate or appropriate

This publication is printed on acid-free paper

Typeset by Fakenham Prepress Solutions, Fakenham, Norfolk
NR21 8NN

DEDICATION

To the memory of my mother Dr Amita Das

CONTENTS

ILLUSTRATIONS

The editor, contributors and publishers are grateful to all the institutions
and persons listed for permission to reproduce the materials in which they
hold copyright. Every effort has been made to trace the copyright holders;
apologies are offered for any omission, and the publishers will be pleased to
add any necessary acknowledgement in subsequent editions.

PREFACE

This entirely original work, unpublished until today, was drawn mainly from the private papers of the first Earl of Minto in the National Library of Scotland, Edinburgh and were unavailable to the general reader until 1958. Additional references were taken from official records in the Raffles and Elphinstone Collections in the Commonwealth Relations Office Library (now British Library, India Office Records), London; the Foreign Office records and the Admiralty Papers in the Public Record Office, London; and John Malcolm's papers in the British Museums. The subtitle of this book is taken directly from the title of the doctoral thesis 'Lord Minto's Administration in India (1807–1813) with Special Reference to his Foreign Policy', written by Ms Amita Majumdar under the supervision of then Reader in Indian History at Oxford University, Cuthbert Collin Davies and submitted toward fulfilling the requirements for a DPhil degree earned in October 1962.

The author passed away in January 2014 and in tribute to her memory and to get this important work out in the public domain, I presented a proposal outline to Boydell and Brewer. Following extensive discussions with Peter Sowden and input from Professor Huw Bowen at Swansea University, it was decided to extend and update the work for publication using a framework of defence of the British Empire against the threat of Napoleon as the basis for Minto's foreign policy. This would accomplish two primary objectives: i) emphasising a strategic and economic scope of the establishment and jockeying for power of British and French colonial influence in a global context; and ii) updating the work to include current scholarship and new perspectives and opinions which enhance and serve to interpret the thoughts and actions of Lord Minto and the East India Company. Contemporary publications of tracts, periodicals, biographies, published memoirs and correspondence have been valuable sources of information. Full lists of the primary and secondary sources used in this book are listed in the Bibliography and as footnotes where applicable in each chapter.

The story begins with a preamble bracketing the political and economic situations faced by the East India Company including the victory of Robert Clive at the Battle of Plassey and the award of the Diwani of Bengal by Emperor Shah Alam that set in motion both expansion and increasing expenditure on the part of the East India Company, defining imperial strategy throughout Asia. Perspectives provided by recent works such as Anthony Webster's *The Twilight of the East India Company* (2009) and Huw Bowen's *The Business of Empire: The East India Company and Imperial Britain* (2006) show how the strategic interests and financial constraints of the Directors of the East India Company, coupled with political outcomes, for example, the establishment of the government of William Pitt the Younger in 1784, allowed the creation of a Board of Control. Minto's period of office coincided with the last years of the Napoleonic Wars in Europe, and their inevitable repercussions in the colonial sphere clearly influenced the shaping of Minto's foreign policy on all fronts. Napoleon's treaty with Russia at Tilsit (July 1807), the treaty of Finkenstein (May 1807) with Persia, and the predominance of French influence in Turkey and Persia, created an alarm for the security of British interests in India. Iradj Amini's *Napoleon and Persia* (1999) shows the intricate diplomatic moves between the French, Persians and Russians including Napoleon's promise to the Shah to liberate his Caucasian possessions in Georgia from Russian occupation. Napoleon's failure in Spain and the sacrifice of Persian interests following a peace treaty with the Tsar at Tilsit in July 1807 resulted in the British eventually being able to establish their influence and dislodge the French in Persia.

Under Minto's direction, diplomatic relations were opened for the first time with the Amir of Kabul in 1808–09. The treaty concluded with Shah Shuja (April 1809) couldn't be enforced as the Afghan ruler lost his throne before the British envoy Mountstuart Elphinstone reached Delhi. Minto's policy toward Sind was more open to direct diplomatic communications with the Amirs of Sind than to form any specific defensive treaty with them. Minto's settlement with the Sikhs was certainly a departure from the policy of non-interference pursued by his predecessor Sir George Barlow and largely influenced by his mentor Burke's doctrine of trusteeship. The diplomatic mission to Ranjit Singh of Lahore was originally sent in order to negotiate an anti-French defensive treaty. However, the original purpose of the mission was shortly afterward replaced by the question of mutual frontiers. The relatively small Sikh and Pathan states in the area between the Yamuna and Sutlej Rivers were taken under British protection. A treaty was concluded with Ranjit Singh (April 1809) which confined his power to the right bank of the Sutlej. A British military post was established at Ludhiana, all of which served to build a buffer zone between Persia and the frontiers of the British Empire in India against a possible French overland invasion.

The main aims of Minto's foreign policy were the defence of the Company's trade and territories in India, and the expulsion of the French from the neighbouring states of Asia and the Indian Ocean. Patrick Crowhurst's *The French War on Trade: Privateering 1793–1815* (1989) details how Napoleon's Berlin Decree of 21 November 1806 and the first Milan Decree eventually resulted in isolating the French from free trade owing to a counter British naval blockade virtually closing the ports on the Atlantic coast, thus isolating them from markets in Northern Europe and restricting the supply of French imports of cotton and cotton thread. In 1806, French merchants were also disconnected from Central Europe due to Napoleon's military campaigns. French privateers operating from the Indian Ocean islands of L'Ile de France, Bourbon and Rodriguez had severely impacted British merchant shipping to the tune of £3,000,000 between 1793 and 1796 and the importance of the islands as outposts of strategic importance to the French in a potential invasion of India was undeniable. It was therefore imperative for Minto to consider British occupation of these islands, not only to protect merchant shipping, but also to lay the foundation for the invasion and occupation of Java to protect trade routes to China by preventing French reinforcement and interference.

Minto's policy with regard to the other European powers in the East was regulated by their relations with France. In January 1808, Portuguese and Danish settlements in India were captured. The annexation of Holland by France brought the Dutch East Indies under French control. Minto therefore planned to occupy the Dutch East Indies by sending an expedition from India. His motive was basically to protect the Company's China trade, for it was feared that under stricter French control, Java might become another centre of sanctioned piracy. However, he did not intend the occupation of the Dutch East Indies to be temporary. He aimed at its permanent annexation to the Company's possessions in India. The value he attached to Java is shown by the fact that he personally accompanied the expedition in order to settle the civil administration of the newly conquered territories. He urged the permanent retention of Java as a British colony to the home authorities. Exports from Java were mainly coffee, sugar, arrack grain and tobacco, while imports were opium, piece goods and other sundry articles. Minto visualised an expansion of the Company's markets in the East Indies and the trans-ference of the Dutch trade with Japan to the Company was also an important point of consideration. The Ministers were however opposed to colonial expansion and the Court of Directors inclined to regard more territories as a threat to their profits. The Dutch East Indies were therefore restored to Holland at the end of the war.

Minto's relations with the home authorities were not happy. He found little support, encouragement or appreciation from Britain. His recall has been associated with the army troubles in Madras which broke out in 1809 and whose aftermath extended to the end of 1812. Minto was recalled a year before he intended resigning office for no other reason than to make room for a personal friend of the Prince Regent, Lord Moira. However, it is clear that the foundation of ideas relating to a network of buffer states and spheres of influence around a primary core as a 'protective rind', and that of a gradual decentralisation of power via formal and informal trading houses operating according to their own skill-sets and specialisation to create global connectivity and facilitate free trade, were first evaluated and outlined by Gilbert Elliot-Murray-Kynynmound, the first Earl of Minto.

The author in her own words:

> I owe a debt of gratitude to Dr C.C. Davies, Reader in Indian History at Oxford University, for his unfailing encouragement, helpful criticism and guidance during the preparation of this thesis. I am extremely grateful to Mrs V. Mazumdar and Mr B. De for their valuable advice and criticism of my work; to Miss C. Gowan and Mr P.K. Das for helping me to read the French works; and to Mrs V. Mazumdar, Mr and Mrs T. Bose and Miss V. Moore for reading the typescript and assisting me generously in making the corrections. I would like to thank the staff of the libraries in London, Edinburgh and Oxford in which I have worked, for their cordial cooperation. The generosity of my father (Mr J. M. Majumdar) and a grant from the Commonwealth Scholarship Commission in the United Kingdom have enabled me to do this research.

It is a rare privilege and a great honour for me to have been given the opportunity to update and provide a perspective to this unique and original work. I am deeply grateful for the consideration, guidance and support I have received from Peter Sowden (Series Editor) and Profesor Huw Bowen (founding editor of the research monograph series 'The Worlds of the East India Company') at Boydell and Brewer. Their vision and belief in the value of this book has allowed me to bring it to a global readership.

Grateful thanks are also extended to Professor Sabyasachi Bhattacharya (former Tagore National Fellow, Ministry of Culture, Government of India and Vice-Chancellor, Visva-Bharati University, Shantiniketan), Professor Michael Dockrill (Emeritus Professor, Department of War Studies, King's College, University of London), Professor Stanley Wolpert (Emeritus Professor, Center for India and South Asia, UCLA) for their support, encouragement and regular feedback on reading the early drafts. Above all, I am indebted to my parents Amita and Pradip Das for their love, affection, inspiration and an encouragement of scholarship in a spirit of inquiry and analysis, a foundation that I believe has led to a deep interest and enthusiasm for learning. The support, affection and faith expressed by my family, particularly my wife Ashidhara and our sons Anirban and Ayan, my brother Pramit, sister-in-law, Shatabdi and my nieces Sharmila and Onjoli, have also been instrumental in bringing out this book as it is certainly intended as a legacy for them.

ABBREVIATIONS

Add. MSS.	Additional Manuscripts
Adm.	Admiralty Records
App. Court Minutes	Appellate Court Minutes
Asiatic Ann. Reg.	Asiatic Annual Register
Ben. Sec. Cons.	Bengal Secret Consultations
Ben. Pol. Cons.	Bengal Political Consultations
Ben. Sec. & Pol. Cons.	Bengal Secret and Political Consultations
Ben. Sec. & Sep. Cons.	Bengal Secret and Separate Consultations
Ben. Sec. Letters	Bengal Secret Letters
BL	British Library
BL, IOR	British Library, India Office Records
Bodl.	Bodleian Library
Corr. Pol. Perse	French Political Correspondence related to Persia
E.I. Accounts	East India Accounts
Fac. Rec.	Factory Records
FO	Foreign Office
HM	His Majesty
Hist. MSS. Comm.	Historical Manuscript Commission
Hist. MSS. Comm. Fortescue	Historical Manuscript Commission (Documents of Fortescue, J.B.)
Home Misc. Series	Home Miscellaneous Series
M.	Minto Papers
NLS	National Library of Scotland
NLS M	National Library of Scotland, Minto Papers
NY	New York
PGR	Punjab Government Record
TNA	The National Archives
Raff. Col.	Raffles Collection

One

SETTING THE STAGE

Preamble

Founded in London in 1600 as a monopolistic joint stock venture to engage in speculative trade with India and the Far East, the East India Company struggled through its first 150 years of existence. The effects of the civil war in the 1640s and the disintegration of the Mughal Empire from the early eighteenth century onward, beginning with the death of Aurangzeb in 1707, caused major problems of stability and a reorientation from a commercial trading organisation to a military focus. The turning point was the Battle of Plassey in 1757 when hostilities with Siraj-ud-Daula, Nawab of Bengal prompted the annexation of the province by the Company. The process of expansion and resultant military expeditions caused recurrent financial strain, forcing the Company to solicit the help of the British state, which although forthcoming, resulted in greater government control over the organisation.[1]

A major breakthrough occurred in 1765, when Robert Clive accepted on behalf of the Company, the Bengal *diwani* (right to collect revenues) from the emperor Shah Alam II. This modus operandi was also followed in other areas, with alliances being established on the basis of military protection in return for the rights for revenue collection. However, this resulted in a cycle of increasing expenditure as new commitments and expansions pushed up costs.

At the time of acquisition of the Bengal *diwani* the mood in London and Calcutta suggested that Indian revenues could alone finance further expansion of the Company's trade, particularly with regard to the purchase of tea from China. However, the Company was unable to manage its new political and military role, combined with uncontrolled private trading of its employees. Specifically, Company bills of exchange were transmitted back toward proceeds of their private adventures and this precipitated

[1] Lawson, P., *The East India Company: A History* (London, 1993). Webster, A., *The Twilight of the East India Company: The Evolution of Anglo-Asian Commerce and Politics 1790–1860* (Woodbridge, 2009).

a severe financial crisis in 1771. In that year the costs of the Company's militarism, declining sales of Indian produce in London and a sudden rise in reimbursement expenses on the excessive bills issued on behalf of Company employees and dividends to shareholders all resulted in undermining the Company's liquidity.[2]

The Company was forced to seek emergency assistance from the Government, which was forthcoming under Lord North's Regulating Act of 1773, but at a price. Although the Company received a loan of £1.4 million, the Government imposed a regime of Cabinet supervision of its affairs. A new system of government was created for India, comprising the governor-general and his council of four who were to be jointly appointed and answerable to the British Government and the Company's Court of Directors.[3] Other reforms included a rotation system for elections for the directorate under which a quarter came up for election each year rather than all being subject to annual elections. Voting rights for the largest shareholders were amended to include greater control especially on payout of unreasonably large dividends and created a stable political environment.[4] The Fox-North coalition governed Britain in 1783 and owing to the problems incurred by the East India Company Fox proposed nationalising it, providing the Government with direct control of appointments. The East India Bill was passed in the House of Commons, but King George III was deeply opposed and informed that House of Lords that any peer who voted for the Bill would be regarded as an enemy. The Bill was defeated in December 1783 and the king immediately dismissed the coalition. In March 1784, a general election was held following which a government was formed by William Pitt the Younger. The East India Company Act of 1784 (also known as the Pitt's India Act of 1784) sought to address the shortcomings of the Regulatory Act of 1773 by bringing the East India Company's Administration in India under the control of the British Government. Pitt's India Act provided for a Board of Control and provided for joint government of British India by both the Company and the Crown with the Government holding ultimate responsibility.

On 15 July 1785, Dundas wrote to the Chairmen pointing out that any far reaching reform of the Company must include a financial reorganisation. On Dundas's suggestion, the Directors agreed to set up in each Presidency standard, reduced establishments, which were to be unaltered without clear sanction from the home government. The debts of the Company in India in November 1784 had been estimated at approximately £8,000,000. The

2   Bowen, H.V., *The Business of Empire: The East India Company and Imperial Britain, 1756–1833* (Cambridge, 2006), pp. 31, 37, 40.
3   Webster, *Twilight of the East India Company.*
4   Cain, P.J. and Hopkins, A.G., *British Imperialism 1688–2000* (Edinburgh, 2001), p. 84.

anxiety expressed in Parliament caused Dundas to suggest to Pitt that the Company's debts in India be funded and transferred to Britain.[5]

According to the system proposed by Dundas, the annual surplus revenues in British India were used to provide a stock of goods called the Investment, which was transferred to Britain on the Company's ships. These goods were then sold at India House, and after the expenses and dividends had been paid, the surplus would be used to supply the Company's settlements in India with writers, cadets, military stores, British manufactured goods and bullion in the form of silver. It was decided that the annual Investment in India should be increased in value from about £1,000,000 to £1,500,000. This Investment, it was calculated, would realise £2,400,000 in Britain. The Company's Indian debts were to be funded at 5 per cent and transferred to Britain by the substitution of bills on the Court of Directors at a fixed rate of exchange, and these bills were to be paid in Britain out of the increased trading profits.[6] This plan failed due to the fact that the annual Investment was dependent on an increase in the amount of bullion sent to India and there was no provision for this aspect. Further, the rate of exchange at which the remittance was fixed was too low for competition with the very favourable channel of remittance through foreign trade with India. Clearly, although Britain's trade with India received a boost following the Seven Years War, with the major markets being India and China, demand for British manufactured goods was insufficient to pay for the products imported into Britain and large amounts of silver had to be exported to China to pay for them.

The Company became an agent of British imperial expansion in Asia securing a chain of control from India throughout South-East Asia and a trading network stretching from China to Southern Africa. However, with military expansion and accompanying responsibilities related to protecting and maintaining possessions, the 'hoped for inflow of Indian wealth to British government coffers did not occur'.[7] The steady decline of the Mughal emperor's power resulted in an evolution to smaller, more controllable territories still owing nominal allegiance to the emperor. However, by attacking Calcutta, the Nawab of Bengal had forced the hand of an 'unwilling foreign trading company into the perilous game of Indian power politics'.[8]

The four major powers which emerged as a direct result of the decline of central rule were the Afghans and Sikhs in the north, the Marathas in central and western India and Mysore to the south. To add to the complexity, France saw a clear opportunity to back these successful states in direct conflict

5   Home Misc. 371, f.1, 15 June 1785. Philips, C.H., *The East India Company 1784–1834* (Manchester, 1961 [1940]), pp. 46–47.

6   Ibid.

7   Ward, P., *British Naval Power in the East 1794–1805: The Command of Admiral Peter Rainier* (Woodbridge, 2013).

8   Ibid.

against the British and began placing its army officers in key positions in the Indian armies of its allies, encouraging diplomatic ties with Mysore and sending military supplies to the Maratha Confederacy.[9] As France no longer had a viable base of operations in the mainland of India, it focused on the island of Mauritius (L'Ile de France), 2500 miles from the west coast of India as a centre of operations for both privateers and national warships to raid merchant shipping. This was the naturally acceptable strategy as the French expenditures in the American Revolutionary War had left them unable to support excessive military investment in India. French attempts at supplying aid to regional rulers opposed to the British such as Tipu Sultan in the 1790s were relatively ineffective and the storming of Tipu's capital of Seringapatam by British troops and the killing of Tipu in 1799 effectively meant the end of independent Mysore and its power was transferred to the Company.

By the 1790s, the value of imports from China, primarily tea, exceeded those from India and this trade was mainly financed by the transfer of silver to Canton. The trade imbalance with India was largely financed by both revenues and taxes generated locally and the cash flows into Britain from the remittance of wealth generated by individual Europeans working on the subcontinent. The trade naturally meant that the shortest route to China from India through the Straits of Malacca needed to be protected from piracy and the Company then obtained the island of Penang from the Sultan following negotiations with a merchant adventurer Captain Francis Light.[10]

In July 1806, £17,500,000 of the Company debt primarily incurred by Wellesley's campaigns was payable at home.[11] This payment could be met either by increasing the Company's Investments and sales or by borrowing from the public. The Directors being reluctant toward a public offering, the Indian governments were ordered to borrow money for this purpose and the value of Investments rose from £5,890,383 in 1800 to £6,052,144 in 1805.[12] However, the institution of the Berlin Decrees by Napoleon in 1806, where British-made goods were not allowed to be imported into countries directly or indirectly dependent on France (following Napoleon's victory against the Prussians at Jena), severely restricted the re-export of Indian goods to Continental Europe. Consequently, whereas in 1798 the Company sold nearly £3,000,000 worth of such goods, in 1807 they sold only £433,000 worth.[13] By April 1808 there were goods worth £7,148,440 lying unsold in the Company's London warehouses.[14]

[9]   Ibid.
[10] Ibid.
[11] Parliament Histories N.S. VII, 1044. Philips, *The East India Company*, pp. 154–55.
[12] EI Accounts, 1813. Ibid.
[13] Select Committee, Report III (1810), I. Ibid.
[14] Asiatic Ann. Reg. (1810–11), p. 308.

In these circumstances, Castlereagh's plan for the transfer of Indian debt to Britain completely broke down. Its main aim had been to save money by transferring Indian debt which stood at 8 per cent interest to Europe at 5 per cent. This transfer took place mainly through the trade in Indian piece goods purchased in India by bills of exchange on the Company at home. The increased import of these goods to Britain, coupled with competition of foreign private traders and British manufacturers, lowered the price as a result of increased supply, and the trade became unprofitable. The consequent loss suffered by the Company's home treasury more than offset the gain anticipated from the transfer of the debt. In August 1807, the Secret Committee ordered the Indian Government to cease transferring debt to Britain.[15] War losses further embarrassed the company with 15,000 tonnes of the Company's shipping sunk between 1803 and 1809 by French privateers operating from their base of Bourbon and Mauritius.[16] As we shall see, the expeditionary costs and administrative costs of taking over these islands, as well as the cost of Minto's conquest of Java in 1811 to prevent it falling into French hands, resulted in additional outlay with no immediate return on investment in the form of land revenue and other revenue collections.

To counteract Napoleon's Berlin-Milan Decrees, which imposed an embargo on all continental trade with Britain, the British Government responded by issuing the Order in Council of November 1807, which forbade all French commerce with Britain and imposed regulations on neutrals trading with the French in that they were routed via British ports and had to pay substantial taxes for engaging in trade with the enemy. This in turn affected American interests, leading in turn to an American law in 1809 forbidding direct trade between America and Britain.[17]

It is from these global developments to the internal processes that led to the East India Company's policy orientation in the middle of the first decade of the nineteenth century, the beginning of the era of Governor-General Minto.

Minto's Appointment and Arrival in India

Minto's appointment as the Governor-General of Bengal in July 1806 was a measure of expediency brought about by a prolonged contest between the Ministers and the Court of Directors over the issue of patronage. Since

---

15 Board's Secret Drafts, Vol. 3, 14 August 1807. The orders were proposed by the Secret Committee.
16 App. Court Minutes, F.25, 16 July 1813. In 1809–10 alone, cargoes to the value of over one million pounds sterling were lost. Home Misc. 817, f.640, 20 January 1810.
17 Tolley, B.H., 'The Liverpool Campaign Against the Order in Council and the War of 1812', in J.R. Harris (ed.), *Liverpool and Merseyside Essays in the Economic and Social History of the Port and its Hinterland* (London, 1969), pp. 98–146.

1 Portrait of Gilbert Elliot-Murray-Kynynmound, First Earl of Minto, by James
Atkinson, 1813, NPG 836 © National Portrait Gallery, London

the passing of the Act of 1784, the Board of Control usually had a voice
in the nomination of a governor-general, but the wishes of the Court of
Directors were not totally ignored. The Act of 1784 granted the king the
prerogative of cancelling all appointments made by the Company,[18] and

18 BL, IOR Home Misc. Series 506, p. 203. Extract from the Act of 1784, 33rd Geo 3. Cap
52, sec. 35.

thereby strengthened the hands of the Ministers. The real difference between Fox's Bill and Pitt's Bill was a struggle for the patronage of India, whether it should be in the hands of the Ministers or of the Company. Fox's Bill was opposed because it left the patronage of India largely in the hands of the Ministers. Pitt's Bill was based on the supposition that it might more fairly be exercised by the East India Company themselves. Although Pitt's Act of 1784 gave the king the power of recall, it was obviously not the intention of the legislature that a bill passed in that spirit should enable His Majesty's Minsters to unilaterally exercise the veto power of the king to gain the entire patronage of India. This is evident from the opposition offered by the Directors by the Ministers' attempt to force them to recall Barlow and nominate the Earl of Lauderdale as governor-general. In the end, a compromise was made and Minto was appointed governor-general to the satisfaction of all parties concerned, except perhaps Fox and Lauderdale. What makes the episode interesting is that Minto as President of the Board of Control carried on Fox's and Grenville's battle with the Directors in a controversy which ended in his own appointment to the contested office.

On the death of Pitt, Grenville formed the Ministry of 'All the Talents'. On 3 February 1806, Minto was appointed President of the Board of Control, without a seat in the Cabinet.[19] In January 1806, news of Cornwallis' death at Ghazipur on 5 October 1805 reached the home authorities. The governor-generalship of Bengal was proposed to Minto by Grenville as early as this time and generally speculated by the public.[20] Minto declined the offer at that time, but it shows that he was considered for the office even before the controversy arose. When Lauderdale's name was proposed to the Directors on Fox's recommendation, Grenville made a superficial apology to Minto as if the proposal ought first to have been made to him, especially after what had passed before on the subject. The fact was that although Grenville wished for Minto's appointment, Lauderdale's nomination was determined 'on Fox's wish to serve and gratify his friend'.[21]

Minto's first act of official duty as President of the Board of Control had been to draw the attention of the Directors to the necessity of appointing the senior member of the Council at Calcutta, Sir George Barlow, to succeed Cornwallis, so that he could continue the business of administration. The Ministers regarded this as a temporary arrangement. This was clearly stated by Minto to Barlow as well as to the two Chairs of the Company.[22] He notified

19 NLS M 33. Minto to Lady Minto, London, 3 February 1806.
20 Ibid., 31 January 1806. Ibid., 4 February 1806. Ibid., 5 February 1806. Spencer, A. (ed.), *Memoirs of William Hickey*, Vol. IV (London, 1925), p. 329.
21 NLS M 33. Minto to Lady Minto, 8 March 1806.
22 NLS M 158, pp. 1–2. Minto to Barlow, India Board, 27 February 1806. BL, IOR Home Misc. Series 506, pp. 215–19. Minto to the Chairman and Deputy Chairman of the East India Company, 14 February 1806.

them 'that the future and permanent settlement of the Government in Bengal in which however at the present moment no change is in contemplation must necessarily be reserved for the more deliberate consideration of His Majesty's Servants'.[23]

Minto did not think any immediate change would be made, but this changed within a month when he was asked by Grenville to inform the Chairs that a new appointment would indeed be made. On 7 March 1806, Minto notified the Chairs of the Government's decision and requested them to see Grenville and himself as soon as possible.[24] Lauderdale's name was not disclosed at first due to the fact that the Ministers felt that the measure required some management at the India House.[25]

The Chairs, Charles Grant and George Smith, resented the assumption by the Ministers of the sole right to nominate the Governor-General, which in the past had been settled by mutual agreement between the President and the Chairs. Moreover, the Court had passed the appointment of Barlow on 19 February 1806 and the order was only sent to India on 25 February 1806. The Chairs therefore wrote to Minto that it would be a considerable shock to the Court to find a change proposed in so very short a time after Barlow's appointment. It was also likely to produce strong repercussions in India, both in the Company's governments and among the Indian states and was certainly harsh to Barlow.[26] Minto maintained that the Government had been very clear that Barlow's appointment was a provisional measure and neither Barlow nor the Company's servants in India would be justified in regarding it as otherwise.[27] At this desire, the Chairs called on him on 12 March 1806 and Minto disclosed the name of Lord Lauderdale as the ministerial nominee, and the same day 'it was blazed all over the town' by the Government, without waiting for the decision of the Directors.[28]

The Directors refused to have their hands forced by the Ministers. They had personal objections to Lord Lauderdale. His sympathies for French Jacobinism and activities as 'Citizen Maitland', along with his views against the Company's exclusive trading privileges, made him an unsafe person in the eyes of the Directors to be sent abroad with the extensive powers of a governor-general. Minto personally believed that Lauderdale had many qualifications for the office and that he would probably have been in reality just as safe as any other. Yet it was found that nothing could be more disagreeable to the Directors.[29] The Directors as a body were not particularly enamoured of

23 Ibid.
24 BL, IOR Home Misc. Series 506, pp. 223–24. 7 March 1806. Minto to the Chairs.
25 NLS M 33. Minto to Lady Minto, 11 March 1806.
26 BL, IOR Home Misc. Series 506, pp. 227–35. 8 March 1806. The Chairs to Minto.
27 Ibid., pp. 239–55, 10 March 1806. Minto to the Chairs.
28 Morris, H., *The Life of Charles Grant* (London, 1904), p. 265.
29 NLS M 33. Minto to Lady Minto, 24 March 1806.

Barlow, whom they regarded as a follower of Wellesley. Barlow had quickly changed his views and policies on the arrival of Cornwallis. This showed a lamentable lack of stability in a person holding a responsible position, and one of the Directors, Sir Francis Baring, felt that another governor-general was absolutely necessary.[30] Barlow however was a protégé of Charles Grant, the Chairman, and the majority of the Directors were decidedly against Lauderdale.[31] Moreover, the Directors were also opposed to the Ministers on account of Wellesley whom they had recalled and who was supported by Grenville. In the House of Commons, Mr Paull was threatening to bring a motion against Wellesley. Grenville wrote to Fox, 'they [the Directors] consider all the Parliamentary proceedings now going on as the triumph of the Court of Directors over the Board of Control, and of the system of governing India by the Company and its servants over that of naming political and public characters to that station'.[32]

Throughout March and April 1806, Minto was preoccupied with this controversy between Grenville, Fox, Lauderdale and the Directors. He found he had 'to mediate amidst three or four different exasperated parties' and the situation was described by him as 'very confused & uncomfortable'.[33] In the new elections in the Court, several of the leading Directors refused to be Chairman, in order to avoid the unpleasant task of having to propose Barlow's recall and Lauderdale's nomination to the Court. In the end on 10 April 1806, the Directors chose W.P. Elphinstone as Chairman on Minto's recommendation. Elphinstone had been acting as a liaison between the Court and the Board, and had no objection to Lauderdale. With Elphinstone at the top of the Court, the Ministers hoped for an amicable settlement of the dispute.[34] They were to be disappointed, for on 20 May 1806 the Directors refused to recall Barlow by a majority of seventeen to four.[35]

Grenville and Fox now decided to exercise the power of recall vested in the king by the Act of 1784 and presented an instrument of recall to the king.[36] By an order issued under the sign-manual of George III and counter-signed by Minto, the Company's commissions to Barlow as Governor-General of Bengal and to the members of the Council, Lord Lake, George Udny and John Lumsden were revoked.[37] In order to avoid embarrassments arising out

---

30 BL, IOR Home Misc. Series 506. Sir Francis Baring to the Directors, 11 June 1806.
31 Morris, *Charles Grant*, p. 263. NLS M 33. Minto to Lady Minto, 26 March 1806. Ibid., 28 March 1806.
32 HIST. MSS. COMM. Fortescue VIII, p. 83. Grenville to Fox, 6 April 1806.
33 NLS M 33. Minto to Lady Minto, 28 March 1806.
34 NLS M 34. Minto to Lady Minto, 9 April, 10 April and 11 April 1806. NLS M 158. Minto to Lauderdale, 22 March 1806. Ibid., Minto to Charles Fox, Whitehall, 12 April 1806.
35 BL, IOR Home Misc. Series 506, pp. 273–80. Extract from Court's Minutes, 20 May 1806. NLS M 34. Minto to Lady Minto, 21 May 1806.
36 HIST. MSS. COMM. Fortescue VIII, p. 160. Grenville to King George III, 27 May 1806.
37 BL, IOR Home Misc. Series 506, pp. 283–87. Instrument of Recall.

of the revocation of the existing government before the arrival of the new governor-general, it was decided that the powers of Barlow and the members of the Council should cease only on the publication of the Instrument of Recall at Calcutta, that is, at the same time as the new governor-general should be there to assume office.

The principle on which the Government acted in this case was explained by Minto to the aggrieved party which also throws light on the prestige and power which had come to be attached to the office of the governor-general. Minto wrote to the Chairs,

> ... His Majesty's Ministers are intimately persuaded, both as a general proposition, and much more application to times of difficulty and crisis, that it is expedient for the due Administration of India, that the Person entrusted with the extensive powers belonging to that distant Government should be one who possesses the cordial confidence of Government at home. They think also that Rank, Weight and Consideration in the Metropolitan Country must add much to the authority and efficiency of those who administer great and remote provinces.[38]

This principle had been formulated during the passing of the Act of 1784, and was sanctioned by practice and the acquiescence of the Company. Experience had shown that Company servants were much too personally involved and open to petty jealousies and intrigues to hold office as successfully as a man from outside was likely to be able to do so. It wasn't that the experiment hadn't been performed earlier. Sir John Shore had held the office from 1793 to 1798, but according to Sir Francis Baring, 'the bark was in the danger of sinking, notwithstanding his very superior abilities, integrity and that he enjoyed the respect and esteem of almost every individual in the service'.[39]

Hence, in the critical state of the Company's affairs – a debt almost too enormous to be mentioned, no sales of Indian manufactures at home with empty treasuries at home and abroad – a man of energy and initiative was urgently required to fill the office of governor-general.

After Barlow's recall was achieved, the question was how to force the Directors to accept Lauderdale. It appeared certain that if his name was proposed it would be rejected immediately. In that case, Fox and Lauderdale insisted that no other name should be proposed and the Directors should be left to their own choice and their own measures. They hoped that the Directors would be so distressed at the difficulty of finding an appropriate

---

[38] BL, IOR Home Misc. Series 506, pp. 291–314. Minto to the Chairs, 29 May 1806. A letter to the same effect from Minto to Barlow, 1 April 1806. NLS M 158, pp. 44–47.

[39] BL, IOR Home Misc. Series 506. Sir Francis Baring to the Directors of the E.I.C., 11 June 1806.

person willing to go to Bengal, that they'd be obliged to accept Lauderdale by default. However, Minto was beginning to see the impossibility of forcing their hand. In this opinion, a person rejected by a majority of the Directors couldn't possibly be fit enough to be posted to India.[40] He succeeded in bringing Grenville around to this line of thought and on his advice Grenville decided to persuade Fox and Lauderdale to be reasonable.

On 19 June, a deputation of the Directors called on the Ministers and signified a decided negative on Lauderdale's nomination although no reasons were given. They requested the Government to recommend another name, inferring from rumours that Minto was the next on the list.[41] Grenville realised that to refuse to cooperate any longer would be inimical to public as well as private interests. He wrote to Fox:

> In the relations between Government and the Company fixed by the existing laws, it is undeniable that the Directors ought to have at least a negative on the choice of a Governor-General... it is too much again to put by Lord Minto's wishes and objects, and to incur at the same time all the odium and mischief of a contest with the Directors on bad grounds.[42]

Grenville wanted his brother Thomas Grenville as the President of the Board of Control with a seat in the Cabinet. He was therefore not without a personal interest in Minto's appointment to India.

In the meantime, Mr Paull had given notice that he would bring the whole matter to discussion in the House of Commons if the Ministers did not communicate on the subject before that time.[43] Lord Melville was also to question Minto on the entire affair in Parliament. This made an immediate resolution necessary. Lauderdale put up a brief fight, but the serious condition of Fox's health at last forced him to withdraw further opposition to Grenville's measure.[44]

On 30 June 1806, Minto's name was formally recommended by the Government to the Directors[45] and on 9 July the Directors appointed him Governor-General of Bengal.[46] It was hoped by both parties that '... such

---

40 NLS M 158. Minto to Lauderdale, London, 25 June 1806. NLS M 34. Minto to Lady Minto, 5 June 1806. Ibid., 6 June 1806; Ibid., 7 June 1806.
41 Ibid., 19 June 1806. The Ministers present were Lords Grenville, Spencer, Henry Petty and Mr Fox. The deputation consisted of the Chairs (Elphinstone and Parry), Sir R. Bensley, Sir Hugh Inglis, Mr Bosanquet and Mr Mills. Also, BL, IOR Home Misc. Series 506, pp. 439–42.
42 Hist. MSS. Comm. Fortescue VIII, pp. 197–200. Grenville to Fox, Downing Street, 23 June 1806.
43 NLS M 34. Minto to Lady Minto, 25 June 1806.
44 Ibid., 27 June 1806. Hist. MSS. COMM. Fortescue VIII, p. 204, Fox to Grenville, 24 June 1806.
45 NLS M 34. Minto to Lady Minto, 30 June 1806.
46 BL, IOR Home Misc. Series 24, pp. 362–68. Appointment of Lord Minto. Home Misc.

a choice would, after what has recently passed, be peculiarly advantageous in marking the cooperation and connection between the different bodies to whose care these important interests have been entrusted by the legislature'.[47]

Minto regarded his appointment with mixed feelings. After long diplomatic service abroad in Toulon, Corsica and Vienna, he was looking forward to settling down in England in a comfortable position. He was fifty-five and did not particularly enjoy the prospect of service abroad which involved long separation from his family. The financial prospects of the office, however, were alluring. This was a vital consideration for him. Although his parliamentary and diplomatic career had brought him a certain amount of recognition in Britain, it had not been financially remunerative.[48] The old family house at Minto was badly in need of repairs, he had daughters to provide for and sons whose careers would be furthered by his appointment to the highest post in India. Minto wrote to his wife:

> I can hardly express the agitation of mine which this subject has kept me... I feel all the personal consequences in their full force. Yet ... it is the only possible way I can imagine to render a great & solid benefit to the children, & barring accidents to myself ... it is a certain way of returning our fortune ... from the pecuniary vexations which have haunted almost the whole of our own lives.[49]

The salary was £25,000 per annum besides other allowances and benefits. He calculated spending at the most about £10,000 per year and saving the rest. His third son John Elliot was a writer at Madras whom he decided to appoint as his private secretary on a salary of £5,000 per year.[50]

Apart from these purely personal motives, Minto was not entirely uninspired by higher ideals. 'There are undoubtedly other strong motives and inducements of quite a different nature', wrote Minto, 'I mean the public call which has been so remarkable in this case and the hope of becoming the instrument of great and extensive good.'[51]

Minto's early views on India were formed during his close association with Burke. From Burke, he imbibed the doctrine of trusteeship. He was one of the managers of the trial of Warren Hastings and moved the motion against Sir

Series 506, p. 455, Extract Minute of the Court of Directors, 9 July 1806. Home Misc. Series 506, p. 459. W. Ramsay (Secretary, E.I.C.) to Minto, 10 July 1806.

[47] BL, IOR Home Misc. Series 506, pp. 447–49. Paper delivered by Grenville to the Chairs on 30 June 1806.

[48] The financial problem of the family was a subject of frequent discussion in the correspondence between Minto and Lady Minto. In a letter dated 7 February 1806, Lady Minto wrote to her husband, 'I hate money thoughts as much as anyone, & never have had my mind free from them for many a long year.' NLS M 58. Lady Minto to Minto, 7 February 1806. NLS M 34. Minto to Lady Minto, 14 June 1806.

[49] NLS M 34. Minto to Lady Minto, 19 June 1806.

[50] Ibid., 28 June 1806. John's salary was later reduced to £3,000 per year.

[51] NLS M 34. Minto to Lady Minto, 19 June 1806.

Elijah Impey in the House of Commons in 1787.[52] Although the motion was defeated because of a lack of adequate evidence and although one of Minto's motives in moving the motion may have been to gain a step up in the party ladder, there is no reason to doubt the sincerity of the views he expressed. He did not believe oppression or corruption indispensable or unavoidable in order to rule over a foreign race. He scoffed at the remark made by one of Impey's adherents that Indians were used to despotic government and to cruelties of the ruling classes. It reminded him of 'the apology for skinning eels – that they are used to it'.[53] His sympathy for the people over which the Company ruled and impatience with corruption and maladministration prevalent in Indian territories were genuine and tinged perhaps with more than a little emotionalism. Burke formed a very high opinion of Minto. He once urged Minto, then Sir Gilbert Elliot, 'You must be all that you can be, and you can be everything.'[54] On his appointment to the Board of Control, Minto had warmly acknowledged his debt to Edmund in a letter to Mrs Burke:

> You know the school in which I was train'd, & the master who taught so many greater & better than myself. That I am a disciple of that dear master, is a reflexion which … is the best security for a faithful if not able discharge of a trust for which I hold myself answerable to his memory as well as to my own conscience.[55]

In July 1806, Minto accepted the office of the Governor-General of Bengal, although he actually took up office more than a year later, in July 1807. His position with the home authorities at the time of his appointment was all that could be desired. His party was in power and the Directors well-disposed towards him despite the recent controversy. Charles Grant wrote about him:

> Lord Minto is considered an honourable man, has the reputation of ability, information, and a cultivated mind in politics and particularly Indian politics. He was of the school of Burke, and thought to be somewhat theoretical … Constitutionally I take him to be a man of sensibility, and in general of mildness and kindness, but liable to be raised to harsher feelings. In the office of the Board of Control I found him most conciliating, easy, affable, frank, with laudable application, and just views on many Indian questions, a man of business, acute too … From what I have experienced of his Lordship, I should be inclined to apprehend that his facility and impressibleness of temper may

52 Countess of Minto (ed.), *Life and Letters of Sir Gilbert Elliot, First Earl of Minto from 1751 to 1806*, 3 vols (London, 1874), Vol. 1, pp. 175–86, 199–203. Magnus, Philip, *Edmund Burke* (London, 1939), pp. 161–62.
53 Minto, *Life and Letters of Sir Gilbert Elliot*, Vol. 1, p. 127.
54 Ibid., p. 113.
55 NLS M 158, pp. 41–43. Minto to Mrs Burke, London, 28 March 1806.

lead him into entanglements from which he may not have the happiest method of extricating himself.[56]

This was a shrewd observation of Minto's character made by Grant who was frequently in and out of office as either Chairman or Deputy-Chairman of the Court of Directors between the years 1794 and 1823. Grant had the opportunity of being in close contact with Minto when he was President of the Board of Control and the opinion he formed of him appears fair and unbiased. Despite his advanced age, Minto brought to the office of governor-general the energy and activity of a younger man. He was naturally mild and kind-hearted, but Grant made a shrewd observation when he said that he was 'liable to be raised to harsher feelings'. This side of his character came out in his quarrels with Harford Jones, Rear-Admiral Drury and the home authorities. He was easily swayed by emotions, either of affection or hatred. Comparing him with Henry Pelham, Thomas Grenville wrote to his brother:

> ... how much more secure from humour, irritation, and eccentricity you would find your correspondence with Pelham that you can hope to find with Lord Minto, and that although Minto's talents were superior to Pelham's in writing a better argument or in making a better speech ... for the average of business, including conduct, discretion and temper, I should have no doubt in preferring infinitely the commoner to the peer.[57]

One thing was certain: Minto was not cut out to be a glorified civil servant devoted to the routine of administration and the task of retrenchment, or in other words another Sir George Barlow. He was essentially a man of imagination and broad outlook. He did not shrink from taking upon himself a large degree of personal responsibility whenever he thought a particular measure necessary. A sense of humour was perhaps the most abiding feature of his character, which never left him, even during the most critical times of his career in India.

On 15 February 1807, Minto sailed for India on the *Modeste*, commanded by his son Captain George Elliot and accompanied by his aides-de-camp Captains Taylor, Stewart and Drinkwater. After a voyage lasting four months he arrived at Madras on 20 June 1807. The strangeness of the land struck him forcibly. 'The novelty of this scene exceeds even my expectations, & appears to me to surpass in strangeness even that of the Cape of Good Hope,' he wrote home.[58] The scantily clad dark people with their strange customs and habits in the sun-baked country aroused his curiosity rather than the

---

[56] Morris, *Charles Grant*, p. 266. Grant to Barlow, London, 26 July 1806.
[57] Hist. MSS. COMM. Fortescue V, p. 85. T. Grenville to Lord Grenville, 10 June 1799, Berlin.
[58] NLS M 35. Minto to Lady Minto, Madras, 22 June 1807.

supercilious contempt which was the not uncommon reaction of English on their first encounter with India.[59]

The memories of the sepoy rising in Vellore in July 1806[60] were still fresh at that time. Minto stopped at Madras for nearly a month while the *Modeste* underwent repairs. During that time he had the opportunity of personal communications with William Bentinck who was then Governor of Madras, Sir Henry Gwillim and other members of the Madras Government in his unofficial capacity, for according to the terms of his appointment he was to assume office as governor-general on his arrival at Calcutta. In Madras, therefore, he was a passing visitor. He was surprised to find the gulf that existed between the administration and the people. The same void was noticeable between the British officers in the army and the sepoys. The army was the chief pillar of British authority in India. It consisted largely of Indians. Sedition and disaffection among the ranks was therefore a matter of serious concern to the Company. Minto judged from Vellore that interference with the religion of the people, Hindu and Muslim, and the alienation of the native officers from the British, were the two causes of sepoy discontent. He wrote:

> Our former faith in the security of India, cannot but have been somewhat imparir'd by that example of disaffection in a considerable body of native troops and by that proof that intrigue and seduction may by possibility succeed, in improving such occasions as chance or improvidence may furnish into motives for mutiny, and spreading, perhaps, disaffection & revolt to an extent that might prove dangerous in a high degree to the British power in India. There is no reason to believe that the Coast Sepoy is in any degree whatever disaffected to the Government ... but he is capable of being practice on by religious pretences and artifice, as well as by the natural influence of his native office ... This unfavourable view of the subject is darkened also, by the reflection that ... there is in the same territories an immense & weighty body of irreconcilable discontent in the higher classes of the Mussulman inhabitants.[61]

The discontent of the Muslims in the peninsula he believed was natural enough, for only recently the British had either totally annihilated or greatly reduced the leading Islamic powers in southern India and 'ruined the individual influence, consideration and fortunes of that powerful race'.[62] The Muslim discontent in the south, Minto expected, would subside in time with

---

59 Ibid. Minto to Lady Minto, dated Madras 22 and 29 June 1807, containing Minto's first impressions of India and its people. They are printed in *Lord Minto in India* by the Countess of Minto, pp. 16–23. The editor has printed the two letters as one and given them the later date.

60 A vivid account of the Vellore mutiny is given in *Memoirs of William Hickey*, Vol. IV, pp. 331–40; Thornton, E., *History of the British Empire in India*, Vol. IV (London, 1843), pp. 57–85.

61 NLS M 159, pp. 164–68. Minto to Edward Parry, Fort William, 19 September 1807.

62 NLS M 159. Minto to E. Parry, Fort William, 19 September 1807.

the decline of the old influence and the growth of new interests originating in the dependence on the British Government.

He regretted the lack of social intercourse between European and Indian officers in the army, which prevented the growth of 'common feelings, which insensibly but firmly cement the union & cordiality of men'.[63] Social relations could hardly be maintained among those who would not on any occasion sit at the same table together. Minto always held that there should be closer understanding and intercourse between the ruling class and the people. He encouraged the younger men in the service to learn Indian languages.

Vellore also impressed Minto with the necessity of non-interference in the religious beliefs of the Company's Hindu and Muslim subjects for the sake of internal security and tranquillity of the Company's territories. He wrote to Edward Parry, then Chairman of the Court of Directors:

> On the Coast, religion is a handle which many have, or feel an interest in employing for purposes of mischief. In Bengal however were are not entirely free from a similar danger, ... more than usually excited at this particular moment by the indiscretion of the well-meaning, & respectable, no doubt, but very mischievous zeal of the European Missionaries... . Religious jealousy, whether provoked, by imprudent acts of our own, or created by designing misrepresentation on the part of our domestic or foreign enemies, appears to me the only possible source of present danger in any part of India.[64]

The views formed at Madras undoubtedly influenced Minto's attitude towards the Baptist missionaries at Serampore. He was not opposed to the spread of the Gospel, but believed that the peace and security of the Company's territories in India were more important in the long run.

Minto reached Calcutta on 31 July 1807 and assumed office the same day. Sir George Barlow reverted back to his position of senior member of the Council. He was invested with the Order of the Bath according to the orders of His Majesty's Government.[65] Minto was relieved to find in him no outward sign of jealousy. On the contrary, until Barlow's appointment to Madras a few months later, he was Minto's principal advisor. Minto formed a high opinion of Barlow's merits. He wrote, 'His good properties are of a high class. A real attachment to his public duties, and ... a naturally sincere & honourable character, secure his best advice & assistance as a colleague.'[66]

He also guessed the reason for Barlow's unpopularity among the Company's

[63] Ibid.

[64] Ibid.

[65] NLS M 159. Minto to Parry, Fort William, 19 September 1807. NLS M 56. Minto to Lady Minto, Calcutta, 31 July 1807. NLS M 159. Minto to Castlereagh, Calcutta, 26 September 1807.

[66] NLS M 93. Minto to G. Elliot, 15 September–8 October 1807, Calcutta.

servants. 'A constitutional coldness & apathy of temper ... has enabled him to discharge many harsh duties pretty inflexibly.'[67]

The other members of his Council were John Lumsden and the Commander-in-Chief General Hewitt. On Barlow's appointment to Madras, H.T. Colebrooke entered the Council. The membership of the Council remained unaltered during Minto's period of office. Lumsden he described as 'a plain, modest sensible man, who having been Chief Secretary, is perfectly conversant with the business of government'.[68] Speaking of his colleagues, he wrote to Edward Parry:

> Mr. Lumsden is fully and minutely versed in the affairs of this Government and is a man of excellent sound judgement; Mr. Colebrooke is you know one of the cleverest men in the world and master above all of one of the great branches of our affairs, the judicial. I am fortunate too in Mr. Edmonstone's continuing another year. One of my greatest felicities and most important advantages is in General Hewitt, a more perfectly honourable, practicable, temperate and judicious mind & character could not be called to his delicate office.[69]

Neil Benjamin Edmonstone, who had been Wellesley's private secretary, was now Chief Secretary to the Government of Bengal. Minto was glad to avail of the advice and assistance of these men, especially in carrying out the routine administration during the first few months of his office. It gave him time to settle down and to form his own views and opinions on the different matters of the Indian administration, after acquiring some knowledge and familiarity of his own with the affairs of the Company's Government in India. If Barlow had been popular among the governmental clique at Calcutta, his removal from office might have created among his adherents a degree of hostility to the new governor-general. This was not the case, as Barlow was far from popular and Minto encountered no opposition on his account.

Minto thought of two ways of maintaining the solidarity of his government: one, by keeping the Council united; and two, by exercising his powers of patronage.[70] He believed that as long as the Council was united, it mattered little what factions were formed against the administration outside it. On the other hand, as the advancement of the careers and fortunes of the Company's servants in India depended largely on the favour of the governor-general, no faction was likely to have a long life. It was the usual practice for the governor-general to have his own men in positions of trust. For the first few months, Minto depended on Barlow for advice and information, but he wrote to Thomas Grenville (who was President of the Board of Control),

67 Ibid.
68 NLS M 93. Minto to Gilbert Elliot, 15 September–8 October 1807, Calcutta.
69 NLS M 159. Minto to Edward Parry, Calcutta, 3 December 1807.
70 NLS M 93. Minto to Gilbert Elliot, Calcutta, 15 September–8 October 1807.

'I am preparing in the meanwhile, by as much study and meditation as the interruptions of current business permit, a staff of my own, which I take it is always the best to walk by, and that indeed by which it is my duty to walk.'[71]

He began by appointing his third son, John Elliot, who was then a junior writer in Madras, as his Private Secretary. Captain Taylor, a young Scotsman and friend of the family who came out with him, was appointed his Military Secretary and aide-de-camp. John Malcolm, Charles Metcalfe and Mountstuart Elphinstone were the budding statesman of the period. They were 'Wellesley's men', but found a wide scope for their talents and activities in Minto's government. Minto favoured a number of his own countrymen, the Scots, and took special pride in their activities. Malcolm, Archibald Seton, Elphinstone and John Leyden were among the outstanding Scotsmen serving in India at this time.

Shortly after Minto's arrival in Bengal, his term of office appeared precarious. News of a change of Ministry at home nearly overtook his own arrival in India. He sailed from England in February 1807 and in March his friends were ousted from office on the issue of the Catholic Bill. The Grenville Ministry was succeeded by a weak administration formed with the Duke of Portland at its head. There were rumours both in London and Calcutta that Minto would soon be recalled.[72] Grenville wrote to Minto that if the Directors had not recalled Bentinck from Madras, the Duke of Portland would have seized this opportunity of appointing him to Bengal by superseding Minto.[73] Minto's family and friends at home did not want him to resign on the first impulse, but to wait and see how far the change was likely to affect his own standing with the home authorities. Grenville gave him a carte blanche to act as he thought best. He wrote to Minto:

> If you think, on a deliberated review of the state of things both at home & abroad, that you can remain where you are with the advantage to the public & with satisfaction to yourself, ... I shall feel sincere pleasure in thinking that one part at least, ... of the interests of the Country is in hands to which one can look with confidence & satisfaction.[74]

He was advised to send a letter of resignation to his son John Elliot, who was to have discretionary powers to present it to the Court of Directors should it be necessary to do so in view of later developments.[75]

---

71 NLS M 159. Minto to T. Grenville, Calcutta, 15 September 1807.

72 NLS M 59. Lady Minto to Minto, 21 March 1807. Ibid., 1 April 1807. *Memoirs of William Hickey*, Vol. IV, p. 365.

73 NLS M 68. Grenville to Minto, Downing Street, 16 April 1807. William Bentinck was a younger son of the Duke of Portland who was Prime Minister from 1807 to 1809. Bentinck was recalled from his governorship at Madras on account of the mutiny of the sepoys at Vellore in July 1806.

74 NLS M 68. Grenville to Minto, Downing Street, 16 April 1807.

75 NLS M 68. Grenville to Minto, Downing Street, 16 April 1807. Ibid., Elliot of Wells to Lady

Several political and personal factors and motives caused Minto to decide not to resign his office in commiseration with his political friends. He believed that the government of India should be independent of the political fluctuations at home. If the governments in India were to change concomitantly with every change in the ministry at home, it would, he believed expose them to danger and weakness. Whatever the political sympathies of the person holding the office of governor-general, it ought not to interfere with his performing the duties of his office. In other words, he believed that the governor-general should be above party politics and that home politics should not be allowed to interfere with the administration of the Company's territories in India. As far as he was personally concerned he did not think he would contract any new political obligation or a new party connection by staying in office. Considering the state of affairs at home he did not altogether give up the hope of seeing the Grenvilles back in power.

Personal considerations were quite naturally uppermost in his mind. To return from India the month after landing was a more serious matter than returning to England from a mission in Europe or resigning a public office at home. He admitted quite frankly:

> ... by my immediate return I must wholly renounce those considerations which could alone justify my embarking in this service ... I must fairly say ... I shall feel it hard to fall back into a struggle with pecuniary difficulties. ... John passes from the most perfect happiness, both in his present condition & his prospects, ... to absolute misery now & despair as to the future.[76]

In view of all these considerations, he decided not to resign but to await his removal if that was intended by the new Ministry. He counted on the goodwill of the Court of Directors. He did not think the new Ministers were personally hostile toward him, although he was rather unsure of the attitude of the new President of the Board of Control, Robert Dundas. Minto expected opposition from the Melvillites, for he stood against Henry Dundas when the latter was accused of embezzlement in the House of Commons. He was afraid Robert Dundas might take up the family feud. The agitation in his mind was naturally great. He wrote to Lady Minto that:

> Although it would argue a strange moral state of a country that Lord Melville's son should recall a Governor-General of India just appointed with the general approbation of the Company & the country, for having pass'd in judgement on his father. ... yet I have lived long enough in the political world of England ... and while Lord Melville is in power, & Lord Eldon is the oracle of our Law, & Morality, no one can have the smallest guess, without knowing much more than

Minto, 20 April 1807. NLS M 59. Lady Minto to Minto, 31 April 1807.
76 NLS M 36. Minto to Lady Minto, 27 September 1807.

the mere merits of the question, whether a man is to be hang'd or rewarded for any given action.[77]

Minto was soon relieved of his anxieties by amicable communications from Robert Dundas. Dundas addressed him cordially and gave him every assurance of support and cooperation.[78] Minto wrote home, 'From what I had heard of the feelings professed by this family towards me, I did not think our correspondence was likely to begin on that footing.'[79] Throughout his period of office, Dundas more or less regarded all Minto's measures with approval, except his treatment of Sir Harford Jones. Grenville was glad that Minto did not resign his office.[80] The Chairman of the Company, Edward Parry, assured Minto that the Board and the Court were disposed to give full support to his administration.[81] However, this favourable state of affairs changed soon after Minto's first year in India.

In 1807, the Company's territories in India consisted of Bengal, Bihar, the Northern Circars, the Coromandel Coast, parts of Mysore, the island of Bombay and some other small ports on the western coast. Wellesley had greatly reduced the independent authority of many of the leading Indian princes. The Nizam of Hyderabad, Peshwa Baji Rao II of Poona and Vizier Ali of Oudh had entered into subsidiary alliances with the British. Wellesley also dealt the final blow to Mysore, and with the fall of Tipu in 1799, the British breathed a sigh of relief. The Raja of Berar ceded the province of Cuttack to the English after his defeat in December 1803. Taking advantage of new accessions to the thrones of Tanjore, Surat and the Carnatic Region, Wellesley had brought them under the Company, leaving empty titles and guaranteed pensions to the princes. The war with the Sindhias and the Holkars was in full swing when Wellesley was recalled in 1805.[82]

Relative peace therefore prevailed in 1807, when Minto arrived in India. The Directors had sent Cornwallis a second time to India to stop the financially ruinous war with the Sindhias and Holkars, but Cornwallis died at Gazipore on his way to Lake's camp on 5 October 1805, three months after his arrival in India. Sir George Barlow followed the line of action proposed by Cornwallis, and made a peace concession with the Sindhias on 23 November 1805 giving back Gwalior and Gohad, and with the Holkars on 7

[77] NLS M 36. Minto to Lady Minto, 27 September 1807.

[78] NLS Minto Papers, Box 56. R. Dundas to Minto, Whitehall, 1 June 1807.

[79] NLS M 36. No. 5. Minto to Lady Minto, 19 November 1807.

[80] NLS M 68. Grenville to Minto, 24 May 1808.

[81] NLS M 192. Edward Parry to Minto, East India House, 15 April 1807, 15 June 1807, 5 September 1807.

[82] Malcolm, Sir John, *The Political History of India from 1784 to 1823*, 2 Vols (London, 1826), Vol. I, Chap. IV, pp. 194–332; Roberts, P.E., *India under Wellesley* (London, 1929), Chaps IV–VIII, X, XI, XVII, XIX–XXI; H.H. Dodwell (ed.), *Cambridge History of India*, Vol. V (Cambridge, 1929), pp. 339–46, 350–54, 357–62, 371–76.

January 1806. Barlow relinquished all territories west of the River Yamuna, except Agra, and withdrew the Company's protection from the Rajput states of Jaipur, Bundi, Machri, Bharatpur and Gohad with whom Lake had concluded treaties.[83]

Barlow's treaties with the Sindhias and Holkars were bitterly criticised by contemporary political colleagues as well as by later British historians, for it postponed the destruction of Maratha power for nearly a decade. The Marathas continued to be a source of alarm and danger to the British. Maratha horsemen ravaged the states of Malwa and Rajputana. Bands of plunderers acting under the Pathan leader Amir Khan and the Pindari leaders Cheetoo and Karim Khan added to the general anarchy. The Raja of Berar was among the first victims of the Pindaris. The Rajput states also suffered from their depredations. The Pindari menace was felt mainly toward the close of Minto's period of office.

According to the settlement made by Barlow with the Marathas, the River Yamuna was regarded as the boundary of the Company's territories in the north-west. Beyond that river, a new power was arising in the shape of the Sikh confederacy under Ranjit Singh, and the Company's Government had soon to adopt a definite policy with regard to the Raja of Lahore. On the whole, Minto had no wish to interfere with the existing state of relations with the Indian states. He wrote to the Chairman of the Court of Directors:

> We are in alliance and in close and intimate connexion with the more powerful Princes of India; the rest are in no condition either of individual force, or of concert and union to give us any present uneasiness … At present therefore a forbearance on our parts, from any active share in their contests may be expect to prevent any interruption from the expense of military operations, to the system of public economy.[84]

He added, 'The impression made upon my mind certainly is, that excluding the case of a European Enemy, no apprehension at present exists of interruption to our tranquility, from the hostility of any of the Native Princes of India.'[85]

Wellesley's unpopularity with the home authorities may be attributed to the principal reason that his wars had proved financially ruinous to the Company. During the years 1799 to 1806, the Company's debt nearly doubled. The India debt increased from £17,000,000 to £31,000,000, an increase of almost £14,000,000, which alarmed the Directors.[86] Much of

---

83 Malcolm, *Political History of India*, Vol. I, pp. 354, 357–69. Dodwell, *Cambridge History of India*, Vol. V, p. 375.
84 NLS M 159. Minto to E. Parry, Fort William, 19 September 1807.
85 Ibid.
86 Smith, V.A., *Oxford History of India*, 3rd edn (Oxford, 1958), p. 558. Philips, *East India Company* (Manchester, 1940), p. 142.

the Company's financial embarrassments arose from the war in Europe. The Company's warehouses in London were full, sales in Leadenhall Street had fallen very much short of what they usually produced before the war, and yet there was always a hope that a change in political events in Europe might bring about an increased demand for the Company's goods.

After Wellesley's recall, the Court of Directors unceasingly urged their Government in India to practise cutbacks in every branch of the adminis-tration. Barlow diligently carried out the Court's orders of non-interference with the Indian states and of economy and retrenchment. Minto received similar instructions from the home authorities as the only means of lessening the load of debt.[87] The company had gone to Parliament for aid. A Committee of the House of Commons was investigating the affairs of the Company. It was therefore all the more necessary to pursue a policy of economy in all branches of administration. Edward Parry wrote to Minto that although HM Government might pay a considerable amount of money in part payment of the debts the Court had long claimed, 'We must look to your Lordship's administration of our Government in India for permanent relief for unless a considerable surplus revenue is created we never can recover.'[88]

The Directors demanded a million sterling surplus in the place of a million sterling deficit in the accounts of the Government of India every year. Minto agreed that peace and economy should be the main aim of his adminis-tration. He was not at all in sympathy with Wellesley's policies of annexation and war.[89] The Directors had sent a million sterling annually to Wellesley to reduce the India debt, but he had used it for his wars.[90] Minto however agreed with the Directors that:

> ... the primary object of your Government in India must be the improvement
> of your financial situation; ... a diminution of debt, a balance between your
> receipt and expenditure, followed by a surplus applicable to investment, are
> the ends to which our general system and our particular measures must be
> directed, ... On this principle my first duty must be to reject and avoid every
> project however plausible as to remote benefit, that involves immediate expense
> of serious amount. Amongst such projects War is unquestionably the Chief,
> and is forbidden by many other motives scarcely less powerful than economy.[91]

[87] NLS Minto Papers Box 56. R. Dundas to Minto, 1 June 1807. NLS M 192. E. Parry to Minto, 15 June 1807. Ibid., 5 September 1807.

[88] Ibid., 30 April 1808.

[89] As the President of the Board of Control, Minto had refused to have anything to do with Wellesley, although Grenville openly supported him. When the Grenvilles left office, Wellesley was described by Lady Minto as 'the only Rat from the Grenville party'. NLS M 59. Lady Minto to Minto, 31 April 1807.

[90] Philips, *East India Company*, p. 142.

[91] NLS M 159. Minto to Edward Parry, Fort William, 19 September 1807.

Minto was therefore inclined to carry on a policy of peace and economy. 'This does not offer a very brilliant career,' he wrote to the Earl of Caledon, Governor of the Cape, 'but if it is a useful one it will satisfy my ambition.'[92] He however soon realised that his administration might not be as peaceful and as devoid of war as he had hoped.

The Napoleonic Wars in Europe had their inevitable repercussions in the East. During Wellesley's administration, Napoleon's Egyptian expedition had aroused the fears of the English regarding the safety of their territories in India. Before 1800, the importance of the land frontiers of India had scarcely been realised. This was perhaps natural enough because the British territories in India extended far short of the natural frontiers. However, the probability of a French overland invasion of India through Turkey and Western Asia, either singly or in collaboration with Russia, brought the problem of the defence of the north-west frontier into focus. The European War forced on Minto a more active and consequently a more expensive line of policy. In December 1807, he wrote to W.F. Elphinstone, one of the Directors, 'Find employment for Bonaparte in Europe and you shall have a surplus revenue in a year.'[93] Again in May 1808, 'you shall have the million surplus to a certainty, provided Europe does not come to Asia to run us deeper and deeper in debt'.[94] In the interim, Napoleon's treaty with Persia at Finkenstein (4 May 1807) and with Russia at Tilsit (7 July 1807) threatened to bring the European War to the door of India via the north-west.

92 Ibid., Minto to the Earl of Caledon, Fort William, 15 December 1807.
93 NLS M 159, pp. 93–95. Minto to W.F. Elphinstone, Calcutta, 3 December 1807.
94 NLS M 160, p. 97. Minto to W.F. Elphinstone, Fort William, 21 May 1808.

Two

POSITIONING IN PERSIA

Britain's West Asia Policy and Strategies against the French Threat

The French East India Company (*Compagnie des Indes Orientales*) had been founded at the instigation of Jean-Baptiste Colbert with investment capital amounting to fifteen million *livres tournois* (approximately £600,000) in 1664. A decade later, Francois Martin established its Indian headquarters at Pondicherry, eighty-five miles south of Madras on the Coromandel Coast. Following the British pattern of settlement, the French established subsidiary factories at Surat (Gujarat) and Chandarnagar (Bengal) on the banks of the Hughli River (Ganges delta) and by the end of the century were competing with the English factories for the Indian market. By seizing the islands of Ile de France (Mauritius) and Bourbon in the Indian Ocean after 1721, France was able to keep its fleet ready for offensive and defensive action against any Indian port. The French reached their peak profit in India in the late eighteenth century with average rate of return of 25 per cent annually on their investment, while the much larger and more cumbersome British company profits were down to under 10 per cent in the same period, although British imports from India were valued at over one million pounds annually. The era of fellow European cooperation and friendship in the 'hostile Orient' was rapidly being replaced by tensions of competitive trade, national rivalry and jealousy. In 1741, Pondicherry came under the presidency of Joseph Francois Dupleix (1697–1764), son of his company's director-general and a statesman of foresight. Its population at the time was about the same as that of Madras, close to 50,000. Five years later, the European war over Maria Theresa's disputed claim to the Austrian succession lured Britain and France into a conflict that erupted in southern India in the summer of 1746. The British captured several French ships, which provoked Dupleix to call for the fleet under the command of Admiral Mahe de la Bourdonnais at Ile de France, swiftly turning the tide along the Coromandel Coast in France's favour. Madras was easily captured by the French in September 1746 and among those taken prisoner at Fort St George was young Robert Clive (1725–74), a 'writer' in the company's civil service who had earlier been so bored with his counting house job that he had tried unsuccessfully to blow out his own brains with a pistol that misfired.[1]

The importance of a French presence in Egypt and Syria (the Levant) as a springboard to expansion of French trade and against British possessions in India was first articulated by Charles Magallon, the French consul in Cairo, who wrote a report to the ambassador dated 17 June 1795:[2]

> I repeat to you citizen, once we are masters of the Red Sea, we shall soon control the English and drive them out of India, if an operation of the kind is envisaged by our government. Through Suez, during a good monsoon, we can transport a large number of troops to India with only a few ships. Our soldiers would at most spend sixty days at sea, while around the Cape of Good Hope it often takes six months to arrive.[3]

At the end of June 1797, the French, who had already conquered Venice, occupied its Ionian possessions. Bonaparte wrote to the Directoire on 16 August 1797:

> The islands of Corfu, Zante and Cephalonia are more interesting to us than the whole of Italy... The empire of the Turks is crumbling day by day; the possession of these islands will enable us to support it as far as that will be possible, or to take our share of it... The time is no longer distant when we shall feel that, to destroy England truly, we shall have to capture Egypt. The vast Ottoman Empire which is perishing day by day will soon force us to think about ways in which to preserve our trade in the Levant.[4]

Bonaparte appeared to have decided to take advantage of the friendly attitudes of certain Indian princes such as Tipu-Sahib (the Sultan of Mysore, who wished to initiate a campaign against the occupiers of his homeland[5]) with regard to France, since both in his official declarations and in his private conversations, the invasion of India stood out as a continuation of the Egyptian campaign.[6] Indeed, he assured the Directoire that 'as soon as he has conquered Egypt, he will establish relations with the Indian princes and together with them, attack the English in their possessions'.[7] Talleyrand outlined this project in the 'Report on the question of Egypt' which he submitted to the Directors on 13 February 1798. 'Having occupied and

1   Wolpert, Stanley, *A New History of India* (Oxford, 2009), Chap. 12, pp. 180–81.
2   Amini, Iradj, *Napoleon and Persia (Franco-Persian Relations under the First Empire)* (Odenton, MD, 1999), Chap. 1, p. 5.
3   Charles-Roux, F.J., *Les Origines de l'Expedition d'Egypte* (Paris, 1910), p. 272.
4   Napoleon I[er], *Correspondance generale* (Paris, 1858–70), 32 Vols, Letter 2103.
5   Amini, *Napoleon and Persia*, Chap. 1, p. 11.
6   Ibid.
7   Barras, vicomte de, *Memoires* (Paris, 1895), p. 11.

fortified Egypt, we shall send a corps of 15,000 men from Suez to India to join the forces of Tipu-Sahib and drive away the English.'[8]

The urgent problem therefore facing Minto in India was the security of the Company's trade and territory from the Bonapartist threat. By the middle of 1807, Napoleon had subdued the greater part of Western Europe, made peace with Russia, and established French influence at Constantinople and Tehran. The overland route to India therefore appeared open to the advance of his troops. Under the pressure of this external danger, the Company's Government in India under Minto was forced to think about the security of its north-west frontier.

Prior to Napoleon's Egyptian expedition of 1798, the problem of the north-west frontier defence had scarcely arisen. An idea had lingered since the days of Robert Clive and Warren Hastings that so long as the British navy maintained its superiority, all external attempts to subvert British power in India could be thwarted by this powerful navy. The natural land frontiers of India in the north, north-west and north-east aroused little political interest until Wellesley took charge. The geography and politics of the neighbouring states – Persia, Afghanistan, Tibet and Burma – were neglected until then. The only source of information about these countries was obtained from missionaries, tradesmen and travellers who ventured there of their own volition and risk.

The earliest contact between France and Persia dated back to the Middle Ages, but it was under Louis XIV and Colbert that a political and commercial character began to be defined. A concession was initiated covering all of the countries and seas east of the Cape of Good Hope, and applied to all activities extending to the Persian Gulf. In 1665 Messrs Lalain and Laboulaye were instructed to go to Isfahan as leaders of a delegation of the new Company in order to promote French influence and interests with the Shah of Persia. The shah in turn welcomed their presence as a counterbalance to the English and the Dutch and granted them a three-year exemption from customs duties and accorded them the privileges that the other foreign powers enjoyed.[9] However, in reality, trade between France and Persia by way of the Persian Gulf was not given much stimulus, since French shipping came under threat of attack from both the English and Dutch, who were at war with France. Further, the merchants of Marseilles were displeased with the establishment of an organisation that chose the ports of the Atlantic Ocean rather than their own, so they focused on the older trade routes via the Levant. Thus, despite the continued presence of the French Company's agents at Bandar Abbas and Isfahan, trade between France and Persia remained mainly symbolic and the French presence manifested itself through Capuchin

8   Lacour-Gayet, Georges, *Talleyrand, 1754–1838* (Paris, 1930), Vol. 1, p. 310.
9   Amini, *Napoleon and Persia*, Chap. 2, p. 16.

and Jesuit missionaries.[10] The frustration was best expressed by Comte de Pontchartrain:

> If France had really had a Compagnie des Indes consisting of merchants who were able to sow in order to reap, the treaty signed in the name of the king by M. Michel with the Sophy of Persia in the month of September 1708 could have opened up trade between the two nations through the Red Sea and the Persian Gulf, as practised by the English and the Dutch. But Providence has decided otherwise... The French are tired of being in India and will stop at nothing to be driven out of that country.[11]

A new treaty that was significantly beneficial to the French was signed at Versailles on 13 August 1715, contingent on their aiding Persia with the proposed conquest of Muscat and Oman, which the French wished to avoid at all costs. The impasse continued until April and May 1722 at which point the shah finally agreed to ratify the treaty without the precondition of a French alliance in the conquest of Muscat and Oman, but it was too late. The Afghan Chief Mahmud and his troops were at the gates of Isfahan and the Safavid dynasty's reign was coming to an end. For three-quarters of a century after that, Persia was to be no more than a combat area of internal rivalries and external greed.[12]

The Afghan invasion of Persia and the ensuing anarchy offered the Turks and Russians a pretext to satisfy their territorial ambitions. While the Ottoman Empire occupied its northern part, including the city of Tabriz, Peter the Great seized the ports of Derbent and Baku on the Caspian Sea, as well as the provinces of Daghestan, Mazandaran, Guilan and Astarabad (present-day Gorgan).[13]

With the rapid expansion of the British East India Company's territories under Wellesley, practically the whole of northern India came under its jurisdiction, although the westernmost limit at the time Minto came to India was the River Yamuna. Beyond the Yamuna were the independent kingdoms of Sind, the Punjab and Rajputana. The expansion of the Company's territorial and political interests brought new liabilities as it brought the Company's territories closer to the natural frontiers of India.

The threat of an external danger first drew the attention of the Government to the north-west frontier; the danger that prompted Wellesley to open diplomatic relations with Persia was a threat not from a European enemy, but from the Afghan ruler Zaman Shah. Zaman Shah invaded the Punjab in 1798 and it was rumoured that the Company's territories were next on his list. Mehdi Ali

---

10 Ibid., p.17.
11 Affaires Etrangeres, Memoires et documents perse, Vol. 2. p. 25.
12 Amini, *Napoleon and Persia*, Chap. 2, p. 24.
13 Ibid., p. 24.

Khan, a Persian agent of the Company at Bushire, suggested to the Bombay Government that a way of diverting Zaman Shah's designs on the Company's territories and checking his progress was by encouraging the Shah of Persia to continue his war with the Afghans. This wily diplomat succeeded in working upon the religious and dynastic animosities of the Persians and the Afghans without giving away that the British were actually afraid of an Afghan invasion.[14] The Afghan menace disappeared due to the internal weakness of that country, but simultaneously a new threat to the security of British territories in India was felt due to the perceived ambitious designs of Bonaparte.

It was a long established maxim of French policy that a method of undermining British strength was to attack their colonial possessions. Napoleon was by no means the originator of the French plan of an overland invasion of India. After 1792, the French Directoire considered a plan of securing a passage to India via Egypt and the Red Sea.[15] Napoleon's Egyptian expedition in May 1798 was directed to the same objective. The route through Egypt and the Red Sea to the Persian Gulf was much shorter and less exposed to danger than the route around the Cape, which was closely guarded by the British.

Napoleon's Army of the Orient landed on Marabout beach, a few miles from Alexandria, between 1 and 2 July 1798 and within three weeks had conquered major portions of Egypt including the capital Cairo, had reordered the administration and established a new government.[16] Admiral Brueys d'Aigailliers (Francois Paul), the commander of the French Fleet, fearing a return in force of the British Fleet, had sheltered his boats in Aboukir Bay, a short distance north-east of Alexandria. However, Admiral Horatio Nelson, who had scoured the nooks and crannies of the Mediterranean for the French Fleet, was finally informed of its location and around six o'clock in the evening of 1 August fought the battle that destroyed the French Fleet. Admiral Brueys was also killed in action. Bonaparte heard the news of the Aboukir disaster on 15 August 1798 and was overwhelmed by it. He was now cut off from all communication with France; and concerned about the potential benefits the British would reap from establishing supremacy in the Mediterranean. Indeed, the British were forming an alliance that was soon to include Russia, Austria, the Kingdom of the Two Sicilies and Turkey. The Ottoman Sultan was incidentally so furious at seeing a traditional friendship betrayed by the sudden invasion of Egypt that on 9 September 1798, before the Second Coalition had been formed, he declared war on France.[17]

Nelson's victory at Aboukir Bay and the success of the British army in Egypt relieved the immediate anxiety. However, while the British authorities

---

[14] Sykes, Sir P., *History of Persia*, Vol. 2 (London, 1921, 2nd edn), Chap. LXXV, pp. 299–300.
[15] Charles-Roux, *Les Origines de l'Expedition d'Egypte*, p. 341.
[16] Amini, *Napoleon and Persia*, Chap. 1, p. 29.
[17] Ibid., p. 31.

in India were trying to predict Napoleon's next strategic moves, the latter marched to Suez on 26 December 1798 to examine a potential expedition to India and to establish French supremacy over the Red Sea region. Soon after returning to Cairo, he sent a letter to the Sultan of Mysore:

> You have already been informed of my arrival on the shores of the Red Sea with an innumerable and invincible army filled with the desire to free you from the iron yoke of England. I hasten to inform you of my wish to have you provide me with news, by way of Muscat and Mocha, of the political situation in which you find yourself. I even wish that you might send some clever man whom you trust to Suez or to the great Cairo, so that I may confer with him.[18]

This letter was intercepted by the British and immediately precipitated the invasion of Mysore by General Harris and his troops on 11 February 1799. After a little less than two months of fierce fighting, one of the battalions under the command of Colonel Arthur Wellesley, the brother of the governor-general and future Duke of Wellington, stormed the town of Seringapatam and Tipu was killed during the siege. The Afghan king Zaman Shah in the meantime threatened to invade India from the north and this was of particular concern since Bonaparte could easily assist Zaman Shah after forming an alliance with Persia. In a letter to Jonathan Duncan, the Governor of Bombay, dated 13 February 1799, Wellesley sought his advice with regard to developing relations with Persia and outlining a treaty covering commercial and political aims.[19] The activities of the British East India Company in Persia, which had been interrupted after the fall of the Safavid dynasty, had started again under the reign of Karim Khan Zand. From 1763, the Company's headquarters, which had been located at Bandar Abbas, were transferred to Bushehr, another port of the Persian Gulf. The agent in place was given the rank of 'resident' at the end of the eighteenth century and to that of 'political resident in the Persian Gulf' a few years later and reported directly to the Governor of Bombay.[20]

In 1800 Wellesley sent Malcolm to negotiate a political and commercial treaty with the Shah of Persia and one of the main objectives of Malcolm's mission was 'to counteract the possible attempts of those villainous but active democrats the French'.[21] Two treaties were concluded with Persia, one political and the other commercial. The political treaty of 1801 was primarily a defensive treaty against the Afghan ruler Zaman Shah. The fifth article of the treaty provided that should a French army attempt to establish itself in

---

18   Napoleon I[er], *Correspondance generale*, Letter 3901.
19   Martin, Montgomery (ed.), *The Despatches, Minutes and Correspondence of the Marquess of Wellesley K. G.* (London, 1836), p. 432.
20   Amini, *Napoleon and Persia*, Chap. 3, p. 35.
21   Kaye, J.W., *The Life and Correspondence of Sir John Malcolm* (London, 1856), Vol. 2, p. 90.

any part of Persia, the two contracting parties were to act in cooperation 'for their expulsion and extirpation'.[22] It must be noted that there was no mention within the treaty of possible Anglo-Persian cooperation against Russia, although it was precisely this country that the Persians feared above all others.[23]

In France, Bonaparte had reached the height of his glory. The victory at Marengo (14 June 1800), followed by the Luneville peace that was to be signed within a few days, sealed the fate of Austria and consolidated the gains of Campo-Formio. Tsar Paul I, until then the implacable enemy of the First Consul, now showed endless admiration and friendship for him. A joint military operation was proposed against the British in India. A French expeditionary force of 35,000 men was to advance through Russia and the steppes to Astrakhan, then cross the Caspian Sea on Russian boats until Astarabad, where it would join a Russian army and advance by way of Herat and Kandahar to southern Afghanistan and the mouth of the Indus. At the same time, another Russian army was to leave Orenburg and advance directly by way of Khiva, Bukhara and northern Afghanistan to the upper Indus.[24]

The French reverses in Egypt and Syria eased the anxiety of the Company's Government regarding the security of its north-west frontier. During the years 1802–07, no attempts were made by the British to keep hostile European influences out of Persia, and during these years French spies and agents infiltrated into Persia, at first in various disguises and later through diplomatic channels.

The Franco-British rapprochement initiated by the Peace Treaty of Amiens (27 March 1802) was hardly more than a truce. London was unhappy with the French occupation of Belgium and Holland, which signified a threat to Britain's vital interests in Europe, and on the French side, the continual postponement of the promised evacuation of British troops from Malta obstructed its Mediterranean ambitions. The end of the French occupation of Ottoman territories in Egypt and the Adriatic had paved the way for a renewal of friendship between France and Turkey and negotiations between the two countries which began at the end of 1801 led to the Peace Treaty of Paris on 25 June 1802 and the resumption of diplomatic relations.[25]

---

[22] Aitchison, C.U., *Treaties, Engagements and Sanads Relating to India and Neighbouring Countries* (Calcutta, 1909), Vol. XII, p. 41. It is doubtful if these treaties were actually ratified by the Government of India or not. The Shah of Persia, Fateh Ali Shah, declined to put his seal to the treaty as he regarded the governor-general to be of much inferior rank to him. Instead he issued a *firman* ordering all his officers to fulfil the conditions of the treaties. It failed to be ratified by the Supreme Government as a result of the confusion which arose on the assassination of the Persian envoy, Haji Khalil Khan, who came to Bombay in 1802. The next Persian envoy, Aga Nabi Khan, who came to Calcutta three years later, met with indifference from the Government of Bengal and went back to Persia in January 1807.

[23] Amini, *Napoleon and Persia*, Chap. 4, p. 43.

[24] Rouire, *La rivalite anglo-russe au XIX⁰ siècle en Asie* (Paris 1908), p. 89.

[25] Amini, *Napoleon and Persia*, Chap. 5, p. 47.

The project of an overland invasion of the British territories in India was not given up by Napoleon after Egypt. In 1803, General Decaen was sent out as the Governor-General of the islands of Bourbon and L'Ile de France and one of his principal instructions was to prepare for the eventual invasion of the British territories in India.[26] At the beginning of 1805, Napoleon appears to have toyed with a vague plan of sending a large number of French and Spanish troops to act conjointly with Decaen's forces against British India.[27] In 1807, Napoleon appeared better prepared than ever before to carry out this expedition. French influence was uppermost in both Turkey and Persia. Sebastiani, the French ambassador to the Porte, was so successful in building up a spirit of resistance to the British among the Turks that in February 1807 Admiral Duckworth had to retreat for safety after giving up the attempt to penetrate the Dardanelles. 'From Trafalgar to the Dardanelles was a plunge from the sublime to the ridiculous.'[28]

Nearer to India, French influence was predominant in Persia. Napoleon was eager to secure Persia's alliance as it was an ideal and strategic location from which to harass his two enemies, Britain and Russia. In 1804, war broke out between Persia and Russia over Georgia and from then on the one main aim of Persia's foreign policy was to procure military or diplomatic aid against Russia. Persia received no aid from the British, for before the treaty of Tilsit, Russia was Britain's ally. Thus, indifference from the British meant an opening for the French. The first overtures for an alliance were made by a French agent in 1802, but were ignored by the shah. In 1804, the French made proposals for an alliance against Russia and in October 1805, M. Romieu came to Tehran, followed by M. Jaubert in June 1806, who brought more precise proposals of military and financial aid against Russia.[29]

Napoleon had decided to step up the process of a rapprochement with Persia. Two different but politically related circumstances caused him to do so. The first was the imminent signature of a treaty of alliance between Russia and Britain in St Petersburg, which was to be a prelude to the Third Coalition; second was the message of Fath Ali Shah brought by Marshal Brune, which opened up the prospect of a diversion in Asia.[30]

Fath Ali Shah received Alexandre Romieu with great pomp on 30 September 1805. When Romieu handed him Napoleon's letter, the shah inquired about the emperor's health and said:

[26] Prentout, H., *L'Ile de France sous Decaen* (Paris, 1901), p. 15.

[27] Sen, S.P., *The French in India* (Calcutta, 1958), p. 578.

[28] Ward, Sir A.W. and Gooch, G.F. (eds) *Cambridge History of British Foreign Policy* (Cambridge, 1922), Vol. 1, p. 358.

[29] Gardane, Alfred de, *Mission du General Gardane en Perse sous le premier Empire* (Paris, 1865), pp. 16–22.

[30] Amini, *Napoleon and Persia*, Chap. 6, p. 56.

When the Emperors of Persia and France are united, the universe will not be able to resist them. I very much desire to form an alliance with your Emperor; he is the only European monarch whose word can be counted on, because he is really great and the others are liars.[31]

Romieu fatally succumbed to an illness he had contracted in the Persian capital on 12 October 1805. He was said to have died after 'constantly vomiting for three days and suffering from shivers and great heat'.[32] The report he wrote is noteworthy as it outlines interesting perspectives and insights on the personality of Fath Ali Shah:

Although he is a despot, he consults his ministers on all important occasions, working regularly, twice a day with those of them who like Mirza Reza Gholi and Mirza Mohammad Shafi are entrusted with the administration of the Empire. He is said to be very just and very charitable toward the poor, but very severe with regard to prominent people, to the point of having them executed if they commit a serious offence. He is religious without being excessively devout or fanatic. All Christians of different sects spread across his Empire are happy with the protection he grants them.

Additionally, there follows an analysis of the approach of the Persian government with regard to Russia and the advantages France could derive from an alliance with Persia:

Its greatest and truest worries come from Russia. This country is a fearsome enemy of Persia, and whenever it wants to attach Persia in strength, it is an acknowledged truth that it will easily penetrate to the centre of the Empire. Until now it has only been waging a defensive war for several years; it has never had more than ten to twelve thousand men in Georgia. Most of them are Georgians disciplined in the Muscovite manner and the rest are Cossacks. Yet, with such insignificant forces, it has stood up to an enemy force of fourteen, fifteen, sixteen and eighteen thousand Persians.[33]

Referring to the most recent battles that had taken place between the Russians and Persians in Georgia, Romieu attributed Persian defeat to a lack of training and obsolete techniques of warfare. Romieu's observations about the strategic approach of Russia with respect to Persia are also interesting as they are contextually placed within the balance of power in Europe. He thought, for example, that the Russians would have acted promptly to conquer Erivan if the political situation in Europe had allowed them to do so. However, since the resumption of their struggles with the Persians in January 1804, they were preoccupied with the demands of the Third Coalition. On

---

[31] Foreign Office, London, FO 60/1 January 1807–December 1808, pp. 11–13.
[32] Ibid.
[33] Affaires Etrangeres, Corr. Pol. Perse, Vol. 9, Doc. 14.

11 April 1805, just after Romieu had left Paris, Britain and Russia signed a treaty of alliance in St Petersburg forming the prelude to this new coalition, which was joined by Austria and Sweden. Romieu further believed that the capture of Erivan, which Russia had been coveting for a long time, was not so much intended as a step towards its conquests within Persia than as a way of opening the road to Turkish Armenia and Anatolia and its eventual designs on Ottoman territory.[34] In Romieu's opinion, the only advantages of an alliance with Persia were on one hand to prevent the growth of Muscovy, and on the other to preserve the remains of the Ottoman Empire. 'The other advantages which France might derive from this union,' he added, 'are either precarious or very remote; in fact, Persia's influence on the Afghans to launch them against the English is less than nil.'[35]

Pierre Jaubert, Napoleon's second envoy, arrived in Tehran on 5 June 1806. In 1794, Agha Mohammad Khan, who wanted to be closer to the centre of his empire without being too far away from his native province of Mazandaran where the inhabitants were devoted to him, had made Tehran the new capital of Persia. It was built on low ground with Mount Damavand looming above it and had a population at the time of about 30,000.[36] Jaubert was hosted at the home of Mirza Reza Gholi who, having lost some of his influence at court, was due to be appointed minister of Prince Mohammad Vali Mirza, the shah's fourth son and governor of the province of Khorasan. Jaubert met him on the first evening of his stay in the Persian capital and found him well informed about the affairs of Europe.[37] Prior to his first audience with the shah, Jaubert paid other courtesy calls on the leading personalities of the empire, such as Mirza Mohammad Shafi, who since Romieu's visit was devoting more of his time to foreign affairs and especially to the promotion of Franco-Persian relations.

At the meeting with Fath Ali Shah, Jaubert conveyed Napoleon's letter contained in a brocade bag. The grand vizier Mirza Mohammad Shafi recited the Persian translation in a modulated tone to bring out the rhythm of the sentences. The shah showered Jaubert with particular honours and talked to him about the affairs of Europe (the capture of Naples and the peace between France and Turkey had impressed Persia), about Napoleon's greatness and about his own friendship with France. The audience lasted for more than an hour with the shah taking pleasure in conversing with a Frenchman who knew Persian so well.[38] Jaubert also accompanied the shah to his annual summer camp at Soltanieh and was lavished with the same attention as at Tehran. He even accompanied the shah on a hunt and on 11 July 1806, the day before his farewell audience, was presented with the *khalaat* (robe of honour) and

34 Amini, *Napoleon and Persia*, Chap. 7, p. 74.
35 Affaires Etrangeres, Corr. Pol. Perse, Vol. 9, Doc. 14.
36 Amini, *Napoleon and Persia*, Chap. 8, p. 78.
37 Ibid., Chap. 8, p. 79.
38 Ibid., Chap. 8, p. 83.

was also given a portrait of the shah along with various Persian manuscripts which he deposited at the Bibliothèque imperiale when he returned to Paris.[39]

As the British appeared to care so little for his affairs, the shah did not feel that the Treaty of 1801 restricted his diplomatic actions with other powers in any way. In response to the French proposals, he sent an envoy, Mirza Reza, to Napoleon's camp in Poland. He was to negotiate the terms of a Franco-Persian alliance.[40]

The death of Pitt in January 1806, followed by a new British policy with respect to France initiated by Fox, ushered in a period of peace in Europe. Following the example of his British friends, Alexander I of Russia had also taken steps to establish a rapprochement with France by sending an emissary, Baron d'Oubril, to Paris. However, despite the goodwill displayed on either side, negotiations between France and Britain were at an impasse due to Napoleon's desire to take over Sicily from the Bourbons. The death of Fox on 13 September 1806 brought an end to the process.[41]

Negotiations between France and Russia had followed a more positive course to the point that a peace treaty had been initiated by d'Oubril on 20 July 1806. However, the response of Alexander I to accepting its terms was clearly dependent on relations between France and Britain, which in turn depended on the Prussian stance. Prussia in the interim had allied itself (albeit reluctantly) with France by the Treaty of Paris on 15 February 1806. Indeed, soon after ratifying it, Frederick William III had sent the Duke of Brunswick to St Petersburg to apologise to Alexander for having signed the treaty.[42]

Napoleon in the meantime, managed to consolidate his ascendancy over Europe by having its key states pledge allegiance to France. By June of 1806, he had entrusted the sovereignties of Naples and Holland, the principality of Lucca, the grand duchy of Berg and Cleves and the principality of Neuchatel to his brothers Joseph and Louis, his sister Elisa, his brother-in-law Marshal Murat and his chief of staff Marshal Berthier, respectively. On 16 July 1806 he had concluded a treaty of alliance with the princes of southern Germany by becoming Protector of the Confederation of the Rhine, and the treaty of Pressburg which was imposed on Austria after his victory at Austerlitz made Napoleon the master of Venetia, Istria and Dalmatia, all adjoining the Balkan peninsula.[43]

These transformations in Europe, which were certainly not to the liking of the Britain and the continental powers, had on the other hand aligned the policy of the Ottoman Porte toward France. As soon as the news of the Pressburg treaty reached Constantinople, the British ambassador was

---

[39] Ibid., Chap. 8, p. 85.
[40] Affaires etrangeres, Corr. Pol. Perse, Vol. 10, Doc. 13.
[41] Amini, *Napoleon and Persia*, Chap. 8, p. 86.
[42] Ibid.
[43] Ibid.

informed that the renewal of the Anglo-Turkish treaty was no longer a consideration. On 5 June 1806, Selim III finally recognised Napoleon as emperor through his ambassador in Paris, thus confirming a new orientation.[44]

While Napoleon, who arrived in Mainz on 29 September 1806, was paving his way to Berlin through lightning victories at Jena and Auerstaedt, Talleyrand, who was with him, wrote to Sebastiani about his master's intentions regarding the Orient from Mainz on 18 October:

> If you have satisfactory news from M. Jaubert and if the officer whom the king of Persia has sent to the Emperor has arrived in Constantinople, tell him to ask his court for full powers to deal with the alliance between the three Empires. Find out from him what the best conditions for the alliance are, what kind of advantage it might offer against English establishments in India and if one might draw the Afghans into the same cause and have some guarantee about their dispositions. Let Persia know, either through M. Rousseau or through M. Jaubert if he is in Tehran, that it must consider itself factually as an ally of France and use all its forces against the enemy. The war in Europe cannot last long. That of Asia, carried on with the same activity, should soon come to an end. This campaign must free from Russian domination Georgia and all the provinces of the Caspian Sea where they have penetrated. The honour and the interests of Persia depend on it. It should act with vigour. France will abandon it neither in war nor in peacetime.[45]

While Napoleon's campaign against Prussia proved to be a resounding success, the war against Russia presented problems of climate and logistics for which the Grande Armée was not prepared. Hence the alliance with Turkey and Persia was crucial in terms of both countries being able to provide a diversion against Russia in Asia to alleviate the pressure brought to bear on the French armies in East Prussia. On 20 January 1807, Talleyrand again emphasised the importance of this step. 'In the struggle against the Empire of the North,' he wrote to Sebastiani, 'Turkey must form our right and Persia our extreme right wing.'[46] Following additional negotiations and after some hesitation, Turkey declared war on Russia on 24 December 1806.[47]

In January 1807, Napoleon was in Warsaw. He had just driven back the Russians at Pultusk and Golymin. The Russians would have probably suffered a crushing defeat were it not for the thick mud that prevented the French army from pursuing the retreating defenders. At the same time he ordered Talleyrand to find a man capable of carrying out the mission of minister in Persia. Talleyrand proposed several people including Vigouroux who had served at Corfu; Seguier the consul at Trieste who had travelled

44 Ibid., p. 87.
45 Affaires etrangeres, Corr. Pol. Turquie, Vol. 212, Doc. 130.
46 Vandal, Albert, *Napoleon et Alexandre Ier* (Paris, 1898), Vol. 1, p. 24.
47 Amini, *Napoleon and Persia*, Chap. 8, p. 89.

widely in India; and Bergeret, a close friend of Admiral Burix. A member of the navy himself, Bergeret had recently arrived in Paris from the Ile de France (present-day Mauritius) after having spent three years in India. Napoleon, however, wanted to know more about Persia before making his choice.[48] In the meantime, Jaubert had arrived in Warsaw and had reported to Talleyrand about his mission. He was joined there a few days later by the Persian ambassador, Mirza Mohammad Reza Khan, who was accompanied by Outrey, Romieu's former interpreter. Talleyrand summarised his meetings with Jaubert and Outrey in a letter to Napoleon:

> Persia and Turkey are willing to enter into a mutual alliance with France, either on a temporary or lasting basis against Russia. But would they as willingly enter into an alliance against England? This is what M. Outrey and M. Jaubert are unable to confirm. Persia does not even have the shadow of a navy. So it cannot attack the English by sea. By land it does not border on any of England's possessions. It could only arrive there [India] through the country of Afghanistan or through Baluchistan. So before carrying out the stipulations of the alliance it will have formed with us, it would have to form others with several nations. M. Jaubert thinks that once it is rid of the war with Russia, it will quite easily carry these nations along through its influence. But in a war with Persia would not the English always and as it were necessarily have the Russians as allies? In a war against both, Persia would have to defend its northern borders against the Russians and its southern borders against the English, who could always attack it with their ships. Would it be able at the same time to take a sizeable army into India? Such ventures would be a great deal above its forces. It can levy and maintain a sufficiently large number of troops; but in these armies there are men rather than soldiers. The sixty thousand men it has on its northern frontiers and who M. Jaubert has seen can be held in check by ten thousand Russians... On the other hand, by barring the passage to its States against English convoys and carriers, and by stopping all inland communications between England and India, it can cause enormous harm to the English. This is why M. Jaubert wishes Persia to be made to adopt an attitude not of declared hostility, but of aloofness and discord with respect to England, so that, without compromising itself too much, it may do as much harm to the English as it really can... Turkey would have little to expect and much to fear from a maritime war; if it fights another war, it will not even have the means to resist the Russians on the Black Sea, which it can do today without too many disadvantages. It appears natural that the alliance, under whatever conditions it is formed, should be common and reciprocal among the three empires. M. Jaubert nevertheless thinks that Your Majesty had better make a separate alliance with Persia and another with Turkey; he bases his opinion on the fact that Persia and Turkey have such different interests that it might become almost impossible to make them agree. In any event, I have outlined the draft of a treaty following the ideas I have just expressed and will have the honour to address it to Your Majesty tomorrow.[49]

---

[48] Ibid., Chap. 9, p. 91.
[49] *Lettres inedites de Talleyrand a Napoleon, 1800–1809*, CCXXXVIII.

On 12 April 1807 the emperor finally decided to conclude a treaty with Persia and to send a minister plenipotentiary there. Without considering any of Talleyrand's recommendations, Napoleon decided to select his aide-de-camp, General Gardane, with instructions to proceed on three fronts:[50]

1. Gather intelligence regarding Persia's resources both from a military and commercial perspective and conduct a study regarding the nature of obstacles to be surmounted by a French army of 40,000 men on its way to the Great Indies and which would be favoured by Persia and the Porte.
2. Consider Persia as a natural ally of France due to its rivalry with Russia, direct the efforts of the Persians toward improving troop training, artillery and fortifications.
3. Use diplomatic channels to hinder the trade of the British East India Company, its communications via dispatches or couriers and maintain links with Ile de France by fostering its trade to the maximum possible extent and maintain links with the French ambassador in Constantinople and strengthen ties between Persia and the Porte.

On 4 May 1807, the Treaty of Finkenstein was concluded between France and Persia, which provided for Franco-Persian cooperation against both Russia and Britain. In May 1807, Napoleon initiated a peace treaty with Russia, which was concluded in July 1807. Therefore, the promises of military aid against Russia to Persia could be considered deceptive in order to gain Persia's acquiescence to the clauses directed against the British. This was a crucial weakness, which was very soon to dissolve the Franco-Persian alliance, but at the time, the combination appeared formidable to British observers. By this treaty of sixteen articles, Napoleon guaranteed the territorial integrity of Persia, including Georgia, and agreed to secure the evacuation of Russian troops from Georgia. There was also a military pact that France should provide ammunition to the shah, send officers to train Persian recruits and engineers to manufacture artillery in Persia. Articles 8 and 12 were directed against the British. Article 8 stated that the shah agreed to break off diplomatic relations with the British, to recall his envoy from Bengal and not to receive any British agents in future. Although the shah agreed to order all British agents in Persia and the Gulf region to quit immediately and to seize all British merchandise in his ports, these steps were never actually carried out. At the time, Gardane was in Tehran, the Company's agents were still at Bushire and commerce between Persia and India was quietly carried on as before. In addition, Fath Ali Shah was also to try to secure the cooperation of the Afghans and other tribes of Kandahar in an attack on British territories in India. He was to provide port facilities should a French squadron arrive in

---

[50] Napoleon I[er], *Correspondance generale*, op. cit.

the Gulf. Article 12 indicated that the shah allow the passage of French troops through his dominions.[51] It is doubtful if the shah would have hazarded his own independence by allowing a large body of foreign troops into Persia. The Persian minister Mirza Shafi later told Sir Harford Jones that the shah did not intend to allow more than 5,000 French troops into Persia.[52]

Napoleon's instructions to General Gardane, who arrived in Tehran on 4 December 1807, reveal how he intended to use his Persian alliance against the British. The French officers of the mission, while instructing the Persians in up-to-date military tactics and discipline to fight the Russians, were to study the routes to India either by way of Aleppo or the Persian Gulf and survey not only the shores of the Gulf but also those of the Caspian Sea. Gardane was to ascertain the force Persia would be able to provide to unite with a French force of 20,000 men in an attack on India. An important objective was to attempt to establish a triple alliance between France, Turkey and Persia.[53] The Treaty of Finkenstein was ratified by the shah but a military and commercial convention which Gardane drew up shortly after his arrival that France should supply 20,000 rifles to Persia and the shah should cede the island of Kharak in the Persian Gulf to the French was never actually ratified.[54] The significance of the Treat of Tilsit (July 1807) was not immediately perceived by either the French agents in Persia or by the Persians. Gardane during his first months spared no pains to fulfil his duties. His officers trained about 4,000 Persian recruits in the European style, inspected the border fortresses and set up a canon foundry at Isfahan. He sent Trezel and Dupre to inspect the ports in the Persian Gulf. They surveyed Bandar Abbas and other places on the Gulf and at Shiraz conferred with the envoys from Sind who were on their way back. From Tehran, Gardane established communications with the French legations in Constantinople, St Petersburg and L'Ile de France.[55] He zealously drew up plans for the march to the Indus. He calculated that an army of 50,000 of which 30–40,000 would be Asian, would take seven or eight months from Aleppo to the Indus via Kabul and Peshawar. The Afghans, the Sikhs and the people of Sind were to be encouraged to join in by holding out prospects of plunder. According to his plan, Decaen would land

---

51   Gardane, *Mission du General Gardane*, pp. 71–80. Traite d'alliance entre S.M. Napoleon et Feth Ali Shah, fait a Finkenstein, le 4 mai 1807.

52   TNA, FO 60/2. Harford Jones to Canning, 4 April 1809.

53   Gardane, *Mission du General Gardane*, pp. 81–94. Instructions pour le general Gardane, 10 mai 1807. Gardane was appointed minister plenipotentiary at Tehran on 12 April 1807. He was a high-ranking officer of the emperor's household and a distinguished French general of the army. For his services, Napoleon granted him the title of a count with holdings in Hanover and Westphalia. His mission to Persia consisted of four lieutenants, five captains, three secretaries, six interpreters, an attaché, a physician, two chaplains and an escort of about 300 soldiers.

54   Ibid., pp. 38–39.

55   Ibid., pp. 42–45. BL, IOR Fac. Rec. Persia 29, pp. 44–48.

troops from L'Ile de France near Bombay in order to act concomitantly with the northern invasion.[56]

Another French emissary, M. de La Blanche, First Secretary at the French embassy in Constantinople, was expected at the court of Fath Ali Shah. Following the emperor's orders immediately after the battle of Eylau, General Sebastiani had told him to persuade the Persians to operate a diversion against the Russians in Georgia, while the latter were engaged on the Vistula. He was also to persuade the shah to declare war on Britain. La Blanche arrived in Tehran in June 1807 and was immediately granted an audience with the shah and delivered the letter written by Napoleon on 17 January following his victories at Pultusk and Golymin. The emperor exhorted the shah to proceed with a vigorous attack on the Russians, 'whom my victory delivers to you weakened and discouraged,' adding, 'Take Georgia and all the provinces that were your empire back from them, and close against them the Caspian gates that had long guarded its entrance.'[57]

The second part of his mission was not straightforward. The Persians didn't want to risk the hostility of the British without being sure of the positive support of France in their war against Russia. The shah's response to Napoleon's letter was noncommittal:

> In this year, it has reached the ears of our *mehraban* [dear] brother [i.e. Napoleon] that the Russian government has several times sent persons charged with negotiating peace with us and determining its conditions, but we have sent them back with the answer that the affair of peace can only be broached when the Russians have completely left Persian territory... May it be above all recognised and manifest that the Kings of Europe who seek and cultivate the friendship of this Prince (who only aims at unity and harmony) are by that very fact assured of our affection; but let it also be known that we have broken relations with the enemies of his Empire.[58]

While La Blanche was negotiating with the shah in Tehran, major events had radically changed the situation in Europe. Napoleon's military operations against Russia had started again and on 14 June, after the fierce battle of Friedland which cost the lives of 25,000 Russians, they had fallen back on the Niemen. On 25 June 1807, Napoleon and Alexander I met on a raft palace in the middle of the river for the event and had negotiated the terms

56 Gardane, *Mission du General Gardane*, pp. 107–08; pp. 11–128: Idees du general Gardane sur une expedition dans l'Inde par Delhi et Patna en traversant la Turquie et la Perse. Envoye le 24 decembre 1807; pp. 129–44: Notes sur certains details suite aux idees sur un expedition dans l'Inde, addressees par le general Gardane, le 24 decembre 1807, a S. Exe. Le Ministre des relations exterieures.

57 Affaires etrangeres, Corr. Pol. Perse, Vol.9, Doc. 57.

58 Ibid., Doc. 128.

of a peace treaty which was signed at Tilsit on 7 July 1807.[59] Despite France's commitment in accordance with Article 4 of the Treaty of Finkenstein to 'make every effort to force Russia to evacuate Georgia and Persian territory, and to obtain this by the coming peace treaty', no reference to this point was made in the Treaty of Tilsit. Napoleon was merely seeking to secure the supremacy of Europe even it meant giving the Russians a free hand with regard to the Asian continent.

Napoleon's interest in Persia as the natural enemy of Russia subsided as soon as he had concluded a peace with Alexander I. Nevertheless, he continued to attach great importance to Persia as a passageway for an expedition to India. This was why General Gardane was formally asked to proceed to his destination despite the radical change in the nature of his mission. Some of the instructions given in November 1807 to General Caulaincourt, the Duke of Vicence, who was appointed French ambassador in Russia after the treaty of Tilsit also confirm this:

> There might be a plan for an expedition to India. The more fanciful it sounds, the more the attempt to do it (and what can France and Russia not do?) would frighten the English; striking terror into English India, spreading confusion in London, and to be sure, forty thousand Frenchmen to whom Persia will have granted passage by way of Constantinople joining forty thousand Russians who arrive by way of the Caucasus, would be enough to terrify Asia and make its conquest. It is with such views in mind that the Emperor has let the ambassador he appointed for Persia travel to his destination.[60]

The shah ratified the Treaty of Finkenstein and approved the conclusion of a commercial treaty based on the terms of the earlier treaties of 1708 and 1715. Additionally, he promised to have freedom of religion respected in all the towns where there would be French consuls and to yield the island of Kharg (Kharak) in the Persian Gulf to France. The latter promise was subject to the execution of Article 4 of the Franco-Persian treaty of alliance, namely the evacuation of Georgia and Persian territory by Russian troops.[61] At the same time, Gardane began to deal with the question of the expedition to India. He dispatched officers to prepare topographical accounts. Captains Verdier and Lamy were sent to train Persian soldiers on European tactics. Lieutenants Fabvier and Reboul were sent to Isfahan to have cannons made for the Persian artillery. The impasse was essentially the lack of follow-through on the reciprocity of Article 4 as mentioned previously and the shah's obligations with regard to Article 8. This article was precisely what mattered most to France for it included the anti-British measures to be taken by Persia. By finally

---

[59] Amini, *Napoleon and Persia*, Chap. 10, p. 110.
[60] Archives privees du general de Caulaincourt, Archives Nationales.
[61] Amini, *Napoleon and Persia*, Chap. 11, p. 122.

agreeing with the shah that this clause was not 'enforceable until Article 4 was carried out', Gardane won the trust of the Persians, but no realistic progress could be made due to the recently concluded Treaty of Tilsit. On 21 January 1808, Gardane signed an agreement with Mirza Shafi for the sale of 20,000 French guns to Persia, at the price of thirty francs apiece; the entire sum was to be paid at the time the goods were delivered at the port of Bushehr (Bushire) or any other port of the Persian Gulf (the negotiation of this agreement formed part of his secret instructions). The Persians had in turn asked for French workers such as clothiers, painters, printers, glaziers, clockmakers, etc., to help them establish these crafts in their country.[62] On 28 January he received a *firman* (command) from the shah confirming the terms of the commercial treaty he had concluded with his ministers. The treaty, which was based on those of 1708 and 1715, contained 23 articles and granted a three-year tax exemption to French merchants in Persia and Persian merchants in France.[63]

Within six months of Gardane's arrival however, Franco-Persian relations began to cool. The peace of Tilsit changed the direction of French policy with regard to Persia. Instead of assisting Persia to resist the Russian forces in Georgia which the shah demanded, France could now merely offer to mediate. Gardane succeeded in bringing about a cessation of hostilities, but the claims of Persia and Russia over Georgia were irreconcilable. Persia complained that France had not taken Persian interests into account while establishing a treaty with Russia, while the French responded by indicating that at the time of concluding the Treaty of Tilsit, the Treaty of Finkenstein had not been ratified by the shah and Persia had at that time no accredited envoy at the French court. The Persian Government pointed out that as Napoleon's influence was not inconsiderable he could at least have conditionally stipulated clauses taking care of Persia's interests. The Treaty of Tilsit gave the tsar complete freedom of action in the East. Gardane tried to bring about truce for a year over Georgia, so that the French plans with regard to India could be tried. The fears of the British, aroused by the Treaty of Finkenstein and Gardane's mission to Persia, would have been greatly allayed had they know that Gardane had agreed that the stipulations of Articles 8 and 12 of the Treaty of Finkenstein were not to be executed by Persia until the evacuation of the Russian troops from Persian territory and the conclusion of a peace between Persia and Russia.[64] The shah was not willing to commence hostilities against the British on the bare promises of the French.

It was only toward the end of October 1807 that Napoleon himself informed his ally of the peace treaty he had concluded with Russia. In a letter from Fontainebleau dated 26 October, he wrote to the shah:

---

[62] Affaires etrangeres, Corr. Pol. Perse, Vol.9, Doc. 164.
[63] Affaires etrangeres, Corr. Pol. Perse, Vol. 9, Doc. 171.
[64] BL, IOR Fac. Rec. Persia 26, p. 113.

After the friendly letter Your Majesty wrote to me in the month of Rebiol-Aghir, God has continued to bless my armies, and having taken them from the western regions to the banks of the Niemen, I made an honourable peace with Russia, and that country and the Sublime Porte have ceased their hostilities. I regret not having had with me a Persian ambassador invested with full powers and the necessary instructions to have your Empire included in this peace treaty. But I took care of your interests. In my conversations with the Emperor of Russia, I was assured that he did not aspire to any conquest over you and I shall intervene, if you so desire, in your peace treaty with this Prince. Then there shall remain a single enemy, and that is England. Let us remain allies against it. Let us constantly have the same friends and the same enemies.[65]

At the beginning of February 1808, Gardane received a letter from Napoleon in Paris which enabled him to convey better news to the shah. Napoleon authorised him to intervene as the French mediator between Persia and Russia during the negotiations which were to take place in Tehran between the shah's government and a Russian ambassador. In doing so, the emperor was only partly following the objective of Article 4 of the Treaty of Finkenstein, for instead of reaffirming his promise 'to make all efforts to force Russia to evacuate Georgia and Persian territory, and to obtain this through the coming peace treaty', he now stated that 'this evacuation would constantly be the object of my policy and of all my solicitude'.[66] In return, he expressly asked the shah to end all commerce between Persia and Britain and to ban British agents and factors from Persian cities and ports and to have all correspondence between Britain and India intercepted.[67] Fath Ali Shah had to be satisfied with this assurance, as he realised that he had essentially put his country's destiny into Napoleon's hands and as such had nothing substantial to offer in return in the game of rivalry between France and Britain.

It is unnecessary to repeat the obvious practical difficulties that rendered a French overland invasion of India an impracticable proposition. The extent and difficulties of the intervening land and sea routes, the mountain and desert barrier, the difficulties of transporting a large European army, the uncertainties of the European situation and the problem of holding a stable rearguard all weighed heavily against such a project. Napoleon's agreements with the shah and the tsar, instead of forming a formidable coalition against the British, actually contributed to vitiate his project. Hoskins points out that at this time the control of the sea routes were nearly equally shared by Britain and France. After Trafalgar (21 October 1805), British naval supremacy was unchallenged in the Mediterranean, but French influence was predominant

---

[65] Affaires etrangeres, Corr. Pol. Perse, Vol. 9, Doc. 151.
[66] Affaires etrangeres, Corr. Pol. Perse, Vol. 9, Doc. 171.
[67] Amini, *Napoleon and Persia*, Chap. 11, p. 125.

in Egypt and Turkey, so the British had no control of the Red Sea route to India. Consequently, although Napoleon was unable to send an expeditionary force to India due to the geographical distance and British control of the Mediterranean, the British, despite their naval supremacy, were in constant fear for the security of their territories in India as they were unable to prevent the French totally from gaining access to the approaches to India.[68]

The concern the British felt at the idea of a French invasion of their territories in India is perhaps to be understood not by weighing the pros and cons of its practical execution, but rather by placing it in the context of European, Middle Eastern and Indian situations. The two former cases have been discussed, but the British were by no means confident of their position in India. British rule was not yet firmly established and in the attempt to do so, Wellesley had alienated the Indian powers. It can be safely said that the British had no friends in India. The sepoy uprising in Vellore in July 1806 had been a shattering experience. The Marathas, the Sikhs and every independent and dependent Indian power were a potential source of danger. In northern India there were bands of mercenaries who wandered continually from service to service and were willing to fight for any power as long as they were paid.[69] A foreign invader with sufficient funds could therefore raise an army at will. Winning allies among the Indian powers was an old policy of the French and the British were constantly on the lookout for 'French agents' in the courts of the princes.

The internal insecurity of the Government was one of the chief causes of anxiety to the British in India. Minto wrote to Dundas:

> We must not forget the nature of our tenure in this Empire, and that it would not require a great European army to disturb our security in India. A body of Twenty thousand French troops, commanded by French officers,... and preceded by French intrigue, I am firmly convinced would not subdue us, but would create a struggle which... must however be attended with great present calamity and followed by signal and unavoidable distress in our affairs. I should for these reasons be sorry that half the number of French regulars I have mentioned were landed in India, to head the confederacy which with that support we might expect to see united against us.[70]

This sentiment was echoed by the Court of Directors. The Chairman wrote to Minto that:

> The political system pursued by our Indian Govt. from the year 1800 to 1805, has unquestionably destroyed the friendship & cordiality of the Native Powers

---

68 Hoskins, H.L., *British Routes to India* (Philadelphia, PA, 1928), Chap. 3, p. 61.
69 Tract 69, pp. 3–37. A letter on the present crisis of affairs in India, addressed to Edward Parry by R.L. Ambrose (London, 1807).
70 NLS M 159. Minto to R. Dundas, Calcutta, 1 November 1807 (Secret).

towards us, & rendered an Invasion from the French far more formidable than it would otherwise be;... Powers who are still controuled by our subsidiary forces and political Residents must be impatient for liberty.[71]

The home authorities formed an exaggerated idea of the danger of a foreign invasion of India and believed that the treaties of Finkenstein and Tilsit had resulted in a formidable coalition against the British. *The Times* took up the subject of a French invasion of India and a private correspondent wrote to Minto that 'the Papers have been amusing the publick with Reports of a joint attempt to attack India with a Gallo-Russian Army by the line of Persia... there are some who think that Proposal not so chimerical as the generality are inclined to consider it'.[72] In September 1807, the Secret Committee wrote to the Governor-General-in-Council:

> The events which have recently taken place in the north of Europe, and the conclusion of a Peace between Russia and France on terms which are certainly not favourable, and may possibly be highly prejudicial, to the interests of the British Empire renders it our indispensable duty to call your early and serious attention to the defence of our Indian Territories; not merely to meet an attack from any of the native Powers, aided by an inconsiderable body of Europeans, but to withstand the efforts of France, in conjunction perhaps with Persia, and even with Russia, and the invasion of Hindostan, on its north western Frontier, by a numerous and powerful European Force.[73]

The Secret Committee admitted that there were many difficulties in the way of the execution of such a plan, but Napoleon's prestige was so high that nothing he attempted could be safely ignored as impossible.

In December 1807, Robert Dundas, President of the Board of Control, wrote to Minto:

> The recent proceedings of Russia will leave you no longer in doubt as to the absolute necessity of being on your guard against an attack on your North Western Frontier... It is known, that French officers have proceeded from Russia towards Persia, and there are many rumours in circulation as to a large force having been detached from Poland... Perhaps the dismemberment and partition of European Turkey will be the first and immediate effort of Buonaparte; but whatever may be his views in that quarter of the world, I cannot bring myself to doubt that the overthrow of the British power in India is one constant object of his hostile ambition.[74]

71 NLS M 192. Charles Grant to Minto, 10 June 1809.
72 NLS M 94. Col. Drinkwater to Minto, Kensington, 3 February 1808.
73 BL, IOR Board's Secret Drafts, Vol. 3, No. 31. Secret Committee to the Governor-General-in-Council, East India House, 24 September 1807.
74 NLS M 172. R. Dundas to Minto, Whitehall, 9 December 1807.

It was believed that if Russia cooperated in the scheme and allowed an army to advance from Astrakhan to Astrabad, the rest of the march from the Caspian Sea to the banks of the Indus would be performed with the cooperation and assistance of Persia. The English had been scared of a Russian threat to India in 1800–01, when on the outbreak of hostilities between the two countries, Tsar Paul actually ordered his Cossacks to march towards India without as much as procuring maps or taking account of the practical difficulties. The army advanced as far as the Volga but its further progress was stopped by the assassination of the tsar.[75] The result of the Russian scare was that the overland routes to India, either from the Black Sea or from Syria to Persia, became the subject of discussion in Britain. Malcolm's letter dated 23 March 1801 to Elgin (then ambassador at Constantinople), was the most important document on the subject.[76] In this letter, Malcolm discussed the overland routes by which it might be possible for Russia either independently or in conjunction with other powers to attack the British possessions in India from the north-west. Two routes were discussed: one from an eastern port in the Caspian to the banks of the Indus and the other from the port of Orenburg through Tartary to Bukhara followed by either an attack on Oudh by marching through the Punjab or on Bombay by coming down the Indus, respectively. However, the success of a project of attacking the British territories in India by either of these two routes depended on the cooperation of the intermediate states – Persia, Afghanistan and the Uzbeks – with whom Russia had no connection. In 1800–01, the Russian designs on India did not cause any serious alarm. The Persians were acutely concerned of Russian objectives in the region as Empress Catherine had sent an army into Georgia in 1796 and Tsar Paul also pressed Russia's claim over Georgia, which the shah regarded as a part of his own dominion. The Afghans and Uzbeks were also unlikely to admit a large foreign force into their countries. After the Treaty of Tilsit however, the British suspected the tsar would assist Bonaparte in his objectives with regard to India. It is useful to mention that during these years, the British were so preoccupied with what Rawlinson calls 'Gallophobia' that the significance of Russian pressure on Georgia was not recognised. During the years 1801–07, Persia's repeated applications for aid against Russian encroachments were ignored by the British. After the Treaty of Tilsit, vague fears of a joint French and Russian invasion were revived, but Britain's bête noire at this time was Bonaparte and not Russia.

In November 1807, before the news of Tilsit reached India, Minto wrote to Dundas:

---

75 Sykes, *A History of Persia*, Vol. 2, p. 300.
76 NLS M 181. Col. Malcolm to the Earl of Elgin, Camp on the banks of the Tigris near Baghdad, 23 March 1801.

The views of Buonaparte have long been known to be directed towards India; but they have of late begun to unfold themselves more sensibly. Success in this present contest with Russia... an absolute ascendancy at the Porte, or a positive conquest of Turkey; a confederacy or understanding with Russia, in Oriental Schemes, if such a prodigy in politics can happen, twice in so short a period; any one of these events must tend to the furtherance, for I am far from saying, the accomplishment, of this last and fondest projects against the British power in India.[77]

News from Europe trickled through Constantinople via the Company's agents at Baghdad, Basra and Bushire to Bombay and Bengal. Although the details of these reports and information could not always be relied upon, the main items of news were usually creditworthy. By the beginning of 1808, the Government of Bengal gathered news of an alliance between France and Persia, of peace between France and Russia and between Russia and the Porte, and also that war had broken out between Britain and Denmark.[78] The Danish settlements of Serampore and Tranquebar were promptly occupied.[79] The Portuguese settlements at Goa, Daman and Diu were also occupied in consequence of the war between Britain and French-occupied Portugal, and an unsuccessful expedition was sent to occupy Macao under Rear-Admiral Drury in 1808, contrary to orders from the Secret Committee.[80]

Napoleon's diplomatic and military successes in Europe increased Minto's anxiety about the practicability of a French attack on India. He wrote to Dundas:

the unfortunate turn that events appear to have taken in Europe, had... accelerated the approach of those difficulties, which although not... out of our contemplation, did not appear at least so impending as there is now reason to consider them.... It appears pretty well established that... a cessation of hostilities or a long truce has taken place between France and Russia, and that either peace, or a truce has been made between Russia and the Porte. A war between Great Britain & Denmark appears the least doubtful of any.... From this state of things arises that degree of leisure and opportunity which France required for the prosecution of hostile designs against India. The relation in which the War between Russia & Persia and the political use made of it by the French Government, places the more Eastern Nations of Europe and the Western Powders of Asia with regard to France, has removed many of the principal obstacles to the prosecution of such designs.[81]

---

[77] NLS M 159. Minto to R. Dundas, 1 November 1807.

[78] NLS M 159. Minto to R. Dundas, Fort William, 10 February 1808 (Secret).

[79] BL, IOR Fac. Rec. Persia 28, pp. 16–17. Governor-General's minute, Fort William, 27 January 1808. Ibid., Letter from Governor-General to the Danish Governor at Serampore, 27 January 1808. Ibid., Instructions to Lt Col. Carey, 27 January 1808. NLS M 335. G. Barlow to Minto, Fort St George, 16 February 1808.

[80] BL, IOR Board's Secret Drafts, Vol. 3, No. 40. Secret Committee to the Governor-General-in-Council, 11 December 1807 (Secret). Ibid., No. 41. 22 December 1807 (Secret).

[81] NLS M 159. Minto to R. Dundas, Fort William, 10 February 1808 (Secret).

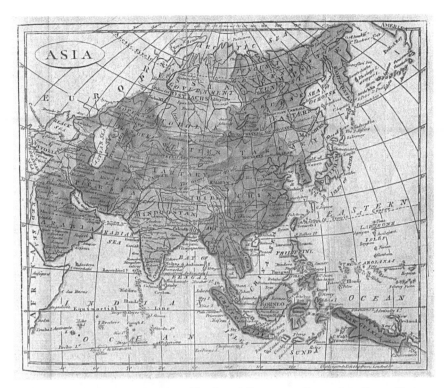

2 'Asia' in 1808 (from R. Brookes, *The General Gazetteer; or Compendious Geographical Dictionary*, Eighth Edition, Dublin, 1808. Courtesy of the University of Texas Libraries, The University of Texas at Austin)

Minto recognised the fact that the inability of the British to offer aid to Persia to fight the Russians had turned the shah towards the French. Intelligence about French activities in Persia were gathered from reports, mostly exaggerated and sometimes false, sent by the Company's agents at Muscat and Bushire. In July 1807, the resident at Bushire, N.H. Smith reported the cession of Gombroon in the Persian Gulf to the French by the shah and that a French squadron from L'Ile de France was probably on its way to take possession.[82] He also reported the actual arrival at Tabriz on the western side of the Caspian, of 300 French troops and twenty-four French officers.[83] He was presumably referring to Gardane's escort. The resident at Muscat, David Seton, reported the probable cession of either Bandar Abbas or Kharak to the French.[84] In order to find out exactly what was happening in

82 NLS M 193. Governor-General-in-Council to the Secret Committee, 26 September 1807.
83 NLS M 194. Governor-General-in-Council to Secret Committee, Fort William, 9 February 1808.
84 BL, IOR Ben. Sec. & Pol. Cons, 202. Cons. of 26 October 1807, No. 2. David Seton to J. Duncan, 25 September 1807.

3 The Emperor Napoleon in his Study at the Tuileries, by Jacques-Louis David,
1812, 1961.9.15, Samuel H. Kress Collection. Courtesy National Gallery of Art,
Washington

the Gulf, Rear-Admiral Pellew sent HMS *Pitt* to reconnoitre Gombroon and a squadron of four ships was kept in readiness at Bombay to sail for the Gulf at the shortest possible notice in order to prevent the French from occupying a post in the Gulf.[85]

Another report caused quite a stir. Captain Ben Hallowell in a letter dated Aboukir, 22 September 1807, reported that the French General Menou was advancing with an army of 12,000 French troops towards Persia from Poland.[86] He did not mention the source of this information and neither did he present any supporting data. The home authorities received the same intelligence from Sir Arthur Paget, who was probably under Captain Hallowell's authority. Sir Arthur Paget's source of information was a Turkish officer on board his ship at Aboukir Bay. It is extremely unlikely that Gardane's party, which travelled through Turkey to Persia, was magnified by this officer into such a large body of French troops. General Menou was actually in Italy at the time. It appears that the march of Gardane's escort to Persia was the foundation of all these reports that the British received with regard to the advance of a French army into Persia. Minto was by no means willing to ignore this report altogether for he believed that:

> ... the march of a body of French troops from some quarter or other towards Persia, is a measure corresponding so much with those of which we have a positive knowledge, that I conceive we cannot prudently exclude some such event from the general state of facts on which our conduct should be regulated.[87]

Minto was willing to believe that an actual French invasion of the British territories in India was within the range of possibility and decided to adopt measures of defence accordingly. He wrote to Dundas:

> It is unnecessary... to consider minutely which of the many advices and rumours we have received are established on perfect and undoubted evidence. It is enough to collect from the whole, those circumstances which we think established with sufficient probability to become data in that case on which we are to act.[88]

Taking this point of view he concluded that the French were aiming at using Persia as a base of operations against the British territories in India and

85 BL, IOR Ben. Sec. & Pol. Cons. 202. Cons. of 9 November 1807, No. 1. Pellew to Minto, HMS *Culloden*, Madras Roads, 15 October 1807.
86 NLS M. 194. Governor-General-in-Council to Secret Committee, 9 February 1808. BL, IOR Fac. Rec. Persia 28, p. 15. Capt Hallowell to John Barker, Aboukir, 22 September 1807. BL, IOR Ben. Sec. & Sep. Cons. 205. Cons. of 30 January 1808, nos 3–5, 7.
87 NLS M 159. Minto to R. Dundas, Fort William, 10 February 1808.
88 Ibid.

that they would gradually collect an army in Persia for eventual hostilities in India.

Minto wrote:

> ... the Military Embassy which is now in Persia, ought, I think, prudently to be considered as the advance guard of an army... The 12,000 of which Captain Hallowell has advised us, are evidently insufficient for the ultimate purpose. I am led therefore to suppose either that a much greater force on the whole is approaching form different quarters; or that some such force as Captain Hallowell describes may be sent before to consolidate the French power & influence in Persia, to fix themselves firmly in such points... as they think adapted to their views, to collect information, to form plans, and to set on foot preparatory measures, whether political or military in furtherance of the main design.... On the whole... I adopt the opinion, that, we ought to prepare for a contest with a French army in the East.[89]

As long as the European war should engage Bonaparte on the Continent, the dispatch of a large number of French troops to the east was obviously impracticable. However, his peace with Russia and the submission of the other continental countries gave rise to a speculative fear that he would be able now to concentrate on this eastern project. The Governor-General-in-Council therefore wrote to the Secret Committee:

> Arduous as such an undertaking must necessarily be and great as are the obstacles and difficulties which oppose its execution in every stage of it, we are not warranted in deeming it in the present situation of affairs to be altogether chimerical and impracticable under the guidance of a man whose energy and success appear almost commensurate with the boundless extent of his ambition.[90]

Minto proposed to adopt both political and military measures of defence. The most important of these was a political mission to Persia. He felt it was no longer safe to remain without 'a suitable representative of the English nation' in Persia and Turkish Arabia. He also decided to send political missions to the countries between Persia and the Indus – Afghanistan, Sind and Lahore. With these states the Supreme Government had previously no direct diplomatic relations.

The Secret Committee wrote to Minto in June and September 1807 that they had decided to send Harford Jones to Persia in order to counteract the activities of the French in that country.[91] They strongly recommended that

---

89 NLS M 159. Minto to R. Dundas, Fort William, 10 February 1808.
90 NLS M 194. Governor-General-in-Council to Secret Committee, Fort William, 9 February 1808.
91 BL, IOR Board's Draft of Secret Letters to India, Vol. 3, No. 28. Secret Committee to the Governor-General-in-Council, 1 June 1807 (Secret).

Minto should win allies among the states occupying the intermediate area between Persia and the Yamuna. As a preliminary measure, they recommended employing 'native Emissaries... to procure constant intelligence of the state of affairs in those countries, and of the dispositions and views of their rulers'.[92] Although the Marathas were greatly reduced in power, they were potential enemies. The Secret Committee therefore advised Minto to keep a watchful eye on them and sanctioned the total annihilation of their power should they be found communicating with the French for the overthrow of the British in India. Such a drastic measure was only to be undertaken if their connection the French could definitely be proved.[93] In other words, the governor-general was not to consider himself authorised to embark on war of annexation on the basis of these orders.

The military measures of defence were not to be neglected. The European force in India at this time was little short of 24,000 men, of which about 2,000 were cavalry and about 3,800 artillery. Some reinforcements were sent from Britain and more promised at the shortest notice in case of an actual invasion. In the meantime, the army, fortifications and magazines in India were to be maintained in a state of preparedness. The Secret Committee recommended increasing the number of sepoys and suggested 'the expediency of raising... a large body of irregular Horse, in part officered, or at least commanded by Europeans with a view to impede the march of the Enemy's Army, by cutting off their supplies, laying waste the countries through which they must pass, and incessantly harassing them in every mode and direction'. Gunboats and other vessels should be assembled at Bombay in order to block the passage of a hostile army attempting to cross or navigate the Indus.[94]

These recommendations were followed by others in a dispatch dated 2 March 1808. Defensive alliances with the independent Indian powers and with the Afghans and the border tribes guarding the Indus at fordable points, and the establishment of a British post at Attock, were recommended as the most effectual means of counteracting a French invasion.[95]

Before these broad and general instructions reached Bengal, the Governor-General-in-Council had already adopted their own plan of defence. It cannot be said that Minto or his advisors in the Council believed that the Company's territories stood in any danger of an immediate actual invasion, but they rather expected a sort of cold war on the north-west frontier in consequence

---

92 Ibid., No. 31. Secret Committee to the Governor-General-in-Council, 24 September 1807 (Secret).

93 BL, IOR Board's Secret Drafts, Vol. 3, No. 49. Secret Committee to the Governor-General-in-Council, 14 September 1808 (Secret).

94 BL, IOR Board's Secret Drafts, Vol. 3, No. 31. The Secret Committee to the Governor-General-in-Council, East India House, 24 September 1807 (Secret).

95 Ibid., No. 43. Secret Committee to the Governor-General-in-Council, 2 March 1808 (Secret).

of the spread of French influence over Turkey, Persia and probably also over the Afghans and the Sikhs.

In the opinion of the Governor-General-in-Council, the route of a foreign invasion from the north-west must lie either through Afghanistan and the Sikh country into northern India, or through Sind to Bombay, traversing therefore the territories of several independent tribes and chiefs situated between Persia and the Company's territories in India.[96] The Supreme Government had so far had little inducement to enter into any kind of diplomatic negotiations with these neighbouring principalities. However, since the French had established their influence in Persia, it was feared that they might soon forestall the British in these intervening countries unless the British Government anticipated their efforts by opening negotiations for friendly agreements with these countries, and if possible, by installing a British agent at each of these courts. It was no longer advisable to rely on native agents and news writers either for information or for accomplishing any political objectives which the interests of the British might require. Fully-fledged British representatives were to be sent. Minto wrote to Dundas:

> It has appeared to me extremely desirable to push forward a British Agency as far beyond our own frontiers and as near the Countries from which the Enemy is to take his departure as possible.... Regular and avowed Embassies which would furnish occasion to the fixed residence during periods like the present of Europeans properly qualified in those Countries would undoubtedly be best calculated to fulfil my present views, which aim, first at obtaining correct & early intelligence of the enemy's designs and movements, and secondly at creating opposition to his progress.[97]

Hence, besides sending a political agent to Persia to counteract Gardane's influence, the Supreme Government decided to send diplomatic envoys to Kabul, Lahore and Sind 'with a view ultimately to combine the power and interests of the Western States with our own in resisting the advance of a French force in that direction'.[98] These diplomatic missions were also to facilitate the adoption of military measures on the frontier should the progress of the French demand it. The Governor-General-in-Council wrote to the Secret Committee:

> the missions to Sinde [sic], to Cabul and Lahore are calculated to afford us that information as well as to pave the way for the advance of a British force to that river and even beyond it, if that measure should ultimately appear to form an advisable part of a general system of Defensive arrangement.[99]

[96] NLS M 159. Minto to R. Dundas, Fort William, 10 February 1808 (Secret).
[97] Ibid.
[98] NLS M 194. Governor-General-in-Council to the Secret Committee, 31 March 1808.
[99] Ibid., 26 September 1808.

It is generally held by historians that Minto aimed at forming a diplomatic confederacy of these states against the French and failed in his objective. In fact, the Company's Government was well aware of the mutual jealousies and enmities existing between Persia, Afghanistan and Sind and between the Afghans and the Sikhs. Far from trying to form a confederacy of these hostile elements, Minto aimed rather to take advantage of the jealousies and rivalries of these states to serve his purpose. He hoped to be able to engage at least some of these powers in defensive alliances against the French. His objective was to secure unilateral agreements with each of these states, not a multilateral entente. This is quite clearly stated by Minto in his letter to Robert Dundas, dated 10 February 1808.

Minto pointed out to the Secret Committee, in answer to their recommendations for forming defensive alliances with the Marathas and other Indian powers, that not much reliance could be placed on the cooperation of the latter against the French. The states whose powers and territories had been reduced by the British were more likely to be disposed to listen to the proposals of the French, than to unite with the British to oppose them. On the other hand, some Indian powers might have been willing to enter into defensive alliances with the Company provided it was operative against the enemies of both parties, which would have the effect of involving the British in wars within India. Taking all these considerations into account, the Governor-General-in-Council concluded that alliances with the weak country powers against the French would be of little value.[100] The Government had no desire to be involved in war with either the Sikhs or the Marathas at a time when its entire attention was focused on the French.

The military measures of defence were not neglected, although they occupied a position of secondary importance to the diplomatic measures because Minto felt 'no apprehensions of an immediate invasion of India',[101] and wished to avoid all unnecessary expense. There was of course the question of whether an invasion was at all practicable, but aside from that consideration, it was Minto's opinion that should a large French army assemble in Persia, an army of at least 20,000 should be advanced to Persia from India in order 'to oppose it at every step of its progress'. This was however merely a vague proposition. The military and financial resources of the Company's Government were appallingly inadequate to meet the exigency of a foreign invasion. 'If we are to meet a French army in Asia,' Minto wrote, 'the Contest is beyond the faculties of the East India Company and of this individual Government.'[102]

An actual French invasion could only be successfully resisted with the aid of large reinforcements from Britain and financial aid of at least two million

---

[100] NLS M 194. Governor-General-in-Council to the Secret Committee, 16 May 1808.
[101] NLS M 159. Minto to R. Dundas, Fort William, 10 February 1808 (Secret).
[102] Ibid.

pounds sterling.[103] The threat to the security of the Company's territories in India was purely a backwash of the European war, and consequently the Government of India could justifiably claim every aid from the home government for its defence. Minto made this quite clear to the home authorities in a letter to the Chairman of the Company:

> If India is invaded by a French and Russian army, that event cannot be ascribed to the character or Councils of your Indian Government. It is to the disasters of Europe to battles in Poland, to the Peace of Tilsit that the necessity of waging a burthensome war in India must be traced... We can provide for our own contests by our own resources, but the contests of the Empire cannot be maintained by one of its provinces for although Asia may become the field of battle the War is purely European. The quarrel is European, the war is waged for European interests; and it is proportioned in its extent and therefore in its charge to the resources of two great Empires and not to the limited & circumscribed means of the East India Company's territorial possessions. If it were proposed to defend India against France & Russia upon that footing the whole scheme of our measures would be grounded in a false & impracticable principle and the success would correspond with it accordingly.[104]

Minto had to be very careful as to what measures of defence to adopt without plunging the Company deeper into debt. The Directors had urged economy in every department of administration so that in a year or two the deficit of a million pounds sterling could be replaced by a surplus of equal amount. On the other hand, it was impossible not to adopt any precautionary measures at all against the prospective danger. In view of all these considerations, Minto decided to adopt only those measures of defence which did not demand a large immediate expenditure, and to suspend others till they could no longer be postponed safely. Some financial aid was derived from the China trade, and Minto made a further application to the supra cargoes at Canton for a supply of bullion to the extent of 30 to 35 lakhs of rupees.[105] No troops could be sent at once to Persia because of the lack of funds to pay for the transport and the troops. The military measures of the Government consisted in assembling a larger proportion of troops than usual on the western part of India, for the French attack was expected to come from that side, and also in order to be prepared for action in Persia on Malcolm's call. Towards the end of 1807, reinforcements had arrived from Britain: HM 14th and 56th Regiments had reached Bombay and the 47th and 87th were detailed at the Cape.[106] The

[103] NLS M 159. Minto to R. Dundas, 1 November 1807. Ibid., Minto to Castlereagh, Calcutta, 3 November 1807 (Secret). Ibid., Minto to R. Dundas, 10 February 1808.

[104] NLS M 159. Minto to Chairman of the East India Company, Fort William, 21 May 1808.

[105] NLS M 160. Minto to J.W. Roberts (President of the Select Committee, Canton), Fort William, 6 February 1808.

[106] NLS M 159. Minto to R. Dundas, Calcutta, 26 November 1807.

total number of European forces in India was about 24,000 of whom 2,000 were cavalry and 3,800 artillery.[107] Although the Secret Committee recommended it, the Supreme Government decided not to increase the number of sepoy troops, for already the proportion of Europeans to Indians in the army was very low. Nevertheless, steps were taken to increase the number of cavalry, horse artillery and pioneers. In order to avoid unnecessary expense, no considerable movement of troops from cantonments were undertaken and the greater part of the army continued in their usual establishments.[108]

The measures of defence which Minto thought prudent to adopt against the so-called French menace provide a clue to his attitude towards that danger. No large-scale military preparations were undertaken, not only because they were expensive, but because they were not regarded as either urgent or necessary in view of the uncertainty and improbability of the danger against which they were to be adopted. On the other hand, measures although equally if not more expensive, were adopted which could be justified not only in view of the extraordinary exigency, but which were expected to produce more permanent results. The regulation of the Government's relations with the states on the north-west frontier was necessary in view of the more permanent interests of the Company than opposition to an uncertain danger. Minto's decision to conquer and annex the French Islands and French-occupied Java and its dependencies, was also largely determined by his desire to secure lasting and permanent benefits to the Company and Britain.

Diplomatic missions to Persia, Afghanistan, Sind and Lahore were undertaken almost simultaneously. Minto devised a frontier policy in which Persia was regarded as the first line of defence of the north-west frontier of the British territories in India, and alliances with the intervening states of Afghanistan, Lahore and Sind were to provide additional means of security. Persia was the crucial factor in the orientation of the Government's frontier policy and the overall policy with regard to the other three states fluctuated in direct proportion to changes in policy and attitudes toward Persia. Minto's diplomatic missions to the Amir of Afghanistan, the Amirs of Sind and the Raja of Lahore were the first attempts of the Supreme Government to open direct diplomatic negotiations with these states. Previously, relations with the Amirs of Sind were conducted by the Government of Bombay, while the resident at Delhi was in charge of all affairs connected with the Sikhs and the Afghans.

A political mission to Persia in order to counteract the efforts of the French and to woo the shah back to his earlier connection with the British was one of the obvious courses which the Governor-General-in-Council decided to

---

[107] BL, IOR Board's Secret Drafts, Vol. 3, No.31. Secret Committee to the Governor-General-in-Council, 24 September 1807 (Secret).

[108] NLS M 159. Minto to R. Dundas, 26 November 1807, 10 February 1808, 15 May 1808.

adopt. Shortly after assuming office, Minto wrote to Dundas on the subject of French activities in Persia and what steps should be adopted to remove that danger. He wrote:

> The mission of an able minister to the Court of Persia is undoubtedly one of the first measures that presents itself... With regard to other measures to counteract the schemes of France in that quarter... we cannot and ought not to embark on military expeditions either to Persia or Baghdad, or any part of the Persian or Arabian Coasts.[109]

His views about a military expedition to the Gulf were however to change quite significantly.

In view of the fact that Persian politics had become closely involved with European politics, Minto had no objection to the proposition that the British envoy to the shah should represent the king and receive his instructions from His Majesty's ministers. At the same time, since the Company's interests in India were so much concerned in Persia's attitude towards the French, he did not favour the idea of diplomatic relations with Persia being conducted solely and exclusively by the Government of Britain. Minto had two suggestions to make. First, that the king's envoy to Persia should hold 'a close, confidential and constant correspondence with the Supreme Government in India, and should receive from that Government instructions in all matters of local concern'; and second, that the person nominated for the office should be selected from among the Company's servants in India, and he recommended Malcolm as the person best qualified for the office.[110]

Minto knew that one of the last acts of the Ministry of All the Talents had been to appoint Sir Harford Jones, former resident at Baghdad, as Envoy-Extraordinary and Minister-Plenipotentiary to Persia in February 1807. The name of John Malcolm had then been recommended by his friend Sir Arthur Wellesley, but Malcolm was unpopular in Leadenhall Street for his extravagance during his mission to Persia in 1800–01. Harford Jones had a much longer earlier association with Persian politics. He first arrived in Basra in 1784 as assistant to the British Residency. He learned Persian, visited Shiraz in 1786 and Bushire in 1791. He was attached to the Residency at Baghdad for nine years during which he carried on private trade along with his political duties as resident at Baghdad. He carried on regular correspondence with the home authorities from Baghdad – particularly with Henry Dundas on Persian and Central Asian affairs, especially on subjects such as the Afghan threat and the Russo-Persian War and the beginnings of French infiltration into Persia. He was therefore eager to be appointed envoy to the Persian Court. In February 1806, he left Baghdad for England and reached London

[109] NLS M 159. Minto to R. Dundas, 1 November 1807.
[110] NLS M 159. Minto to R. Dundas, 1 November 1807.

in December 1806.[111] Shortly thereafter he presented a memorandum on the state of affairs between Britain, Russia, France and Persia to the Secretary of State for Foreign Affairs, in which he suggested that the negotiations with Persia should be conducted in the name and under the authority of the king for 'Neither Russia nor Persia can be expected to conduct a treaty with a person vested only with Powers from the India Company.'[112] Jones was selected as His Majesty's Envoy to the Court of Persia under the patronage of Henry Dundas, Grey and Tierney in February 1807.[113] In August 1807, he received his appointment from Canning, then Foreign Secretary. The interesting aspect of the controversy that was later to develop between Minto and Harford Jones was that the latter was appointed as a Royal Envoy on the representation made by the Court of Directors to the Foreign Office, that an envoy with royal credentials would carry greater weight at the Persian court. Canning's appointing instructions to Jones, however, made it clear that he was to receive his instructions and guidance 'from the Court of Directors of the east India Company or from their Government in India', to which he should conform.[114] Harford Jones was thus in the peculiar position of being an agent of both the Foreign Office and the East India Company. His final instructions were drawn up by the Secret Committee. He was to counteract French intrigues in Persia, and to find out the exact nature of their hostile measures against the British territories in India. He was to cultivate friendly relations with the Pasha of Baghdad, and communicate with the British Ambassador at Constantinople. The Secret Committee also directed him to be particularly cautious about the clauses relating to military aid and assistance to Persia and to define clearly the extent of British obligations. He was however not to consent to any specific stipulation to furnish military or naval aid without previous reference to the Ministers or the Indian Government.[115] The treaty was to be concluded in His Majesty's name.[116]

Although Minto knew that Harford Jones had been appointed His Majesty's Envoy to Persia, he was unsure of the basis on which the king's envoy was to stand with regard to the Company's Government in India, and the time of the latter's arrival in Persia was uncertain. On the whole, Minto preferred to send his own nominee to Persia and expected many advantages from such a mission. He wrote to Dundas:

111 *Dictionary of National Biography*, Vol. VII (London, 1886).

112 TNA, FO 60/1. Memorandum from Harford Jones, 7 January 1807.

113 Brydges, Sir H. Jones, *Account of His Majesty's Mission to Persia* (London, 1834), pp. 3–17.

114 TNA, FO 60/1. G. Canning to Sir H. Jones, Foreign Office, 28 August 1807.

115 TNA, FO 60/1. Robert Dundas to George Canning, Whitehall, 20 August (Secret). FO 60/2. Draft of Instructions from the Secret Committee to Sir Harford Jones, 8 September 1807 (Secret). Harford Jones was also instructed to discover the means of expanding the sale of British manufactures in Persia, and to ascertain the possibility of selling British woollens, metals and chinaware to Persia.

116 TNA, FO 60/1. Canning to Jones, Foreign Office, 2 September 1807.

We should then have a central point in which the political concerns of Europe and India would meet; not only authentic and early accounts from Europe and India would be constantly exchanged, but a knowledge of events and designs on the extensive and intermediate space now scarcely known to either, be obtained by both, and we might reasonably expect to establish an influence there extremely favourable to our security interests both in the East and West.[117]

The choice of Malcolm[118] as Minto's political agent to Persia was perhaps inevitable. He had been on a mission to Persia before and was regarded by many as an authority on Persian affairs. During his earlier mission, Malcolm had come to the conclusion that 'the two great necessities of diplomacy in Persia were the giving of presents and the stickling for forms'.[119] However, when he tried to apply the same formula in 1808, to his great annoyance, he failed to make any headway with the Persian Government. In 1807, Malcolm was resident at Mysore and not very happy in what he considered a minor position. He did not altogether give up hope of securing a wider field of activities either in Bengal or in a foreign country. In May 1807, he applied to Edmonstone, Chief Secretary to the Government of Bengal, recommending himself for employment 'in charge of any important political mission and command of any expedition' in order to oppose the French in Turkey.[120] He found no response from Barlow. In June 1807, when Minto reached Madras, Malcolm tried to establish contact with him through his son John Elliot. In his letter to John Elliot dated 28 June 1807, Malcolm complained about the lack of appreciation of his services by the Directors, and while expressing a desire to spend the rest of his career in India quietly at Mysore, broadly hinted that he was as full of ambition and zeal for 'the high and important duties of the Empire' as before.[121] Minto personally replied to this letter expressing his desire to profit from Malcolm's knowledge and experience in Persian affairs.[122]

Malcolm promptly took up the cue and brought up the subject of a political mission to Persia. He wrote to Minto, 'I had hoped that my claims to be employed (if a second mission was to be sent to that country) were from their nature exempt from invasion, but the personal solicitations of Sir Harford Jones are I find likely to succeed in obtaining him that appointment... it was

[117] NLS M 159. Minto to R. Dundas, Calcutta, 26 November 1807.
[118] As early as 1803, Malcolm was called 'Lord Wellesley's factotum and the greatest man in Calcutta.' BL, IOR Home Misc. Series 831 ©-4. Also quoted in Kaye, *Life of Malcolm*, Vol. I, p. 175. He was a personal friend of Minto's son, John Elliot.
[119] Kaye, *Life of Malcolm*, Vol. I, p. 111.
[120] Ibid., pp. 382–84.
[121] NLS M 182. Malcolm to J. Elliot, Mysore, 28 June 1807 (Private and Confidential). Quoted in Kaye, *Life of Malcolm*, Vol. I, pp. 384–85
[122] NLS M 158, pp. 173–75. Minto to Malcolm, Madras, 8 July 1807.

not possible I could have suffered a greater mortification than to have the pretentions of that Gentleman brought in competition with my own.'[123]

He was ceaseless in his efforts to impress on Minto the necessity of sending a mission from India to counteract the French in Turkey and Persia. In October 1807, he wrote again that if either the home authorities or Minto should appoint him on a mission to Persia, he would proceed zealously to oppose the 'French rascals', provided he was trusted with ample powers and funds to follow his own methods. His only fear was the Harford Jones had already won the nomination of the home authorities 'by offering to do their work cheap'.[124] He was not at all sure that Minto would be bold enough to act on his own responsibility and send a mission to Persia without orders from England. He expressed his anxiety to his friend Colonel Barry Close, then resident at Poona:

> You may suppose that I am not a little anxious; but from what I have lately heard from Bengal, Lord Minto's character is more of a smooth and cautious than a bold and enterprising cast, and he will be satisfied with preserving what we have without attempting further security, particularly if that is to be purchased by any disbursement.[125]

However, he did not give up hope. He sent a long letter to Minto, dated 23 November 1807, on the subject of French activities in Turkey and Persia. He wrote that Turkey was totally on the side of the French, and if the Porte's power over the rebellious provinces of Egypt, Syria and Baghdad could be re-established with the aid of the French, the latter would be able to direct their anti-British activities from those places. In Persia, French influence was already established and there could be no doubt that Napoleon meant to utilise this connection to strike at the British in India. 'This danger though prospective is very serious and I am satisfied it will require the most early and spirited measures on the part of the British Government to defeat it. The first measure that would suggest itself is the deputation of a mission to the Persian Court.'[126]

His other suggestions were not very practicable. He suggested that an effort should be made to prevail upon the tsar to admit the mediation of the British Government in settling his dispute with the shah and believed that 'there would be little difficulty in obtaining the assent of Russia to so equitable a proposition'.[127] Malcolm overlooked the fact that Russia was no longer an

---

[123] NLS M 182. Malcolm to Minto, Mysore, 13 August 1807.
[124] Ibid. Malcolm to J. Elliot, 27 October 1807 (Private and Confidential).
[125] Kaye, *Life of Malcolm*, Vol. I, p. 391. Malcolm to Col. B. Close, Mysore, 10 November 1807.
[126] NLS M 181. Malcolm to Minto, 23 November 1807. Quoted in Kaye, *Life of Malcolm*, Vol. I, pp. 395–98.
[127] NLS M 181. Malcolm to Minto, 23 November 1807.

ally of the British and that if the British should mediate between Persia and Russia, they had been in a better position to do so before the Treaty of Tilsit. He also saw no reason why the shah should not be easily prevailed upon to consider the British as his only true friends and to regard his allies the French as inveterate enemies. He felt that it was obvious that the shah should recognise Persia's strategic location in this potential conflict – that is, as a buffer to attacks on India as an ally of the British and as a nation possibly subjugated by the French and Russians first in order to act as a rearguard for the same objective – an attack on India. Malcolm felt that if the shah failed to be impressed by this line of reasoning, that stronger measures could be used:

> Should however the King of Persia be ever so far deluded as to give openly and decidedly a preference to the Enemies of Great Brittain [*sic*] that nation should instead of having recourse to measures of fruitless conciliation which would undoubtedly be mistaken for proofs of weakness take such steps as were calculated to awaken that Monarch to a just sense of the Importance of its friendship. The establishment of a more intimate alliance with the Bashah [*sic*] of Baghdad, the withdrawing of the Factory from Abusheher, the formation of a settlement in the Gulph (a point which is under every view of importance) and the temporary Interruption of the Intercourse between India & Persia would either oblige the King of Persia to alter his Policy or throw his Dominions & life into great hazard.[128]

This was actually the line of action that Malcolm wanted to adopt after he failed to persuade the Persian Government to allow him to proceed to Tehran in 1808. Malcolm's opinion of the Persians and their Government was not at all complimentary or fair. He regarded the Persians as the meanest, money-grabbing, dishonest race and their Government he credited with little ability. In his opinion, 'the King of that Country like all Barbarous and despotic monarchs will be found to act oftener from motives of caprice and pride than of policy and judgement'.[129] Such a sweeping judgement was characteristic of Malcolm, who once confessed that he liked to make up his mind quickly and once decided he did not like to think that his judgement was not infallible.[130] During these years, the Persian Government, pressed on all sides by the French, the Russians and the British, showed considerable diplomatic finesse and ability in keeping its head above troubled waters.

On 30 January 1808, Minto proposed to the Council the appointment of Malcolm as the Government's political agent in Persia and Turkish Arabia.[131] His hands were tied by two considerations: the alliance between Britain and

[128] NLS M 181. Malcolm to Minto, 23 November 1807.
[129] Ibid.
[130] Malcolm, John, *Sketches of Persia*, Vol. I (London, 1828), p. 169.
[131] BL, IOR Ben. Sec. & Pol. Cons. 205. Cons. of 30 January 1808. No. 1 Governor-General's minute, 30 January 1808/ Also Fac. Rec. Persia 28.

Russia and the actual appointment of Sir Harford Jones to Persia, who was known to be on his way to Persia via St Petersburg. He now felt free to act 'by the separation... between Great Britain and Russia; and by the growing necessity of the case in Asia'.[132] Russia's volte face at Tilsit gave the British substantial ground to stand upon in their negotiation with Persia for they could now offer aid against Russia.

The Government of Bengal had received no news of Harford Jones's movements as yet, and the time of his arrival in Persia appeared uncertain. Besides, Minto formed an opinion that 'By Col. Malcolm, if by any man living we may admit the hope of detaching Persia from her hostile alliance with our enemy.'[133]

Malcolm's commission was framed in such a way as to not clash with Harford Jones, and to enable Malcolm to continue in the Gulf region and in Persia after Jones's arrival. Specifically, Malcolm was to withhold his own credentials and diplomatic powers in Persia, but he was to continue as 'Political Agent to the Governor General or in other words the political (not diplomatic) representative of the East India Company and of the British Affairs in India'. Minto saw no reason why the king's envoy and the Governor-General's political agent should not be able to act harmoniously with mutual advantage to each other. This was theoretically quite possible, but Minto did not consider the personal rivalry and ideological differences between Malcolm and Harford Jones. A clash between the two representatives he regarded as possible but not inevitable. He wrote to Dundas, 'If any evil seems to result from the clashing of these commissions (a thing I confess not impossible) the natural remedy, I mean the recall of Col. Malcolm may be applied.'[134]

Minto wrote to Barlow:

> I confess also, that I should still consider Colonel Malcolm's residence in the countries to which his mission extends, highly desirable, even if we knew that Sir H. Jones were actually in Persia. I look to many essential benefits from Colonel Malcolm's mission, besides the negotiation with the Court of Persia. Because it is evident, that correct information, opinions & advice, I mean, on which we may securely rely, must if anything can, prevent the omission of measures necessary for our interests, or the adoption of false and prejudicial ones. I am aware that great inconvenience may naturally perhaps unavoidably arise from the clashing of these commissions but, I think Colonel Malcolm's mission, or agency in the countries bordering on the Persian Gulph so essential that the experiment ought to be made.[135]

---

[132] NLS M 159. Minto to Malcolm, 31 January 1808 (Most Secret). Quoted in Kaye, *Life of Malcolm*, Vol. I, pp. 402–04.

[133] NLS M 159. Minto to R. Dundas, Fort William, 10 February 1808 (Secret). Partially printed in Countess of Minto, *Lord Minto in India* (London, 1880), pp. 108–09.

[134] NLS M 159. Minto to R. Dundas, Fort William, 10 February 1808 (Secret).

[135] NLS M 160. Minto to Sir G. Barlow, 3 March 1808.

Malcolm was vested with plenipotentiary powers in order to enable him to negotiate with the Persian Government and the rulers of Turkish Arabia. He was authorised at any time he might consider it necessary to do so, to supersede and exercise the powers of the residents at Baghdad, Basra and Bushire. In addition to the general powers of control over all political affairs and concerns of the British in Persia and Turkish Arabia, he was also given the credentials of an envoy from the governor-general to the court of Tehran and to the Pasha of Baghdad, to be presented in the event of his finding it practicable and expedient to do so in the absence of Sir Harford Jones or any other person similarly accredited by His Majesty in Persia.[136] It appears clearly that Malcolm's commission was divided into two parts of which only one part was to become obsolete if Harford Jones should be in Persia before he could achieve that objective.

The main purpose of Malcolm's mission was to obstruct the progress of the French towards India and with that object in view to detach the states in the Gulf region from any alliance with the French and to prevent their participation in French schemes against the British. Malcolm was to detach the shah from his French alliance and prevail upon him to refuse to admit French troops into Persia, and to prevent the French from occupying any port in Persia or the Gulf. This aim was to be accomplished if possible by negotiations, but the Government was willing to use force if necessary. 'One great benefit which we expect to derive from Lieutenant Colonel Malcolm's observation and discernment is the suggestion of such means whether of persuasion or force as may be employed more efficaciously for the accomplishment of the main purpose.'[137]

As Gardane's mission to Persia was a military one, Malcolm's mission was also given a military character. He was given the rank of Brigadier-General at his own suggestion, and Minto wanted him to be escorted by a respectable force. Such a force, it was hoped, would be able to prevent the occupation of any port in the Gulf by the French and also give weight to Malcolm's negotiations in so far as it would indicate to the shah that the British meant to oppose the French in Persia seriously and vigorously. On the other hand, if the shah was already getting tired of his French allies and wanted to shake them off, the presence of an British envoy with a considerable force would give him confidence to do so.[138]

Malcolm was particularly instructed to report on the actual state of affairs in Persia and the disposition of the shah with regard to the French projects

[136] NLS M 194. Governor-General-in-Council to the Secret Committee, 9 February 1808. BL, IOR Fac. Rec. Persia 28, pp. 39, 40–48. BL, IOR Gen. Rec. & Pol. Cons. 205. Cons. of 30 January 1808, No. 1, Governor-General's minute, 30 January 1808. BL Add. 37285 34–35, Summary of letter from Edmonstone to Malcolm, 29 February 1808.

[137] NLS M 194. Governor-General-in-Council to the Secret Committee, 9 February 1808.

[138] NLS M 159. Minto to R. Dundas, 10 February 1808. NLS M 160. Minto to G. Barlow, 3 March 1808.

against British India. On his advice, Minto was prepared to send a large army into Persia to oppose the French, preferably with the cooperation of the Persians. If a body of 10,000 or 12,000 French troops were actually advanced into Persia, Minto understood that it would be necessary to send 20,000 troops from India to oppose it. If on the other hand, the French should follow the tactics of gradually assembling a force in Persia and forming an establishment in the Gulf, a smaller force of 4,000 to 5,000 men would be sent from India to the Gulf on the first summons from Malcolm. In Minto's opinion, the first opposition to the French arms, if that contingency should arise, should be made as far away from the actual British frontiers as possible. He wrote to Malcolm:

> In my view of these transactions, our opposition to France in Persia is the anchor on which our hopes must rest; for if we permit that country to be the depot of preparations against us, and wait at home till the enemy thinks himself that he is equal to the undertaking, we shall give him a great and, as it appears to me, a most manifest advantage.[139]

No large force actually accompanied Malcolm to the Gulf as it would have excited alarm in Persia and would have impeded instead of assisting Malcolm's negotiations. Malcolm's escort was formed in such a way as to preserve its character as an escort without assuming that of an expeditionary force. About 500 troops accompanied Malcolm as marines and a large force was assembled at Bombay to await his call.[140]

The instructions given to Malcolm show that the Government of India had no clear idea of the real state of affairs in Persia or what actually the French plans of invasion (if any) were. One of the primary duties assigned to Malcolm was to collect accurate information about the political state of the region and to advise the Government about the disposition of the shah towards the French and the British, whether troops should be advanced from India to Persia to oppose the French and what measures should be adopted if Persia was found to be definitely hostile. The Supreme Government's instructions to Malcolm were of a very general nature and from it Malcolm later claimed that he was left at liberty to proceed to any station in the Gulf or to Basra and that all his movements were left to the dictates of his own judgement.[141]

Malcolm readily accepted office and sailed from Madras on 17 February 1808 in order to be in Bombay by the first week of March and reach Bushire by the middle of April. In March, when Malcolm was on his way

[139] NLS M 160. Minto to Malcolm, 9 March 1808 (Most Confidential). Quoted in Kaye, *Life of Malcolm*, Vol. I, pp. 409–11.

[140] Ibid.

[141] BL, IOR Home Misc. Series 831 (c)-1. Malcolm to Minto, Fort William, 25 September 1808.

from Madras to Bombay, Minto heard from Rear-Admiral Drury who had recently arrived from England, that Harford Jones was preparing to leave England by sea at the time Drury sailed.[142] Minto could have sent orders for Malcolm's detention at Bombay on receipt of this news, but he did not want to do so. Through the *Georgiana*, which arrived at Calcutta on 13 April 1808, the Supreme Government received the Secret Committee's dispatch dated 24 September 1807 containing official information of Harford Jones's departure from England on HMS *Sapphire* for Bombay on his way to Persia. The Government also received copies of his instructions from the Secretary of State for Foreign Affairs, Canning, and from the Secret Committee and that his credentials were both from the Foreign Office as well as the East India Company. Additionally, a few days later, Minto received Harford Jones's letter dated 7 January 1808 from the Cape, informing him of his arrival there on his way to Bombay.[143]

This state of affairs threatened to upset Minto's arrangements. 'It is impossible to imagine anything more importune and unseasonable than the probable arrival of Sir Harford Jones at Bombay, just at the moment of Malcolm's embarkation', Minto wrote in exasperation to Barlow.[144] New instructions were sent to Malcolm that were to reach him at Bombay if he had not already sailed for the Gulf. Minto realised that he had no other alternative but to cancel Malcolm's Persian mission altogether, but confirmed his other duties in Turkish Arabia.[145] If Harford Jones had been deputed by His Majesty's Government alone, there might still have been room for a political agent of the Company in Persia who might have assisted and cooperated with him. However, since Harford Jones represented the interests of both the king and the Court of Directors, Minto came to the conclusion that Malcolm's presence in the same scene would produce 'a collision of authorities calculated to impede the arrangement adopted by the Government in England, and to embarrass the public interests'.[146] He wrote to Malcolm:

After perusing all that has been written to us from England on the subject of the mission, and after considering the authorities (the East India Company as well as Government) from which his powers are derived, I confess I feel that no authority in this country can be competent to delegate similar powers for precisely the same purpose to any other person... there is no deceiving

---

[142] NLS M 159. Minto to R. Dundas, 15 May 1808.

[143] NLS M 159. Minto to R. Dundas, 15 May 1808. BL, IOR Fac. Rec. Persia 25. Minto to H. Jones, Calcutta, 21 April 1808. Ben. Sec. & Sep. Cons. 206. Cons. of 25 April 1808. No. 1. H. Jones to Minto, Cape Town, 7 January 1808.

[144] NLS M 160. Minto to G. Barlow, 21 April 1808.

[145] Ben. Sec. & Sep. Cons. 206. Cons. of 25 April 1808. No. 8. Governor-General's minute, Fort William, 19 April 1808. Ibid. No. 12. Edmonstone to Malcolm, Fort William, 21 April 1808. Ibid. No. 13. Minto to H. Jones, Fort William, 21 April 1808.

[146] NLS M 194. Governor-General-in-Council to the Secret Committee, 3 May 1808.

oneself on this point, and it is clear that your mission to Persia must be abandoned.[147]

Minto though was clearly unwilling to withdraw Malcolm altogether from the Gulf region and his opinion was that Malcolm was to retain that part of his commission which related to Baghdad and the neighbouring states which did not fall within the scope of Harford Jones's duties. Minto wrote to Malcolm:

In the material articles of information and advice, your province will still comprise the same extent, and will embrace all the territories from the Indus to Constantinople, and I may say to Petersburg including Persia itself for I may venture to name that country in this private and confidential communication.[148]

According to these new instructions, Malcolm was to take charge of the Company's political affairs and interests in a wide and important field westward of Persia, and he was to observe and report on 'the whole range of politics from the Indus to Constantinople'.[149] It was necessary to safeguard British interests with the Pasha of Baghdad and other rulers of Turkish Arabia. Minto hoped that from Baghdad Malcolm would be able to establish a reliable channel of communication between Europe and India. Malcolm was also to supervise the residencies at Baghdad, Basra and Muscat. On the establishment of French influence in Constantinople, it was at first feared that the Porte might demand the withdrawal of the British residencies from Baghdad and Basra. Although Sulaiman Pasha, the new ruler of Baghdad, received his office by bribing Sebastiani, he was quite amicably disposed towards the British. Mr Hine, the acting-resident at Baghdad, observed that the French menace to the British territories in India was to be feared not from the quarter of Baghdad and Basra, but from Persia. Additionally, owing to trouble between the Imam of Muscat and the British resident David Seton, which resulted from the Imam's refusal to grant a building permit for a personal residence, and following Seton's recall to Britain, Malcolm was in turn entrusted with the Residency of Muscat.[150]

It appears that the Government was aware of the growing decline of the relationship between the Persians and the French due to the Treaty of Tilsit (between France and Russia) and wanted the envoys to take full advantage. Harford Jones immediately realised this favourable turn of events and used it in his negotiations with the Persian Government, whereas Malcolm stubbornly maintained that the Persians were as closely attached to their French allies as ever and consequently, there was no hope of success in the negotiations of the British with the Persian Court.

[147] NLS M 160. Minto to Malcolm, Fort William, 23 April 1808 (Private & Confidential).
[148] NLS M 160. Minto to Malcolm, Fort William, 23 April 1808 (Private & Confidential).
[149] Ibid. Minto to G. Barlow, 21 April 1808.
[150] NLS M 194. Governor-General-in-Council to the Secret Committee, 3 May 1808.

The tone Malcolm meant to adopt in Persia was described by him as not one of 'conciliation and solicitation', but one which would force the Persian Government to choose between the British and the French once and for all. He wrote to Minto:

> I mean to withhold my mission to the Court of Persia till such concessions are made as I may conceive from the state of circumstances I have a right to demand and my language instead of solicitation will be that of temperate remonstrance and offended friendship.[151]

According to Malcolm, until the shah showed a preference for the friendship of the British, it would be a mistake to send a mission to his Court from the king. He wrote to Minto:

> ... nothing could be supposed more injurious to our Interests (if the French Influence still prevails at Tehran) than an immediate & direct mission to that Court... I most earnestly recommend to your Lordship if you do not think yourself at liberty to suspend the mission of Sir Harford Jones... to keep it in India till you were satisfied from my report that the Conduct of the King of Persia merited such a proof of favour and friendship of his Britannic Majesty.[152]

Since Malcolm left before Harford Jones reached Bombay on 24 April 1808, all parties agreed that his mission should be represented as preliminary to His Majesty's mission. Whatever annoyance Harford Jones felt at this state of affairs he decided not to proceed to Persia immediately, but to wait in Bombay for Minto's instructions. From Minto's instructions to Malcolm, it is quite clear that Minto did not intend either to suspend or supersede Harford Jones's mission, although he was eager that Malcolm should reach Persia before Harford Jones did. As this was what actually happened, Harford Jones had no other alternative but to suspend his own departure for the present, for he realised 'nothing could be more impolitic than to suffer even the appearance of clashing authorities in Persia, and nothing more unjustifiable than putting the public to the expense of separate missions to the same Court'.[153] At the same time he added:

> I... consider it unnecessary... to do more than barely mention that since the French have appeared at Tehran the Persians are aware that National Ministers can only be accredited by His Majesty... I am on every account fully determined to pay the most respectful obedience to your Excellency's orders as far as can be compatible with those Instructions which I have received from His Majesty's Ministers and the Hon'ble the Secret Committee.[154]

---

151 NLS M 182. Malcolm to Minto, 15 April 1808, Bombay.
152 Ibid.
153 BL, IOR Fac. Rec. Persia 25. H. Jones to Minto, Bombay, 28 April 1808.
154 Ibid.

Harford Jones made his position clear at the outset. He declared himself willing to cooperate with the Government of India, and at the same time emphasised his status as HM envoy. By deciding to wait at Bombay, he also showed consideration for Malcolm's personal feelings and his position in Persia, which unfortunately were not reciprocated by the latter.

Minto also realised that this was the only way of adjusting the difficulties that had arisen or were expected to arise from the deputation of two separate British missions to the same court. He was relieved to hear that Harford Jones had decided to wait at Bombay and had expressed a desire to cooperate in every way with the Supreme Government. Recounting the reasons for Malcolm's appointment to Persia, Minto wrote to Harford Jones, 'It never was the intention of this Government to supersede the mission on which you have been deputed by His Majesty's Ministers and by the Honorable the Secret Committee nor do I consider this Government to possess the authority for that purpose.'[155]

He further added:

> A short previous Residence of Brigadier General Malcolm in Persia and his preliminary and introductory negotiation in which he would profess himself not to supersede, but to precede and announce your Mission would in our judgement add to the dignity and value of your functions while it would give unity and concert to the two missions, as forming part of one and the same plan, instead of exhibiting a conflict of two unconnected, if not discordant authorities.[156]

Armed with rich presents and an escort of nearly 500 men, Malcolm reached Bushire on 10 May 1808. He started to act in Persia on the assumption that he had full powers to negotiate and conclude a treaty with Persia and that Harford Jones's mission had terminated at Bombay. Eight days after his arrival at Bushire, he issued instructions to his cousin and second-in-command, Captain Charles Pasley, deputing him to carry a letter from himself to the shah at Tehran announcing his appointment and arrival at Bushire. Pasley was to make his way to Tehran by encouraging a false impression among the Persians that he was empowered to exercise more powers than were usually vested on a letter-bearer. This Malcolm believed would keep the Persian Court 'in a state of anxious suspense' and induce them to consider seriously the position they were in, being placed between two rival European powers. Pasley was not given any particular political designation, but was given full liberty to declare himself an accredited agent at his discretion.[157] Malcolm expected that Pasley would either

[155] BL, IOR Fac. Rec. Persia 25. Minto to H. Jones, Fort William, 23 May 1808.

[156] Ibid.

[157] BL, IOR Fac. Rec. Persia 25. Malcolm to Pasley, Abusheher, 18 May 1808. Brit. Mus. Add. 37285, ff. 50–69.

lay the foundation of the success of his mission or failing that would at least be able to collect correct information regarding the progress of the designs of the French on India and to what extent the Persian Government was involved in it. In short, he expected to derive from Pasley's preliminary reconnaissance the same advantages that Harford Jones expected to derive from his.

Malcolm was confident that he would be able to accomplish the objectives of his mission 'by an extraordinary liberality'.[158] Pasley was instructed to secure his progress from Bushire to Tehran not by making actual grants of money to influential officials, but by holding out promises of ample remuneration afterwards. Malcolm told him:

> it is an essential principle in the line of proceeding that I have adopted, to excite but not to gratify the hopes of the Ministers and great men of Persia until I have every prospect of success; and my knowledge of their general character leads me to hope this rule of conduct will aid considerably in the accomplishment of the great object of my Mission.[159]

The main objective of Pasley's mission was to secure the expulsion of the French embassy from Tehran. He was to notify the Persian Government that Malcolm would not come to the court unless General Gardane was officially rejected and asked to leave. As inducements, Pasley was to assure the shah that the British would replace every French officer and artificier who should be dismissed from Persia and would make a gift of arms and ammunition including twenty pieces of cannon, 5,000 stands of small arms, 2,500 carbines and 2,500 pairs of pistols in addition to training the Persian cavalry. Malcolm added that:

> ... perhaps you can use no argument that will more effectually accelerate this object than by pledging yourself that the day I hear of the departure of the French Embassy, I will move towards Tehran and you may hold out if necessary to those who are active in our Cause, a hope of benefitting by liberal presents.[160]

If the Persian Government would refuse to sever its connection with the French, Pasley was to return to Bushire after making it clear that the British would adopt certain drastic measures. He was to inform the Persian Government that the British would establish 'a fleet, a small body of Troops, and a depot of stores in some of the Islands in the Gulph' in order to act more promptly and effectively against the French.[161]

The most interesting part of Malcolm's instructions to Pasley was that relating to Sir Harford Jones's mission. Malcolm had offered to announce

---

[158] NLS M 182. Malcolm to Minto, Bombay, 15 April 1808.
[159] BL, IOR Fac. Rec. Persia. 25. Malcolm to Pasley, Abusheher, 18 May 1808. Brit. Mus. Add. 37285, ff. 50–69. Ben. Sec. & Sep. Cons. 208. Cons. of 15 August 1808. No. 11.
[160] Ibid.
[161] BL, IOR Fac. Rec. Persia 25. Malcolm to Pasley, Abusheher, 18 May 1808.

Harford Jones's mission to the Persian Government, but actually had no intention of doing so. In answer to the Persian Government's inquiries about Harford Jones's mission and the probable date of his arrival in Persia,[162] Pasley was directed to inform them that Harford Jones had orders to proceed to Persia via India and on his arrival there to become subject to the governor-general's orders, who was to direct his future proceedings. Malcolm added:

> You will at the same time… explain the impossibility of the existence of any different object in my mission from what there would have been in that of Sir Harford Jones if he had arrived in Persia, as we are both officers of the same Government acting under and receiving our instructions from the same superior.[163]

Malcolm believed himself to be in sole charge of the Persian negotiation and as far as he was concerned, Harford Jones might not have been there at all. Pasley was given a copy of Malcolm's credentials which he was to show to the Persian Ministers if necessary as proof that Malcolm had full powers to enter upon any negotiation and to conclude any treaty with the shah. He also carried a declaration from Malcolm to the ministers of the shah containing consequences for disregarding the treaty of 1801, warning them against the dangerous repercussions of an alliance with the French, and informing them that whatever common interest the French might have had with Persia against Russia had disappeared the moment Napoleon signed the Treaty of Tilsit with Russia. The declaration also contained a threat indicating that if Persia should continue to show a preference for the French, the British would be forced to suspend all commercial transactions and advance a naval and military force to the Gulf.[164] It was a curious declaration containing supplication as well as threat.

Pasley however was not able to go farther than Shiraz, capital of the province of Fars, which was ruled by a younger son of the shah, Prince Hussein Ali Mirza. Pasley reached Shiraz on 30 May 1808, and sensed the alarm and embarrassment felt by the Persians at the arrival of a British mission when they least wanted one. He wrote to Malcolm that he would be detained at Shiraz until the Government of Fars received orders from the shah.[165]

The Persian Government had received news from Constantinople that an embassy from Britain was on its way to Persia. When the Prince of Fars inquired about the whereabouts of that embassy, Pasley informed him, as

---

162 The Persian Government heard of Harford Jones's mission from Constantinople.
163 BL, IOR Fac. Rec. Persia 25. Malcolm to Pasley, Abusheher, 18 May 1808.
164 BL, IOR Fac. Rec. Persia 25. Pp. 177–97. Declaration from Brigadier General Malcolm… to the exalted Ministers of His Majesty Fetteh Ally Shah, King of Persia. Also, Brit. Mus. Add. 37285 ff. 150–67. Also Ben. Sec. & Sep. Cons. 208. Cons. of 15 August 1808, No. 12.
165 BL, IOR Fac. Rec. Persia 29, Pasley to Malcolm, 30 May 1808.

directed by Malcolm, that Sir Harford Jones had arrived at Bombay, 'where his mission would at present terminate'. He explained that although Harford Jones had received his credentials from the King of England, yet due to the distance between Britain and the states of Asia, the British Government had decided to leave the conduct of affairs relating to these states in the hands of the governor-general, and since the governor-general had already sent Malcolm to negotiate, Harford Jones's mission would not be necessary.[166] This was a gross misrepresentation of facts, which Pasley was prompted into making according to the instructions given to him by Malcolm. Harford Jones, when he heard of it, complained bitterly against it.[167]

The Persian Government was in a predicament. It could ill afford to alienate either the French or the British. The only way for it was to improvise a diplomatic solution and above all not to have both the British and the French envoys at court at the same time, for the Persians saw, as Mirza Sheffee Khan, chief minister to the shah did when he wrote to Nasrullah Khan, chief minister to the Prince of Fars, that 'The Enmity which these two nations bear each other is greater than my Pen can express.'[168]

Gardane was at Tehran and a Russian minister had just arrived at Tabriz, so that the Persian Government was most unwilling to let this opportunity of a settlement of the Georgian questions through Gardane be lost because of the untimely arrival of a British envoy. Mirza Sheffee therefore directed Nasrullah Khan that 'if he (Malcolm) is really sent as an ambassador... you must prolong his stay at Bushire in a friendly manner till such time as orders for his advance are received from the King'.[169]

The Persian Government appears to have entertained some doubts about the character of Malcolm's mission and probably suspected his warlike motives. The Shiraz Government received Pasley cordially. Prince Hussein Ali Mirza informed him that as his brother Abbas Ali Mirza was entrusted with the conduct of relations with the French, and he was entrusted with the conduct of relations with the British.[170] This was misinterpreted by Malcolm as signifying that the British would have to negotiate with the minor government of Fars and would not at all be allowed to negotiate with the Government of Persia at Tehran. Actually the Persian Government was merely asking the British mission to wait for a while at Shiraz, where it was favourably received, until the result of Gardane's peace talks with the Russian minister was known. The Shiraz Government was tolerably pro- British, mainly because of its

[166] BL, IOR Fac. Rec. Persia 25. Pasley to Malcolm, Shiraz, 2 June 1808, pp. 199–203.
[167] Ibid., H. Jones to Pasley, Bombay, 2 September 1808, pp. 445–48.
[168] BL, IOR Fac. Rec. Persia 25. Pasley to Malcolm, Shiraz, 2 June 1808, pp. 211–12. A letter entirely in Mirza Sheffee's hand received by Nasrullah Khan at Shiraz on 1 June 1808 and confidentially communicated to the British by Nasrullah Khan.
[169] Ibid.
[170] BL, IOR Fac. Rec. 25. Pasley to Malcolm, Shiraz, 2 June 1808.

commercial relationships with the East India Company. Both Nasrullah Khan and Muhammed Nabi Khan urged Pasley to stay at Shiraz and await further developments which they assured him would be favourable to the British.[171]

To wait at Shiraz or Bushire until the shah could ask him to come to Tehran meant delay, and Malcolm grew anxious about the success of his mission. If Gardane should be successful in arriving at an agreement with the Russians acceptable to the shah, his position at Tehran was likely to become impregnable. Malcolm had to act quickly and decisively if he was not to fail totally. He therefore made a great show of impatience at the 'intrigue' and 'deceit' practised by the Shiraz Government and by his erstwhile friends Nasrullah Khan and Muhammed Nabi Khan, who he said were playing a double game in order to gain their own ends. He ordered Pasley that if he should not be allowed to advance to Tehran by 15 June, within a fortnight of his arrival at Shiraz, he should refuse to stay at Shiraz and join Malcolm at Bushire.[172]

Malcolm had a plan outlined on which he proposed to act. This was his favourite project of having a British naval and military post in one of the islands in the Gulf. In a letter to Wellesley, dated 26 July 1800, he had discussed this subject at great length. He had initially selected the island of Kismah or Qishm as the most suitable spot from the perspectives of both strategy and commerce. However, in 1808, he preferred the island of Kharak, situated at the mouth of the River Basra, as 'it was the most advanced and presented the probable scene of military operations'.[173]

On 8 June 1808, Malcolm sent a lengthy dispatch to Minto on the French activities in Persia and the Russian pressure on Georgia. According to Malcolm, the route a French army was most likely to take would be from the Mediterranean through Baghdad, and then would either seize Basra or march through Persia. Due to the Russian presence on the north-western frontier of Persia, it would take a longer transit if the French were unaided by the Russians.

In his opinion, Russia's means of invading were much greater, and Persia's resources to assist either France or Russia in an invasion of India were 'very considerable'. Until, however, the schemes of the French and the Russians took specific shape, the British could do no more than try to conciliate those who were attached to their interests and arouse fears of retaliation in those who were on the side of the enemy. In Malcolm's estimation, Persia fell in the latter category.[174] Consequently, he proposed to Minto in letters dated 5

171 BL, IOR Fac. Rec. Persia 25. Pasley to Malcolm, Shiraz, 5 June 1808, pp. 229–32. Ibid. pp. 235–47. Extract from Capt. Pasley's journal, 5 June 1808, Shiraz.
172 BL, IOR Fac. Rec. Persia 25. Malcolm to Pasley, Abusheher, 9 June 1808. Ibid. Malcolm to Minto, Abusheher, 10 June 1808.
173 NLS M 182. Malcolm to Minto, Abusheher, 5 June 1808 (Private).
174 BL, IOR Fac. Rec. Persia 29, pp. 35–108. Malcolm to Minto, Abusheher, 8 June 1808. Also

and 8 June 1808, even before he received any news of Pasley's progress in Shiraz, that Kharak should be occupied. He proposed that an officer vested with authority and control over the British interests in the Gulf should be posted at Kharak with 'a well-equipped force of five or six hundred infantry, fifty artillery and two hundred cavalry, with a depot of military stores' and that 'for the security of these Stores and the safety of the detachment, a small but strong and compact Fort or Post should be built with a house for the Superior Officer and Barracks for the Troops'.[175] Kharak was selected as it would afford shelter to ships in all seasons, had an abundant supply of fresh water and was a strategic and central position between Basra, Bandar Abbas and Bushire. The total population of Kharak was about six hundred and it fell within the jurisdiction of the Sheikh of Bushire. Malcolm had no prima facie evidence, but believed that the Sheikh would welcome the British flag.[176]

The advantages of such a post was described by Malcolm as follows:

> Our Establishment at Kharak would fix us in that position in this quarter which it appears to me indispensible for our Interests we should assume and we should be enabled to act with that Spirit Independence and prompt decision which the times require, and be able to affect everything with the half barbarians of this quarter when they see us possessed of such effectual local means of either injury or support of their Interests... the jealousy excited by such a step would be considerable but it would be exceeded by their fears.[177]

According to Malcolm's proposal, Kharak was to be the centre and focal point of British activities in the Gulf region. From Kharak, the British would also be able to deal effectively with the Pasha of Baghdad, to ruin his power and commerce 'in a week' if he was hostile to the British, or to assist him against Persia if he were disposed to be friendly.[178] The factories at Bushire and Basra could be withdrawn and established at Kharak. The superior officer at Kharak (an office which Malcolm visualised for himself) was to hold the title of resident, superintendent or lieutenant-governor and be placed under the direct control of Bengal. The residents and Baghdad and Tehran (if one could be so established) were to be entirely under the orders of the superior officer at Kharak who would have the power of visiting either of these courts in times of emergency and also to enter into any engagements with them which he might consider necessary. A civil servant acting under

Brit. Mus. Add 37285, ff. 70–116. Also Ben. Sec. & Sep. Cons. 208. Cons. of 15 August 1808. No. 10.

[175] NLS M 182. Malcolm to Minto, Abusheher, 5 June 1808.

[176] Ibid.

[177] Ibid.

[178] BL, IOR Fac. Rec. Persia 29. Malcolm to Minto, Abusheher, 8 June 1808, pp. 104–08.

the superior officer might be given charge of everything connected with the commercial interests of the Company in the Gulf region.[179]

On 3 July, Malcolm directed Pasley and Dr Andrew Jukes, surgeon at the British residency at Bushire, to inform Abdul Rasul, Sheikh of Bushire that Malcolm would land with his escort and retinue at Kharak, the objective being to browbeat the sheikh into letting Malcolm occupy the island without any opposition. The sheikh was told that Malcolm would not submit to any insult or show of suspicion, and that 'the English Government could... make itself master of it at any moment it chose nor could all the world combined prevent its doing so, while that nation preserved the superiority at Sea'.[180]

However, the Persian Government was already considerably alarmed and the Sheikh of Bushire had orders to keep a close watch on Malcolm's activities. Consequently, the sheikh refused to grant him permission to land troops at Kharak without orders from the shah. Pasley, in order to persuade the sheikh, used an extraordinary argument that since the shah was eager that Malcolm should not quit Persian territory, what objection could he possibly have if instead of staying at Bushire, Malcolm preferred to establish himself at Kharak.[181] The sheikh made his position very clear that Malcolm would be opposed if he attempted to land at Kharak and steps were taken to strengthen the garrison at Kharak. Additionally, the sheikh declared that anyone who assisted Malcolm would be severely punished.

Malcolm realised that he could not bluff his way to Kharak without being involved in hostilities with the Persians. He had made it impossible for himself to continue at Bushire and since he couldn't proceed to Kharak, he came to the conclusion that the only other alternative was to go back to Calcutta with a show of offended dignity.

Minto regretted that Malcolm had decided to intimidate the Persian Government instead of treating it on the basis of 'common interest'. He wrote to Malcolm:

> I cannot help regretting that you should have judged it advisable to adopt the principle of Intimidation... Our intercourse with Persia in the present circumstances should be tempered with indulgence... The dignity of our sovereign and of our national character has not been impaired, but on the contrary has been exalted by that indulgent forbearance which in the strong towards the weak is a feature of true magnanimity. In my opinion the sound, the Wise, & for those reasons the most dignified basis on which we could treat and openly profess to treat with Persia was that of a Common Interest.[182]

[179] NLS M 182. Malcolm to Minto, Abusheher, 5 June 1808.

[180] BL, IOR Fac. Rec. Persia 25. Malcolm to Minto, HMS *Doris*, Abusheher Roads, 10 July 1808, pp. 365–418.

[181] BL, IOR Fac. Rec. Persia 29, pp. 616–19. Translation of a letter from Capt. Pasley to Sheikh Abdul Russoul Khan (undated).

[182] BL, IOR Fac. Rec. Persia 25. Minto to Malcolm, Fort William, 12 August 1808.

Minto wrote to General Hewitt, the Commander-in-Chief:

> I am sorry to say (in strict confidence) that Malcolm has disappointed me
> extremely in the opening of his mission.... I am compelled to say that my
> confidence is entirely shaken by the injudicious course he has pursued....
> Persia is now in the hands and in the very bosom of France, and was to be
> weaned from that connection by good and convincing reasons, urged in a
> conciliatory form. Intimidation, which Malcolm has chosen as the character
> of his negotiation, cannot succeed against the united force of the French &
> Russian Empires.[183]

Minto at this time had no intention of backing Malcolm's threat of
attacking Persian territory. Neither did he think that Persia would suffer very
much if the British stopped their trade, for the Arab ships would provide
Persia with articles of Indian produce and manufacture. It should be noted
that although Minto had by this time received Malcolm's dispatches down
to that of 10 June 1808, he refused to comment on the Kharak plan in his
letter to Malcolm of 12 August 1808. He was particularly anxious for the
continuance of amicable negotiations with Persia and Minto saw no reason to
obstruct Harford Jones's mission to the Persian court any longer.

In a letter of the same date Minto authorised Harford Jones to proceed
to Persia in the event of Malcolm actually leaving Bushire or 'his having
succeeded in establishing his Mission and prosecuting his Negotiations in
a manner introductory to your Mission on the principle prescribed in the
Instructions of Government of the 23rd of May'.[184] The date of departure
was left entirely to Harford Jones's discretion. Harford Jones, Minto expected,
would be able to break fresh ground in Persia for he was not hampered by
'personal declarations inconsistent with any compromise or indulgence' as
Malcolm now was.[185]

At Calcutta, several conferences took place between Minto and Malcolm
during which Malcolm persuaded Minto to believe that there was no hope
of any future negotiations with the Persian Government as the shah was
dominated by the French and Russian ambassadors at his court and that
even if a British envoy agreed to negotiate at Shiraz, there was little hope
of his achieving any of the objectives of his mission. Minto now agreed that
Malcolm would have compromised national dignity by continuing in Persia.
On 29 August 1808, Minto wrote to Harford Jones, suspending his mission
altogether. He declared that:

---

[183] NLS M 160. Minto to Hewitt, Fort William, 30 July 1808 (Private & Confidential). Printed
in Countess of Minto, *Lord Minto in India*, pp. 114–55.

[184] BL, IOR Fac. Rec. Persia 25. Minto to H. Jones, Fort William, 12 August 1808. Also Ben.
Sec. & Sep. Cons. 208. Cons. of 15 August 1808. No. 41.

[185] BL, IOR Fac. Rec. Persia 25. Minto to Sir Harford Jones, Fort William, 12 August 1808.

… his [Malcolm's] determination to retire was in the end adopted in consequence of the discovery he had made, and of the certain knowledge he had
obtained, I may say, indeed of the plain avowal that the Court of Persia has
fallen so entirely & irreclaimably under the control of the French & Russian
ambassadors, that his own mission & every other from any British Authority
whatever must have been… wholly & absolutely dependent on the mandates
of those hostile Ministers… the final & ultimate object of our proposed
intercourse with Persia, was evidently subject to the exclusive decision of our
enemies.[186]

Minto decided to maintain the general tone of Malcolm's proceedings in
the Government's future relations with Persia, and the prosecution of Harford
Jones's mission was in direct contradiction to it. He therefore notified Harford
Jones that his mission must be suspended at least for the time being, with a
hint that:

the character of the measures which it may be necessary to pursue will probably
be such as to exclude the prospective contemplation of any assignable period
of time at which the prosecution of your Mission could be consistent with the
dignity or conducive to the interests of the British Nation.[187]

Minto once again wanted Malcolm to go to Baghdad or Basra and take
charge of the Company's affairs in Turkish Arabia so that he would be close
at hand to resume the Kharak plan at the earliest opportunity. Pasley and all
other members of Malcolm's earlier mission were to be recalled from Bushire
as Minto wanted 'no possibility of jostling between anything that is yours
[Malcolm's] and Sir Harford Jones".[188]

It is quite evident that Minto was at this time undecided whether to recall
Harford Jones from Persia or not. He was willing to afford him a chance to
gain the objectives of the British in Persia through negotiation. According to
Canning's directives to Harford Jones, he was to be guided by the instructions 'from the Court of Directors of the East India Company, or from their
Governments in India',[189] and this power Minto was determined to exercise.
He wrote to Malcolm, 'Sir Harford Jones will probably be at Shiraz before
anything from hence can reach him; but I doubt very much the power of
controlling him from Bengal although I certainly possess a right to do so &
shall assert it.'[190]

---

[186] BL, IOR Fac. Rec. Persia 25. V.2. Minto to Harford Jones, Fort William, 29 August 1808.
[187] Ibid.
[188] NLS M 160. Minto to Malcolm, Barrackpore, 30 September 1808. Printed in Kaye, *Life of Malcolm*, Vol. I., pp. 437–38. Also partly printed in Countess of Minto, *Lord Minto in India*, p. 128.
[189] TNA, FO 60/1. G. Canning to Sir Harford Jones, Foreign Office, 28 August 1807.
[190] NLS M 160. Minto to Malcolm, Barrackpore, 30 September 1808.

In defence of Harford Jones's conduct, it may be said that he had shown every respect for Minto's orders and had demonstrated patience in waiting nearly five months at Bombay for his directives. He had, however, no means of predicting how Minto would so suddenly and totally change the opinions expressed in his letter of 12 August 1808.

The relations between the governor-general and the king's envoy became steadily worse. Harford Jones left Bombay on board HMS *La Nereide* on 12 September 1808 and reached Bushire on 14 October.[191] Pasley had left Bushire for Basra in August and Lieutenant Bruce was in charge of the commercial and political affairs in that place. Harford Jones must have realised that his best chance of success would be to assume a totally independent stand instead of following the lead proposed by Malcolm. He instructed the British agent in Shiraz, Jafar Ali Khan to inform the Persian Government that his departure from India was not in any way connected with Malcolm's return, 'nor any other circumstances, unconnected with His Majesty's commands'.[192] He wrote to Mirza Sheffee and to the Prince of Shiraz to arrange for his speedy journey to Tehran.[193] In his negotiations with the Persians, Harford Jones was determined not to offend or take offence easily. He advised the members of his mission to be careful in their interactions with Persians. His motto was 'whatever can conciliate will be uniformly practised, whatever can offend or irritate studiously avoided'.[194]

Minto's letters of 22 and 29 August 1808 reached Harford Jones at Bushire on 30 October.[195] These letters he found merely instructed him to suspend his departure from Bombay, but contained no further instructions related to diplomatic positioning. Consequently, he did not think it was his duty to return on receiving these letters. Moreover, he saw a prospect of success and signs of decline of the French ascendancy in Persia. He therefore decided not to leave Persia, and simultaneously requested Minto to send him advice and instructions in matters relating to his mission.[196] The French influence at the court was very much on the decline due to the fact that Gardane had not yet succeeded in coming to any arrangement with the Russian ministers over Georgia that would be satisfactory to the Persians. Russia had sacrificed her

---

[191] BL, IOR Fac. Rec. Persia 25. Vol. 2. Harford Jones to Minto, Bushire, 15 October 1808. Harford Jones's mission consisted of James Morier, private secretary; T.H. Sheridan, political assistant; Capt. J. Sutherland, surveyor; C. Willock; and a Persian secretary. Major Smith, public secretary to the mission was then at Calcutta. Brydges, *An Account of H.M. Mission to Persia*, pp. 19–20.

[192] BL, IOR Fac. Rec. Persia 25. Vol. 2. Harford Jones to Jafar Ali Khan, Bushire, 24 October 1808.

[193] Ibid., Harford Jones to Mirza Sheffee. Enclosed in Harford Jones's letter to Minto, 15 October 1808. Ibid., Harford Jones to Prince Hussein Ali Mirza, Bushire, October 1808.

[194] Ibid., Harford Jones to the Gentlemen of the Mission, Bushire, 14 October 1808.

[195] Ibid., Harford Jones to Minto, Bushire, 30 October 1808.

[196] Ibid., 1 November 1808.

European interests by the peace of Tilsit and had been promised compensation in the East, mainly at the expense of Persia. If the French tried to mediate a peace between Persia and Russia at Persia's cost, the shah would naturally be eager to break off relations with the French, and Harford Jones proposed to take advantage of that situation. He also proposed to work on the fears of the shah for the safety of his throne and treasures by inculcating a fear that the shah would not be a master of either once he allowed a foreign army into his territory. The anglophiles in court were also likely to represent to the shah that he would incur a grave risk by refusing to receive a mission from the King of England. On the whole, Harford Jones believed that he had a reasonable chance of success.[197]

Through Jafar Ali Khan, he negotiated with the Shiraz Government for his journey to Tehran. The Prince of Shiraz sent Mohammed Hussein Khan to Harford Jones to find out from him the powers and authority he was vested with and whether he would confirm the promises of military aid which Malcolm had held out the Persian Government through Pasley.[198] Harford Jones agreed to comply with these promises although he did not at that time know what they actually were. He was later criticised by Minto for making such a rash promise, but he obviously acted on the assumption that Malcolm could not have made any promises that would not be in accordance with the governor-general's instructions. In any case, the Shiraz Government forthwith sent a mehmandar, Mohammed Zikia Khan,[199] to conduct him from Bushire to Shiraz. On 17 December 1808, Harford Jones left for Shiraz and reached it on 30 December.[200]

Towards the end of December 1808, Minto received Harford Jones's dispatches of October and November from Bushire. He was annoyed to find that his letters of 22 and 28 August 1808 had not induced him to withdraw or even to suspend his negotiations with the Persian Government. Minto now began to have doubts whether Harford Jones would obey the positive orders to withdraw contained in the letter of 31 October 1808. Harford Jones was likely to receive that letter in December. In the meantime, Minto decided that 'everything will proceed just as if Sir Harford Jones were in England'.[201]

It was now Malcolm's turn to wait at Bombay. Neither Minto nor Malcolm thought Harford Jones would be bold enough to disobey the orders

[197] BL, IOR Fac. Rec. Persia 25. Vol. 2. Harford Jones to Minto, 3 November 1808.
[198] BL, IOR Fac. Rec. Persia 25. Vol. 2. p. 328. Jafar Ali Khan to Harford Jones, Shiraz, 28 Ramazan.
[199] Mohammed Zikia Khan was the favourite General of the Prince of Shiraz and Chief of the Nooree Tribe. BL, IOR Fac. Rec. Persia 31. No. 79. p. 145.
[200] BL, IOR Fac. Rec. Persia 25. Vol. 2. pp. 313–16. Harford Jones to Minto, Bushire, 13 December 1808. BL, IOR Fac. Rec. Persia 26. pp. 47–49. Harford Jones to Minto, Shiraz, 10 January 1809.
[201] NLS M 161. Minto to Sir E. Pellew, Fort William, 2 January 1809.

of 31 October 1808. Preparations for the military expedition were kept up in Bombay.[202] Malcolm had no intention of giving up the Kharak expedition but he began to have misgivings. From his correspondents at Bushire, Juke and Bruce and from Harford Jones's friends in Bombay, he heard that the latter was determined to go on to Tehran if he saw the least chance of success.[203]

On 30 December 1808, Malcolm wrote to Harford Jones that he would in conformity to the Supreme Government's orders sail for the Gulf within a fortnight and occupy Kharak either by means to an arrangement with the garrison and inhabitants of that island or simply by force. He requested the king's envoy to leave Persia prior to this event for his own safety.[204]

The news that the Government of India was sending an expedition to occupy Kharak reached Shiraz through other channels some hours before Harford Jones received Minto's letter of 31 October 1808 on 5 January 1809.[205] Harford Jones was then about to leave for Tehran and had received the shah's *firman* inviting him to the court.[206] Various rumours spread, one of which circulated by Muhammed Nabi Khan that Malcolm was going to place a prince of the Zand family on the throne of a new kingdom consisting of the southern provinces of Persia.[207]

It was a tricky business reconciling the presence of an envoy from the King of England in Persia with the resolution of the Supreme Government in India to occupy Persian territory. Harford Jones tried to explain to the Shiraz Government that it was intended as a purely defensive measure which the Governor-General-in-Council had been forced to adopt on strong representations made to the Government by Malcolm. The Shiraz Government had told him earlier that the shah might wish Shiraz to be the seat of the British negotiations. Harford Jones therefore told the Shiraz Government, 'If it can be managed that I am acknowledged, and admitted by His Persian Majesty as the accredited Minister to him by my King, my power in Persia, from that instant, becomes superior to the Governor-General's; and I will undertake to keep peace between England and Persia.'[208]

---

[202] NLS M 182. Malcolm to Minto, Bombay, 2 December 1808 (Private). Ibid., 8 December 1808 (Private and Secret). Ibid., 22 December 1808.

[203] Ibid., 23 December 1808. Ibid., 25 December 1808.

[204] BL, IOR Fac. Rec. Persia 26. Malcolm to Harford Jones, Bombay, 30 December 1808.

[205] Brydges, Sir Harford Jones, *Account of H.M. Mission to Persia*, p. 130. BL, IOR Fac. Rec. Persia 26. Harford Jones to Minto, Schyras, 5 January 1809.

[206] BL, IOR Fac. Rec. Persia 26, pp. 63–66. Firman from Fath Ali Shah to Sir Harford Jones, received 28 December 1808 at Khanazungoon.

[207] BL, IOR Fac. Rec. Persia 26, pp. 149–50. Harford Jones to Minto, Koush Khana, 7 February 1809.

[208] Brydges, *Account of H.M. Mission*, p. 139.

He also signed a bond pledging his life and property to the Shiraz Government that no act of hostility would be committed by Malcolm until at least the result of his negotiations at Tehran was known.[209]

The signing of that bond was an extraordinary and unparalleled act, but nonetheless a clever one. On one hand, it put a deterrent on any hostile move on Malcolm's part while Harford Jones was negotiating; and on the other, it left the British free to act as they pleased if his negotiations should be unsuccessful. The threatened attack was therefore turned by Harford Jones to his own advantage, and by doing so, he proved himself a wiser diplomat than Malcolm, who was basically a soldier. Malcolm had confidently predicted that Harford Jones would never be able to make any foolproof explanation to the Persian Government 'as will reconcile it to the sight of an amicable mission & a hostile Expedition from the same nation at the same period'.[210]

Concomitantly, the favourable turn of the war in Europe as a result of the Spanish uprising and Napoleon's reverses, removed the fears of a French war in India and in the opinion of the Government of India, the proposed establishment of a base of operations in the Persian Gulf become a matter of less importance than previously considered, and certainly not worth risking hostilities with Persia. The essential difference in the attitude of Minto and Malcolm towards the Kharak plan was that Malcolm considered it an object of importance to the interests of the British irrespective of the emergency situation, whereas Minto regarded it as a measure of defence against a probable French advance.

On 17 January 1809, Minto sent orders to Malcolm cancelling the Kharak expedition.[211] Owing to the change of circumstances, Minto believed that it would now be the turn of Persia to solicit an alliance with the British, and that therefore instead of employing force, Kharak might possibly be gained by negotiation. He wrote to Malcolm that 'so small a sacrifice would be refused if it were thought expedient to make it an object of negotiation'.[212] Even if Kharak was acquired by negotiation, the establishment on that island was not to be on such a grand scale as Malcolm had proposed. In view of the changed circumstances, Minto believed a much smaller post at Kharak would be adequate to look after the Company's political and commercial interests in the Gulf in addition to the residencies at Baghdad and Bushire. Minto indicated to Malcolm that he was sorry to disappoint him, but that in view

[209] BL, IOR Fac. Rec. Persia 26, pp. 25–29. Harford Jones to Minto, Schyras, 5 January 1809. Ibid. p. 39. Translation of Bond given by Sir Harford Jones to the Persian Government at Shiraz, 8 January 1809. Ibid., pp. 31–33. Harford Jones to Nasrullah Khan, Schyras, 5 January 1809.

[210] NLS M 186. Malcolm to Minto, 5 January 1809.

[211] BL, IOR Fac. Rec. Persia 26. pp. 261–64. Minto to Malcolm, Fort William, 17 January 1809.

[212] NLS M 161. Minto to Malcolm, Fort William, 7 March 1809.

of the new situation he had no further justification for entering into hostilities with Persia.[213]

Harford Jones's proceedings in Persia were justified by his success, but it cannot be denied that he overstepped the letter of his instructions. It was by no means the intention of His Majesty's Government to oust the Government of India from the field of Persian diplomacy or to deprive it of a voice in the Persian negotiations, although an alliance was to be formed in the name of the two kings. Harford Jones had a 'concurrent' commission to represent both HM Government as well as the East India Company in Persia, but he preferred to be known as the 'king's envoy' only.

Another major complaint that Minto had against Harford Jones was that he unnecessarily degraded the position and powers of the governor-general, and the Company's Government in India in the eyes of the Persian Government. He not only disavowed his subjection to the orders and instructions to the Indian Government and acted in direct opposition to them, but he also made 'an invidious and degrading comparison' of the rank of a minister appointed by the King of England and an envoy of the Government of India. Minto's contention was that the Supreme Government in India was virtually a sovereign power or at least exercised the powers attached to sovereignty. The Governor-General-in-Council wrote to the Secret Committee:

> By the Laws which have been framed for the management of the honourable Company's affairs, the local Government of this country is vested with the power attached to sovereignty. It is empowered to administer civil and criminal justice, to levy war, and to conclude peace. It is equally essential to the preservation of this valuable branch of the British Empire that the States of Asia should consider the British establishment in India in the light of a sovereign State, as that the Government should actually exercise the powers annexed to it.[214]

It was very important that the British Government of India should be regarded in the light of a sovereign state by neighbouring states. It is also true that neither the Shah of Persia nor the King of Burma recognised the governor-general as their equal. However, they at least recognised his authority to conduct diplomatic relations or negotiations with all stages and

---

[213] Ibid. The question of a naval demonstration in the Persian Gulf in order to coerce Persia was a subject of controversy both at this period and later. In 1838, at the time the Persians besieged Herat, the Government of India sent troops to occupy Kharak rather than marching an army to Tehran. Kharak was evacuated in 1840 after an agreement was reached with Persia. See Davies, C.C., *The North West Frontier* (Cambridge, 1932), p. 154. Rawlinson, Sir H., *England and Russia in the East* (London, 1875), pp. 58, 65.

[214] NLS M 195. Governor-General-in-Council to the Secret Committee, 3 April 1809. Also quoted in Countess of Minto, *Lord Minto in India*, pp. 135–36.

to employ the resources of the British territories in India either in the aid of an ally or in war on an enemy. Minto wrote to the Secret Committee:

> It is in this character alone that we have been enabled to obtain those manifestations of respect that regard to the claims of dignity, which, amongst all nations of the world, but in a special degree among Asiatic States, are essential to the maintenance of real power in the scale of political interest. This acknowledged character as it constituted the basis, so it must form the cement of our external relations. To deprecate therefore that estimation of the power, and the dignity of the British Government in India... is... to expose us to much of the danger arising from a real loss of power and authority, by diminishing that awe and respect with which this Government has hitherto been contemplated, and on which the tranquillity and security of the British dominion in India mainly depend.[215]

Harford Jones had made rapid progress from Shiraz to Tehran. The Persian Government arranged that Gardane should leave Tehran on the day fixed for Harford Jones's entry into the city. Gardane left on 13 February 1809 as arranged although Harford Jones did not reach until the following day. On the 17th the audience with the shah took place, and the King of England's letter and presents were delivered to the shah. Without further delay, the shah appointed Mirza Sheffee, the Prime Minister and Kazi Muhammad Hussein Khan, the Ameen-ud-Daula or Minister of Finance, as plenipotentiaries to draw up the terms of the treaty in consultation with the British minister. Numerous discussions were held, all of which hinged on the aid which the British would provide to enable the Persians to fight the Russians.

Harford Jones had already committed himself to fulfilling the offers that Malcolm made in his declaration to the Persians in 1808 and it was on that basis that he was received by the shah and the French were expelled. Harford Jones found that the Persian Government asserted those proposals to be much more extensive than what Malcolm had specifically mentioned in any of his communications to the Persian Government. For instance, the Persian representatives wanted an unqualified offensive and defensive alliance, assistance of 25,000 to 30,000 troops, 100 pieces of artillery and 20,000 muskets; additionally, a repayment to the shah of the expenses incurred during the Afghan campaigns of 1800–01 which were undertaken for the benefit of the British.[216] To these difficulties were added the fact that the threat to Kharak had made the Persian Government slightly uneasy about the motives of the British, and although the French legation had left Tehran, Gardane and his assistants were still within Persian territory at the time the British negotiations were being conducted in Tehran. The Persian envoy to Paris, Askar Khan,

---

[215] NLS M 195. Governor-General-in-Council to the Secret Committee, 3 April 1809.
[216] BL, IOR Persia 26. Harford Jones to R. Dundas, Tehran, 16 March–31 March 1809.

was soon expected back and if he brought back any new proposals from Paris regarding an arrangement respecting Persia and Russia, it might have totally changed the shah's attitude. The Treaty of Dardanelles signed between Britain and Turkey on 5 January 1809, on the other hand, gave some confidence to the British negotiator at Tehran.

On the matter of aid to Persia against Russia, Harford Jones's opinion differed from that of Minto. In his letter of 12 August 1808 to Malcolm, Minto had instructed him that Persia may be offered the aid of a British force against the French and the Russians, but any aid offered to Persia against the Russians must have in view the restoration of peace between Britain and Russia.[217] In his letter of 7 March 1809 to Malcolm, Minto wrote that 'assistance against Russia... cannot be granted', since the disappearance of the French danger the Government was unwilling to spend its resources on Persia.[218] Minto did not appear to think that the British in India had anything to fear from Russian encroachments on Georgia. Harford Jones, however, was of the opinion that the interests of the British would be served ultimately by offering aid to the shah to keep the Russians out of Persian territory. He wrote to Dundas, 'we are essentially interested no European Power should establish herself in the Possession of any of the Provinces of Persia... it occurs to me the only difference between France or Russia acquiring such possessions, is that the latter,... would be a more formidable Neighbour to our Indian Government than the former'.[219]

If Persia was to be used as a buffer between India and the pressure of either the French or the Russians, it was imperative to provide significant financial and military aid. In a letter to the Chairman of the East India Company, the financial provisions of the proposed Treaty were as follows:

Annual expense of 16,000 troops	£103,846
16,000 muskets rated at 20 rupees each	£36,000
20 pieces of field artillery at 7,000 rupees each	£15,750
Total	£155,596[220]

Harford Jones wrote to the Chairman that 'this is to prevent Persia falling into the hands of Russia and France, to preserve a trade of near £600,000 pounds sterling p.a. and to secure a barrier to our possessions in India. It is to

[217] BL, IOR Fac. Rec. Persia 25. Minto to Malcolm, Fort William, 12 August 1808.

[218] NLS M 161. Minto to Malcolm, Fort William, 7 March 1809.

[219] BL, IOR Fac. Rec. Persia 26. Harford Jones to R. Dundas, Tehran, 16–31 March 1809.

[220] BL, IOR Fac. Rec. Persia 27. Detail of the subsidy and aid offered by Sir Harford Jones to Persia, enclosed in his letter to the Chairman of the East India Company, 6 May 1809. The rate of exchange was Rs. 1 = 2 *s* 3*d*.

be observed that the aid once given, ceases forever and the subsidy remains at £103,846 until Persia has peace with Russia.'[221]

On the whole, Harford Jones could probably justifiably claim that he had succeeded in making 'a cheap and politic bargain for the East India Company'.[222] The Persian Government had demanded much more than they received and Harford Jones provided much less than what Malcolm had offered and what he later agreed to fulfil. In the discussion on the subject of subsidy and aid which followed the signing of the Preliminary Treaty, he stuck to his proposition of 16 March 1809 to the Persian ministers, and they in turn thought it prudent to accept what was offered. The subsidy was to be granted only as long as the Persians would have to fight the Russians in self-defence and no longer. It was agreed that the conclusion of the definitive treaty should be postponed until Harford Jones's proceedings were confirmed by the home authorities and further orders were received from Britain.[223]

Harford Jones had written to Dundas that although Gardane had left Tehran, 'the struggle whether His Majesty's Mission or the French Legation was to reside at Tehran, was not finished'.[224] Gardane sent a note to Mirza Sheffee informing him of the firm alliance between France and Russia, the capitulation of Madrid and the retreat of the British from Spain, and also that in India the Maratha powers, Sindhia and Holkar were united against the British.[225] Jones warned Minto that the effect of his orders of 30 January 1809 might be to increase Gardane's hopes of return, and that in order to prevent it, the terms of the Preliminary Treaty must be fulfilled without further delay.[226] At the time that Jones was negotiating with the Persian Government, not only was Gardane at Tabriz, but the French chargé d'affaires, Monsieur Jouannin, was at the capital and the Persian ministers emphasised the shah's right to permit the French to reside at Tehran.[227] The Persian Government was undecided whether to trust the British implicitly or not, and the French ministers at the Persian court were regarded as a likely guarantee of the fulfilment of the terms of the treaty by the British. Gardane left Tabriz on 16 April 1809 for France via Constantinople.[228] In order to give the shah confidence in his new alliance and to send away the remaining part of the French embassy from Persia, Jones immediately offered to pay

---

[221] BL, IOR Fac. Rec. Persia 27. Harford Jones to the Chairman of the East India Company, 6 May 1809.

[222] BL, IOR Fac. Rec. Persia 27. Harford Jones to the Chairman of the East India Company, 6 May 1809.

[223] BL, IOR Fac. Rec. Persia 26, p. 101.

[224] BL, IOR Fac. Rec. Persia 26, pp. 129–30. Harford Jones to R. Dundas, Tehran, 31 March 1809.

[225] Ibid., p. 137. General Gardane to Mirza Sheffee (Copy) (in French).

[226] BL, IOR Fac. Rec. Persia 26. Harford Jones to Minto, Tehran, 9 June 1809.

[227] TNA, FO 60/2. Harford Jones to G. Canning, Tehran, 12 April 1809. No. 6.

[228] Ibid. Translation of a note from Mirza Sheffee to Harford Jones, received 20 April 1809.

six months subsidy to the Persian Government. Jouannin and his secretary, Monsieur Nerciat left Tehran on 19 April 1809.[229] They took up quarters in Tabriz with the permission of the Prince Royal, but holding out a prospect of settlement of the Georgian question with Russia,[230] and also on the pretext that the Persian Government owed 51,334 piastres to the French legation.[231] On their financial demands being fulfilled by the Persian Government with the money provided by Harford Jones, Jouannin and his party left Tabriz on 12 September 1809.[232] Jouannin was to return again to Tabriz and finally left in December 1809.

The Preliminary Treaty was sent to the governor-general for ratification. Minto did not approve of some of the articles of the Treaty, namely those related to Kharak and to the Afghans. With regard to Kharak, Article 5 of the Preliminary Treaty stipulated that if any British troops landed in Kharak, they might be employed in the service of the shah to fight in Georgia, so that if Malcolm had actually gone there, the shah could have demanded the services of the troops serving under him. Minto strongly objected to this article for it prevented the Government of India from pursuing or reviving the Kharak plan based on its original intent. Article 7 of the Preliminary Treaty was contradictory to the Government's Afghan policy, as it prohibited the interference of the British in any war between Persia and the Afghans, other than by mediation. This was contrary to Article 2 of Elphinstone's treaty with Shah Shuja at Peshawar, ratified on 17 June 1809. That article stipulated British aid to the Afghans against the French and the Persians.

Notwithstanding his dislike of Harford Jones's proceedings in Persia and of the terms of the Preliminary Treaty, Minto did not think that he had any other option but to ratify it. On the basis of his engagements with the British, the shah had renounced his alliance with the French, recalled his envoy from Paris, dismissed Gardane and Jouannin and had provoked the resentment of the powerful ruler of France.

Minto was probably aware that he might place himself in further difficulties with the home authorities if he refused to ratify a treaty endorsed by them. He therefore wrote to Malcolm:

> Persia has been induced by an accredited minister to fulfil the principal engagement, contracted on her part, upon the faith of a Preliminary Treaty, and has established an onerous Title to the performance of ours. My opinion, therefore, is that we are bound to execute the principal & leading conditions

---

[229] Ibid. Harford Jones to G. Canning, Tehran, 2 May 1809, No. 10. BL, IOR Fac. Rec. Persia 26, pp. 187–98. Harford Jones to R. Dundas, Tehran, 2 May 1809.

[230] Ibid. Harford Jones to Minto, Tehran, 9 June 1809. TNA, FO 60/2. Harford Jones to G. Canning, Royal camp near Tabreze, 28 August 1809, No. 17.

[231] Ibid. Harford Jones to G. Canning, Tehran, 12 September 1809.

[232] Ibid.

of Sir Harford's Treaty. By these I mean the stipulated succours against France and Russia, or against Russia singly, during war between Great Britain and Russia.[233]

The Preliminary Treaty does not appear to have removed all fears of a return of the French to Persia. The peace treaty signed between France and Austria on 14 October 1809, news of which was received from Constantinople in December once again aroused misgivings about Napoleon's next move. The Persian Government certainly took the utmost advantage of the jealousy of the British for the French. Mirza Sheffee told Jones that Jouannin was returning from Trebizond by the express orders of the French Government and that he was the bearer of letters to the shah and the Prince Royal. Prince Abbas Ali Mirza promised to dismiss him without reference to the shah provided Jones assured him that the British Government would fulfil the terms of the Preliminary Treaty and provided that he would immediately furnish six months subsidy. Harford Jones not only paid 25,000 tomans through the British agency at Constantinople, but also drew a further bill of 5,000 tomans on the Government of India.[234] It was later found by Jones that Jouannin's letter was merely a duplicate of an old letter written by the French Minister Champagny, dated Vienna, 8 June 1809, a copy of which the Persian Government had already received in September 1809.[235] Hence it was not only Jouannin who was trying to hoodwink the Persian ministers, the latter were no less eager to use him to squeeze the British.

The state of British diplomatic relations with Persia became once again very confusing due to Minto's decision to send a second mission to Persia while the king's envoy was still residing in the Persian court. Captain Pasley arrived at Bushire in December 1809 to take charge of affairs until Malcolm arrived. He in turn informed Harford Jones of his orders and that he should stop making any further payments of the subsidy.[236] The Persian ministers were puzzled at receiving Minto's communication to them accepting the Preliminary Treaty, but disavowing Harford Jones's conduct and his bills. They decided to continue to transact business with the king's envoy, until they heard from the Persian minister in London or from the British Government.[237] Jones's bills drawn in payment of the subsidy were protested by Mr Bruce, the acting-resident at

---

[233] NLS M 162. Minto to Malcolm, Barrackpore, 27 June 1809 (Private).

[234] BL, IOR Fac. Rec. Persia 27. Harford Jones to Minto, Tauris, 10 December 1809. No. 35. The rate of exchange was 14 piastres = 1 toman, 17 piastres = 1 pound sterling; 8 sicca rupees = 1 pound sterling.

[235] Ibid.

[236] BL, IOR Fac. Rec. Persia 27. Capt. Pasley to Harford Jones, Bushire, 3 December 1809.

[237] Ibid. Translation of a letter from Hajee Mohammed Hossein Khan (Ameen-ud-Dowlah) to Sir Harford Jones, received 31 December 1809. Ibid. Translation of letters from Mirza Sheffee and Mirza Bozurg, received 31 December 1809.

Bushire.[238] Fortunately for him, Harford Jones received confirmation of his powers from the Foreign Office towards the end of January. In a letter dated 6 November 1809, the Secretary of State for Foreign Affairs, Lord Bathhurst, informed Harford Jones that in consequence of the representation of the Court of Directors through the President of the Board of Control, the instructions given him by Canning of 28 August 1807 and the full powers vested in him on 3 September 1807, were confirmed, and Minto's orders of recall to him were cancelled.[239] This strengthened Harford Jones's hands considerably, so he immediately ordered Pasley to stop all communications with the Persian Government and informed him that he was in sole charge of the negotiations.[240] He also informed Minto of the confirmation of his powers and stated categorically 'I cannot, nor will not act in any shape with Brigadier General Malcolm in this country. Our ideas and sentiments on Persia are so essentially different that such a coalition can lead to nothing but confusion and distraction.'[241]

Aside from the personal and professional jealousy between the two British envoys there was a fundamental difference in their methods and policies. Harford Jones emphasised Persia's connection with European politics. He stressed the fact that he was an envoy from the British Government, concluded a treaty between the two crowns of Britain and Persia and encouraged the dispatch of an envoy from Persia to Britain. He also devoted significant effort to bring about a rapprochement between Persia and the Porte in order to create a bulwark and create a diversion in Eastern Europe to the detriment of Britain's enemies.

Malcolm, on the other hand, supported a policy of military aggression and display of superiority as a fundamental operating principle and for Persia to gain an appreciation of the regional power of the British in India, particularly as Britain's position in Continental Europe was weak, whereas in India, Britain was a paramount power. The French had initially sought a diplomatic connection with Persia as it was in their interests to do so, while Malcolm was of the opinion that their objective was to focus the attention of Persia on India as a strategic partner. Malcolm regretted that a Persian envoy had gone to Britain for that would expose an analysis of Britain's resources and weaknesses. The Persians would learn that Britain was not a land-based power and that British strength and safety depended on an insular position and their navy, which would not strictly be of much use to the Persians.[242]

The orders from the Foreign Office dated 6 November 1809 confirming Harford Jones's powers were received by him in January 1810. Wellesley was

238 Ibid. Translation of a letter from Ameen-ud-Dowlah to Harford Jones, received 7 January 1810.
239 TNA, FO 60/2. Lord Bathurst to Harford Jones, Foreign Office, 6 November 1809.
240 BL, IOR Fac. Rec. Persia 27. T. Sheridan to Capt. Pasley, Tauris, 27 January 1810.
241 Ibid. Harford Jones to Minto, Tauris, 30 January 1810. Also Foreign Office 60/3.
242 NLS M 188. Malcolm to Minto, Bushire, 10 April 1810 (Private & Secret).

now Foreign Secretary and Jones expected his support on account of the good relations and friendship that existed between them. Malcolm on his part expected the new Foreign Secretary would be inclined to support the course of measures adopted by the Indian Government because of his personal experience of eastern diplomacy and the fact that he had been Malcolm's patron and as governor-general had sent Malcolm on a mission to Persia in 1800–01.[243]

On 2 July 1810, Harford Jones received dispatches from the Foreign Office, announcing the appointment of Sir Gore Ouseley[244] as ambassador to Persia holding the same rank as the British minister in Constantinople, and directing Jones to remain in charge of affairs till his arrival in Persia.[245] The Foreign Office notified the Persian ministers that Harford Jones's proceedings were entirely in conformity with the orders he had received from HM Government and that the conduct of the governor-general arose from 'accidental error'. They were told that, 'the Interests of the East India Company & of His Majesty are inseparable. Any appearances of separation... are to be imputed exclusively to the mistakes and unfortunate incidents to which all human administration is subject.'[246]

The new ambassador was instructed to consider the wishes of the Company's Government in India so that there might be no further conflict between the two. The appointment of a minister of ambassadorial rank to conclude the definitive treaty with Persia confirmed the trend of British foreign policy with regard to Persia which began with Harford Jones's mission to that country, and deprived the Government of India of any independent course of action in that quarter. In order to avoid any further clash between the envoy to Persia and the Government of India, Gore Ouseley was vested with a commission totally independent of the latter. The ambassador and secretary of the embassy were to receive their salaries from HM Government.

[243] NLS M 188. Malcolm to Minto, Bushire, 15 April 1810. Ibid. Ispahan, 31 May 1810 (Private & Secret), No. 12.

[244] Gore Ousley (1770–1844) had spent nearly seventeen years in India, although not as a servant of the Company. He was attached to the Court of Oudh as an oriental scholar and knew Farsi. He was appointed by Wellesley to act as interpreter and 'mehmandar' to Mirza Abul Hassan in London, and appointed Ambassador-Extraordinaire and Plenipotentiary to Persia to conclude the Definitive Treaty (completed on 14 March 1812). Although the home authorities had ratified the Preliminary Treaty of 1809, they annulled Gore Ousley's treaty of 1812 and ordered another one to be drafted. The Definitive Treaty with Persia was finally concluded by James Morier and Henry Ellis on 25 November 1814. Reynolds, Rev. J., *Memoir of Sir Gore Ousley* (London, 1846), pp. xi, xv–xli, xviii–lxxvii. Atchison, *Treaties, Engagements and Sanads*, Vol. XIII, pp. 56–63.

[245] TNA, FO 60/3. Wellesley to Harford Jones, Foreign Office, 14 April 1810 (Draft). BL, IOR Fac. Rec. Persia 26. Harford Jones to the Secret Committee, Tauris, 12 July 1810.

[246] TNA, FO 60/2. Draft of a letter to Mirza Sheffee and Ameen-ud-dowlah, Foreign Office, Downing Street, 6 March 1810. Letter to the same effect from George III to Fath Ali Shaha, 13 July 1810. TNA, FO 60/4.

Ouseley was to receive orders and instructions from the Foreign Office and be responsible to it only. He was however to keep the interests of the Company in Persia always in view and not to be derogatory to the power and prestige of the Company's Government in India.[247]Harford Jones's efforts to bring about a closer understanding between Turkey, Persia and Britain against France and Russia has largely been overlooked. He regarded the Persian campaign in Georgia as serving the interests of both Britain and Turkey for it served the common cause of diverting the attention of the Russians from the eastern frontier of Turkey.[248] He encouraged the Persians to keep fighting the Russians in Georgia rather than settle an armistice. The Russian General Termasoff made tentative overtures to the Persian Government for the renewal of talks on armistice, but Jones advised the Prince Royal not to agree to any of his proposals until the politics of St Petersburg were better understood.[249] Russia was the common enemy of Britain, Turkey and Persia, and a hostile movement on the part of any one of these powers benefitted the other two. The appearance of a British fleet in the Baltic in 1808, where it remained for the next five years, had the effect of drawing the Russian troops toward the neighbourhood of Riga, which operated to a certain extent in favour of Persia and Turkey. It was the change in the course of European politics a few years later beginning with Napoleon's retreat from Moscow and the reconciliation of Britain and Russia in 1812 that prompted the British to bring about the Treaty of Gulistan between Persia and Russia in October 1813 on terms which were highly disadvantageous to Persia.

In bringing about a rapprochement between Persia and Turkey, Jones received the cooperation of the British ambassador at Constantinople, Stratford Canning, who succeeded Robert Adair to that office. When Suleiman Pasha of Baghdad revolted against the Porte and sought assistance from the Persian Prince-Governor of Kirmenshah, the Shah of Persia on Jones's advice, issued a *firman* that 'in consequence of the good understanding existing between Persia and Turkey we have not thought proper to comply with his request. On the contrary we are most anxious daily to strengthen our alliance with Turkey.'[250] Mirza Ameen, the francophile Persian envoy at Constantinople was withdrawn and the new Persian envoy, Aga Hossein, was directed to act in concert with the British ambassador.[251]

Jones and Canning also actively cooperated with each other to ensure that the French were kept out of Constantinople and Persia. A French agent, Monsieur Outrey accompanied Askar Khan the Persian envoy to Paris who

[247] TNA, FO 60/4. Draft of HM Instructions to Sir G. Ousley, 13 July 1810.

[248] BL, IOR Fac. Rec. Persia 27. Harford Jones to Minto, Tauris, 15 October 1810.

[249] BL, IOR Fac. Rec. Persia 27. Harford Jones to Minto, Tauris, 19 January 1811.

[250] Ibid. Enclosure in Harford Jones's letter to Wellesley, Tauris, 3 November 1810. Also FO 60/3.

[251] TNA, FO 60/3. Harford Jones to G. Canning, Tauris, 13 November 1810.

was then on his way back to Tehran via Constantinople. Canning warned Jones that although Outrey was ostensibly to act as a French agent at Baghdad, he might possibly be charged with a special mission to the court of Persia. He also pointed out that the Persian agent in Constantinople, Mirza Ameen, and Askar Khan who were both suspected of being francophiles, might create intrigue with the French in Constantinople and should therefore be removed without delay.[252] Outrey was sent back from Erzeroom in December 1810 by the Persian Government.[253]

Harford Jones was not only instrumental in clinching political ties between Britain and Persia, he also visualised Persia as a market for the British as distinct from the East India Company's goods. In December 1809, he wrote to Canning about his ideas of opening a new and lucrative commerce between England and Persia. He found that the whole of the northern and western provinces of the Persian Empire were supplied with European goods by Russian vessels which despite the war between the two countries entered the Persian ports on the Caspian. Ports in the Persian Gulf were far away from Tehran and the northern provinces, hence the British could not success-fully compete with the Russians. Jones suggested that if British goods could be imported into a port in the Black Sea, namely Trebizond, then the whole Persian market might be captured with the East India Company supplying the southern and eastern provinces, and the London merchants the northern and western.[254] Although this ambitious project was not attempted, he succeeded in expanding the market for British woollens in Persia for the clothing of the army which added to the revenues of the Company.[255]

Minto offered every support and cooperation to the new ambassador to Persia. The only suggestion he had to make with regard to the definitive treaty was that Ouseley should avoid any agreement with Persia which might be incompatible with the treaty recently concluded between the Government of India and the King of Kabul.[256]

The appointment of a British ambassador to Persia temporarily provided a solution to the dispute whether HM Government or the Government of India should conduct diplomatic relations with that country. Britain's interest in the Middle East during the Napoleonic Wars and rivalry with France and Russia were the determining strategic factors, but Persia's importance to and connection with India could not be totally disregarded. According to

---

[252] TNA, FO 60/3. S. Canning to Harford Jones, Pera, 22 August 1810.

[253] BL, IOR Fac. Rec. Persia 27. Harford Jones to the Secret Committee, Tauris, 29 January 1810.

[254] TNA, FO 60/2. Harford Jones to G. Canning, Tauris, 14 December 1809. No. 25.

[255] BL, IOR Fac. Rec. Persia 27. Harford Jones to the Secret Committee, Tauris, 16 October 1810.
Ibid., 4 November 1810.

[256] TNA, FO 60/6. Minto to G. Ouseley, Fort William, 3 February 1811. Also NLS M 162.

Sir Reader Bullard, the question of principle was not settled until 1860, and that between 1810 and 1860, on several occasions there was 'a shifting of responsibility, backwards and forwards, between London and Calcutta'.[257] In 1859, with the transfer of power from the East India Company to the queen, relations with Persia were at first entrusted to the Secretary of State for India instead of the Secretary of State for Foreign Affairs. The British representative at Tehran was to remain under the direct control of the Crown, although the subordinate members of the establishment were to be filled by members of the Indian Political Service. The Government of India not only contributed toward the cost of the British legation in Persia, but the British consulates in Persia, posts in the Persian Gulf and the residency at Baghdad continued to be filled by members of the Indian Service, and the Government of India until 1947 had an important voice in the all matters relating to British policy in Persia. This was 'the principle' that Minto emphasised at the beginning of the nineteenth century – he did not demand that the conduct of diplomatic relations with Persia be the exclusive domain of the Government of India, but that due to its regional political, economic and strategic role must necessarily be consulted on all matters prior to any decisions being made by the Crown.

---

[257] Rawlinson, *England and Russia in the East*, p. 96.

Three

CREATING A BUFFER ZONE

Defending the North-western Frontier of India

Toward the beginning of 1808, Minto decided to open diplomatic relations with Ranjit Singh, the Sikh ruler of Lahore. His objective was to form a defensive alliance against the French. It was believed that an army of invasion from Persia must necessarily march 'through the Kingdom of Cabul and the territories of Lahore as well as through the countries of several independent Chiefs'[1] before it could reach the Company's possessions in the Doab.

In a note dated 17 June 1808, Minto wrote:

> The more I reflect upon the progressive activity of the intrigues & exertions of the French Embassy in Persia directed to the ultimate execution of their hostile designs against the British possessions in India,... the more I am convinced of the immediate necessity of adopting those additional measures of counter-action which have long been in the Contemplation of Government but of which the actual prosecution has been hitherto suspended by a Consideration of apparent obstacles and difficulties. I allude to the Mission of British agents to the Courts of Lahore and Caubul.[2]

It was believed in India that an attack on the British territories from the north-west might be directed by two possible routes: the northern route through Persia, Kandahar, Kabul and the Punjab into Oudh, and the southern route through Persia, Kabul and Sind into Bombay.[3] The importance of the Sikh country, situated on the banks of the Sutlej, for the defence of the British territories in India was discussed in a memorandum by David Hopkins, a member of the Company's Bengal Medical Establishment. Comparing the potentialities of Sind and the Punjab, Hopkins wrote that Sind was distinguished neither for its wealth nor its strength and was of importance 'only

[1] NLS M 159. Minto to Robert Dundas, Fort William, 10 February 1808 (Secret).
[2] BL, IOR Ben. Sec. & Sep. Cons. 207. Cons. of 20 June 1808, No. 2. Governor-General's minute, 17 June 1808.
[3] NLS M 159. Minto to Robert Dundas, 10 February 1808.

as it commands the navigation of the river Indus'. The Punjab, on the other hand, not only commanded the upper Indus valley but was 'uncommonly fertile… and inhabited by a hardy and brave but an uncivilized and rapacious race of people'. An enemy in possession of the Punjab could easily advance upon Delhi.[4] The presence of the French in Persia and a look at the map of India convinced Minto of the necessity of first sending a political mission to Lahore. Minto had to formulate his cis-Sutlej policy shortly after Metcalfe commenced the negotiations with Ranjit Singh.

The Company's Government had first come into contact with Ranjit Singh in 1805, when Lord Lake, in pursuit of Holkar, entered his territory and the Treaty of Lahore (1 January 1806) was concluded.[5] On the expulsion of the Marathas from the country between the Jamuna and the Sutlej, the petty Sikh chiefs of the cis-Sutlej area welcomed British protection. Both Lake and Wellesley regarded it essential to defend the Sutlej. However, Wellesley was recalled and all the British battalions were withdrawn from the area. As a result of Barlow's settlement with the Marathas, the Jamuna became the limit of the Company's territories in the north-west. The relations of the British with the Sikh chiefs of Sirhind and Malwa came virtually to an end. Minto resumed diplomatic relations with Ranjit Singh in 1808, not as a result of the Maratha menace, but the fear of a foreign invasion form the north-west which caused the Government to shape its policy in the area between the Jamuna and the Sutlej.

Ranjit Singh rapidly consolidated his power after 1805. Taking advantage of the weakness and constant discord among the cis-Sutlej states, he tried to bring them under his own supremacy and to unite them all into a well ordered state.[6] In 1806–07, Ranjit made two incursions on the left bank of the Sutlej. He took *nazrana* or tribute from a number of cis-Sutlej chiefs and occupied Ludhiana. The cis-Sutlej chiefs in despair turned to Seton, the resident at Delhi, as they had turned in 1800 to General Perron who was then in charge of Sindhia's affairs in northern India, against the pressure of the Irish adventurer George Thomas. In March 1808, a deputation of cis-Sutlej chiefs consisting of Bhag Singh of Jind, Bhai Lal Singh of Kythal, Bhagwan Singh of Jagdari, Dulcha Singh of Radhur, Chyn Singh, confidential agent of Raja Sahib Singh of Patiala, and the vakil of Raja Jaswant Singh of Nabha, came to Delhi to see Seton. At the same time, Ranjit Singh's Lawyer, Mohar Singh came to find out what sort of reception the Raja was likely to receive from the British during his proposed visit to Haridwar. Seton sent a cordial invitation to Ranjit to visit Haridwar and proposed to the Supreme Government

---

4   NLS M 333. Hopkins's Memorandum on the defence of India, 1808. Hopkins was also the author of the work entitled *The Dangers of British India from French Invasion and Missionary Establishments* (London, 1809).

5   Aitchison, *Treaties, Engagements and Sanads*, Vol. I, 5th edn, p. 33.

6   Cunningham, J.D., *History of the Sikhs* (Calcutta, 1903, reprint of 1st edn), p. 134.

that Charles Metcalfe, the first assistant at the Delhi Residency should be sent to attend the Raja at Haridwar.[7] As soon as Mohar Singh left Delhi, the cis-Sutlej chiefs appealed for British protection against Ranjit Singh's encroachments.[8] They presented a paper to Seton containing their wishes and expectations.[9] Seton was courteous and attentive toward the Sikh chiefs at Delhi, but each time they raised the question of British protection against Ranjit Singh, he observed that it was the policy of the British Government to adhere to the principle of non-interference. He also tried to discourage their frequent visits to Delhi, for the object of their visit was apparent to all.[10] The Government of Bengal fully backed Seton.[11] In answer to the propositions presented by the cis-Sutlej chiefs, the Supreme Government replied that although the rulers of Delhi and Agra had usually exercised overlordship over the cis-Sutlej Sikhs, the British had:

> ... resolved to restore to the Sikhs the independence which they had a right to enjoy and expressly disclaimed all interference in their concerns all rights of supremacy over them and all claims to tribute or Revenue from them... The British Government therefore cannot recognize the existence of those corresponding relations of authority and dependence which might be considered to impose on it a positive obligation to guarantee their possessions and consequently in the case to which the chiefs have averred, the conduct of that Government must be regulated according to the circumstances of the occasion.[12]

The cis-Sutlej chiefs appeared to prefer the British to their co-religionist Ranjit Singh. However, in 1808 it was not in the interest of the British Government to stand forth in their defence against the Raja of Lahore. Minto wrote to the Secret Committee:

> the certain resolution of the Rajah of Lahore to subjugate the States situated between the Sutlege and the frontier of our dominion would, under other circumstances than the present, constitute a case on which, on grounds of self-defence, the interposition of the British power, for the purpose of preventing the execution of such a project, would be equally just and prudent. Yet

---

7   BL, IOR Ben. Sec & Sep. Cons. 206. Cons. of 4 April 1808, No. 6. A. Seton to Edmonstone, Delhi, 18 March 1808. Ibid., No. 7. Translation of a letter from the resident at Delhi to Ranjit Singh of Lahore, written on 17 March 1808.
8   Ibid., Cons. of 18 April 1808, No. 8. A. Seton to Edmonstone, Delhi, 3 April 1808.
9   Ibid., No. 9. Translation of a paper of proposals rendered to the resident at Delhi by the Sikh chiefs Rajah Bhaug Singh and Bhye Laul Singh and Cheyn Singh.
10 BL, IOR Ben. Sec. & Sep. Cons. 206. Cons. of 2 May 1808, No. 16. A. Seton to Edmonstone, Delhi, 16 April 1808.
11 Ibid., No. 17. Edmonstone to Seton, Fort William, 2 May 1808.
12 BL, IOR Ben. Sec. & Sep. Cons. 206. Cons. of 2 May 1808, No. 18. Note of reply to the propositions of the Sikh chiefs communicated in the dispatches from the resident at Delhi of 3 and 8 April 1808.

the accomplishment of the more important views already described seems evidently incompatible with such a course of policy.[13]

The rise of a strong military power on the borders of the Company's territories could not be overlooked by the British, especially after their bitter experience with the Marathas and Tipu Sultan. It must however be remembered that Ranjit Singh's kingdom in 1808 did not extend very much beyond his two capital cities of Lahore and Amritsar.[14] His status might have been considered to be ranked between a petty chieftain and a formidable rival. However, due to the increasing importance in 1808 of the counteraction of the French threat and the mobilisation of Ranjit's cooperation for that purpose, Minto was unwilling to alienate him. Although therefore he had no intention of allowing Ranjit Singh to complete the subjugation of the cis-Sutlej states, he wanted that question shelved for the time being. Minto's primary aim was to enter into an anti-French agreement with Ranjit Singh. He was willing to make some sacrifice if absolutely necessary, but initially not prepared to commit himself to any definite policy with regard to the cis-Sutlej states. Minto did not agree with Seton's recommendation that the Government should inform Ranjit Singh that the Sutlej should be regarded as the boundary of his territories to the southward, that Karnal should be regarded as the boundary of the Company's territories in the north-west, and that the territory occupied by the cis-Sutlej chiefs should be independent of both the Raja of Lahore and the British. In this opinion, 'under a knowledge of the Rajah's designs a declaration of absolute neutrality would be a virtual invitation to the prosecution of them, and the signal of commotion, warfare and destruction in the vicinity of our Dominions'.[15]

The hostility between Ranjit Singh and the Afghan ruler Shah Shuja had also to be taken into consideration by Minto as he sought to establish connections with both these powers. Minto was afraid that Ranjit Singh might refuse to grant a passage to the Kabul mission through his territories. The opening of diplomatic relations with Ranjit Singh therefore presented certain problems because of his hostility toward the cis-Sutlej chiefs as well as toward the Afghan ruler. Minto wrote to the Secret Committee about his dilemma:

> the difficulties which oppose the intercourse and connection... are occasioned... by the jealousy, ambition or conflicting interests of the Western States... the local position of the Rajah's territories would evidently render a close connection with that Chief necessary to the success of those ultimate views which dictate the policy of a direct intercourse and union of interests with the Government of Cabul. On the other hand the practicability of forming the

[13] NLS M 194. Governor-General-in-Council to the Secret Committee, 31 March 1808.
[14] Davies, C.C., *An Historical Atlas of the Indian Peninsula* (Oxford, 1959, 2nd edn), pp. 62–63.
[15] NLS M 194. Governor-General-in-Council to the Secret Committee, 31 March 1808.

species of connection with the Rajah of Lahore which our interests appear to require is impeded by the nature of his views with respect to the Sikh Chieftains to the Southward of the Sutledge.[16]

In April 1808, Minto, on Seton's recommendation, agreed that the foundations of a closer relationship with Ranjit might be laid down at the time of Ranjit's intended visit to Haridwar. It was decided that Metcalfe should be deputed to attend the Raja as the agent of the governor-general. Metcalfe was instructed to gratify and conciliate the Raja in every way and to ascertain his attitude toward a British embassy to Kabul. He was also to try 'to lead Runjeet Sing to invite him to accompany him on his return to Lahore or to propose an Embassy to his Court on the part of the British Government'.[17] Metcalfe was at least to ascertain whether such an embassy would be acceptable to the Raja or not. However, Ranjit cancelled his trip to Haridwar and another proposed trip to Thaneswar, another place of pilgrimage in northern India, was also uncertain. A political mission to his court was therefore the most direct manner of contacting and negotiating with him.

Minto thought of adopting preliminary measures to find out what sort of reception this mission to Lahore and Kabul was likely to receive from the states in question, but this meant a necessary delay which he was anxious to avoid. He was confident that both the Amir of Kabul and the Raja of Lahore would be highly flattered by such attention from the British Government. Any reluctance or apprehension that Ranjit might entertain with regard to a political mission from the British Government would, in his opinion, be superseded by 'a sense of honour and distinction which the mission would confer upon him in the eyes of the states of India'.[18] It was also extremely unlikely that Ranjit Singh would be bold enough to display a hostile attitude toward a power of which he was already wary.

Metcalfe was selected to lead the mission to Lahore in view of his ability and local knowledge, and the fact of his being acquainted with the details of the previous transactions with the Sikh chiefs at Delhi. Minto thought of entrusting Metcalfe with both the mission to Lahore and to Shah Shuja, but opted for a focused approach.[19]

The main object of Metcalfe's mission was to impress on Ranjit Singh the dangers of a French attack on the Punjab and eventually on the British territories in India, and the consequent expediency of forming a defensive alliance between Ranjit Singh and the British Government against the French. The

---

16 NLS M 194. Governor-General-in-Council to the Secret Committee, 31 March 1808.

17 BL, IOR Ben. Sec. & Sep. Cons. 206. Cons. of 4 April 1808, No.8. Edmonstone to Seton, Fort William, 4 April 1808.

18 BL, IOR Ben. Sec. & Sep. Cons. 207. Cons. of 20 June 1808, No. 2. Governor-General's minute, 17 June 1808.

19 Ibid.

time at which this 'ultimate purpose' of the mission should be announced to the Raja was left to the envoy's discretion. Metcalfe was advised to get acquainted with the character and attitude of Ranjit Singh and his principal advisers and to try to win their confidence and goodwill before making any communications to them on the subject.

The object of the mission, in the meantime, was to be represented as the improvement of friendly relations between the two states. The Raja was to be told that his letter congratulating Minto on his arrival in India had encouraged the Government to cultivate and improve the connection between the two states, and that an envoy was sent to his court 'for the express purpose of cementing the bonds of mutual friendship'.[20]

These instructions suggest that Minto was not entirely unaware of the diffi-culty of convincing Ranjit Singh of the danger from the French. Ranjit was likely to be suspicious about the objectives of the British if the counteraction of the French was declared to be the primary motive of Metcalfe's mission, especially when there was no immediate or apparent threat from the French and additionally no French representatives in his court or territory. Metcalfe was therefore advised that the circumstances under which he might enter immediately on the actual objectives of his mission were:

a) If any French agent had already arrived or was expected shortly to arrive at Lahore or any part of the Punjab, and
b) If the activities of the French in Persia had already attracted the Raja's notice or if any reliable information should be received of the advance of a French army toward Persia.

The general principles on which an anti-French alliance was to be negotiated with Ranjit Singh were the same as those of the negotiations with the Amirs of Sind and Kabul, namely that it was the 'common interest' of Ranjit Singh and the British to oppose the French. Ranjit Singh's cooperation was to be sought by arousing his apprehensions about the fate of his own kingdom if the French were allowed to enter it either as friends or enemies. Metcalfe was instructed by Minto that:

> the primary object of your attention must be to alarm his fears at the eventual approach of the Enemy and to endeavor to convince him that the preservation of his Country from devastation and subjection is concerned in cooperating with the British power for the destruction of an invading force, equally hostile to his territories as to our own.[21]

---

[20] BL, IOR Ben. Sec. & Sep. Cons. 207. Cons. of 20 June 1808, No. 3. Edmonstone to Metcalfe, 20 June 1808. Also Home Misc. Series 592, pp. 23–65.
[21] BL, IOR Ben. Sec. & Sep. Cons. 207. Cons. of 20 June 1808, No. 3. Edmonstone to Metcalfe, 20 June 1808.

If the threatened invasion actually were to occur, Minto thought of advancing an army beyond the Indus to oppose it. With regard to that contingency, Ranjit's consent was to be sought for the advance of a British army through his territories. Metcalfe was to obtain Ranjit's promise to furnish supplies and to allow the British Government to establish military posts in his dominion. Minto did not pay sufficient attention to the fact that in view of the recent activities of the British in India, the Raja of Lahore was unlikely to view with favour either the establishment of a British resident at his court for an indefinite period of time or the advance of British troops into his territories to oppose a foreign enemy from whom he felt no danger.

Minto was not altogether unaware of the possibility of Ranjit Singh demanding certain concessions. While reiterating that it was contrary to the principles of the Company's policy to unite with any of the states of India in projects of conquest or ambition, or to conclude defensive engagements that might involve the Company in internal warfare, Minto expressed himself willing to make some sacrifices to Ranjit's wishes in proportion to the emergency. He was, in case of extreme necessity, willing to concede the demand for British restraint in Ranjit's campaign related to subjugating the cis-Sutlej chiefs. Edmonstone wrote to Metcalfe, 'Our acquiescence in this negative demand however would not... constitute a violation of our political principles; on the contrary our rejection of it would in fact be a deviation from those principles because it would involve the protection of states unconnected with us by the obligations of defensive alliance.'[22]

Minto left the question open until it could be known to what degree the Company's own interests might require a cordial union with Ranjit Singh, and what sacrifices might be expedient to make for that purpose. Minto's cis-Sutlej policy clearly depended on the pressure of the French threat in the north-west. The two possibilities were that Ranjit be given a free hand over the cis-Sutlej Sikhs if the danger of a French attack became imminent and it was essential to secure Ranjit's cooperation in opposing it. Alternatively, the objective of the British Government could be to thwart the increasing power of the Sikh ruler and to prevent his subjugation of the cis-Sutlej states.

As Metcalfe's mission to Lahore preceded the mission to Afghanistan, one of his duties was to facilitate the progress of that mission. He was authorised to start preliminary communications with the Amir of Kabul or with some of the leading men at his court to prepare for the favourable reception of Elphinstone's mission. However, he was not to announce the Kabul mission or to volunteer any information about it to Ranjit Singh until after Elphinstone was on his way. If Ranjit heard of it from other sources and displayed any suspicions about it, Metcalfe was to assuage his fears and declare that the mission to Afghanistan involved nothing injurious to his

---

22   BL, IOR Ben. Sec. & Sep. Cons. 207. Cons. of 10 June 1808, No. 3.

interests. He was to also secure, if possible, the Raja's assent to the passage of Elphinstone and his escort through his territory and directed to obtain information about the political state of affairs in Afghanistan and in all the political dominions and regions through which he was to travel to Lahore. He was to collect geographical information about these geo-political areas west of the Indus and about the route through which an army might march from Persia to the Indus. Metcalfe was also to ascertain the actual disposition of Ranjit Singh toward the British Government and to verify the nature of the correspondence Ranjit was supposed to maintain with Holkar and Sindhia. He was to gather information about Ranjit's resources, troops, the constitution of his government, the extent of his dominion and his relations with other states.

The Commander-in-Chief at Fort William, Major General Hewitt, proposed that two officers, the Adjutant and the Quarter-Master-General of the King's troops, should be sent with Metcalfe's mission but not attached to it, to the Punjab, and an officer of the Engineers with Elphinstone to Afghanistan to collect information of a military nature and report it directly to headquarters. The lack of accurate information to guide the movements of the troops on the frontiers of the newly acquired Company's territories was acutely felt. In Hewitt's words, 'beyond the Jumna all is conjecture'.[23]

Minto objected to these secret military commissions owing to the fact that the dispatch of military officers of high rank through the territories of independent states without permission or intimation of their objectives would have aroused suspicion and resentment. He felt that if it should be found necessary to advance an army to the Indus, greater advantage would be gained by the friendship and assistance of these states than by precise topographical knowledge of the ground or of the resources of these states at the cost of their friendship. In his opinion, the same objectives could be attained by less objectionable means, that is, by a proper selection of persons regularly attached to the two missions and by special instructions to the envoys themselves and to the officers attached to the missions.[24]

The unauthorised proceedings in Lahore of Captain Mathews, an officer attached to the Company's army at Fatehgarh, who was at the time travelling through the Punjab to Kashmir was a source of uneasiness to the Government. Although Captain Mathews was travelling unofficially, he collected all sorts of information for the future use of the Government at the request of General Hewitt. He was regarded as an authorised agent of the British Government both by Ranjit Singh and his enemies and was approached by Ranjit Singh's mother-in-law, Rani Sada Kaur, through his *munshi* (agent or clerk) to win his

---

23 BL, IOR Ben. Sec. & Sep. Cons. 207. Cons. of 4 July 1808, No. 1. Minute by Sir George Hewitt, Commander-in-Chief, 22 June 1808. Also Home Misc. Series 592, pp. 79–82.

24 Ibid., No. 2. Governor-General's minute, Fort William, 2 July 1808. Also, Home Misc. Series 592, pp. 85–93.

connivance in a plot to overthrow Ranjit Singh. At a time when Minto was seeking to establish official communications with Ranjit Singh, the presence of Captain Mathews and his activities in Lahore was a source of serious embarrassment. Minto ordered his immediate return from the Punjab and Metcalfe was directed to disavow his proceedings in Lahore.[25]

On 6 July 1808, Minto received a letter from Ranjit Singh expressing his desire to enter into an amicable arrangement with the Company through the agency of Captain Mathews. From letters and representations of the cis-Sutlej chiefs, Rani Ratan Kaur, Raja Bhag Singh, Bhai Lal Singh, Bhai Chyn Singh, and Raja Jaswant Singh, Ranjit had gathered that the British were intending to go to war against him. This suspicion probably caused him to cancel his trip to Haridwar in April. Ranjit claimed that the country west of the Jamuna, with the exception of the posts occupied by the Company, was subject to his authority and invited Minto to recognise this. He also proposed that the enemies of one state should be regarded as the enemies of the other, and that 'the relations of amity and friendship, as established by Treaty, shall continue daily to improve from generation to generation until the latest posterity'.[26]

In reply to his letter, Minto took the opportunity of announcing Metcalfe's mission to the Raja, and described its objective as improving the friendly relations and good understanding existing between the two governments. Captain Mathews was dismissed as a mere traveller.[27] Edmonstone wrote to Seton that the conduct of the cis-Sutlej chiefs in threatening Ranjit Singh with British arms was thoroughly reprehensible, and that if found to be true, Seton should require from them a written retraction and forward it to Metcalfe.[28]

In reply to Seton's letter of 17 July 1808 announcing Metcalfe's mission, Ranjit Singh wrote that the deputation of an envoy from the governor-general to his court was 'a source of the most animated satisfaction to my friendly heart', and that he was anxious to cultivate the friendship of the British, the foundations of which were established by Lord Lake in 1805. Ranjit sent one of his highly regard confidantes Imamuddin to Patiala to receive Metcalfe and conduct him to his court.[29]

Metcalfe became assistant to the resident at Delhi on October 1806, but he was not very interested in 'the Politics, Police, Revenue and Justice of this

25 NLS M 160. Minto to Edmonstone, Barrackpore, 11 May 1808 (Confidential). NLS M 194. Governor-General-in-Council to the Secret Committee, 15 September 1808.

26 BL, IOR Home Misc. Series 592, pp. 147–52. Ranjit Singh to the Governor-General, Lahore, received 6 July 1808.

27 NLS Minto Papers, Box 59. Original letter from Minto to Ranjit Singh, 11 July 1808, with a translation attached. Also BL, IOR Home Misc. Series 592, pp. 155–57.

28 BL, IOR Home Misc. Series 592, pp. 157–69. Edmonstone to Seton, 11 July 1808.

29 BL, IOR Ben. Sec. & Sep. Cons. 208. Cons. of 29 August 1808. Translation of a letter from Ranjit Singh to Seton, 28 July 1808, received 6 August 1808.

quarter' and was disconcerted as he was 'getting so deep into the Revenue line, and so far from the Political'. He was also burdened with a load of debt.[30] The appointment as Minto's political agent to Ranjit Singh, with a salary of Rs 2,000 per month, therefore afforded him a wonderful opportunity. He set out from Delhi on 28 July 1808 with a small staff and escort.

Metcalfe reached Patiala on 22 August and exchanged visits with Sahib Singh of Patiala. The latter tried to prevail on him to receive the keys of his fort and to restore them as a gift on the part of the British Government. It was obviously Sahib Singh's intention to obtain the appearance of the guarantee of the British Government to his dominion. Metcalfe refused to do so, but assured him of the friendship of the British Government. He refused to believe in Sahib Singh's report that Ranjit intended shortly to cross the Sutlej to occupy Faridkot.[31] Soon afterwards, he heard from other sources that Ranjit was moving to Kasur in order to cross the Beas on a military expedition. He received a letter from Ranjit Singh inviting him to join him at Kasur instead of at Amritsar.[32] Imamuddin, Ranjit's confidential agent who met Metcalfe at Patiala, told him that Ranjit's movement to Kasur was not a sudden action, but based on a prior plan based on an appropriate season.[33] While Metcalfe was on his way to Kasur, Ranjit Singh's army was assembling there from all quarters, leading Metcalfe to believe that 'his principal motive in collecting his forces at this period is his desire to make a grand display of military power before the British mission'. Metcalfe had to admit that from Kasur an expedition could be launched against either Multan to the north or the Sikh territories south-east of the Sutlej.[34]

On 11 September 1808, Metcalfe reached Ranjit's camp at Kasur. Ranjit's principal minister, Diwan Mokham Chand, and Sirdar Fateh Singh came out a few miles with a body of cavalry to receive him. The mission was encamped on the deserted bed of a river, on either banks of which Ranjit's troops stood on guard. On the 12th, Metcalfe visited Ranjit Singh, and presents and compliments were exchanged. A salute was fired in the evening in honour of the day. Metcalfe was quite pleased with his reception.[35] However, he wrote to the Government that Ranjit showed many signs of jealousy toward the British Government, and felt more suspicion than pleasure at the mission sent to his court. All communications between Ranjit's camp and the British

---

[30] Kaye, Sir J.W., *The Life and Correspondence of Charles, Lord Metcalfe* (London, 1854), Vol. 1, pp. 223–24, 228, 231. Metcalfe's salary as assistant to the Delhi residency was only Rs 750 per month, which was less than what he received as Wellesley's assistant.

[31] BL, IOR Ben. Sec. & Sep. Cons. 209. Cons. of 19 September 1808. Metcalfe to Edmonstone, Camp Patialah, 24 August 1808.

[32] Ibid., Cons. of 26 September 1808, No. 6. Metcalfe to Edmonstone, 2 September 1808.

[33] Ibid., No. 8. Metcalfe to Edmonstone, 4 September 1808.

[34] Ibid., Cons. of 3 October 1808, No. 20. Metcalfe to Edmonstone, 5 September 1808.

[35] BL, IOR Home Misc. Series 593, pp. 1–4. Metcalfe to Edmonstone, Camp Qusoor, 13 September 1808.

camp were strictly prohibited on the pretext of not disturbing the mission. The cis-Sutlej chiefs who were in Ranjit's camp sent messengers to Metcalfe that although they wished to pay him a visit, they could not do so from fear of the Maharaja. Metcalfe found the greatest difficulty in trying to procure intelligence. He wrote to Bengal, 'it would appear that I am regarded as a dangerous enemy to be guarded against rather than an Envoy from a friendly state charged with the most amicable duties'.[36]

Ranjit seemed to expect that Metcalfe would depart in a short time. His ignorance of the actual objective of the mission was the main cause of his anxiety. The recent visit of the cis-Sutlej chiefs to Delhi, the reports of the British Government's intention of taking up their cause against him and the late proceedings of Captain Mathews were factors which caused him to regard the British Government as his enemy and a major obstacle to his dream of a united Sikh kingdom. He might also have suspected that Metcalfe's mission and Captain Mathew's journey were both undertaken in order to obtain information about his dominion, power and resources.

On an interview with Ranjit Singh on 22 September Metcalfe declared that the governor-general had received authentic information that the French were trying to establish themselves in Persia and had formed a strategic plan to invade Hindustan and to seize Kabul and the Punjab. The primary responsibility of the British Government therefore was to warn these states of the impending danger and feeling their interests to be the same, the governor-general had commissioned him to negotiate with the Raja arrangements for a defensive alliance against a common enemy.

The draft of a treaty presented by Metcalfe to Ranjit Singh on 4 October 1808, consisted of three articles. The first provided for joint action against a French army or the army of any power in league with the French attempting to invade the territories of either of the contracting parties. The second article demanded the passage of the British army through the territories of Ranjit Singh and that the Raja should furnish supplies and allow the establishment of depots in his country should it become necessary to advance troops beyond the Indus. The third article stipulated the establishment of a regular postal system by the British Government through the territories of Ranjit Singh in order to maintain communications with Persia and Afghanistan and to collect information about the designs of the enemy. It was indicated that agents, messengers and runners employed in that service should enjoy free movement and protection throughout Ranjit Singh's territories.[37] The first two articles were in conformity with Metcalfe's instructions, and the third he

---

[36] BL, IOR Ben. Sec. & Sep. Cons. 210. Cons. of 17 October 1808, No. 12. Metcalfe to Edmonstone, Camp Qusoor, 15 September 1808. Also, Home Misc. Series 593, pp. 7–18.

[37] BL, IOR Home Misc. Series 593, pp. 319–21. Plan of a Treaty between the British Government and Ranjit, transmitted to the Raja by Metcalfe on 4 October 1808.

thought advisable in order to maintain communications with Kabul after his own mission ceased.

On 8 October, Ranjit delivered counter-proposals, also drawn up in the form of a treaty of three articles. The first article proposed that there should be perpetual friendship between the British and his Government, that the friendship of any other power should not be preferred to his, and that the British Government should not interfere in his disputes with the Amir of Kabul. The second article proposed that the friendship of the two states be continued from generation to generation. The third proposition contained a declaration of Ranjit Singh's right of sovereignty over the whole Sikh dominion and required the acknowledgement of that right by the British Government. No Sikh chiefs should be given protection by the latter. Ranjit used the terms 'Surkur Khalsujeo' to refer to his own government, meaning the Sikh nation of the Confederacy of the Sikhs. It is naturally implied that he was the head of the Sikh nation.[38]

The two drafts could not have been wider apart showing the complete difference in perspective and objectives that existed between the two governments. Ranjit seized upon Metcalfe's mission as the most favourable opportunity for the settlement of the question of the position of the cis-Sutlej states and to place his relations with the Company on a secure and advantageous footing, whereas Metcalfe focused exclusively on the necessity of a defensive alliance against the French, perhaps even against his own convictions.

Metcalfe wrote to the Government about Ranjit's actual views regarding the pending negotiations. He wrote:

> It appears to me, that he wishes sincerely to have a Treaty of perpetual friendship with the British Government, to be maintained hereafter with his Heirs and Successors; that he is indifferent to the proposed alliance against the designs of the French as the danger is not near nor perceptible to him; that to that alliance generally however he has no objection, although he wishes to make his agreement to it, the means of obtaining concessions from the British Government;... at the same time, he does not view without uneasiness,... the probability of the Introduction of British Agents into his territories, the disclosure of the actual State of his dominion, army and resources, and other imagined consequences of opening the means of communication between the British Government and the disaffected Chiefs whom he oppresses.[39]

Ranjit Singh's crossing the Sutlej in force in September 1808 forced Minto to make a decision related to the cis-Sutlej states. It was evident that Ranjit could only be stopped by a strong declaration by the British Government of

---

[38] BL, IOR Home Misc. Series 593, pp. 322–25. Proposals delivered by Ranjit Singh to Metcalfe on 8 October 1808.

[39] BL, IOR Home Misc. Series 593, pp. 301–19. Metcalfe to Edmonstone, Camp Rajkot, 20 October 1808. Also Ben. Sec. & Sep. Cons. 210. Cons. of 14 November 1808, No. 14.

its determination to protect the cis-Sutlej states, which of course the latter had to be prepared to back up by force if necessary. The only snag was, as Seton pointed out, it would be resisting the execution of plans which were neither directed immediately against the British nor against their allies.[40] Minto adopted the view that opposition to Ranjit Singh would be a defensive measure as it was inimical to British interests to have his dominions too close to their own frontiers. If Ranjit was allowed to complete his plans of extending his authority south-east of the Sutlej, his frontier would converge on the British frontiers, and it would also bring him to the immediate neighbourhood of the Marathas, a circumstance which the British could not but regard as highly prejudicial to the equilibrium of the Company's territories. Although there was no evidence of any understanding between Ranjit Singh and Holkar, yet from their common enmity toward the British, an alliance might easily mature. Ranjit Singh has been circulating a report that both Holkar and the Raja of Bahawalpur had approached him for a joint effort against the British.[41] Edmonstone wrote to Metcalfe:

> By annexing to his dominion, the territories of the Sikhs between the Soutledge and the Jumna, the State of Lahore would become (what it cannot at present be considered) one of the substantive powers of Hindostan, possessing territories more extensive, a dominion more firm and absolute & resources more efficient than those of any other native State in India not actually under the influence and control of the British Government & place in a position contiguous to the most vulnerable quarter of the Company's possessions... the pride of conquest might lead him to meditate... projects of hostility against the British power.[42]

With the extension of Ranjit's authority over the cis-Sutlej states, his dominion would extend to the frontier of Haryana, which was nominally under Abdul Samad Khan, but who was incapable of either resisting the predatory incursions of the neighbouring tribe of Bhuttis or of controlling the turbulent zamindars. He would be easily conquered by Ranjit. The extension of Ranjit's territories would also bring him close to the territories of the allies of the British, the Rajas of Macheri and Bharatpur, and might threaten the stability of those alliances as well. The expansion of Ranjit's dominion south of the Sutlej would remove the buffer between the Company's territories and those of the independent states beyond the Jamuna. This fear was clearly expressed by Minto to General Hewitt. Minto wrote:

[40] BL, IOR Home Misc. Series 593, pp. 373–91. Metcalfe to Edmonstone, 1 November 1808. Ibid., pp. 167–82. A. Seton to Edmonstone, Delhi, 14 October 1808.
[41] BL, IOR Ben. Sec. & Sep. Cons. 210. Cons. of 31 October 1808, No. 1. Metcalfe to Edmonstone, 1 October 1808.
[42] BL, IOR Home Misc. Series 593. Edmonstone to Metcalfe, Fort William, 31 October 1808. Also, Ben. Sec. & Sep. Cons. 210. Cons. of 31 October 1808, No. 3.

By this extension of Rajah Runjeet Sing's dominion and influence over the North of Hindostan, the Barrier which now separates the most vulnerable quarter of the Company's dominions, from the Collision of any powerful neighbour would be removed, & be added to the resources of a Chief whose professed views are those of ambition; whose pursuits are those of conquest & military renown and who in that Situation may be said to hold in his possessions the Key to our North Western dominions.[43]

Minto added:

The establishment indeed of the dominion of Runjeet as that of a Substantive power in Hindostan, must necessarily produce a material change in the political System of that country & tend to disturb those relations of combined or conflicting interests among the various States to the Northward of the Nerbudda [Narmada] on the operation of which in a considerable degree depends the tranquillity & even the Security of the Company's possessions.[44]

Minto carefully considered the pros and cons of giving in to Ranjit's wishes in return for his acquiescence in an anti-French alliance. From Metcalfe's reports it was evident that the French threat had made no impression on Ranjit Singh, and that on the contrary, he regarded it as 'a fiction invented by the British Government with a view to designs against his independence'. Under such circumstances, Minto concluded that 'no reliance should be placed on the efficacy of an engagement contracted by the Rajah... to cooperate in opposing a danger, the Existence of which he disbelieves'.[45] On the contrary, Ranjit was likely to secure his own safety by agreeing to assist the French and affording them a passage through the Punjab. Edmonstone wrote to Metcalfe, 'By yielding therefore to the expectations which the Rajah has announced, as the Condition of the proposed alliance we should be exposed to all the eventual evils of that Concession without any security for the expected advantages of it.'[46]

Although Minto was not seriously thinking of subverting Ranjit Singh's power on the pretext that he might be a likely ally of the French, a pretext not so long ago employed by Wellesley to overthrow Tipu Sultan of Mysore, yet such a contingency was not entirely overlooked. Metcalfe was told that circumstances might yet arise of a nature both to justify and require British support of the efforts of those whose rights were encroached upon and territories usurped by Ranjit, to subvert his power.

[43] BL, IOR Home Misc. Series 593. Minto-in-Council to General Hewitt, Fort William, 14 November 1808. Also Ben. Sec. & Sep. Cons. 210. Cons. of 14 November 1808, No. 1.

[44] Ibid.

[45] Ibid.

[46] BL, IOR Home Misc. Series 593, pp. 129–53. Edmonstone to Metcalfe, 31 October 1808.

It is clear that from the outset, the British viewed the question and decided upon the policy toward the cis-Sutlej states purely from the point of view of self-interest. Minto had previously refused to grant them any assurance of protection. However, he now declared that upon the British succession of the Marathas in northern India, the Sikh chiefs on the left bank of the Sutlej considered themselves 'on grounds of usage & prescription as the vassals of this State'. He declared that in pursuance of the policy of non-interference, the British had absolved them from that state of subjugation and had declined any obligation to guarantee their possessions, without however relinquishing the right to interfere in future. The Sikh chiefs had been assured though, that the mission to Lahore involved no objectives hostile to their interests. The Government wrote to Metcalfe, 'It may therefore justly be observed that to suffer their Country to be overrun & their independence to be subverted by a foreign State, is at least to depart from the principles which we professed & to convert an intended benefit into an instrument of Destruction.'[47]

It was declared that although the British Government was not bound to guarantee the possessions of these chiefs, yet it could not without some degree of discredit expressly sanction the conquest of their territories.

The British based their claim over the cis-Sutlej states on their inheritance of the Maratha hegemony over northern India. However, as N.K. Sinha has remarked, 'In the dispatches of Wellesley, Maratha rights in the cis-Sutlej Sikh country which the British later claimed to have inherited have been variously referred to as Perron's "influence", his "personal connection" or as his "ascendancy". The British succeeded to this position which was really indefinable.'[48]

The withdrawal of the British to the Jamuna in 1806 had left British relations with the cis-Sutlej states in an equivocal situation. Sinha points out that in opposition to the British claim that the country between the Sutlej and the Jamuna was historically a part of the territory belonging to Delhi and that the British had inherited the right enjoyed by the Marathas until the subversion of their power in northern India by the British, Ranjit could also have appealed to historical unity of the Khalsa and his supremacy at Lahore and Amritsar which carried with it a de facto title to the country south of Lahore.[49] It was however not a battle of de jure or de facto rights. With reference to an age when the might of the sword was the only right, all such arguments are purely academic. If the power in possession of Delhi owed a duty to protect the cis-Sutlej chiefs, no excuse was offered as to why the British Government had neglected its duties during the past years. On the contrary, the Government tried to make a merit out of its neglect by declaring that it

[47] BL, IOR Home Misc. Series 583. Edmonstone to Metcalfe, 31 October 1808.
[48] Sinha, N.K., *Ranjit Singh* (Calcutta, 1951, 3rd edn), p. 20.
[49] Ibid., pp. 33–34.

had wished to afford the cis-Sutlej states an opportunity to be independent. It would have been closer to the truth to suggest that the Company wished to avoid new commitments unless forced by circumstances to do so.

The advantages to be derived from the protection of the cis-Sutlej states and the establishment of a British post on the Sutlej were described by Edmonstone as follows:

> By protecting these Chiefs we seek their attachment to our interests & by establishing a force on the North Western frontier of the territory between the Sutledge and the Jumna we afford an earnest of that protection and obtain the command of those territories for any purposes connected with a system of defensive arrangement. In that advanced position also we shall be prepared to take immediate advantage of any event in the Rajah's territories in which the support or employment of the British troops may be required by the exigency of the public Interests without infringing those principles of Faith & Justice which must ever govern the policy of the British Government in India.[50]

Metcalfe was directed to avoid concluding any treaty with Ranjit Singh, as it might restrict the Government's future proceedings with regard to the Raja. Ranjit was however to be assured that the Government was willing to continue friendly relations with him if he complied with all the demands and withdrew from the left bank of the Sutlej. Metcalfe was to remonstrate with Ranjit for the various acts of indignity and suspicion shown toward the British mission. If Ranjit refused to comply with the British demands, Metcalfe was to leave his territory.[51] Minto also wrote a letter to Ranjit Singh informing him of his decision to protect the cis-Sutlej states.[52]

The advancement of a detachment to the territories of the southern Sikhs was a necessary consequence of Minto's decision to protect them, for it afforded both to Ranjit and the Sikh chiefs the only satisfactory evidence that the Government meant what it said. It was definitely intended to put armed pressure on Ranjit Singh to make him yield, but even after the advancement of Ochterlony's detachment to Ludhiana, it is a stretch to claim that either Metcalfe or Minto won a diplomatic victory over Ranjit Singh.

A detachment of two battalions of sepoys with a proportion of cavalry and artillery was considered adequate for the purpose of occupying a post in the territory of the Raja of Patiala. The advantages to be secured by this military movement did not solely relate to the protection of the cis-Sutlej states. Minto wrote to General Hewitt:

[50] BL, IOR Home Misc. Series 593. Edmonstone to Metcalfe, 31 October 1808.
[51] Ibid.
[52] BL, IOR Ben. Sec. & Sep. Cons. 210. Cons. of 31 October 1808, No. 4. Minto's letter to Ranjit Singh, 31 October 1808.

The protection of the Sikh Chiefs however... is not the only object of this proposed movement, as a post of observation and a situation which will enable us to watch & to control the proceedings of the Rajah of Lahore and to take advantage of any events in that country... & to obtain more accurate information of the nature & resources of the Country through which a hostile army may approach or our own may advance, a Military Station in that quarter may be expected to prove of essential importance.[53]

The commander of the detachment was entrusted with political as well as military duties. Lieutenant-Colonel David Ochterlony, who was then stationed at Allahabad, was considered highly eligible for both sets of duties in view of his military experience and former interactions with the cis-Sutlej chiefs. It was decided to take advantage of the march of the detachment to obtain a complete survey of the area between the Jamuna and the Sutlej. Lieutenant White was entrusted with the task of making a geographical survey of the regions through which Ochterlony's detachment would march. The post to be occupied on the Sutlej was left to the decision of General Hewitt, Seton and Ochterlony.[54]

Seton informed the cis-Sutlej states, Raja Sahib Singh of Patiala, Raja Bhag Singh of Jind, Bhai Lal Singh of Kythal, Bhanga Singh of Thaneswar, Bhagwan Singh of Buria and Dulcheh Singh of the Government's decision to protect them.[55] Seton reported that Ranjit had lately tried to procure a seemingly voluntary written agreement from these chiefs acknowledging him as their overlord. Ranjit also employed the exertions of one of the Sikh gurus Bedi Shahib Singh in order to arouse the religious patriotism of the cis-Sutlej chiefs.[56] Seton was directed to notify the cis-Sutlej chiefs of the advance of British troops to the Sutlej for their benefit, but they were not allowed to entertain any hopes of hostility against Ranjit Singh.[57]

The cis-Sutlej states were informed that their active cooperation would be required for the defence of their territories both now as well as in the future. No subsidy or pecuniary contribution was demanded for the aid given, but the Government reserved the right to demand such contributions in future. Ochterlony was advised to obtain accurate information regarding the attitude, condition and military strength of the several chiefs and to advise the Government about the way in which their power might be advantageously

---

[53] BL, IOR Home Misc. Series 593. Minto-in-Council to General Hewitt, 14 November 1808.

[54] BL, IOR Ben. Sec. & Sep. Cons. 210. Cons. of 14 November 1808, No. 4. Edmonstone to Ochterlony, Fort William, 14 November 1808.

[55] BL, IOR Home Misc. Series 593, pp. 498–99, Seton to the Sikh Chiefs, 21 November 1808.

[56] BL, IOR Home Misc. Series 593, pp. 493–97, Seton to Edmonstone, Delhi, 11 November 1808.

[57] BL, IOR Home Misc. Series 593, pp. 253–61, Edmonstone to Seton, Fort William, 14 November 1808.

utilised in any defensive arrangements against an invading army or in military operations against Ranjit Singh if that should become necessary.[58]

From Metcalfe's dispatches, Minto learned that Ranjit was anxious to conclude a treaty of perpetual amity, but that he would not consent to the free introduction of British troops into his territory or the adoption of other defensive measures proposed by the British except under restrictions. Ranjit had reluctantly agreed to concede the latter point only under the condition of the British Government's acceptance of his cis-Sutlej claims which Minto refused. Minto also vetoed the idea of two separate treaties with Ranjit and nor was he disposed to conclude a mere treaty of amity with Ranjit Singh. Metcalfe was instructed that if the Raja was still eager for a treaty he should be told that the only admissible basis of negotiation would be a defensive agreement against the French.[59]

Toward the end of November 1808, Ranjit returned from his successful campaign and hurried to Amritsar, making and breaking two appointments with Metcalfe on the way. On 10 December, Metcalfe reached Amritsar and presented Ranjit with Minto's letter of 31 October 1808 declaring that the cis-Sutlej states had been taken under British protection in reply to Ranjit's reference of the question to the governor-general. Ranjit might have viewed that reference and Minto's answer to it as superfluous, as two of the cis-Sutlej chiefs, Jaswant Singh of Nabha and Bhai Lal Singh of Kythal followed him to Amritsar in order to solicit a share in the territories of the Rani of Ambala. Bhai Lal Singh also obtained a detachment of troops from Ranjit to take possession of Mohilan, a part of Ranjit's former conquest between the Sutlej and Jamuna which he had assigned to another chief. Ranjit followed a clever policy of conciliating the Sikh chiefs and creating their personal interest in the new arrangements by assigning parts of the newly conquered territories among his dependents. He retained the fort of Ambala but the districts of Ambala were to a large extent distributed, and Faridkot and its lands were also assigned to a chief. Saniwal, a late conquest about 15 miles from the Sutlej, was under the management of Diwan Mokham Chand, or in other words in actual possession of the Raja.[60]

Metcalfe realised that during the early part of the negotiation he had been too amenable and had allowed the Raja to hope for a recognition of his cis-Sutlej claims. He wrote to the Government that he had given in to the Raja's wishes at that time as his objective was to get the alliance against the French signed unconditionally and that he could not forget that he had been sent to establish an alliance and not to bring about a war. On the receipt of

[58] PGR II, Edmonstone to Ochterlony, Fort William, 29 December 1808.
[59] BL, IOR Home Misc. Series 593, pp. 443–65. Edmonstone to Metcalfe, Fort William, 28 November 1808.
[60] BL, IOR Home Misc. Series 594, pp. 73–77. Metcalfe to Edmonstone, Camp Amritsar, 11 December 1808.

the orders of 31 October and 14 November 1808, however, he saw that a more forceful conduct was now required of him and this suited him well. He wrote, 'I shall have a selfish gratification in paying him for all the uneasiness he has caused to me.'[61]

On 23 December, Metcalfe informed Ranjit Singh of the Government's resolution to advance a detachment of troops to the banks of the Sutlej.[62] The Raja was naturally greatly agitated on hearing this and wanted to march at once to Amritsar. On Metcalfe's remonstrance however, he postponed his movement to Amritsar and continued discussions in Lahore. Ranjit now proposed a compromise that the cis-Sutlej area should be placed in the same state and condition in which it was before Metcalfe's arrival. He also offered to undo his own handiwork provided the British Government should agree to adopt no new measures in that area, and that later an arrangement may be arrived at to mutual satisfaction.[63] Metcalfe insisted on his unconditional compliance with the requisitions made by the Government.

After long procrastination, Ranjit agreed on 2 January 1809 to withdraw his troops from Ambala and to restore it to its former owner Rani Daya Kaur. Metcalfe wrote to the Government that Ochterlony could now advance to a post on the Sutlej without any risk of immediate hostilities, for while Ranjit's troops were at Ambala, the British detachment could not have advanced without either compelling those troops to retreat or leaving them in its rear. About Ranjit's attitude, Metcalfe wrote, 'his Conduct hitherto has had all the effect of a refusal... notwithstanding that he has been careful not to express any intimation of a disposition to oppose, he has not made any real advance towards compliance... I cannot regard his conduct as otherwise than hostile.'[64]

During the entire month of January 1809, Metcalfe wrote vociferous letters to the Government insisting on the point of view that entering into a treaty with Ranjit Singh was not only unnecessary, but contrary to the interests of the British Government. He wrote:

> Ranjit Singh, I conceive, can have no right to demand in the manner in which he pressed the point, the conclusion of an engagement, the effect of which would be, to give stability to his unlawful, new and doubtful ascendancy, and to bind the British Government to witness without notice or interruption, the extension and establishment of a power decidedly hostile in disposition. This concession on the part of the British Government would be no neutrality, but a

---

61 Ibid.
62 BL, IOR Home Misc. Series 594, pp. 209–11. Metcalfe to Edmonstone, Camp Lahore, 24 December 1808.
63 BL, IOR Home Misc. Series 594, pp. 228–29. Translation of a note from Ranjit to Metcalfe, received 25 December 1808.
64 BL, IOR Home Misc. Series 594, pp. 303–13. Metcalfe to Edmonstone, Lahore, 3 January 1809.

partiality, in favour of an enemy against friends, for purposes evidently injurious to its own interest.[65]

Ranjit's anxious desire for a treaty and his efforts to prevent Metcalfe leaving his court without concluding one, were disregarded. On the contrary, the measures he undertook on hearing of the approach of a British force to the Sutlej were played up by Metcalfe as proof of his decided hostility. Perhaps Metcalfe was erring in interpreting his instructions from Calcutta. During the early part of his negotiations, failing to judge the actual intention of the Government with regard to the cis-Sutlej states from his instructions of 20 June 1808, he had all but given in to Ranjit's claim of sovereignty over these states. He was pulled up for that and new instructions were sent to him defining Minto's cis-Sutlej policy more clearly. In the instructions of 14 November 1808, he was told that a treaty with Ranjit Singh was not required, and that in the event of the French threat becoming real, Minto might consider the subversion of Ranjit's power if he proved too troublesome, not by the actual invasion of his territories, but by aiding the discontented chiefs and the subversive elements within his dominion. On the basis of these instructions however, Metcalfe advocated war on Ranjit Singh. In the true spirit of one of Wellesley's brigades, he regarded a war with Ranjit and overthrow of his power as a logical and legitimate outcome of the failure of his mission.

At the time Metcalfe was calling for war on Ranjit Singh, the Government at Calcutta was revising its policy toward the Sikh ruler. The news from Europe of Napoleon's reverses was the cause of this change in perspective as it was also the mainspring of the revision of Minto's policies with regard to Persia, Afghanistan and Sind. The latest news received from Europe removed the anxiety regarding the advance of a European force toward Turkey or Persia for the ultimate invasion of India and the Government could now safely surmise that Bonaparte's projects against the British territories in India had been suspended if not entirely abandoned. In such circumstances, the extraordinary defensive preparation and arrangements that Minto had undertaken could be suspended and the expenses reduced. In Minto's opinion:

> This intelligence also materially alters the condition of our interests relatively to the state of Lahore and enables us in our judgement to accede to arrangements of a nature calculated to facilitate an adjustment of our differences with Rajah Runjeet Sing. It was not at any time in the contemplation of Government to effect the subversion of his power by force of arms,... Under the circumstances of the recent intelligence from Europe it is still less an object of necessity to adopt the settled purpose of extermination of the power of the Rajah Runjeet Sing.[66]

[65] BL, IOR Home Misc. Series 594, Metcalfe to Edmonstone, 26 January 1809.
[66] BL, IOR Home Misc. Series 594, Minto-in-Council to Hewitt, 23 January 1809, p. 279.

In view of the more permanent interests of the security of the north-west frontier, Minto decided to retain the cis-Sutlej states under British protection and to confine the territories of Ranjit Singh to the Sutlej. Force might be employed to expel Ranjit's troops from the left bank of the Sutlej, but Minto did not consider it advisable to carry out military operations beyond that river. In his opinion, Ranjit could only be induced to engage in hostilities by a fear that the British aimed at the complete subversion of his power, and not merely his exclusion from the area between the Jamuna and the Sutlej. Minto wrote to Charles Grant:

> Our impending struggle with Runjeet Sing will I think soon terminate in a pacification as satisfactory as the actual state of our affairs now require. We must insist of restraining him within the Sutledge but I would now carry my views no further even in my wishes, or in speculation. To these terms there will probably be little difficulty to obtain or to compel his assent.[67]

The disappearance of the French threat therefore may have served to save Ranjit Singh from greater loss than the limitation of his kingdom to the Sutlej. Minto wrote to Hewitt:

> Whilst the danger of a European invasion could be considered to be impending we should perhaps have had no reason to regret the occurrence of a contest, the successful result of which would be the extinction of a power unquestionably favourable to the Cause of our Enemies, but under the certainty that this danger, if not permanently removed, is at least greatly and indefinitely remote, our interests require the earliest practicable accommodation with the state of Lahore.[68]

As a first step toward smoothing out the differences with the Raja, Minto was willing to fix the advanced military post further away from the Raja's frontier than Ludhiana, even to withdraw it to Karnal. He was afraid that if the British advanced post was maintained too close to the Raja's territories, the latter might also decide to maintain a large body of troops on his frontier for defensive purposes, and such a state of affairs would be a permanent source of distrust and suspicion between the two governments. Hewitt was therefore directed to establish the military post as far away from the Sutlej as possible without frustrating the objective of its formation.[69]

In the meantime, Ranjit expressed his anxieties about the advance of the British troops and the military preparations at Karnal. On 2 February, orders were given for the restoration of Khur and Faridkot. Ambala had already

---

67 NLS M 161. Minto to Charles Grant, Fort William, 21 January 1809.
68 BL, IOR Home Misc. Series 594, p. 281. Minto-in-Council to Hewitt, Fort William, 23 January 1809.
69 Ibid., Edmonstone to Ochterlony, Fort William, 30 January 1809. Also, PGR II, No. 17.

been restored to Rani Daya Kaur and measures were in progress for the dissolution of the Raja's army on the Sutlej.[70] Alarmed at the advance of the troops under Major-General St Leger, Ranjit proposed to send his vakils to Ochterlony's camp.[71]

Ochterlony crossed the Jamuna on 16 January 1809. He reached Patiala on 1 February and Nabha on 5 February and was received with heartfelt expressions of relief by Sahib Singh of Patiala and Jaswant Singh of Nabha. From Patiala, Ochterlony marched to Malerkotla, followed at a short distance by the division under St Leger. Abdullah Khan, the Pathan chief of Malerkotla was freed from paying tribute to Ranjit Singh,[72] Ranjit's vakils, Sirdar Sada Singh and Nizamuddin Khan arrived at Ochterlony's camp on 13 February, when he was within a day's march of Ludhiana.[73] They wished to know if Ochterlony would actually march to Ludhiana or not, and informed him that they would not be answerable for the consequences of that step. They entered into a discussion and criticism of Metcalfe's proceedings and expressed Ranjit's suspicions of British motives. Minto disapproved of Ochterlony's conduct in listening to these 'improper' representations, and for suspending the march of his troops for five days on the promise of the vakils that they would secure Ghynda Singh's retreat from the left bank of the Sutlej.[74] Ghynda Singh had already moved on the orders of Ranjit Singh and the objective of the vakils was merely to delay Ochterlony's march.

Ochterlony reached Ludhiana on 19 February. He had earlier referred to the Government that he was at a loss as to what reply he should give to chiefs who were in possession of grants of land from Ranjit or those who might claim the restitution of their lands on the grounds of ancient rights.[75] For example, Ludhiana was an old conquest of Ranjit Singh from the widow of Rai Ilyas, which he had assigned to Bhag Singh. The latter was willing to give it up to the British, but hoped to gain either Karnal or Panipat in exchange. Ochterlony recommended Bhag Singh's request.[76] Although the cis-Sutlej states had been taken under protection, Minto refused to enter into their disputes about the ownership of lands and ancient rights. Minto explained to the Secret Committee:

> the utmost extent of our views only went to the exclusion of the sovereignty and control of Rajah Runjeet Sing from the territories to the Southward of the Sutledge and that object being accomplished any claims to the occupation of

[70] BL, IOR Home Misc. Series 594, pp. 451–60. Metcalfe to Edmonstone, Amritsar, 3 February 1809.

[71] Ibid., pp. 467–76. Metcalfe to Edmonstone, Amritsar, 6 February 1809.

[72] PGR II, No. 20. Ochterlony to Edmonstone, Camp near Malerkotla, 9 February 1809.

[73] Griffin, L.H., *The Rajahs of the Punjab* (London, 1873, 2nd edn), pp. 114–17.

[74] NLS M 195. Governor-General-in-Council to the Secret Committee, 15 April 1809.

[75] PGR II, No. 11. Ochterlony to Edmonstone, Camp Dadoopur, 18 January 1809.

[76] Griffin, *The Rajahs of the Punjab*, pp. 303–04.

those territories were to be considered as points which the claimants must be required to adjust among themselves. ... our interposition for the protection of the Chiefs was gratuitous and that therefore we were not required by any principle of justice to extend our interference beyond the limits of our convenience.[77]

He decided to leave the Sikh chiefs in possession of territories they may have acquired during Ranjit's earlier conquests south of the Sutlej. The chiefs at whose expense others had benefitted had to be satisfied with the prospect of future security against Ranjit Singh. Minto had no wish to involve the Government in the difficulties and embarrassments of an investigation into the intricate claims and disputes of the cis-Sutlej chiefs.

The treaty of 1809 contained no specification of the districts in the cis-Sutlej area over which Ranjit's sovereignty was to extend. The territories under Diwan Mokham Chand, Ghurba Singh and Uttar Singh and the districts of Gongrana and Nara acknowledged Ranjit Singh's sovereignty; the territories under Fateh Singh, Danna Singh and the districts of Machiwara and Makhowal were in dispute; and the remaining cis-Sutlej states were under British protection.[78] As a general principle Minto decided to acknowledge Ranjit's sovereignty over territories which were under his direct rule as well as those which were held in jagir by his dependents.

Minto was pleased with the outcome of the negotiations with Ranjit Singh. He was glad that the display of force had accomplished its purpose without actual hostilities. He wrote to the Chairman of the East India Company:

> We are now at peace throughout India. Runjeet Sing has executed all his engagements... I trust the pacification in that quarter as complete. The general treaty of amity... will I trust remove the jealousy concerning our views in the late proceedings... and together with the demonstration which he has seen of our power afford a prospect of permanent tranquillity beyond the Jumna.[79]

Ranjit had been thwarted and a buffer generated between his territories and the British provinces by taking the cis-Sutlej states under British protection. Minto decided to avoid entanglement with the internal troubles and jealousies of these states. In his opinion, the British Government would repel any attempt of Raja Ranjit Singh to extend his dominion south of the Sutlej, but the cis-Sutlej chiefs would have to look to their own protection against petty wars amongst themselves. The protection afforded to the cis-Sutlej states was to be of a general nature so that the British Government would not be involved in every petty dispute or boundary quarrel among

---

[77] NLS M 195. Governor-General-in-Council to the Secret Committee, 15 April 1809.

[78] Sinha, *Ranjit Singh*, p. 73.

[79] NLS M 161. Minto to the Chairman of the East India Company, Fort William, 25 April 1809. Also, NLS M 209.

the Sikh chiefs.[80] Ochterlony, in a letter dated 17 March 1809, made certain suggestions about the Government's future relations with these states, also giving an idea of their revenue and military resources and some symptoms of fear and jealousy on their part with regard to the views and intentions of the British Government. Ochterlony pointed out the necessity of informing the cis-Sutlej chiefs, by a formal written Instrument, the exact nature of their relationship with the British Government and the obligations imposed on them in return for protection. The conditions proposed by Ochterlony appeared to Minto to involve a degree of interference in their internal affairs and of a closer control over them than he wished to actually exercise.[81] In Minto's opinion, opposition to Ranjit Singh's encroachments south of the Sutlej was the basis of the connection between the British Government and the cis-Sutlej states, and this was to be the principal if not the only relation between those states and the Company. He did not intend to interfere in their internal affairs or to place them under total subjugation to the Company.[82] His aim was primarily 'to establish a practical recognition of our paramount authority without creating the necessity of an embarrassing and vexatious interference in their relative claims, disputes and dissentions or in any manner abridging their anterior independence within the limits of their own possessions, to maintain the privilege of marching our troops into their country whenever occasion should require'.[83]

Ochterlony was directed to make a declaration to the cis-Sutlej chiefs along the following lines: a) an assurance of permanent protection from Ranjit Singh; b) exemption from all pecuniary tribute; c) enjoyment of all rights and authority which they had so far exercised within their respective territories; d) free passage of British troops through their territories; and e) cooperation with the British against any invasion of their country.[84] On 3 May 1809, Ochterlony issued an *Ittilanama* (Declaration) to all the vakils of the cis-Sutlej chiefs in attendance on him at Ludhiana along the above lines and copies of it were sent to the chiefs of Khur, Faridkot and Malerkotla as well as to the dependents of Ranjit Singh who had territories on the left bank.[85] Bhag Singh, Bhai Lal Singh, Sahib Singh of Patiala and Jaswant Singh of Nabha

---

[80] NLS M 161. Minto to Chairman, 25 April 1809.

[81] PGR II. Ochterlony to Edmonstone, 17 March 1809. NLS M 195. Governor-General-in-Council to the Secret Committee, 15 April 1809.

[82] BL, IOR Home Misc. Series 595, pp. 93–98. Edmonstone to Ochterlony, Fort William, 10 April 1809.

[83] NLS M 195. Governor-General-in-Chief to the Secret Committee, 15 April 1809.

[84] BL, IOR Home Misc. Series 595, pp. 93–98. Edmonstone to Ochterlony, Fort William, 10 April 1809.

[85] BL, IOR Ben. Sec. & Pol. Cons. 216. Cons. of 3 June 1809, No. 24. Ochterlony to Edmonstone, Ludhiana, 6 May 1809. Ibid., No. 26. Translation of an Ittilah Nameh addressed to the Chiefs of the Country of Malwah and Sirhind on the side of the River Sutluge. Printed in Aitchison, *Treaties, Engagements and Sanads*, Vol. I, 5th edn, pp. 156–57.

had refused to leave Ochterlony's camp until the surrender of Faridkot and the conclusion of the treaty finally convinced them that Ranjit Singh had been curbed by the British.

On reviewing the whole of the transactions with Ranjit Singh, Minto observed that although the mission to Lahore had failed in its objective of securing a defensive alliance with Ranjit Singh against the French, it was not entirely unproductive. The advantages derived from the mission were stated to be the collection of information regarding the internal condition of the Punjab, the disposition of the Sikh chiefs toward the Company's Government and a knowledge of the form and constitution of Ranjit's Government, army and external relations. Above all, 'The extension of his power had been prevented, the limits of his possessions defined and fixed at a distance from our frontier and the interval occupied by chieftains sensible of the benefit of the British protection... the jealousies and suspicions of the Rajah himself in respect to our ultimate views removed. The Treaty however is admitted to be beneficial only as it defines the limits of his dominion to the south.'[86]

The home authorities fully approved of Minto's policy toward Ranjit Singh and the cis-Sutlej states, although the President of the Board of Control remarked that it carried 'the appearance of a deviation from the line of policy prescribed by orders from the Secret Committee of 30th October 1805 and 27th February 1806'.[87] The Secret Committee wrote, 'We agree with you in deeming it an object of general importance to prevent the subjugation of the Rajahs of these petty states, and chieftains in the immediate neighbourhood of our frontier, and do not disapprove of the course which you have resolved to pursue for that purpose.'[88]

Minto's Afghan Policy

Minto's aim was to make Persia the main bulwark in the defence of the Company's territories in India. Nevertheless, he sent a political mission to Afghanistan to form a defensive agreement with the Amir of Kabul due to Persia's uncertain attitude toward the British and to secure a second line of defence against the much speculated French threat.

Prior to 1809, there was practically no political or commercial inter-action between the British and Afghan Governments. The Company's Government possessed very little accurate information about the state of affairs in Afghanistan as there was no reliable source of information. In 1783,

86 BL, IOR Home Misc. Series 511. Memorandum on mission to Lahore, 18 August 1810, p. 79.
87 NLS M 172. R. Dundas to Minto, Whitehall, 3 September 1810 (Private).
88 BL, IOR Home Misc. Series 511, Memorandum on the mission to Lahore, 18 August 1810, p. 50.

a civilian from Madras, George Forster travelled at his own risk and cost through Kashmir and Afghanistan to Russia and collected some facts about the commerce and resources of Afghanistan.[89]

Later in the century, the Afghan ruler Zaman Shah (1793–1800) was a source of alarm to the Company's Government. Zaman Shah made frequent descents on the Punjab in punitive expeditions. Although he didn't advance farther than Lahore, both Sir John Shore and Wellesley viewed his incursions with considerable anxiety, particularly because the Durrani ruler was invited by both Vizier Ali of Oudh and Tipu Sultan of Mysore to attack the territories of the Company, and some of the Hindu rajas also offered to assist him against the British.[90] In 1799–1801, Wellesley sent Malcolm to conclude a treaty between Persia and the Company which was directed at both the French and the Afghans. The Durranis of Afghanistan and the Persians were sworn enemies and the treaty of 1801 not only provided a defensive alliance against the Amir of Kabul, but also encouraged Persia to attack the Afghan territories. In 1799–1800, Zaman Shah was defeated and blinded by his half-brother Mahmud Shah who was supported by the powerful Barakzai clan. However, Mahmud Shah's authority was disputed by the other rival claimants to the throne. His rival Shuja-ul-Mulk, brother of Zaman Shah, was in power at the time Minto sent Elphinstone to the Afghan court.[91]

With Zaman Shah's fall from power, Afghanistan became weak and torn by civil war. This state of affairs was quite satisfactory to the British until they realised that this confusion and chaos might render it a field open to the French. In February 1808, Minto wrote to Dundas about the necessity of sending 'regular and avowed Embassies' not only to Persia, but also to Kabul and Lahore.[92] The Secret Committee was also notified of his intention in a dispatch dated 31 March 1808.[93] The thoughts of the home authorities ran along similar lines, and in March 1808, the Secret Committee wrote to Minto, 'we cannot impress too strongly on your attention the necessity of cultivating to the utmost of your power the favourable opinion and cooperation not only of all the States and Countries to the Eastward of the Indus but also of the Afghan Government, and even of the Tartar Tribes to the Eastward of the Caspian'.[94]

The actual dispatch of the mission to Kabul was delayed mainly due to the civil war raging in Afghanistan. The period of Shah Shuja's rule (1803–09)

---

[89] Forster, G., *A Journey from Bengal to England, through the northern part of India, Kashmire, Afghanistan and Persia, and into Russia, by the Caspian Sea* (London, 1798), Vol. 2.

[90] Kaye, J.W., *History of the War in Afghanistan* (London, 1851), Vol. 1, pp. 2–3.

[91] BL, IOR Home Misc. Series 511. Mission to Cabul, pp. 536–37.

[92] NLS M 159. Minto to R. Dundas, Fort William, 10 February 1808 (Secret).

[93] NLS M 194. Governor-General-in-Council to the Secret Committee, 31 March 1808.

[94] BL, IOR Board's Secret Drafts Vol. 3, No. 43. Secret Committee to the Governor-General-in-Council, 2 March 1808 (Secret).

was one of chronic disorder. The majority of his subjects were in revolt, and his chief difficulty was the lack of money due to the non-payment of tributes and revenues. Kashmir was in rebellion, Sind virtually independent, and Mahmud Shah and Fath Khan, the Barakzai leaders were trying to seize Kandahar and Kabul. In May 1808, Minto wrote to Dundas, 'Caboul is unfortunately still distracted by civil war and by a contest for the sovereignty of the Country and the moment is not yet arrived when we can prudently address ourselves to either of the contending parties.'[95]

Minto was aware that the opening of diplomatic relations with Afghanistan presented certain difficulties. The civil war in Afghanistan was the major obstacle to the sending of a diplomatic mission and although the treaty of 1801 with Persia was no longer operative, the Amir of Kabul could always refer to the hostile intentions of the British as embodied in that treaty.[96] Such impressions were not at all favourable to the establishment of a close connection between the two Governments. The British Government, however, was no longer interested in supporting the Amir's enemies. It was now its policy 'to unite with it for the purposes of common interest and common security'.[97] The conflict of interests between the Amir of Kabul, the Raja of Lahore and the Amirs of Sind also presented considerable difficulties. Ranjit Singh had overthrown Afghan overlordship, and only recently had partly subdued and then relinquished for a ransom a portion of the Afghan territories. He naturally looked with suspicion on any attempt on the part of the British to form a connection or an alliance with the Afghans. Shah Shuja on the other hand, might solicit British aid to recover lost territories in the Punjab. Sind was tributary to Afghanistan, but taking advantage of the internal disorder, the Amirs of Sind refused to pay tribute and became virtually independent as early as 1793.[98] The Afghan ruler however did not give up his right of overlordship and tried to enforce it from time to time. The objective of the Amirs of Sind was to gain assistance from other powers to resist the efforts of their Afghan overlord successfully. The latter on the other hand might demand British aid to enforce rights over Sind. In Minto's opinion, response to Shah Shuja's demands for aid against Persia, Lahore or Sind should depend on British relations with these powers.

At first Minto thought of making preliminary enquiries about the attitude of Shah Shuja toward a British political mission to his court. Later, in a memo dated 17 June 1808, he declared that the missions to Lahore and Kabul should not be delayed any longer and that a preliminary intimation to these

95 NLS M 159. Minto to R. Dundas, 15 May 1808.
96 NLS M 194. Governor-General-in-Council to the Secret Committee, 15 September 1808.
97 BL, IOR Home Misc. Series 657. Edmonstone to Elphinstone, 29 August 1808.
98 Dodwell, *The Cambridge History of India*, Vol. V, p. 484.

courts was not essential. Minto was confident that 'the pride of the King of Caubul would be highly gratified by an embassy on the part of a power so high in the Scale of political ascendancy and so celebrated as that of the British Government in India'.[99]

Mountstuart Elphinstone, who was then the acting British agent at Sindhia's court, was selected to lead the political mission from Minto to Shah Shuja. Elphinstone visited Calcutta on holiday in August 1807 and met Minto. He wrote his impressions of 'Gibby Elliot' in a mildly amusing fashion to his friend Strachey.[100] In the early part of 1808, the French threat to India was the favourite topic of conversation among the Company's servants in India. Elphinstone volunteered his services to be employed in any one of the diplomatic missions which were known to be in the process of being contemplated by the governor-general. He wrote to Strachey:

> You will have heard of the intended invasion of this country by the French, with the assistance of the King of Persia. I have written to Adam to try to get me sent on some one of the missions which will be the consequence of this impending danger. I take it for granted Gibby and Edmonstone have the worst possible opinion of me... but I trust to being a volunteer, and to their not readily finding people ready to go.[101]

Elphinstone, like Malcolm and Metcalfe, was ambitious. He sought a wider and more exciting field of action than Sindhia's camp, and felt that he could do better than watch the intrigues of a Maratha court. Although Elphinstone held a junior rank in the diplomatic service, he was nevertheless regarded as qualified for the office in view of 'His ardent character, his distinguished abilities, his enterprising Spirit, his current services and long experience in the diplomatic line.'[102]

Elphinstone was appointed in June 1808 and ordered to proceed immediately to Delhi to await further instructions.[103] Elphinstone received his letter of appointment on 10 July 1808 and set out for Delhi the next day and arrived on 20 July.[104] In his usual high spirits he wrote to Strachey, 'Omadeh meeroud beh Caubul [a great man is going to Kabul]'.[105]

99 BL, IOR Ben. Sec. & Sep. Cons. 207. Cons. of 20 June 1808, No. 2. The Governor-General's minute, 17 June 1808. Fort William. Also Home Misc. Series 657.
100 Colebrooke, Sir. T.E., *Life of Mountstuart Elphinstone* (London, 1884), Vol. I, pp. 159–61. The Countess of Minto wrote that Elphinstone was personally unacquainted with Minto before the Kabul mission: *Lord Minto in India*, p. 159.
101 Colebrooke, *Life of Elphinstone*, Vol. I, pp. 169–70.
102 BL, IOR Ben. Sec. & Sep. Cons. 207. Cons. of 20 June 1808, No. 2. Governor-General's minute, 17 June 1808.
103 Ibid., No. 5. Edmonstone to Elphinstone, Fort William, 20 June 1808.
104 BL, IOR Ben. Sec. & Sep. Cons. 208. Cons. of 1 August 1808, No. 6. Elphinstone to Edmonstone, 10 July 1808.
105 Colebrooke, *Life of Elphinstone*, Vol. I, p. 184.

The detailed instructions to Elphinstone were not drawn up until August 1808. His mission was placed on a grander scale than the mission to Lahore in view of the dignity of the court to which he was being sent and also to give a flattering impression of the power from which it was sent. He was accompanied by an escort of 200 mounted troopers and 100 sepoys, whereas Metcalfe's escort to Ranjit Singh consisted of only 20 mounted troops and two companies of sepoys. In addition, Elphinstone also carried rich presents for Shah Shuja, but was otherwise advised to practise economy.[106]

The selection of Elphinstone's escort and other members of his mission was left to the resident at Delhi, Archibald Seton. Seton of course offered to waive his right to nominate the envoy's family, but Elphinstone declined the offer. The members of his mission were specially chosen to acquire information about the geography and peoples of the area. Apart from Richard Strachey who was appointed Secretary to the Mission, Elphinstone complained that the rest of the party consisted of men with whom he was entirely unfamiliar. He also thought it strange that the mission to Afghanistan should consist of a smaller number of Europeans than there were in Nagpur or any other residencies he had experienced.[107]

The principal objective of the mission to Shah Shuja was to encourage the Afghans to resist or impede the progress of a French army in cooperation with the British Government. In 1808, Persia was a potential enemy and was regarded by the Government as a firm ally of the French. Another goal prior to the conclusion of the Preliminary Treaty with Persia in March 1809, was therefore to enter into a defensive, and if necessary an offensive alliance with Shah Shuja against Persia.[108] This was probably why Minto pushed forward the mission to Afghanistan notwithstanding the unsettled conditions and unstable leadership. Between August and December 1808, Minto was determined to occupy Kharak and a diversion from Afghanistan would have been useful. This anti-Persian policy changed after Persia's positive response to the British in the beginning of 1809 and the receipt of news of Wellington's successes in Portugal at the same time.

Metcalfe had been instructed to facilitate Elphinstone's progress through the territories of Ranjit Singh and also to try to establish communications with some of the leading and influential men in the court of Kabul so as to prepare that court for the reception of Elphinstone's mission. The resident at Delhi had already addressed a letter to Koresh Sultan Begum, Shah Shuja's half-sister and had also induced the mother of the king of Delhi to send

106 BL, IOR Ben. Sec. & Sep. Cons. 209. Cons. of 23 August 1808. Edmonstone to Elphinstone, 19 August 1808. Also, Home Misc. Series 657.

107 Colebrooke, *Life of Elphinstone*, pp. 185–86. Elphinstone to Strachey, Delhi, 5 September 1808. Also Elphinstone, Hon. Mountstuart, *An Account of the Kingdom of Cabul* (London, 1839, 3rd edn), pp. 1–2.

108 BL, IOR Home Misc. Series 657, pp. 1–24. Edmonstone to Elphinstone, 19 August 1808.

a letter to her which was expected to please the Amir and prepare him to receive the mission.[109]

If Shah Shuja referred to the hostile policy previously pursued by the British Government against the Afghans, he was to be assured that the treaty of 1801 with Persia was purely a defensive measure directed against Zaman Shah's mediated aggression on the Company's territories. As Shah Shuja had now abandoned the hostile views of his brother, the British Government was cordially disposed toward him and wanted 'to establish a permanent alliance with the Afghan power'. Elphinstone was of course advised not to raise the subject of Wellesley's anti-Afghan policy unless the matter was brought up by the Amir.[110] Elphinstone carried a letter from Minto to Shah Shuja announcing that in order to cultivate and improve the amicable relations subsisting between the two states, he was dispatching a special envoy to his court with full powers to generate a treaty on behalf of the Government of India.[111]

In addition to developing a policy depending on the status of relations with the Persia, it was also necessary to synchronise the conduct of relations with Lahore and Afghanistan. By December 1808, the Government was disappointed with Ranjit Singh's response to its solicitations for an anti-French alliance. Far from manifesting a 'sense of common interest and common danger', Ranjit Singh demanded British non-interference in his schemes of conquest over the cis-Sutlej states as well as over territories in the north claimed by the Afghan ruler. However, he did not seem very willing to agree to either the unconditional advance of British troops into his territories or the establishment of depots within it. By December 1808, Minto had declared his intention of opposing Ranjit Singh's ambition of conquering the cis-Sutlej states by force if necessary and he was therefore willing at this time to conclude a treaty with Shah Shuja opposing the interests of or even directly hostile to Ranjit Singh if it should be expedient to do so. Elphinstone was directed to convey information with regard to the general stance of Shah Shuja to the Government of India without independently finalising a proposal.[112]

The greatest defect of Minto's instructions to Elphinstone was that it took no account of a probable application for aid by Shah Shuja against his rival Mahmud Shah in return for his promise to oppose the French and the Persians. Elphinstone's instructions provided him with no clue to Minto's views on this matter. He was to find to his dismay that Shah Shuja sought no aid against Persia, Lahore or Sind, but that his sole concern and persistent

---

[109] BL, IOR Ben. Sec. & Sep. Cons. 209. Cons. of 23 August 1808. Edmonstone to Elphinstone, 19 August 1808.

[110] Ibid., Cons. of 29 August 1808. Edmonstone to Elphinstone, 29 August 1808. Fort William. Also, Home Misc. Series 657, pp. 57–63.

[111] BL, IOR Home Misc. Series 657, pp. 25–28. Minto to Shuja-ul-Mulk, 19 August 1808.

[112] BL, IOR Home Misc. Series 657. Edmonstone to Elphinstone, 5 December 1808.

demand was to obtain financial aid to enable him to successfully fight his rival Mahmud Shah.

At the end of January 1809, Elphinstone received news that Shah Shuja was coming to Peshawar and that his mission would be received there. Elphinstone's mission was viewed with suspicion by Ranjit Singh, the Chief of Multan and the Amirs of Sind, each imagining that the British had designs on their territories and that an alliance between the British Government and Shah Shuja might be directed against them. The Durrani nobles and chiefs on the other hand were opposed to an alliance which might strengthen the hand of the Amir to the detriment of their powers. In turn, the Amir was equally suspicious of the objectives of the mission, but the tales of rich presents the envoy was carrying with him and the psychological boost it would give him to have a mission from the British at his court at a time when his throne was by no means secure, persuaded him to receive Elphinstone. On the Afghan frontier at Dera Ismail Khan, Elphinstone was met by an agent of Shah Shuja and under his guidance he set out from Dera Ismail Khan for Peshawar on 7 February 1809 and reached it on 25 February.[113] The first week was spent in discussing the form of presentation and on 4 March Shah Shuja received the mission.[114]

Elphinstone presented Minto's letter and disclosed the objective. The Amir was told that the French in conjunction with Persia were determined to attack the British territories in India, that the French had promised the Shah of Persia the whole of the Afghan dominions and parts of India, and that the Russians and Austrians had also been won over to cooperate in the scheme by offering them portions of the Turkish empire. In order to guard against such a calamity, the governor-general proposed an alliance between the Company Government and the Amir. The latter was asked to suggest the mode of cooperation as his dominions were more exposed to the French and the Persians than the British territories.[115]

Shah Shuja agreed to enter into an alliance with the British, but he hoped to derive greater advantages from the mission than the gifts that were brought when he saw that the other party was anxious for a treaty. There were two leading parties in Shah Shuja's court. The most influential group was headed by Akram Khan, a Durrani lord who was the Ameen-ul-Mulk or chief minister to the Amir and also the general of his army. The other group was composed of the Persian courtiers who were always within earshot of the Amir and possessed a degree of influence which they used in opposition to

---

[113] BL, IOR Home Misc. Series 657, pp. 197–209. Elphinstone to Minto, Peshawar, 8 March 1809.

[114] BL, IOR MSS. Eur. F.88, Box 13 F. Vol. h. MSS. Journal of Mountstuart Elphinstone, 1 November 1808–6 August 1809, pp. 189–202.

[115] Ibid. BL, IOR Home Misc. Series 657, pp. 197–209. Elphinstone to Minto, Peshawar, 8 March 1809.

Akram Khan. The leader of this faction was Mir Abul Hassan Khan, Keeper of the King's Wardrobe, Commander of the King's Guards and Governor of Peshawar. He managed to secure the office of *mehmandar* (Guest Attendant) to Elphinstone in Akram's absence, but he was soon displaced by Akram Khan's nominee Musa Khan. Akram Khan, Abul Hassan Khan and Mirza Sherif Khan were the principal advisors of Shah Shuja. Elphinstone was approached by both parties, for both were in favour of an alliance with the British. Akram Khan was away fighting the rebels in Kashmir, hence Elphinstone communicated with Akram Khan's brother and also with Mir Abul Hassan Khan.[116] One of the leading courtiers was Mirza Gurami Khan.[117] Elphinstone found that Gurami Khan kept himself well informed about Indian and European affairs. He asked some awkward questions about Bonaparte's successes and the plight of the British in Europe. He also referred to the successes of the French privateers in the Indian Ocean and inquired 'why the insurance of ships should be raised so high by the success of the French privateers when we (the British) had so manifest a superiority at sea'.[118] The Afghans were therefore not entirely ignorant of what was happening beyond their frontiers and it is doubtful if they were convinced by Elphinstone's representations that their country was in danger of being overrun by the French and the Persians. On the contrary, they demanded specific and quantifiable advantages in return for their friendship – financial aid to Shah Shuja against his rival Mahmud Shah.

The negotiations for a treaty were carried on despite the fact that each party failed to see the other point of view. Elphinstone rejected a proposal for an offensive and defensive treaty, and stated that even the defensive agreement was to be of a limited nature, for if the Persians singly attacked the Afghans, British help would not be forthcoming. The British were to come to the assistance of the Amir only if there was French involvement in the aggression against the Afghans. On 18 March 1809, Elphinstone presented a draft treaty along these lines.[119]

---

[116] BL, IOR Home Misc. Series 657, pp. 197–209. Elphinstone to Minto, Peshawar, 8 March 1809. BL, IOR MSS. Eur. F.88. Box 13 F, Vol. h. MSS. Journal of Mountstuart Elphinstone, p. 213.

[117] Gurami Khan was in India in the early part of 1808 and had offered his services to Mr Brooke, acting-agent at Benaras, to act as Company's agent at Kabul under the plea of possessing a lot of influence at the court of Shah Shuja. As Minto was thinking of sending an official mission to Kabul, Brooke was advised not to employ Gurami Khan. Brooke however authorised Gurami Khan to announce Elphinstone's mission to Shah Shuja on his return and to prepare for its reception. The Government disapproved of Brooke's conduct and advised Elphinstone to be on his guard against the intrigues of Gurami Khan and to find out his real character and intentions.
BL, IOR Home Misc. Series 657, Edmonstone to Elphinstone, 5 December 1808, pp. 158–62.

[118] Elphinstone, *An Account of the Kingdom of Cabul*, Vol. I, p. 82.

[119] BL, IOR Home Misc. Series 657, pp. 268–72. Draft Treaty. Elphinstone to Minto, Peshawar, 15 March 1809.

The comments of the Afghan ministers on the draft proposals were caustic. Elphinstone wrote to Minto that the ministers complained that 'all the advantage was on our side and all the danger on the King's'.[120] They pointed out that the Amir was to renounce all communication with the enemies of the British and oppose them with all his resources, while the British were to give him only such assistance as they found convenient. They regretted not having had an opportunity to listen to the proposals of a French envoy, so that the Amir could then have made a free choice between the two. Elphinstone tried to maintain his ground by saying that although the British Government would undoubtedly gain some advantages if Shah Shuja opposed the French, the Amir, for the sake of preserving his own independent power must also oppose the French; that if the French were allowed to enter his territories, they would set up depots and bases and the whole country would be overrun by foreign troops; that the policy of the French was first to send their emissaries, then their ambassadors and finally their armies to foreign countries. To this, one of the Afghan negotiators, Mullah Jafar replied that the British were not as straightforward as they pretended to be. Elphinstone wrote to Minto:

> He [Mullah Jafar] frankly owned that we had the character of being very designing and that most people thought it necessary to be very vigilant in all transactions with us… that the present proposal would never succeed and that if we did not wish to have all our pains thrown away, we must introduce something more enticing to the King than what we have offered.[121]

Elphinstone applied for instructions about granting financial aid to the Amir. Shah Shuja may have been lazy and pleasure-seeking, but his main difficulty was his lack of funds. Kabul was besieged by Mahmud Shah, while the greater part of his army was away fighting in Kashmir. Elphinstone wrote to Minto that although it would have been preferable to keep clear of the domestic troubles in Afghanistan, yet in order to make the connection with that country worthwhile, it was necessary to support either Shah Shuja or Mahmud Shah, or to give up the connection entirely. He thought it advisable to support Shah Shuja in preference to Mahmud Shah and in his opinion, an aid of 15 lakhs of rupees (1.5 million rupees), would ensure Shah Shuja's success, although a much smaller sum of about 2 lakhs (200,000 rupees) would obtain his consent to a treaty.[122]

The Afghan negotiators proposed alterations in almost all the articles of the draft treaty presented by Elphinstone. In the 1st Article, they objected to the

---

[120] Ibid., pp. 255–66. Elphinstone to Minto, Peshawar, 19 March 1809.
[121] BL, IOR Home Misc. Series 657, pp. 255–66. Elphinstone to Minto, Peshawar, 19 March 1809.
[122] BL, IOR Home Misc. Series 657, pp. 221–29. Elphinstone to Minto, Peshawar, 22 March 1809.

friendship being forever between the British and the Durrani state and would only agree to its being between the British and Shah Shuja during his life and with his son after him. In the 2nd Article, they objected to the total exclusion of French emissaries, as they indicated they needed to know what was proposed before they could reject it! Elphinstone conceded this point, and the ministers tried to conciliate him by proposing to carry on any such negotiations at Herat. One of the ministers, Mullah Sher Muhammad, brought up the question of the French applying to the Amir for cooperation without the Persians, and offering to pay a sum of money for the passage of an army through any part of the Afghan territories into India. Elphinstone answered that the proposed treaty was directed only against a confederacy of the French and the Persians, and that if that alliance was dissolved, the British Government would meet any subsequent events by new treaties and other means.[123] Elphinstone lost sight of the fact that the main objective of his mission was to form a defensive alliance with the Amir against the French, whether joined by the Persians or not. He was criticised by Minto for this oversight. Edmonstone wrote to him, 'the principle of Cooperation which precluded the King of Cabul from promoting the invasion of India, by the united forces of France and Persia, seems equally applicable to the single efforts of France directed to that object'.[124]

Elphinstone wrote to Minto:

> it seems… possible to restore the vigor of this Government by supplying it with money and if those means were supplied by the British, that Nation could not fail to acquire a decided ascendancy in the King's Councils. By this we should derive the following advantages. We should command the Northern route from Persia to India and a great extent of the Navigation of the Indus and we should influence the Chiefs of Sistoun and Mekraun and of the hills between those Countries and the Indus all of them being in different degrees subject to the King of Caubul.[125]

An annual subsidy of 15 to 20 lakhs of rupees would in his opinion go far toward the establishment of British ascendancy in Afghanistan. The scheme that Elphinstone had in mind was that the Company should agree to pay Shah Shuja an annual sum as the revenue of Sind on condition of his ceding all his rights over that country to the British. Such a proposal, though, would have to first come from the Afghan ministers.[126] The annual revenue of Sind was estimated at 80 lakhs of rupees which would enable the Company to pay the 'rent' to the Afghan ruler as well as meet the cost of holding Sind. Apart from the strategic advantages to be derived from occupying Sind, Elphinstone

---

[123] Ibid., pp. 283–94. Elphinstone to Minto, Peshawar, 23 March 1809.
[124] BL, IOR Home Misc. Series 657, p. 361. Edmonstone to Elphinstone, Fort William, 29 April 1809.
[125] BL, IOR Home Misc. Series 657. Elphinstone to Minto, Peshawar, 28 March 1809.
[126] Ibid., 23 March 1809.

pointed out the commercial advantages which would accrue to the Company by the free and uncontrolled trade via the Indus.[127]

The proposal of acquiring Sind by paying an annual revenue to the Amir of Kabul was rejected by Minto. Edmonstone informed Elphinstone:

> ... considerations intimately connected with those fundamental principles of political discretion as well as political morality by which alone the true honour and prosperity of the British Empire in India can be permanently maintained would under any circumstances oppose the adoption of that project, whilst its practicability and success are too doubtful to warrant the attempt, even if it were unopposed by dictates of prudent policy and the obligations of public justice.[128]

Whatever may have been the claims of the Shah Shuja over Sind, that country was actually independent of his control. Sind acknowledged only a tributary relation to Kabul, and even under that acknowledgement had only yielded occasional tribute under duress. The Amir of Kabul's sovereignty over Sind was obsolete for practical purposes. If the British tried to impose their authority over Sind on the basis of the arrangement with Shah Shuja, they would most certainly have found themselves involved in a war of conquest and usurpation. T.E. Colebrooke prepared an elaborate defence of Elphinstone's proposal for 'renting' Sind on the basis that he was merely proceeding along the lines of his instructions of 5 December 1808.[129] Elphinstone's fallacy was in assuming that the Amirs of Sind were hostile toward the British from his belief in a false report that the Amirs of Sind had expelled a British envoy from Hyderabad and had refused to negotiate with the Company. He also took the word of the Afghan ministers at face value when they indicated to him that Shah Shuja possessed and exercised full sovereignty over Sind.

The news from Spain, and the amicable turn in the negotiations with Persia, caused a revision of Minto's policy toward Shah Shuja. New instructions were sent to Elphinstone in March 1809. Any offensive alliance with Shah Shuja against Persia was now out of the question. With regard to a defensive alliance, Elphinstone was told that the interests of the Government were not as directly and immediately concerned as before in concluding one, but if the Amir should insist on it, Minto was willing to concede the point as he still wished to form a connection with Afghanistan. The home authorities also recognised the fact that the relationship with Persia was the crucial factor in determining the Company's relations with the other states between Persia and the Sutlej. The Secret Committee wrote to Minto:

---

[127] Ibid., 28 March 1809.
[128] BL, IOR Home Misc. Series 657, p. 396. Edmonstone to Elphinstone, Fort William, 13 May 1809.
[129] Colebrooke, *Life of Elphinstone*, Vol. I., pp. 218–25.

The great hinge upon which the whole system turns, both from its local situation and its comparative strength, is Persia, and no plan can be formed which has not for its basis, a knowledge of the part which that power is likely to take. Your plans have been ultimately formed upon the supposition that Persia is hostile... But the prospect which has arisen from the reception of Sir Harford Jones's Embassy, and from the retreat of General Gardane from Tehraun to Europe,... may have given a very different turn to our affairs in that quarter of the Globe. In this case, the negotiation with Cabul, which was begun with a view to joint operations against Persia, considered as an ally of France, will probably proceed no further than a general expression of amity; even a defensive alliance (if against Persia) much more an offensive one, might become incompatible with the relations we should... have established with the Court of Tehraun.[130]

It may be speculated that had the British Government provided aid to Shah Shuja, and stabilised his power, British influence may have been established in Afghanistan, which in view of later events would have been highly advantageous to them. However, Minto's refusal to pursue that policy reveals that his Afghan approach was founded on the temporary exigency of a foreign invasion and was intended to provide security against that particular emergency instead of creating a more permanent influence with the Amir. The extension of the Company's territories northward and Russian expansion in Central Asia were later on to influence the policy of the British Government in creating Afghanistan as a buffer state.

Minto ratified the treaty of Peshawar on 17 June 1809. He objected to the insertion of the name of George III in the preamble and reiterated his views about 'the powers attached to sovereignty' vested on the Governor-General-in-Council and that it was essential that 'the states of Asia should consider the British Establishment in India in the light of a Sovereign State'. In his opinion, the maintenance of this impression among the neighbouring states was 'essential to the maintenance of real power and real ascendancy in the scale of political interest'.[131]

The treaty with Shah Shuja became abortive almost at the same time as it was ratified. Although it was ratified by both parties, Shah Shuja lost his throne soon after it was concluded. The entire expense of the mission was therefore a loss to the Company. Minto's sagacity in deputing a mission to Shah Shuja at a time when his throne was insecure and a civil war was in progress in Afghanistan is questionable. Although Shah Shuja was defeated and became an exile in the Punjab, his conqueror Mahmud Shah's power was by no means secure. He was essentially a pawn in the hands of the powerful

[130] BL, IOR Board's Secret Drafts Vol. 3, No. 56. Secret Committee to the Governor-General-in-Council at Bengal, 2 October 1809 (Secret).

[131] BL, IOR Home Misc. Series 657, pp. 445–54. Edmonstone to Elphinstone, Fort William, 17 June 1809.

Barakzai faction. The issue of the civil war in Afghanistan was not decided until the Barakzai leader Dost Muhammad became the King of Kabul in 1826.[132] The British Government in India ceased all diplomatic relations with the ruling power in Kabul after 1809 until 1836, when Alexander Burnes was sent to Kabul.[133] The interest of the British in Afghanistan revived due to the alarm created by the Russian pressure on Central Asia where the focus then became on treating Afghanistan as a buffer state.

Minto's Policy in Sind

The East India Company maintained intermittent commercial relations with Sind in the seventeenth and eighteenth centuries. The Company had a trading factory in Lower Sind for about thirty years in the seventeenth century, and again from 1758 to 1775 when it was withdrawn due to the unfriendly conduct of the Kalhoro ruler.[134] In 1799, Wellesley directed the Government of Bombay to reopen commercial and political relations with the Amirs of Sind, the motive being to encourage the Amirs to revolt against their Afghan overlord Zaman Shah, who was then threatening the Company's territories. A Bombay civilian, Nathan Crow, was deputed to Sind in 1799. Mir Fateh Ali Khan issued an Order granting certain commercial privileges to the British in Sind, as a result of which a factory was established at Karachi.[135] Crow was sanguine in his hopes of inciting the Amirs against Zaman Shah and establishing a firm British influence in Sind which would shut out the French, Afghans or the Marathas from Sind. However, on receiving a threat from Zaman Shah that he would destroy the power of the Amirs if the British were not expelled from Sind at once, Fateh Ali Khan ordered Crow to leave immediately and to close the Company's establishments in Sind. Crow was expelled and the British factory at Karachi plundered in 1800. The Company lost over a lakh of rupees in this abortive venture, and did not protest or respond in any way.[136]

On the death of Fateh Ali Khan in 1801, his successor Ghulam Ali Khan sent an agent to the Government of Bombay in 1803, declaring his wish to make amends for past injury. His objective was to procure British aid to defend himself against an Afghan invasion which he feared. Ghulam Ali's agents were not publicly received by the Bombay Government, but the latter seized this opportunity of renewing communications with the Amirs of Sind. A native

132 Majumdar, R.C., Raychaudhuri, H.C., and Datta, K., *An Advanced History of India* (London, 1946), p. 750.

133 Ibid., p. 752.

134 Lambrick, H.T., *Sir Charles Napier and Sind* (Oxford, 1952), p. 12.

135 Aitchison, *Treaties, Engagements and Sanads*, Vol. VIII, 5th edn, p. 311.

136 NLS M 194. Governor-General-in-Council to the Secret Committee, 31 March 1808.

agent of the Bombay Government accompanied the envoys from Sind to Hyderabad in order to settle the British claims of indemnification for the past injury and also to detect French activities in that quarter. The Amirs of Sind appeared anxious to cultivate good relations with the British Government, but withheld the required indemnification. Barlow declared however, that 'indemnification and atonement' for the conduct observed by Fateh Ali toward Crow must be 'an indispensable preliminary' to the renewal of friendly connections with the Amirs of Sind.[137] In 1808 however, the activities of the French in Persia and the fear of a hostile combination between the French, the Persians and the Amirs of Sind, prompted Minto to ignore the rule laid down by Barlow and to renew communications with the Amirs of Sind. The resident at Bushire reported that vakils from Sind had arrived in Persia to negotiate a treaty with the Shah against the Afghans. The shah was to aid the Amirs against the Afghan ruler in return for their aid to further Persian designs on Kandahar. From this it was deduced that since the French were allies of the shah, they might gain a foothold in Sind through him. In the meeting of the council on 11 March 1808, Minto brought up this subject for discussion. In his opinion,

> with reference to that Intelligence, it would be advisable to endeavor to renew the connection formerly subsisting between the British Government & the State of Sinde & for that purpose to authorize the Government of Bombay to dispatch a person to the Government of Sinde in the Capacity of Resident or Envoy, who might be enabled to ascertain the real nature & extent of the negotiations between the French and Government of Sinde & between the latter Government & Persia.[138]

Minto sent orders to the Government of Bombay to dispatch an envoy to Sind with a suitable escort. Barlow's policy with regard to Sind was therefore completely reversed. The demand for reparation, although it was not formally relinquished, was not to be asserted. If the Amirs refused to agree to the re-establishment of a British factory in Sind, they were to be persuaded at least to allow an agent of the British Government to reside at their court. The main duty of the envoy to Sind was to assess the nature and extent of French influence in that region and to counteract it. In addition, the envoy was also to investigate the practical aspects of marching an army from India to Persia through Sind in order to oppose a foreign invasion. The Government of Bombay was authorised to select the envoy and to draw up detailed instructions.[139]

Interestingly and conversely, in March 1808, another agent from Ghulam Ali (Meher Ali) arrived at Bombay to solicit British aid to prevent Persia's

[137] Ibid.

[138] NLS M 194. Governor-General-in-Council to the Secret Committee, 31 March 1808.

[139] BL, IOR Ben. Sec. & Pol. Cons. 205. Cons. of 14 March 1808, No. 1. Minto-in-Council to J. Duncan, Governor of Bombay, 14 March 1808.

ascendancy over Sind! The Amirs had sent a deputation to Persia to solicit aid to resist the Afghan claim of tribute from Sind, but before any help was forthcoming, Shah Shuja threatened to attack Sind, and Ghulam Ali purchased his forbearance by paying the stipulated tribute of 13 lakhs of rupees. The Persian envoy, Fateh Ali Khan, was on his way to Sind, but the Amirs repented, having appealed to Persia as they were afraid of being forced in turn to accept Persian overlordship.[140]

Captain David Seton, former resident at Muscat was appointed envoy to Sind. He was directed to gain the confidence of the Amirs and procure their assent to the re-establishment of the British factory in Sind. The Company's claim for an indemnity was to be used to gain concessions from the Amirs. Seton was also directed to make discreet enquiries about the state of affairs in the countries to the north of Sind. He was advised to be cautious in view of the rivalry and enmity between Sind and Afghanistan.[141]

Seton left Bombay on 28 April 1808 accompanied by an assistant Lieutenant Grindley, an assistant surgeon and an officer in charge of sixty sepoys. He reached Mandavi in Kutch on 17 May 1808 and sent a letter to the Amir announcing his arrival. He halted for nearly six weeks at Mandavi and reached Hyderabad on 15 July 1808. The Persian envoy Fateh Ali Khan had arrived at Hyderabad on 4 June 1808 and professed to a joint treaty for the shah and the French. Seton gathered that the Persian envoy had offered Mir Ghulam Ali that if he would favour the view of the French and the Persians, the Shah of Persia would recognise him as the Beglerbeg or Governor of Kabul and Kandahar. The Persian envoy had even brought a Hukum or Order from the shah appointing Ghulam Ali to that office. He told the Amirs that the British by the steady increase of their power in India were becoming a danger to the peace of the world and that consequently the Amirs should join in the effort to crush their power. The Amirs also received a letter from Joseph Rousseau the French agent at Baghdad, proposing an offensive and defensive alliance. All this information Seton received directly from the Amirs and consequently may have been exaggerated. The Amirs declared that the timely arrival of the British envoy had prevented them from accepting the proposals of the French and the Persians.[142]

The motives of the Amirs in trying to impress Seton with the eagerness with which their alliance was supposed to have been sought by the Persians and the French are fairly obvious. The Amirs proposed a close alliance with the British Government without binding them to pay any indemnification for

[140] NLS M 377. J. Duncan to Minto, Bombay, 9 February 1808 (Private). Ibid., 29 March 1808. NLS M 194. Governor-General-in-Council to the Secret Committee, 3 May 1808.

[141] BL, IOR Ben. Sec. & Pol. Cons. 207. Cons. of 30 May 1808. No. 12. J. Duncan-in-Council to Minto, 30 April 1808.

[142] BL, IOR Home Misc. Series 591, pp. 95–100. D. Seton to Malcolm, Hyderabad, 21 August 1808.

their past affair. However, they declared that the reopening of the factory at Tatta or Hyderabad should be subject to the consent of their Afghan overlord which was simply an excuse to prevent its re-establishment. The Amirs proposed that each party was to provide military assistance to the other if required, with the party requesting aid paying the expenses. The Amirs specifically demanded British military aid in order to capture Amarkot, a fort eighty miles east of Hyderabad which they claimed rightfully belonged to Sind. The Amirs also had designs on the neighbouring territory of Kutch. They proposed that the coastal districts of Kutch should be divided between the Company and Sind and were particularly anxious to take Lakhpat Bandar, a port on the west coast of Kutch. Seton agreed to all these proposals except the one regarding Lakhpat Bandar and the division of the coastal territories of Kutch. He agreed to the proposals regarding Amarkot and mutual military aid, for he thought both these clauses would be of utility to the British.[143]

On 18 July 1808, Seton concluded an Agreement with Ghulam Ali Khan which stipulated that a firm alliance should exist between the two states. It provided for mutual military aid and the Government of Sind was allowed to freely purchase military stores from any of the ports belonging to the Company. Seton also agreed to relinquish the claim of indemnification, but he did not succeed in gaining permission for the re-establishment of British factory in Sind.[144]

Seton made a mistake in believing that the Government desired an alliance with the Amirs of Sind at all costs. His instructions were merely to restore communications between the Company and Sind and to endeavour to establish a permanent footing and influence in that territory. He had been directed to gather information and counteract French influence, but not to conclude any specific political treaty with the Amirs. From the reports sent by Seton, it appeared to Minto that neither the activities of the French and the Persians in Sind, nor the need for an alliance with the Amirs, were so immediate as to warrant the establishment of a treaty or justified acquiescence to all of their demands. Seton's treaty with the Amirs was also inconsistent with Minto's Afghan policy. Minto believed that 'the main object of the anxiety of those chiefs evidently was to obtain the aid of a foreign power for their emancipation from their tributary dependence on the State of Caubul'.[145] Seton appears to have misjudged the fact that a mutual military assistance treaty could involve the British in wars that were not their own. In addition, Article 7 of Seton's treaty inflicted additional humiliation on the British Government as it stipulated that the establishment of a British factory

---

[143] Ibid., pp. 5–13. Seton to Duncan-in-Council, 24 July 1808.

[144] BL, IOR Home Misc. Series. 591, pp. 87–89. Agreement concluded with Meer Gholam Ali, Hakim of Sind by Captain Seton at Hyderabad, 18 July 1808. Printed in Aitchison, *Treaties, Engagements and Sanads*, Vol. VIII, 5th edn, pp. 292–93, footnote.

[145] NLS M 194. Governor-General-in-Council to the Secret Committee, 15 December 1808.

at Tatta should be deferred until the Amirs should have 'full satisfaction and perfect confidence' in the good faith of the British. Minto did not consider any partial modification of Seton's treaty to be beneficial and decided to annul it altogether. He wrote to Duncan, 'we are not disposed to authorize the conclusion of any Engagements which are not founded on the solid basis of mutual confidence, common interest and similarity of our view'.[146]

In order to minimise the embarrassment of cancelling the treaty established by Seton, Minto decided to appoint a direct representative of the governor-general to Sind and indicated that the mission conducted by Seton was preliminary in nature. Nicholas Hankey Smith, the former resident at Bushire who had accompanied Malcolm to Calcutta was appointed as the new envoy. Minto wrote a letter to Ghulam Ali Khan to that effect. No mention was made of Seton's treaty or its cancellation by the Government. It merely informed the Amir that the governor-general being encouraged by Captain Seton's reports had decided to open a direct communication with the Government of Sind and was therefore dispatching an envoy to continue Captain Seton's negotiations.[147]

In the beginning of 1809, news of the favourable change of affairs in Europe and Napoleon's reverses in Spain led to a revision of Minto's diplomatic policies with regard to all the states he had opened communications with in order to counteract Napoleon's eastern project. Fresh instructions were sent to the envoys in Persia, Sind, Lahore and Afghanistan. The only political interest that the British Government had in Sind was the counteraction of hostile influences of its enemies in that territory. In Minto's opinion, it was too early to conclude that Bonaparte would not be able to reconsolidate his power in Europe and renew his projects on the British territories in India.

In a letter dated 6 March 1809, Edmonstone informed Smith that in view of the prevailing conditions his instructions of 28 November 1808 were affected 'only in the degree in which the immediate danger of a Foreign Invasion is weakened or removed' and that 'it is an object to establish such a connection with the State of Sind as may afford us the means of counteracting that influence hereafter'. Hence, the connection with Sind was still to have an anti-French bias. Smith was directed to further the primary objective of his mission, that is, to try and establish a permanent friendship and connection with Sind according to his former instructions, but the size and scale of his mission were reduced.

On 14 August 1809, Ghulam Ali Khan received the British envoy ceremonially and demanded to hear the objectives of his mission. Smith sent him

---

[146] BL, IOR Home Misc. Series 591. Minto-in-Council to Duncan-in-Council, Fort William, 5 December 1808.

[147] BL, IOR Home Misc. Series 592. Minto to Mir Gholum Ali Khan, pp. 141–43. Fort William, 10 October 1808.

a written document enumerating the British objectives according to Minto's instructions. The advantages offered to the Amirs in return for the establishment of a British commercial factory or political residency in Sind were a pledge of British neutrality in the event of wars with any other power, the hope of ultimately obtaining a closer connection with the British Government and its active support and commercial benefits. Smith also explained that a government had a right to disavow the actions of their agents if they had overstepped their authority and contrasted the original objective of Seton's mission with his actual actions. Whether convinced or not, the Amirs seemed satisfied by his explanations and there were no further comments.[148]

Ghulam Ali Khan presented counter-proposals through his Munshi Kushal Ram. He consented to the re-establishment of the British factory in Sind on condition that the British should cooperate with him in invading Kutch, and proposed that the revenues of Kutch be divided in the proportion of ten annas in a rupee to Sind and six to the British. If however, the British agreed to be neutral in his war against Kutch, then in return for their neutrality, he offered to enter into an offensive and defensive alliance against the French. The re-establishment of the factory in Sind was to depend exclusively on British cooperation against Kutch. Smith of course refused to entertain any proposal of hostility against Kutch, as the spread of Sind's authority over Kutch would have brought the dominion of the Amirs close to Gujarat and the Maratha kingdom and naturally such a proposition could not be considered even for political and economic gain. The terms were eventually outlined in a 'Promissory Agreement'. The first two articles contained general expressions of friendship which were incorporated in view of 'the childish timidity' of the Amirs; the third provided for the continuous exchange of diplomatic agents between the two governments and the fourth secured the exclusion of 'the Tribe of the French' from Sind. A treaty was signed on 22 August 1809 incorporating these four articles[149] and it was the first political agreement signed between the British Government and the Amirs of Sind. It is clear that the main objective of Minto's policy with regard to Sind was not the formation of a defensive alliance against the French, but to actively counteract any nebulous French or Persian influence in Sind by the strength of commercial enterprise and political connectivity through mutual diplomatic exchange in order to reassert British influence in the region.

The strategy of creating a *cordon sanitaire* that would block the possible approaches to India was carried out well into 1830. Relations with Sind presented few problems. Its amirs were nominally Afghan subjects and they had supported the Company whenever the rulers of Afghanistan showed

---

[148] BL, IOR Home Misc. Series 591, N.H. Smith to Edmonstone, Mandavi, 1 October 1809.
[149] BL, IOR Home Misc. Series 591, pp. 408–11. Conference between Golam Ali and Ellis, Hyderabad, 21 August 1809.

any sign of reasserting their sovereignty.[150] The Punjab under Ranjit Singh, Maharaja of Lahore, was an island of stability and a formidable power with its European-trained and equipped army, the Khalsa. However, the 'Lion of Lahore', who had held absolute power since 1799, was ageing and his vigour was later impaired by a stroke in 1836 coupled with an addiction to brandy and opium.[151] Relations with both the Punjab and Sind were however being strengthened through an economic dependency. Free trade was Britain's new economic orthodoxy and its prophets declared that its spread across the globe would be a foundation for universal peace.[152] In 1836, Lord Auckland predicted that paddle steamers puffing up the Indus with cargoes of British goods would transform the outlook of those who lived on its banks.[153] In future, they would 'look... more to our merchants than our soldiers'.[154]

The attempt by Russia to extend a hand of friendship to the shah in Afghanistan during the 1830s caused panic in Calcutta and London, where Russian diplomatic moves were interpreted as the first stage of the long expected thrust toward India. Russia's attempt at 'destabilisation' by diplomatic leverage was an attempt to pry apart the states which formed India's buffer zone and set them at each other's throats.[155] Afghanistan was an ideal testing ground for Britain's imperial will. Dost Muhammad was acting in an obstructive and wayward manner by refusing to accept British terms and flirting with Russia and this was an opportunity to demonstrate that Britain would not shrink from defending its vital interests in the area.[156]

The decision to invade Afghanistan was taken in May 1838 by Auckland against a background of 'universal panic', prompted by reports of intrigues of Russian agents in Persia and Kabul and fears that Herat would be captured. Auckland was swayed by a coterie of experts, most notably William Macnaghten, the secretary of the Indian Government's secret department. He was a deskbound official with an over-developed sense of his own omniscience and an undeserved reputation for being a diplomatic genius.[157] He proposed that an Anglo-Punjabi army occupy Afghanistan, dethrone Dost Muhammad and replace him with the pro-British Shah Shuja, an exiled pretender then living in India. Details of this plan reached London at the end of October and were warmly endorsed by the Cabinet and the Duke of Wellington.[158]

---

[150] Lawrence, J., *Raj: The Making and Unmaking of British India* (New York, 1998), Chap. 2, pp. 86–87.
[151] Ibid.
[152] Ibid.
[153] Ibid.
[154] Norris, J.A., *The First Afghan War* (Cambridge, 1967), p. 83.
[155] Lawrence, *Raj*, Chap. 2, p. 88.
[156] Ibid., p. 89.
[157] Ibid., p. 90.
[158] Norris, *The First Afghan War*, p. 216, pp. 218–19.

The following month, the Russian Government finally gave way to British pressure and having given Britain a shock, the Russians were prepared to back off and focus on what really mattered – negotiations over the future of the Turkish empire. The disappearance of what had been a largely illusory threat did not change the plans for the march to Kabul. Britain still needed to affirm its power in the traditional way and with Shah Shuja installed in Kabul, a hitherto wobbly state would be transformed into a firm and submissive ally of the Company and the downfall of Dost Muhammad would serve as a warning to other rulers in the region.[159]

[159] Lawrence, *Raj*, Chap. 2, p. 90.

Four

PROTECTING TRADE AND SUPPLY LINES

Conquest of the French Islands

In the 1780s, between the end of the War of American Independence and the outbreak of the French Revolution, French commerce achieved a period of unprecedented prosperity. Trade between the French colonies in the West Indies linked with trade with the United States as a result of the alliance during the War of American Independence was the primary cause of economic growth. Colonial trade was dominated by Bordeaux, which acted as a focal point for distribution of colonial goods throughout Northern Europe and also possessed a range of industries situated along the tributaries of the River Garonne that produced household goods and plantation utensils which were shipped to the colonies.[1] Parts of this manufacturing industry had been modernised along British lines shortly before the Revolution, but in general were not able to compete with industries within France when their colonial markets collapsed. Nantes and La Rochelle played a part in the commerce with the West Indies, supplying slaves for the plantations and importing sugar and other commodities.[2] A specialised organised trade from Bordeaux was that with the East Indies, organised through L'Ile de France (modern-day Mauritius). This demanded larger ships and considerable risk capital. Whereas commerce with the West Indies required ships of around 100–150 tons, East Indiamen were upward of 400 tons and similar in size and armaments to naval frigates.[3] After abandonment of the French East India Company presence in Madagascar, the Mascarene Islands of Bourbon and L'Ile de France grew in importance. Both had been occupied earlier by the French, but became more firmly established with a military garrison during the era of John Law.[4] Each had a governor until 1727, after which the

---

[1] Crowhurst, Patrick, *The French War on Trade: Privateering 1793–1815* (Aldershot, 1989), Chap.1, pp. 1–2.
[2] Ibid.
[3] Ibid.
[4] Wellington, D.C., *French East India Companies: A Historical Account and Record of Trade* (Lanham,

position was demoted to a military commander under the direction of the commandant general stationed in Pondicherry. Seven years later in 1734, a further administrative change created one governor-general in control of civil and military matters on both islands.[5]

In India the French presence was primarily in Pondicherry on the Coromandel Coast and Chandarnagar in Bengal. Both encompassed a territory under French jurisdiction. Elsewhere, the French only had trading posts. A post existed at Masulipatam on the Coromandel Coast while others were added at Yanaon in the Northern Circars in 1721, Mahe on the Malabar Coast in 1725 and Karikal in Tanjore in 1739. Balasore at the mouth of the River Hughli was a settlement for pilots employed in French shipping. Others included Surat in Gujarat and although Calicut was abandoned in 1722, Patna in Bihar was a centre for opium production, Dacca and Jougdia on the River Brahmaputra in Bengal, Cassimbazar and Gigouria. Posts outside India included Bandar Abbas and temporarily Basra covering the Persian Gulf, Moka on the Red Sea and Canton in China. All of these were under native jurisdiction.[6]

Pondicherry was the administrative centre in India as a grouping of enclaves ceded to the French by the Nawab of Arcot. The area under French control eventually reached fourteen enclaves totalling 29,000 hectares in area. The concessions gave the French the rights to levy taxes and customs duties, mint coins, oversee judiciary and executive powers over all inhabitants and fly the French flag.[7]

The entire French East India Company operation both administrative and judicial was under the direction of a governor-general. He was responsible for carrying out the Company's mission and orders in India and also commanded civil, military and naval services in India. The sense of independence was derived from a pattern of longevity in service and the slowness of communication with Paris. Benoit Dumas served for twelve years and Dupleix for twenty years.[8]

The essence of the company's trade between France and India was the exchange of specie (money in the form of coins) for cloth. Specie exports were estimated at about twenty-five million livres worth each year during the twenty years of peace prior to the War of the Austrian Succession. French law prohibited the export of the specie from France. Although the Crown did on occasion rescind the prohibition, the company usually obtained the specie from elsewhere – the main source being Cadiz, which was the point of arrival of Spain's annual convoy of treasure from America. The French East

MD, 2006), Chap. 9, p. 61.
5 Ibid.
6 Ibid.
7 Ibid., p. 62.
8 Ibid., p. 63.

India Company bought mostly silver coin, piastres of Peru and Mexico, which was a Spanish coin stamped at 916 2/3 purity containing twenty-four grams of pure silver. The specie purchases were made through brokers who were primarily French bankers based in Saint Malo, Bayonne and Paris. If France was at war with Spain, silver purchases could be made at Amsterdam. Gold coins purchased from Portugal were also shipped to India. Total company shipments of silver and gold to India amounted to around five million livres tournois per year in the second decade of the eighteenth century, rising to double that figure in the third decade and reaching approximately thirteen million livres in the fifth decade.[9] Trade with North Africa was focused on grain and hides and the company surrendered its monopoly rights for import in 1730. West African trade centred on Guinea and Senegal was related to slaves transported to Caribbean islands, which reached a peak in the mid years of the third decade of the eighteenth century. Trade with Asia was significantly diverse and included coffee from the Mascarene Islands and Moka on the Red Sea. Tea, porcelain, copper, camphor, lacquer, sugar, raw silk and silk textiles from China and saltpetre, drugs, dyes, lacquer, rare metals and shells from India. The main Indian export was textiles which came in a variety of different forms – thread, yarn and unbleached and bleached coloured cloth of cotton, wool, silk or linen. The principal French ports of transhipment in India were Pondicherry and Surat. Pondicherry specialised in cloth, some of which came from Bengal which produced the best of some kinds of cloth. Surat also provided cloth but of a poorer quality. However, Surat was a better source for other products including drugs and spices which were purchased from the Dutch East India Company. On the Malabar Coast, Mahe replaced Calicut as the principal French trading post as a source of pepper. The range of profits from this trade (from sale in France) was between a hundred and two hundred per cent.[10]

Behind the façade of prosperity of Bordeaux was a growing problem. The West Indian colonies were heavily in debt. Productivity was falling due to decreasing soil fertility and there was no new land to bring under cultivation. Additionally goods imported from France by the landowners could not be paid for in full and this situation couldn't be resolved even by the Bordeaux merchants taking control of the plantations. The textile industry in Normandy was also facing serious difficulties and this was the beginning of the pre-Revolutionary crisis.[11] The outbreak of the Revolution caught French commerce facing severe difficulties. Within two years of the outbreak of the Revolution in Paris there was a major slave revolt in the north of

---

9   Ibid., Chap. 10, p. 67.
10 Ibid., Chap. 10, p. 69.
11 Kaplan, J., *Elbeuf during the Revolutionary Period: History and Social Structure* (Baltimore, MD, 1964), pp. 100–01.

Saint Domingue and imports of sugar, coffee and other colonial goods fell. The introduction of *assignats*, which became legal tender in September 1790, rapidly disrupted much of trade as their value declined as it became increasingly difficult for merchants to calculate a price that would provide adequate compensation for the normal delay in payment by bill of exchange.[12] Consequently inflation brought trade to a halt as peasants were also unwilling to bring their produce to sell for a currency they considered worthless. The situation became worse with the outbreak of war with Austria in 1792 and the attempts to raise additional revenue by taxation. The following year, inflation reached dramatic proportions as prices and wages rose steeply. Essentially there was not enough wheat to feed the population and merchants in France were suspected of holding stock that they were unwilling to sell and profiting from the misery of their fellow citizens. At the end of January 1793 after the execution of Louis XVI, Britain declared war on France. This provided merchants and ship owners with the opportunity to fit out privateers and raid British shipping.[13]

In the wars between France and Britain in the eighteenth and nineteenth centuries, the colonial possessions of the two countries were always pawns in the game. During the war of 1793–1814 the European conflict was carried into Asia, Africa and America. India was a prize that was hotly contested by the two rivals. In 1793, the British drove the French out of the Indian mainland, but not from the Indian Ocean. The French fell back on their second line of defence, the French settlements at Madagascar, Seychelles, Bourbon and Mauritius (L'Ile de France), which they hoped to use later as a base for offensive operations against the British in India. The French footholds in the Indian Ocean were suitable for just the sort of operation that the French were aiming at against the British after the short-lived peace of Amiens in 1802, that is, the destruction of Britain's commercial prosperity. A lesson that the Revolutionary War had been that colonial produce could only reach France on American ships, and the trade had also provided excellent cover for illegal activities since the origin of goods which passed through American ports was hidden by the nationality of the ship that had carried them. Additionally the British Government did not try to interrupt American trade with Europe as Britain did not want to risk another war with the United States and also because Britain benefited from American commerce.[14]

Between the years 1806 and 1812, Napoleon despairing of conquering Britain, sought to cripple British commerce. The Berlin Decree of 21 November 1806 and the first Milan Decree that followed inaugurated the Continental System. It stated that Britain was to be blockaded and that all

---

12 Crowhurst, *The French War on Trade*, Chap. 1, p. 5.
13 Ibid., p. 6.
14 Ibid., p. 16.

trade with Britain should immediately cease. British nationals and goods were to be seized and no ship would be allowed to enter a French port after leaving a British one. This was Napoleon's response to the failure of the peace negotiations and the British Order in Council of May, which declared that the European coast from Brest to the River Elbe was formally blockaded. The resultant effect on trade encouraged French merchants to fit out privateers, but the Berlin Decree did make the owners of neutral vessels more cautious and raised insurance rates. The emperor's projects against the British territories in India originated from this desire rather than the expansion of the French empire. While the grand plans of an invasion of India were not brought to fruition, the French were extremely successful in their attacks on British commerce from their outposts in the East. The French privateers operating from Bourbon and L'Ile de France between 1803 and 1810 were successful in their exploits to become a serious threat to the prosperity of Indian trade. Their activities rivalled the exploits of those operations from the ports of Brest, Cherbourg and St Malo. This indeed was an extraordinary phenomenon in view of the fact that the naval superiority of the British was said to been an established fact after Trafalgar. It was not until 1810 that the Government of India under Minto decided to address this situation and added to Britain's colonial territories as a direct result. The conquest of the French Islands and the East Indies, together with Britain's conquests in South America and the West Indies, further extended the British Empire. Europe was so busy facing the challenge of Napoleon's expansions that Britain's fast-growing colonial empire aroused little opposition. J.H. Rose remarks, 'While Napoleon sought to crown his system by the armed coercion of Russia, the British had already completed theirs by the occupation of Java (September 1811).'[15]

The importance of Britain's trade was recognised by both sides and the French attempts to destroy it both by commerce raids and by decrees designed to exclude British goods from Europe ultimately failed, though the margin was slim and the years 1808 and 1811–12 were particularly difficult for the British economy. The figures for the growth in British trade reveal its crucial nature for the capital with which the wars were fought: imports rose from £39.6 million in 1796 to £80.8 million in 1814 and exports and re-exports from £30.1 million and £8.5 million to £45.5 million and £24.8 million in the same time period, respectively.[16]

Holland Rose writes that Britain's chief motive was to secure a monopoly of tropical products as an offset to Napoleon's attempts to exclude all British

---

15 Rose, J.H., *Cambridge History of the British Empire* (Cambridge, 1929–59), Vol. 2, Chap. III, p. 105.
16 Crowhurst, *The French War on Trade*, Chap. 2, p. 31.

produce from the Continent.[17] This explanation of Britain's chief motive is however not borne out by the terms of the peace settlement of 1815. Britain retained only those recent conquests that were strategically valuable and that secured the control of the Mediterranean and the routes to India, China and the West Indies. Further, it was not merely the need for more sugar and cloves that caused Minto to embark on expeditions against the French Islands and the Dutch East Indies in 1810 and 1811, but the need for greater security of the British trade and territories in the East.

The main task was to maintain business confidence and close ties between commerce and government, particularly due to the fact that commercial profits covered the costs of the wars of the eighteenth century. The Board of Admiralty provided defence for trade from the first year of war by the first Convoy Act and made this compulsory in 1798. At the beginning of the Napoleonic Wars, this support became even more critical. Many convoys were particularly large; those to the West Indies of upward of 800 ships were usual and the loss of a single convoy could have a disastrous impact on the Government's standing. The navy also played an important role in restricting the commerce of Northern Europe whenever this was felt to be benefitting Napoleon. In practice however, the problem proved to be less clear cut that many had imagined. In 1803, at the outbreak of the war, the navy instituted a blockade of the Weser and Elbe as a counter to the French occupation of Hanover. In theory this should have damaged or destroyed trade which had formerly passed through the ports on these rivers, notably Hamburg and Bremen. However, this did not achieve the desired outcome following the Berlin Decree and eventually the Foreign Secretary Lord Canning asked the Admiralty to lift the blockade on Hamburg as these ports provided an avenue to evade the Continental System proposed by Napoleon. The eventual seizure of Hamburg in 1807 provided the British merchants with a base for smuggling and it is claimed that in the last half of 1807 no fewer than 1,475 small vessels entered Hamburg laden with British goods.[18]

Naval campaigns overseas also contributed significantly to the establishment of British commerce. The capture of Tobago, part of Saint Domingue and St Pierre and Miquelon in the first year of the war demonstrated British naval strength while weakening the French economically.[19] The naval blockade of the French coast also checked the flow of naval stores to Brest and other ports. Naval shipbuilding was largely dependent on supplies of Baltic materials to construct ships and keep them operational. From the point of view of the French shareholder in privateering ventures, the naval war made it extremely difficult to profit from commerce raiding as there was a shortage of seamen,

---

[17] Rose, *Cambridge History of the British Empire*, Vol. 2, Chap. III, p. 105.
[18] Crowhurst, *The French War on Trade*, Chap. 2, p. 40.
[19] Ibid., p. 42.

of capital to finance voyages, of suitable materials to build and repair the ships and indirectly, the naval blockade damaged neutral trade and drove it away from the Atlantic coast.[20]

The French Islands, a group of three islands in the Indian Ocean, Rodriguez, Bourbon and L'Ile de France, situated about 500 miles east of Madagascar, were a very old settlement of France. In 1715, the French occupied the Dutch island of Mauritius from the neighbouring island of Bourbon, and renamed it L'Ile de France. As a settlement and a centre of trade and as a naval base in times of war, these islands gradually assumed importance especially under their energetic governor La Bourdonnais. Situated about 2,520 miles from Bombay and 2,100 from Colombo,[21] the islands provided the French with a base from where they could sabotage British commerce in the Indian Ocean as well as maintain relations with the Indian princes for purposes hostile to the security of the British territories in India. The strategic importance of the French Islands with regard to the Indian peninsula was rated at varying degrees by different people. Bernadin de St Pierre, an officer of the Engineers, and Sonnerat were sceptical about the strategic value of the islands because they were not self-sufficient, produced no timber for shipbuilding, and were at a considerable distance from India.[22] Others held a different opinion: Abbe Raynal observed about L'Ile de France:

> It is situated in the African sea, just at the entrance of the Indian ocean,... As it lies out of the common track, its expeditions can be carried on with great secrecy... Great Britain sees with a jealous eye her rivals possessed of a settlement where the ruin of her property in Asia may be prepared.[23]

The career of Robert Surcouf opens a new stage in commerce raiding. Surcouf was no ordinary managing owner but one of the most daring and experienced of all privateer commanders. He achieved fame in 1796 as the captain of the *Emilie* in the Indian Ocean and used L'Ile de France as a base. Early in the year, when it was considered dangerous for large ships to be off the east coast of India because of the prevailing monsoon, he appeared off the mouth of the Hughli. He achieved complete surprise and captured two merchant ships and a pilot brig. The latter was the perfect disguise for a privateer because all shipping bound for Calcutta needed the help of a pilot to navigate the constantly changing waterways of the Sandheads in the Gangetic delta. The *Triton* East Indiaman, captured on 29 January by Surcouf and sixteen men, carried a crew of 150 men. In 1799 Surcouf cruised in another

---

[20] Ibid., p. 43.
[21] Grant, C., Viscount de Vaux, *The History of Mauritius* (London, 1801), p. 10. L'Ile de France was 2,295 miles from the Cape, and approximately 3,000 from the East Indies.
[22] Prentout, *L'Ile de France sous Decaen*, p. viii.
[23] Grant, *The History of Mauritius*, p. 507.

ship, the *Clarisse* in the Bay of Bengal, where he took many more prizes and practically blockaded Calcutta. When he took the *Clarisse* back to L'Ile de France to refit, he was offered the *Confiance*. In this vessel, Surcouf was able to out-sail all British warships that came within sight and also further captured over a dozen merchant ships. Surcouf remained in the Indian Ocean for the rest of the Revolutionary War and returned to St Malo in 1802 where he was appointed Colonel in the National Guard.[24] In January 1808 Surcouf returned to the Indian Ocean as the commander of a privateer and sailed from St Malo on the eighteen-gun *Revenant*, which was built as a corsair and was extremely fast. He evaded the British blockade off Ile Bourbon and entered Port Louis on 10 June. He then proceeded to harry the rice trade between Bengal and Madras to provide food for the population of L'Ile de France and cruised off the Sandheads in the frigate *Piemontaise*.[25]

During the Revolutionary and the Napoleonic Wars between Britain and France, the French Islands became a centre of vigorous opposition to the British in India and a focus of profitable trade. Between 1769 and 1785 La Rochelle sent twenty-six vessels to the Indian Ocean, and they obtained slaves from East Africa who were sent to L'Ile de France via Madagascar, coffee from Ile Bourbon, Indian cloths and Bengal silks from Pondicherry, Chinese porcelains and spices from the Dutch East Indies.[26] Their main offensive was directed against English trade, and between 1793 and 1796, the losses of the East India Company as a result of the activity of the French privateers amounted to over £3,000,000. L'Ile de France gained much prestige in the eyes of the enemies of the English. In 1798, embassies arrived at L'Ile de France from Tipu Sultan of Mysore, the Dutch at Batavia, and the King of Pegu, all seeking aid against the common enemy. Wellesley made short work of Tipu and wanted also to act swiftly against Decaen in L'Ile de France. Wellesley wrote to Castlereagh pointing out that the Cape and the French Islands were two strategic points in the Indian Ocean, and the power in possession of these two outposts had the means of either protecting or harassing the sea routes to India. He pointed out that while the French should retain L'Ile de France with the advantage of unrestricted communication with the Cape, they would be a very lively source of trouble. The French and Dutch ships in the Indian Ocean and the Eastern seas, exclusive of those at the Cape, were at the time supposed to be superior in number and weight of metal to the British squadron within the same area. From the French Islands, the French would not only be able to harass British shipping, but also the British settlements at Malacca and Penang, and even establish a liaison with the Court of Ava. Wellesley therefore proposed that while the Cape should

[24]   Crowhurst, *The French War on Trade*, Chap. 4, p. 100.
[25]   Ibid., p. 101.
[26]   Ibid., p. 122.

be occupied by an expedition sent directly from Britain, Mauritius should be taken over by an expedition sent from India.[27] After the Mysore war, Wellesley turned his attention to three objectives: the occupation of the French Islands, the conquest of Java and an expedition to Egypt. Wellesley's project against the French Islands was frustrated by the refusal of Admiral Rainier, Commander-in-Chief of the King's Navy in India, to cooperate with the Government of India without orders from the Lords Commissioners of the Admiralty.[28] Wellesley next turned his attention to Java, but was restrained by the positive injunctions of the home government not to engage in any warlike enterprise in the Eastern seas and the troops assembled for the expedition were sent to Egypt.[29]

Hence Wellesley's projected attempt on L'Ile de France was abandoned and the French Islands were given a fresh lease of life that lasted until December 1801. The occupation of Malta, the Cape and Ceylon by the British generated a feeling of overall security to the British trade and territories in the East, but the French Islands continued to be a source of trouble and embarrassment. The activities of General Decaen and the French privateers finally forced Minto to send an expedition from India to expel the French from these islands.

The French and 'Caballing Natives' in India

Decaen had been sent out by Bonaparte with a strong detachment of troops to take charge of the French territories in India, in accordance with the terms of the Treaty of Amiens (March 1803). Decaen retired to L'Ile de France with his troops at the outbreak of hostilities. The French historian Henri Prentout has given a substantive account of the nature of Decaen's commission and efforts to carry out the instructions of the emperor. Decaen was to observe the British in India closely, establish secret contacts with the Indian princes, and formulate plans for a future war. The scope of intrigues with the Indian powers however was very limited when Decaen arrived on the scene. The major Indian powers had been vanquished before 1803 and the Marathas were on the decline. The reports that Decaen's agents sent from India were more often than not unreliable. Decaen's chief of staff Binot did establish contacts with the Rajas of Tanjore and Travancore and sent a French officer to Sindhia's court, who however gave himself up to the British. Two of

---

27 Owen, S.J., *Selections from the Dispatches of the Marquis of Wellesley* (Oxford, 1877), pp. 585–89. Wellesley to Castlereagh, 25 July 1803, Fort William (Secret).
28 Martin, R.M., *The Despatches, Minutes and Correspondence of the Marquess Wellesley* (London, 1836–37), Vol. 2, pp. 753–58.
29 Ibid., pp. 436–37, 440–52.

Decaen's agents to Sindhia and Holkar were also captured by the British.[30] Yet Decaen did not despair of success. On the basis of the dubious report from his secret agents in India, he drew up plans for an attack on the British in India by joint land and naval forces and also sent several emissaries to France to urge Bonaparte to attack the British in India.[31] In 1807 it appeared that Decaen's dream was about to be realised. In July 1807, the Minister of Marine, Decres, informed Decaen of the conclusion of the Treaty of Finkenstein with Persia, and ordered him to cooperate with General Gardane in Persia in planning a two-pronged attack on the British territories in India. Gardane and Decaen did establish a line of communication through Persia, Muscat and the Seychelles to Mauritius.[32]

The British believed the French had a hand in every trouble they had to face in India at this time, including the belief that the mutiny of the sepoys at Vellore in July 1806 had been fomented by French agents. An unknown observer wrote, 'Monsieur de Caen is repaying with Interest to the successor of Marquis Wellesley, the Intrigues by which that nobleman drove the French from Hyderabad. I have not a Doubt, but at this moment, all India is filled with caballing natives, in the pay of the French.'[33]

Decaen's agents were also traced in the Danish settlements in India, in Tranquebar in the south and in Serampore in Bengal. These neutral settlements served as convenient points of observation for the French. In January 1808, after Denmark declared war on Britain following the attack by the British on the Danish fleet at Copenhagen, Tranquebar and Serampore were captured by the British. The French agent at Tranquebar, Dufayel, was arrested and sent back to France. News of the conflagration between Britain and Denmark was received by a private letter from the acting resident at Baghdad and the Government decided to act on it without delay. The Danish settlements, factories, ships and public property in India were taken over by the British. All civil, military and marine officers and all Europeans in the service of the Danish Government or the Danish East India Company were taken prisoner of war. The Commander-in-Chief's Military Secretary, Lieutenant Colonel Carey was sent to take over Serampore on 27 January 1808.[34] The Baptist missionaries at Serampore, who were highly unpopular with the Government of Bengal, were suspected of supplying information

---

[30] Sen, *The French in India*, pp. 573–77. The author gives an account of the activities of Decaen's agents in India, based mainly on the work of Prentout.

[31] Decaen sent Barois, Cavaignac and Lefebvre to Paris in the course of 1804, followed by Rene Decaen in July 1805 and again in January 1808. Prentout, *L'Ile de France sous Decaen*, pp. 391–400.

[32] TNA FO 60/3, H. Jones to Wellesley, Tauris, 16 September 1810, No. 29.

[33] BL, IOR MSS. Eur. F89. Box 20, Pkt. 5. Written presumably sometime after the Vellore mutiny. Paper entitled 'On Missionaries', undated, unsigned, incomplete.

[34] BL, IOR Fac. Rec., Persia 28, pp. 16–17.

to the French spies at Serampore who were supposed to maintain a regular communication with Decaen. This suspected sympathy of the missionaries toward the French is doubtful and only perhaps underlines their unpopularity.

Threats to British Overseas Trade Interests

It was however neither Decaen's intrigues with anti-British elements in India, nor any projected or prospective attack on the British territories in India from the French Islands, which rendered these islands a source of serious trouble to the British. They were also a base of operations from which French priva- teers raided the British commerce-carriers in the Indian Ocean from the beginning of the war in 1793 until 1810. It is usual to dismiss the exploits of these French privateers as operations that had merely a 'nuisance value'. Yet it cannot be denied that the British losses at sea were considerable during these years,[35] and must have been galling to the side that boasted a superior naval force. The islands could perhaps have been taken before 1810, but the tactics adopted by the home government to reduce them were not very effective. The Admiralty hoped to take L'Ile de France by means of a blockade and after the abandonment of Wellesley's projected expedition against the French Islands in 1803, a blockade was established against the islands. The occupation of the Cape in January 1806 provided a base of operation nearer the islands and the British hoped to enforce the blockade more rigorously. The blockade maintained by a few ships of the Cape squadron for only a few months of the year was totally ineffective. Far from reducing the islands by starvation, it could not stop the French and the neutral ships from coming in and going out of the ports and harbours of Bourbon and L'Ile de France. During the hurricane months, from the middle of December to the end of March, the blockading ships withdrew to the Cape for the lack of a base nearer the islands. The French used the hurricane months to throw in supplies to the islands from Seychelles and Madagascar, and for refitting and replenishing food supplies for the privateers. Their exact number and prizes are not recorded, but the losses encountered by the merchants and traders were generally believed to be considerable. In February 1806 Rear-Admiral Sir Edward Pellew of the East India station in consultation with the Governor-General Sir George Barlow introduced the convoy system for ships departing from Bombay for greater safety of the merchantmen. Many however in their eagerness to secure early markets for their goods took the risk of sailing singly and were consequently easy prey. Pellew proposed to Barlow that an expedition should be sent

---

[35] *The Asiatic Annual Register 1799–1811* contains accounts of naval engagements fought by British ships and French privateers and frigates during the years 1799–1809 in the Indian Ocean.

against the French Islands. Barlow however refused to undertake any measure involving a large expense to the Company. He pleaded lack of finance and the prohibitory orders of the Court of Directors to reject Pellew's proposal for a joint naval and military attack on the French Islands.[36] During 1805–1808 therefore, the navy offered what protection it could to the merchantmen by means of the convoy system, while an ineffective blockade of the islands continued to be maintained from the Cape.

In head to head combat, the larger British Indiamen could beat off or capture the French frigates, but the immunity of the privateers lay in the fact that they used lighter and faster moving vessels. Occasionally one or two of the French ships were taken by the British, but that did little to reduce their overall number. French prisoners were usually exchanged in order to release British prisoners of war, but the ships if sold could be bought by neutrals who could sell them back to the French, so the cycle continued. The British tried to stop this practice by destroying the smaller craft and converting larger ships to its service. On the other hand, captured British ships were converted into privateers and specially built ships, which were lighter and faster moving vessels, came out from France. In 1806, two French frigates – the *Piemontaise* and the *Canoniere* – arrived at L'Ile de France and in May 1807, Robert Surcouf of the *Revenant* returned to the Indian seas. These were joined in 1808 by the *Venus*, *Manche* and *Caroline*. During the years 1807–09, the French Islands became the centre of an increasing 'exchange-trade'. The port of St Louis became the base both for equipping and fitting out the raiders and the centre for the disposal of the prize to the neutral Arab traders and to ships coming from America. The activities of the French privateers almost annihilated the coastal trade of the Coromandel. As the Islanders experienced a shortage of food supplies, the privateers employed themselves chiefly on the trade between Bengal and Madras, especially the Bengal rice ships.

Shortly after Minto arrived at Calcutta in July 1807, the questions of the conquest of Batavia and the French Islands were discussed in the Council. Minto wrote to Dundas, 'The Mauritius and Batavia are the only two establishments possessed by our European Enemies, the local situation of which, afford material advantage in promoting the success of any hostile attempts against British possessions and interests in the East.'[37]

Mauritius was dangerous to the Company not only because it was the centre of French privateering in the Eastern seas, but also because it was a convenient location for the assembly of troops, stores and shipping for eventual hostilities with the British. At the height of the French alarm in 1807, Minto regarded Mauritius as a likely place of rendezvous, depot and a 'point

---

36 TNA Adm. 1/177. Pellew to William Marsden, Admiralty, dated 12 February 1806, HMS *Culloden*, Bombay Harbour.

37 NLS M 159. Minto to Robert Dundas, Fort William, 1 November 1807.

of departure' of the French in their hostile operations against the British. He wrote to Dundas:

> It seems every day more probable that some operation of the Enemy may be directed to the Persian or Arabian coasts, and to the western side of India. In the prosecution of designs whatever they may be, in that quarter, the Mauritius if not entirely indispensable must at least be very particularly adapted to facilitate their execution. ... the capture of Mauritius is the most pressing as well as the most important object in this part of the globe.[38]

Minto therefore proposed to the Secret Committee that Mauritius should be taken, with the ultimate objective of conquering Java. At this time, he recommended that the expedition against Mauritius and Bourbon should be sent from the Cape, without any combination of troops from India.[39] The circumstances in India at that time were not favourable to the dispatch of a large number of European troops for service abroad, as the number of European troops in India was not adequate to both meet the needs of internal security as well as furnish an expedition abroad. The presence of the French in Persia demanded the presence of all available forces in India. Moreover, Minto was unsure of the support of the home authorities in any warlike measures he might adopt. The Grenvillite Whigs went out of office shortly after his arrival in India, and for a time his own continuance in office was a matter of speculation. The Court of Directors' injunctions for financial economy, peace and non-interference were too fresh in his mind to allow him to undertake a military expedition immediately after his arrival in India. The home government on its part, while agreeing with Minto regarding the expediency of attempting to exclude the French and the Dutch from all their settlements between India and China, particularly Batavia, pleaded the lack of means for accomplishing that objective. Robert Dundas wrote to Minto:

> With regard to the Mauritius, the experience of the last year, if nothing more could be stated, would justify the operation that it affords the means of great annoyance to our Trade; but independently of the very large Force which it is supposed would be necessary for its reduction, I know that very high authorities (among others I believe Lord Cornwallis) have doubted the expediency of such an attempt.[40]

The Minister of War, Castlereagh, did not want any operations eastward of the Cape. The occupation of Ceylon in 1796 and of the Cape in January 1806 gave the British two strategically placed vantage points in the Indian

---

[38] Ibid.
[39] BL, IOR Bengal Secret Letters, Vol. 10, Minto to the Secret Committee, 2 November 1807, Fort William.
[40] NLS M 172. No. 6. R. Dundas to Minto, Whitehall, 2 May 1808. Private and Secret.

Ocean, adequate for the purpose of guarding the sea route to India. The expulsion of the French from Bourbon and L'Ile de France was not considered a matter of urgent necessity as these islands in general were wholly unsuited to the purpose of forming or maintaining a large number of European troops for an attack on India. H.W. Richmond writes that Mauritius was barely self-supporting and could not provide for a large number of troops and seamen, especially after its main source of supply was cut off by the British occupation of the Cape.[41] Mauritius was dependent on the Cape and Madagascar for the supply of corn and cattle. After the British occupation of the Cape, the French Islands depended on the neutral traders, the American and Arab ships for their supplies and also on the rich prizes that the French privateers brought into port. The British hoped by means of the blockade to starve the islands into surrender. The blockade however was not strictly enforced as it was not applied against neutral vessels and as Rear-Admiral Bertie of the Cape found it impossible to keep a close watch on all the four ports of the two islands at the same time with the few ships at his disposal.

Neither the blockade nor the convoy afforded adequate protection to the British *merchantmen* from the continued attacks of the privateers. In December 1807, the merchants, ship-owners and underwriters of Calcutta sent a memorial to the Lords Commissioners of the Admiralty, moaning over their losses and charging Pellew with inhumanity for allowing all the rice ships to be taken in September 1807.[42] The Admiral had facts to produce against the charges, indicating that the Bengal merchants, in order to make large profits by securing an early market, took the risk of sailing without convoy, and were easy prey to the raiders. The merchants of Bombay on the other hand, maintained a regular system of convoy for the China trade by which they were effectively protected.[43] During 1805–08, 110 ships ran between Bombay and China, of which only twenty-eight ran unprotected outside the fixed period for the regular convoys.[44] The Bombay Insurance Society refused to insure ships which quit the convoy.[45] During August, September and October 1807, the unprotected situation in the Bay of Bengal resulted in the capture of thirty-three vessels belonging to Calcutta and other ports on their way to Madras, Penang and Canton. On the capture of the rice ships in September 1807, 'little short of Fifty Lacks of Rupees were on that occasion lost to the

[41] Richmond, Sir H.W., *The Navy in India, 1763–1783* (London, 1931), p. 123.

[42] TNA Adm. 1/180. Memorial of the merchants, agents, shipowners and underwriters of Calcutta to the Lords Commissioners of the Admiralty. Calcutta, 10 December 1807.

[43] TNA Adm. 1/180. Sir E. Pellew to Lord Minto-in-Council, HMS *Culloden*, Bombay Harbour, 21 April 1808.

[44] TNA Adm. 1/180. Vote of thanks passed in favour of Pellew at a meeting of the merchants, shipowners and underwriters of Bombay, on 19 December 1808.

[45] TNA Adm. 1/180. Advertisement, Bombay Insurance Office, 7 February 1806.

underwriters and shipowners of Calcutta, a circumstance unparralelled [*sic*] in the Annals of Indian Commerce'.[46]

Pellew reported to the Admiralty in February 1808:

> The Enemy's Cruizers have of late been very successful in their depredations on the Country Trade, passing thro' the Bay,... their Successes are to be attributed in a great measure to the circumstance of the Masters of these Vessels being in the constant practice of running without Convoy... which has hitherto secured the Company's Ships from Capture.[47]

Although six of Pellew's ships were constantly cruising in the Bay of Bengal for protection of trade, none had the good fortune to encounter the French ships. Pellew complained, 'for the most part the first Intelligence of their appearance in the Bay is announced by their Successes'.[48]

In October 1808, Pellew in consultation with the Supreme Government fixed four convoys to the eastward from Calcutta to Penang and four to the westward from Calcutta to Madras to sail at fixed dates in the months of January, March, August and November–December every year. The frigate *Rattlesnake* and three sloops of war, *Dasher*, *Samarang* and *Victor* were appointed to the service.[49]

The convoy system however was not an adequate solution of the problem of affording protection to trade against the French privateers. Rear-Admiral Drury, who succeeded Pellew to the command of the East India Station in February 1808, found his resources unequal to meet demands of the Government and the merchants for protection of trade. Drury had five ships in the dock, and except his flagship the *Russel* and the *Modeste* under Captain George Elliot, no other effective man-of-war was to be found in India. Reinforcements from Britain were badly needed. The disposable part of the navy was assigned to carry out a variety of duties in different parts of the Indian seas. Three frigates and five sloops of war were in the Ganges, stationed for the protection of the trade of Bengal. One frigate was stationed between Cape Negrais and Ceylon; another between Acheen and the Nicobars; and a third with a sloop on the west coast of Sumatra occasionally looking into the Straits of Malacca. A frigate was appointed to convoy the Bombay trade to and from China, and a ship of the line to attend the regular

---

[46] TNA Adm. 1/180. Agents and Secretaries to several Insurance Companies at Calcutta to Lord Minto. Undated. The Government's reply to it was dated 11 March 1808, Fort William.

[47] TNA Adm. 1/180. Rear-Admiral Sir Edward Pellew to Honble W.W. Pole, Admiralty, HMS *Culloden* at Sea, 22 February 1808.

[48] Ibid.

[49] TNA Adm. 1/181. Orders issued by Rear-Admiral Sir Edward Pellew to the Captains of the *Rattlesnake*, *Dasher*, *Samarang* and *Victor*, Madras Roads, 8 October 1808.

China ships. Three frigates were in the Gulf with Malcolm, and another batch was at Bombay waiting to proceed to the Gulf at his call.[50]

The losses at sea could not be checked. In June 1809, the *Rattlesnake*, which was accompanying a convoy from Penang to Bengal was lost to the French. This was followed by the loss of the *Streatham* and the *Europe*. Minto sent a dispatch to Drury accompanied by various complaints from the merchants at Calcutta, who requested the transmission of their grievances through the Court of Directors to the Admiralty, and demanded more effective protection of their trade.[51] Drury however refused to 'satisfy the caprice of the commercial part of Calcutta' or to listen to what he termed their 'imaginary distresses'. His attitude was clearly reflected in the following passage, '... the Gentlemen of Calcutta must recollect that in regard to the Navy they are neither the Law nor the Gospel, and it will never be found by them that the Squadron under my Command is steered by Compass alone'.[52]

Drury was impatient with the merchants' complaints and he also resented Minto's directions to him to suspend the blockade of Java and the Moluccas. The Court of Directors became alarmed at the heavy losses at sea. In April 1810, Bosanquet, then Deputy-Chairman, wrote to Minto that sea losses had recently amounted to at least £1,100,000 and that further losses were encountered at the capture of the *Charlton*, *United Kingdom* and *Windham*.[53]

Strategic Issues in Anglo-French Confrontation

It was becoming increasingly clear that for the safety of the British ships and commerce in the Indian seas, the French must be expelled from their pockets in the Indian Ocean. Naval enterprise in the Eastern seas would be impossible without a naval station. Experience showed that from the nature of the British commerce in the Eastern seas, it was impracticable to provide general convoys except to China and even then there would be ships unable to join the convoy due to scheduling conflicts. The restrictions imposed on the merchants by the convoy system were such as to hamper the free development of British commerce. Hence for the sake of unfettered development and prosperity of unhindered British trade, the French Islands had to be taken and occupied.

The plan to conquer the islands by a joint military and naval attack was recommended by Wellesley in 1803 and by Pellew in 1806. Both efforts were nullified by the non-cooperation of the navy and the Government of India, respectively, without specific orders from the home authorities. In

---

[50] TNA Adm. 1/181. Drury to Minto, HMS *Russel*, 25 April 1809.

[51] TNA Adm. 1/182. The Governor-General-in-Council to Drury, Fort William, 26 June 1809.

[52] TNA Adm. 1/182. Drury to the Hon'ble W.W. Pole, Admiralty, HMS *Russel* off Colombo, 17 December 1809.

[53] NLS Minto Papers Box 67. Bosanquet to Minto, East India House, 23 April 1810.

1810, Minto's will and determination combined with the cooperation of Rear-Admirals Bertie and Drury, brought about the neutralisation of the islands of Bourbon and L'Ile de France, a measure which was long overdue.

From 1807 to 1809, the French Islands enjoyed immunity from attack by the British because during these years the attention of the Foreign Office and the Indian Government was focused on the Persian Gulf. The presence of General Gardane and his entourage in Persia and the alleged pro-French sympathies of the chieftains in the Gulf region was a matter of more grave concern to the British than the activities of Decaen or the privateers in Bourbon and Mauritius. Hence, at the height of the French threat, which may be dated from the Treaty of Finkenstein in 1807 until the departure of General Gardane from Persia in 1809, the French Islands enjoyed comparative immunity. It was only after the disappearance of the apprehension of an invasion of India from the north-western frontier by the French after both Gardane had withdrawn from Persia, and Napoleon was too harassed on the Continent to turn his attention to an eastern expedition, that Minto was able to focus strategically on the French Islands.

In 1810, there was hardly any possibility of large reinforcements being sent from France to Decaen, although from intercepted dispatches it appeared that Napoleon had promised reinforcements and Decaen was anxiously awaiting their arrival. One or two French frigates did slip out from Brest, Toulon and Nantes and arrived at L'Ile de France, but the departure of substantial reinforcements from Europe was practically impossible. The French ports were under close observation of the British navy, and Napoleon clearly needed all available forces in Europe. Minto wrote to the Secret Committee:

> The Establishment of the Enemy at the French Islands, although it affords the means of the most injurious annoyance to the British Commerce cannot be considered to be a source of material danger to our Indian possessions.... The small extent of the Territory of the French Islands, their distance from India and deficient resources, imposed a limit of the aggrandizement of the strength of the French and on their means of injury in that quarter.[54]

The two principal motives that induced Minto to undertake the conquest of the French Islands were to achieve security of commerce and to facilitate the eventual occupation of Java. It was necessary therefore, to stop the commerce raiding operations of the French frigates and privateers. The blockade could continue indefinitely without bringing about the surrender of the islands or stopping the activities of the French privateers. The convoy system was also an inadequate solution to the problem. With regard to the failure of the blockading system, Minto wrote:

[54] BL, IOR Bengal Secret Letters, 1810, Vol. 12, Minto to the Secret Committee, Fort St George, 23 January 1810.

From the Isle of France all the cruisers have been sent out against our trade, against which a very large squadron have done little to protect us. The losses of the Company as well as of the general trade have been enormous. The Islands have been blockaded by a squadron under Admiral Bertie who commands at the Cape and they have experienced some distress from that measure, but none sufficient to produce even a chance, as it appears to me, of their surrender.[55]

From a direct attack on the islands, Minto hoped to secure the Company against the heavy losses it had recently suffered in the capture and sinking of their ships. He saw that the Company would be continually exposed to such losses as long as the French enjoyed the use of the ports of Bourbon and L'Ile de France. Additionally, the neutralisation of the French Islands was the first step toward the neutralisation of Java which was in fact Minto's 'ulterior motive'. The union of Holland and France brought the Dutch East Indies under the French flag. Strategically, Java could be used much more effectively than Mauritius. Java was self-supporting, and under efficient management could become a useful naval base. Its situation on the route to China was such as to render it a highly dangerous weapon in the hands of the enemies of Britain. If the French privateers made Java their base of operations, its effects were likely to be ruinous to the Company's China trade. Java was therefore to be conquered, but it was necessary to first secure a rearguard action.[56] Minto decided 'to prosecute the less arduous enterprise of an attack on the Isle of Bourbon, the success of which may probably lead to the surrender of the principal French Settlement on the Isle of France'.[57]

The decision to attack the island of Bourbon was brought about partly by certain favourable circumstances. In July 1808, Rear-Admiral Bertie of the Cape had written to Minto that the occupation of Rodriguez would facilitate the blockade and requested him to cooperate by providing a troop of fifty Europeans, fifty sepoys and fifty to a hundred lascars.[58] Minto had then replied that he could not provide any considerable force from India except the very skeleton array requested by Bertie.[59]

In December 1808, as the clamour of the merchants and insurance companies for more effective protection of trade increased in volume, and petitions were sent to the Admiralty, the Lords Commissioners ordered Bertie to strengthen the blockade and promised reinforcements from Britain.[60] The

---

55 NLS M 38. No. 5. Minto to Lady Minto, 26 March 1810.
56 BL, IOR Bengal Sec, & Sep. Cons. 230, Cons. of 24 April 1810, No. 4. Minute of the Governor-General, 24 April 1810.
57 BL, IOR Ben. Sec. Letters 1810, Vol. 12. Minto to the Secret Committee, Fort St George, 23 January 1810.
58 BL, IOR Ben. Secret Cons. 204, No. 4. Bertie to Minto, *Leopard* at Sea, 18 July 1808.
59 Ibid., No. 10. Minto to Bertie, Fort William, 7 November 1808.
60 TNA Adm. 2/1367. Secret Orders and Letters. The Lords Commissioners to Admiral Bertie, 22 December 1808.

Secret Committee at the same time wrote to the Government of Bombay that it was considered advisable to occupy the island of Rodriguez by force in order to use it as a naval station and depot. Jonathan Duncan was ordered to furnish the troops required by Bertie. As the blockade of the French Islands affected the trade of the Arab traders from the Persian Gulf, the Secret Committee advised Duncan to make the necessary explanations about the nature and objective of the blockade to them. Duncan also aroused the suspicion of the chiefs of the Persian Gulf, particularly the Imam of Muscat, about the alleged designs of the French to establish themselves in force in the Persian Gulf. The blockade of the French Islands was to be represented to the Arabs 'as calculated for their protection and providing for the security of their interests in common with those of the British Government'.[61] The home authorities entertained an idea that the occupation of Rodriguez and the tightening of the blockade would force the other two islands to capitulate.[62] Bertie's reports to the Admiralty gave an impression that Bourbon and L'Ile de France suffered greatly from the blockade and starvation and would surrender on the first summons. In March 1809, the Secret Committee wrote to Minto that a body of troops should be sent from India to take possession of the islands, if upon Bertie's representations it should appear that either one or both islands were likely to surrender to the blockade.[63] On the urgent request of Bertie, a force consisting of 200 Europeans and 200 sepoys under Lieutenant Colonel Keating of the Bombay Establishment was dispatched from Bombay in May 1809. On 4 August 1809, Rodriguez was occupied without resistance by a joint enterprise led by Commodore Rowley of the Cape Squadron and Keating.[64]

The First Step: Rodriguez Island

The small volcanic island of Rodriguez, inhabited by three French planters and some indentured labour, was situated about 300 miles to the east of L'Ile de France. It was a suitable place for the marshalling of troops for an attack on the two larger islands. It provided the British with a base from where a close watch could be maintained.[65] Keating reported that the Americans

---

61 BL, IOR Board's Secret Drafts, Vol. 3, No. 50. Secret Committee to the Governor-General-in-Council at Bombay, 27 December 1808.

62 NLS Minto Papers Box 69. R. Dundas to Minto, 26 December 1808 (Private).

63 BL, IOR Board's Secret Drafts, Vol. 3. No. 53. Secret Committee to the Governor-General-in-Council in Bengal, 27 March 1809 (Secret).

64 BL, IOR Bengal Secret Letters 1809, Vol. 11, Minto to the Secret Committee, 24 March 1809.

65 L'Ile de France (Mauritius) is to the windward of Rodriguez. The prevailing wind being east-south-east, it took only forty-eight hours to reach L'Ile de France from Rodriguez.

had made repeated efforts since 1794 to buy Rodriguez from the French, and in 1806 an American ship also surveyed the island. In the beginning of 1808 they had offered 9 million dollars to Bonaparte to secure a grant of the island. 'The Emperor refused; remarking Rodriguez is to windward and is the advance-guard to the other islands; and whoever has it must have all.'[66] What the emperor's thoughts were Keating could not imagine, but he wished the Government of India would follow up on the occupation of Rodriguez by the conquest of the other two islands. The supposed strength of Decaen's garrisons and fortifications was the chief defence of L'Ile de France and Bourbon. It was a belief generated by the lack of accurate information. That myth however was soon exploded by the efforts of Commodore Rowley and Keating.

The occupation of Rodriguez was swiftly followed by a successful attack on Port St Paul in the island of Bourbon by Rowley and Keating. Rowley was prompted to attack St Paul in order to recover the two British frigates *Streatham* and *Europe* lying in harbour, and Keating willingly cooperated. On 21 September 1809, British troops landed about seven miles from St Paul and took the French by surprise. However, the French commandant at St Paul, Saint Mihiel, did not surrender without a response, but nevertheless was forced to submit on 23 September. The Governor of Bourbon, General De Bruslys, shot himself in a fit of depression. Rowley and Keating remained on St Paul for a few days and departed for Rodriguez on 2 October with the spoils of victory. They captured *La Caroline*, a frigate of forty-six guns, and *Grapler*, a brig of eleven guns, took five merchantmen – the *Streatham*, *Europe*, *Fanny*, *Tres Amis*, *La Creole* – and destroyed four smaller vessels.[67]

The successful attack on Port St Paul at once revealed the weakness of the French forces and fortifications and their lack of preparedness to meet an attack from the British. The advantages enjoyed by the French were conse-quently largely due to British ignorance regarding the magnitude (or lack thereof) of the actual defences. By observation and from intercepted French dispatches and informers on the islands, Keating collected a mass of infor-mation about Bourbon and L'Ile de France. The captains of the blockading squadron, Rowley, Willoughby, Corbett and Pym, cruised around the islands to select a suitable place for the landing of troops among the coral reefs which surrounded the islands. During the actual operations, it was found that half the battle was won after a successful landing had been made. Keating wrote to General Hewitt:

---

[66] NLS M 337. Keating to J. Duncan, Governor of Bombay, 14 March 1810.

[67] BL, IOR The French in India Series, Vol. 1, Bundle 1, Pkt. 6G. Lt Col. Keating to F. Warden (Chief Secretary to the Bombay Government), St Paul, 29 September 1809. British casualties were fifteen killed and fifty-eight wounded in a force of 368 officers and men. Malleson's account of the attack on Port St Paul is not entirely accurate. See Malleson, G.B., *Final French Struggles in India* (London, 1878), pp. 117–23.

... the Islands are to be conquered more by good arrangement & stratagem than by numbers; besides there is no regular Fortification upon either island, nor is there any post likely to hold out half an hour if properly attacked, all must be carried by the Petite guerre or War of Ports.[68]

The French Islands depended entirely on their naval forces and fortifications for their defence. No inland fort could hold out if an enemy occupied their ports and coasts. The French realised that the only method of defending the colony was to provide for the security of its ports, and so there were no other fortifications on the islands. The exact strength and composition of Decaen's land forces is not known. The French and the British sources give varying figures.[69] According to Keating's report, Decaen, when forced to retreat from Pondicherry in 1803, brought the greater part of the force intended by Bonaparte to form the nucleus of a French army in India to the French Islands. At that period, the European force consisted of nearly 1,200 regulars and a considerable body of officers who were to have organised the sepoy corps. By 1810, the effective strength of this corps was reduced to about 900, divided between the two islands. Many of the officers had returned to Europe while others were dispersed among the militia. According to Keating, besides the European corps, there was in L'Ile de France a battalion of 1,000 regulars composed of Creoles and Mulattos so that altogether there were about 1,600 regulars (600 Europeans and 1,000 Creoles and Mulattos) on the islands of Bourbon and L'Ile de France. Of these, about 500 were at Port Louis in L'Ile de France and the remainder dispersed in the batteries around the coast. Aside from the regulars, there was the National Militia. Before Decaen's arrival at L'Ile de France, the defence of the island was entirely entrusted to the militia. The militia were well organised and disciplined and in 1810, numbered about 3,000 on L'Ile de France and 2,500 on Bourbon. Despairing of receiving reinforcements from France, Decaen had proposed arming the indentured labour of about 4,000, but it was regarded by the planters as too dangerous an experiment and Decaen was obliged to desist. The crews of the French frigates and privateers were also available for military service.[70]

The inhabitants of the islands had suffered much during the years of the blockade and the stoppage of funds from the mother country. They were obliged to find money for public expenses and were heavily taxed. This did not make Decaen very popular and as sources of relief, prizes of various types were anxiously sought to be sold immediately and money raised for the payment of military, naval and civil officers of every department. The success

---

68 NLS M 365. Extract of a letter from Lt Col. Keating to General Hewitt. Fort Duncan (Rodriguez), 10 February 1810.
69 Parkinson, C.N., *War in the Eastern Seas, 1793–1815* (London, 1954), p. 449. Appendix I: The Garrison of Mauritius.
70 NLS M 368. Lt Col. Keating to Minto, Fort Duncan, Rodriguez, 25 March 1810.

of Rowley and Keating at St Paul removed the fundamental basis of their economy and livelihood. Keating wrote to Minto:

> The great mass of the inhabitants are Creoles, who having existed so long without the protection of the mother country, & now suffering from severe & unexampled imposts, ruled over with military tyranny & their commerce annihilated, it could not be expected that they will be hearty in staking the remains of their property, & their persons in defence of a Government they are dissatisfied with, especially when by experience they know that their persons and their property, their religion and their customs would be respected & protected by their enemy; & also the additional inducement of a present market for their colonial products now lying in their warehouses & a provision for the disposal of their future industry.[71]

If the goodwill of the planters and the Creoles could be secured, Decaen would be left to fight with the regular troops. The neutrality of the inhabitants could be secured by assuring them the protection of their rights by the British. The inhabitants in general, particularly the planters, possessed large numbers of slaves. The proportion of slaves to free men on the islands was about 100 to eight. If the islands were occupied by the British, the inhabitants dreaded nothing more than the freedom that they might give to the slaves, which they feared would not only be attended with ruin and loss of their plantations and property, but end in murder and anarchy. Keating therefore recommended that in order to conciliate the inhabitants of the islands, no measure was to be taken for the abolition of slavery in the islands after British occupation.

The two islands could not be attacked simultaneously due to the lack of adequate means. L'Ile de France could be attacked first in preference to Bourbon as it was not only the seat of government, but the principal depot of naval and military stores, and Bourbon was likely to succumb more easily after the larger island was taken. If Bourbon was attacked first it would give ample notice to Decaen to prepare his defences. However, it would also give the British a place from which supplies could be drawn and also where the army could retire if the succeeding attack on L'Ile de France failed. If Bourbon was taken first, the means of the French would be much reduced and the only place of escape lost to them.

Rear-Admiral Drury recommended that the first concentrated and determined attack should be made on L'Ile de France.[72] Minto however refused to sanction a direct attack on L'Ile de France 'without a more distinct knowledge... of the difficulties which may oppose that enterprise, and of the means which may be required to insure success'.[73]

---

[71] NLS M 368. Keating to Minto, 25 March 1810, Fort Duncan, Rodriguez.
[72] TNA Adm. 1/182. Drury to Minto, HMS *Russel*, Madras Roads, 22 February 1810.
[73] TNA Adm. 1/182. Minto to Drury, Fort St George, 12 March 1810.

Admiral Bertie in his letter of 7 December 1809 had supplied information which also encouraged an immediate and direct attack on the main island. Minto gave him the same reason as he had given to Drury for not attacking L'Ile de France immediately, and the advantages he hoped to derive from the previous occupation of Bourbon. An additional reason for deferring the attack on L'Ile de France was that a large portion of the force necessary for the attack was to be drawn from the Cape.

Minto sought Bertie's cooperation in the undertaking and assured him that:

> In the measures which I have thus thought it advisable to pursue for the reduction of the Isle of Bourbon, I have not been unmindful that the Mauritius is an object of still greater importance and the conquest of that Island has from the beginning been directly contemplated in the mediated attack upon Bourbon.[74]

Minto's policy of caution was supported by the two commanders-in chief, General Hewitt of Bengal and Major-General Abercromby of Bombay. The absence of any authentic information about the state of the defences of L'Ile de France made it impossible to draw up any sure plan of attack. Hewitt complained, '... we have not the slightest sketch, plan or memoir, either of the Country of works... the latter is said to be extensive'.[75] The inhabitants had once compelled Decaen to relinquish his design of arming the slaves, but with the enemy on their coast that measure if adopted, could be very effective in a country like Mauritius where the natural defences were strong. In 1794, it was believed that a force of 5,000 Europeans would be sufficient to initiate a successful attack on L'Ile de France, however since that time General Decaen had been busy fortifying Port Louis and might have constructed other defences on the island. Hewitt preferred one of the two alternate suggestions made by Keating, that for a regular attack on L'Ile de France, Bourbon should be occupied first.[76]

Major-General Abercromby subscribed to Hewitt's views. Keating's reports on the state of the garrison and defences of L'Ile de France were not confirmed by any other source. The Government did not possess any information regarding the state of the natural and artificial defences of that island, specifically the strength of Decaen's garrison, showing the approximate number of Europeans, Militia, Caffres and armed slaves if any; the nature and extent of the works at Port Louis; and the different points of disembarkation, their distance from Port Louis and the nature of the intervening geography.[77]

---

[74] TNA Adm. 1/63. Minto to Bertie, Fort St George, 26 March 1810.
[75] NLS M 365. Hewitt to Minto, Madras, 19 April 1810.
[76] Ibid.
[77] NLS M 365. Abercromby to General Hewitt, Bombay, April 1810.

Hewitt roughly estimated that Decaen had about 1,200 Europeans and 8,000 militia, that is, a force of almost 10,000 troops at his disposal, not including the Caffres, armed slaves and seamen that might add another 7,000 to 8,000 troops. The works at L'Ile de France were said to be out of range of the British ships and it was unsafe to rely on treachery, cowardice or famine. Hewitt therefore came to the conclusion that L'Ile de France could not be attacked with fewer than 10,000 troops.[78] Abercromby concurred with Hewitt that a force consisting of 8,000 Europeans and 5,000 sepoys would be adequate for an attack on L'Ile de France.[79] Both Hewitt and Abercromby expected Decaen to put up a strong resistance against the British attack. Events were to prove that they were wrong in their estimation of Decaen and his resources. In a minute dated 24 April 1810, Minto wrote, 'The information acquired by the brilliant and successful exploit of St. Paul's on the Isle of Bourbon in the Month of September, led me to contemplate the expediency of undertaking an Expedition with a view to the conquest, and permanent occupation of that Island.'[80]

The fall of Bourbon might not necessarily lead to the surrender of the main island which was dependent on Bourbon for supplies, yet certain advantages were expected from it. Minto wrote:

> ... the advantage of obtaining possession of Bourbon, in depriving the Enemy of a place of refuge, which has always afforded him the means of securing the fruits of his extensive depradations on our Commerce, and of eluding the vigilance of our Cruizers; in cutting off the chief source of Supplies to the Isle of France, and in enabling His Majesty' Ships, effectually to maintain the blockade of that Island, ... constitute in my opinion a Sufficient inducement to the undertaking; the expense of which also would even in a pecuniary point of view be compensated, by securing the Hon'ble Company against a repetition of such heavy losses as have recently been sustained in the Capture of their Ships, losses to which the Company must continue to be exposed, so long as the French Ships and Privateers shall possess the means of entering and issuing from the Ports of the French Islands, unobserved by the Ships of the blockading Squadron.[81]

Minto's cautious policy related to his war strategy, consisting of three successive steps – each setting the foundation for the next – the attack on Bourbon to be followed by L'Ile de France and finally the occupation of Java. He later wrote to General Grey at the Cape:

[78] NLS M 365. Hewitt to Minto, Madras, 19 April 1810.
[79] NLS M 365. Abercromby to Hewitt, Bombay, April 1810.
[80] BL, IOR Ben. Sec. & Sep. Cons. 230. Cons. of 24 April 1810. No. 4. Minute of the Governor-General, 24 April 1810, Fort William.
[81] Ibid.

This enchainment of the measures now in progress has enabled me to proceed on sure ground, and was necessary for the general interests of the public service, but indispensable in the case of so great an effort compared with our resources and of so burthensome and chargeable an enterprize, undertaken on Individual judgment alone, & unsanctioned by any competent authority.[82]

The Second Target: Bourbon

The earliest practicable time when the operation could be safely under-taken off the French Islands was after the end of the hurricane season in mid-March. As Commodore Rowley of the Cape Station was willing to cooperate with the expedition from India, Drury was only required to cooperate by appointing an adequate naval force for the protection of the ships employed in transporting the troops to Rodriguez.[83] Keating had recommended that a reinforcement of about 2,000 men should be sent from India, which in conjunction with the force at Rodriguez would easily occupy Bourbon.[84] However, Minto taking into account the possibility of Decaen's sending reinforcements to Bourbon, decided to send a larger military force from Madras, consisting of 1,922 Europeans and 1,850 sepoys, shipping required for transport, about 9,000 tons, stores, provisions and ordnance were provided by the three Presidencies.[85]

In sending an expedition against Bourbon in May 1810, Minto overcame a serious obstacle with regard to sending out a European force from India, particularly Madras, at that time. A mutiny had broken out among the officers of the Madras army in April 1809 against the civil government. In August 1809, Minto went to Madras and spent nearly nine months trying to enforce discipline and bring back a measure of harmony between the civil and military authorities. On the night of 7 May 1810, the expedition to Bourbon sailed from Madras and on the following day, Minto returned to Calcutta.[86] The troubles in Madras may well have prevented the expedition to Bourbon as an overseas expedition could only be carried out when there was a measure of stability in internal affairs. Minto wrote to Dundas:

> The fact that such a large armament could be sent out of India, gave satis-factory proof of the Company's resources in India, & the perfect tranquillity

---

82 NLS M 206. Minto to Lt General Grey, Commander of HM troops at the Cape, Fort William, 21 October 1810.

83 BL, IOR Ben. Sec. & Sep. Cons. 230. Cons. of 24 April 1810, No. 7., Drury to Minto, *Russel*, Madras Roads, 8 February 1810.

84 NLS M 38. No. 5, Minto to Lady Minto, 26 March 1810.

85 BL, IOR Ben. Sec. Letters Vol. 12. Minto to Secret Committee, Fort St George, 6 February 1810.

86 NLS M 38. Minto to Lady Minto, No. 8, Calcutta, 31 May 1810.

which was maintained in the absence of so large a body of troops, principally H.M. Regiments, afforded favorable [*sic*] views of the political state without and of security within after the entire suppression of the recent troubles.[87]

In undertaking the expedition against the French Islands, Minto acted against the prohibitory orders of the Court of Directors against any enterprise involving financial burden on the Company. He offered the following arguments in his defence. First, that the objective proposed by the measures adopted by him would be considered desirable by the home government upon their accomplishment. Second, that there was no other way of attaining these objectives except by the course he adopted. Third, that he was confident of success if the measures were adopted at the time that they were in terms of the criticality of the losses of British shipping to the French privateers operating from the islands. He added, 'Fourthly, (and this is the strong point of my defence, without which all the rest would be invalid), I was intimately convinced… that the service would have become impracticable by delay and expecially the delay necessary for asking and receiving instructions.'[88]

Minto could also argue that his warlike measures would in fact be measures of economy. The blockade could not be effectively enforced and the costs for maintaining this attempted surveillance and control were also heavy. Hence, the conquest of the islands would not only secure the Company's trade against further losses at sea, it would also relieve HM Government from a heavy charge and a number of valuable ships would be added to the navy. The commercial value of the colonies as a market of a population of nearly 260,000 for British-made goods was also taken into consideration. Minto calculated that under efficient management, Mauritius would prove a valuable acquisition to the British.

Minto was so confident of success, he appointed Robert Farquhar, a Madras civil servant who had distinguished himself as Commercial Resident at Amboyna and also a Special Commissioner in the Moluccas, to proceed with the troops to Bourbon as the provisional governor. Minto directed him to avoid any pledge in the capitulation that might preclude the future modification of the system of government of the island or the enactment of laws and regulations by the British. Farquhar was vested with civil as well as military responsibilities and was to be paid a salary of £4,500 per annum, an amount usually granted to a resident at a foreign court.[89]

Minto stated certain general principles regarding the internal administration and the government of the colony. The existing system of local laws

[87] NLS M 377. Minto to Robert Dundas, Fort William, 1 January 1811.

[88] NLS M 377. Minto to R. Dundas, Weltervreeden, Java, 4 September 1811.

[89] BL, IOR Ben. Sec. & Sep. Cons. 230. Cons. of 15 May 1810, No. 11. Minto to Farquhar, Fort St George, 30 April 1810.

and administration was to be maintained subject of course to such modifi-
cations as the security of the colony under British authority might require.
The primary objective was to reconcile the minds of the inhabitants to the
change of authority. Hence the laws, usages and privileges to which they were
accustomed were to be retained and oppressive laws and heavy taxes were to
be suspended or modified. The religious establishments of the inhabitants
of the islands and the system of jurisprudence were to be maintained and
Minto sanctioned the continuance of existing tribunals for administration of
justice according to French laws. The Governor of Bourbon was to enjoy such
authority and control with regard to judicial matters as was constitutionally
vested in the local government.

These general principles of policy were to be followed with regard to both
the islands. In an enclosure to his letter of 30 April 1810 to Farquhar and
his letter to the Secret Committee of the same date, Minto stated his views
regarding L'Ile de France. As soon as circumstances would justify and the
necessary information collected, reinforcements would be sent from India to
join the Bourbon contingent to attack the principal settlement of the enemy.
Minto had already written to the Governor of the Cape, Lord Caledon,
asking him to cooperate in the operations against Mauritius by sending a
body of European troops to Madras. After the capture of the main island,
Farquhar was to become the Governor of L'Ile de France and its dependencies and Keating to become the Lieutenant-Governor of Bourbon, acting
under the former.

With regard to Bourbon it was not necessary to burden the British
Government with the payment either of the principal or the interest of the
public debts at that island. With regard to L'Ile de France however, 'if it
should be found to contribute materially to the Surrender of that Island',
Minto authorised Farquhar to engage for the payment of interest only of such
loans as at the time of surrender may be bona fide property of the inhabitants
of the island, to the extent which may be practicable after paying for the fixed
establishments. On no account however, was he to undertake the payment of
the principal of those debts.[90]

The troops from Madras arrived at Rodriguez on 20 June and Keating
took command. The whole armament consisting of 1,800 Europeans and
1,850 sepoys under Keating accompanied by *Boadicea*, *Nereide* and *Sirius* under
Rowley, Willoughby and Pym, reached the point of rendezvous fifty miles
windward from the island of Bourbon on the evening of 6 July 1810. Keating
decided to strike first at the capital, St Denis, in order to avoid protracted
warfare in the interior of the country, and also to ensure the capture of the
island in the shortest possible time by securing the garrison and the governor
who were at St Denis. Before the attack could be made however, the French

[90] Ibid.

Commanding Officer, Colonel St Susanne sent out an officer to demand the suspension of arms and proposed to surrender the island on honourable terms. According to Keating's report St Susanne had 4,193 men at his disposal, of which 576 were regulars, 417 creole militia, 900 National Guard and 2,300 militia, yet he surrendered without resistance.[91]

The capitulation for the surrender of Bourbon was signed by St Susanne, Rowley, Keating and Farquhar on 8 July 1810. Some concessions were made to the honour of the vanquished army. The French troops of the line and the Garde Nationale were allowed all the honours of war. The French officers, 'in consideration of the gallant defence of the island', were allowed to preserve their swords and military decorations. The French troops and officers taken prisoners of war were to be transported to the Cape or to Britain. All public property was taken over. The British declared, 'The laws, customs and religion of the Inhabitants, as well as their Private property of all description shall be respected and insured to them.'[92]

The next day the entire island was delivered to the British. Farquhar took up residence at St Denis as governor. The British grenadiers took possession of the posts vacated by the French and the French vessels at Port St Paul were taken over by Rowley.[93]

The Third Target: L'Ile de France

News of the capture of Bourbon reached Calcutta toward the end of August 1810. Preparations were already in progress for an expedition against L'Ile de France, which Minto had determined to undertake before the end of the year. Minto wrote to the Secret Committee:

> It had now been ascertained that the surrender of the Isle of France would not necessarily follow the loss of the Sister Island. Our occupation of Bourbon would indeed distress the Enemy and facilitate the operations of the blockade, but could not preclude though it might interrupt & render difficult the arrival of succours & supplies at the Isle of France, ... our possession of the former would naturally excite on the part of France the utmost possible exertions to provide for the defence & security of the latter,... which when successful would... require on our part a corresponding augmentation of the local maritime force

[91] BL, IOR Ben. Sec. & Sep. Cons. 230. Cons. of 25 August 1810, Keating to Duncan, 21 July 1810. TNA Adm. 1/63. Rowley to Bertie, HMS *Boadicea*, Road of St Denis, Isle of Bourbon, 11 July 1810.

[92] BL, IOR Home Misc. Series 701, pp. 301–03. Capitulation for the surrender of the Island of Buonaparte, 8 July 1810.

[93] The French ship *Lottery* and associated vessels, *Buchanan*, *Favorite*, *Welcome Return* and the government schooner *La Mouilene* were taken. TNA Adm. 1/63. A List of Vessels captured in the Bay of St Paul's, 11 July 1810.

to place us merely in the same situation relative to the French power in the Indian sea which we held before.[94]

L'Ile de France was the stronghold of the French and the chief centre of Decaen's naval and military force. The loss of Bourbon cut off one of its chief source of supplies, but it did not mean that L'Ile de France would starve. Privateers and neutral traders continued to be suppliers and as long as they managed to evade the blockade, Decaen could hope to maintain the status quo. Minto felt that the delay of a single season in attacking L'Ile de France would be injurious to British interests as he believed that Decaen would receive reinforcements during the hurricane season when it was impossible to maintain a close watch on the island. The safe period of operations off the French Islands was from May until about the middle of December, after which 'violent hurricanes which seem to live in those islands, come out like swallows at certain seasons',[95] made it unsafe for ships to rendezvous off the island without a safe anchor. The French however were known to utilise these months, when the British ships withdrew to safer harbours to throw in supplies. If therefore the attack on L'Ile de France was postponed until the following May, Decaen would have ample time to prepare his defences and also receive the expected reinforcements from France. Minto wrote, 'This is one of several reasons and certainly the strongest which made me "damnatus obstinatus mulier" (vide Cowslip's translation), and determined me to prepare & push off the expedition now, whether it was possible or not.'[96]

In a dispatch dated 27 June 1810, Farquhar wrote to Minto about the amount of force necessary for the reduction of L'Ile de France. It was accompanied by memoranda from Keating and Rowley. Keating, Rowley and Farquhar considered a force of 6,000 Europeans and 3,000 sepoys, with 200 artillery and one troop of cavalry, necessary and sufficient to secure the success of a regular attack on L'Ile de France.[97] Farquhar also wrote that after the capture of Bourbon:

> It is intended vigorously to employ our little force, to distress and harass him [Decaen] at every point, to bombard his Towns and Shipping, and to keep his Coasts in a constant state of alarm... By these means,... it is within the range of possibility that their actual sufferings... and the example... which the Island of Bourbon will hold up to them... of the advantages which are so abundantly enjoyed by those who have the happiness to live under a British Government,

---

94   NLS M 196. Secret & Separate General Letter, 25 October 1810. Also BL, IOR Ben. Sec. Letters, Vol. 12.
95   NLS M 38, No. 13. Minto to Lady Minto, Calcutta, 19 September 1810.
96   NLS M 38. No. 13. Minto to Lady Minto, Calcutta, 19 September 1810.
97   BL, IOR French in India Series, Vol. 14. Farquhar to Minto, Rodriguez, 27 June 1810 (Most Secret). Ibid. Memorandum by Keating, Fort Duncan, 26 June 1810. Ibid. Memorandum by Rowley, Rodriguez, 26 June 1810.

will induce that Colony [L'Ile de France] already discontented... to seize some favorable opportunity of craving the protection of the British Government.[98]

Both Hewitt and Abercromby doubted the soundness of Farquhar's proposal of the desultory and intermittent attacks on the inhabitants of the coast and their property. In their opinion, such a course of action would not only injure the British character with the inhabitants, but was likely to unite the inhabitants and the troops in a general bond of union to resist the British.[99] Minto also would not sanction such a course of action, but he was willing to rely on the recommendations made by Farquhar and Keating with regard to the primary attack on L'Ile de France.

Opinions were widely divided as to the strength of Decaen's force, the nature of the opposition which might be encountered, the time that the expedition could be optimally accomplished (both in terms of available vessels, resources and the season) and the strength and composition of the force to be sent. Hence the final decision had to be taken by Minto and he had to take full responsibility for the consequences. The expedition against Mauritius was pushed forward by him 'sometimes by absolute determination rather than by visible means',[100] so that the conquest was accomplished five months sooner than it would otherwise have been. He wrote to Dundas:

> ... there were great and real difficulties in the way of an immediate execution of the plan, at the time of receiving the reports from Commodore Rowley and Lt. Col. Keating, upon which the final resolution was to be founded; and they were so great that I stood single in the opinion that they might be surmounted by exertion, and the measure was practicable before the tempestuous season.[101]

By September 1810 all preparations were in place. Minto wrote to Lady Minto:

> After many difficulties, doubts and anxieties, our armament is now complete & all afloat. The force is such, both in numbers & quality, as to secure success – nothing but improbable disasters at sea, from weather, can prevent the attack being made immediately after the force arrives & is all assembled at the point of destination. It has required a little wholesome pertinacity on my part to carry this business through all the obstacles, which seem'd to oppose it; and a pretty strong & general opinion of all those who I am bound to consult, of its immediate impracticability, was not the smallest of the difficulties in our way.... I do flatter myself with success in this very important affair, for it will be

98   BL, IOR French in India Series, Vol. 14. Farquhar to Minto, Rodriguez, 27 June 1810 (Most Secret).
99   NLS M 365. Hewitt to Minto, Madras, 20 July 1810 (Private). Ibid., P. Carey to Edmonstone, Fort St George, 20 July 1810.
100 NLS M 38, No. 13. To Lady Minto, Calcutta, 19 September 1810.
101 NLS M 377. Minto to R. Dundas, Fort William, 25 January 1811.

a great public benefit, and I hardly know how the arms of G. Britain could be employed more usefully.[102]

He added, 'It stands however, as yet upon my own single responsibility, & I must expect the opinion of Govt. & possibly that of the public to follow the event & take its colour from the result.'[103]

The Campaign for L'Ile de France

The expedition against L'Ile de France sailed more than a month before Minto received the Secret Committee's dispatch communicating the decision of HM's Government to conquer the islands of Bourbon and Mauritius. According to Lord Liverpool's orders, Mauritius was to be taken by a joint military force from the Cape, India and Ceylon, amounting to 8,000 men of which 5,000 were to be Europeans. The Company's establishments in India were to provide 4,000 Europeans and 3,000 natives, the Cape 1,000 Europeans, 200 artillery and a troop of light dragoons, and Ceylon might afford one battalion of British troops, 100 artillery and a native regiment. The home government appointed Sir Samuel Auchmuty, who was sent out from Britain as the commander-in-chief at Fort St George in command of the expedition. According to Liverpool's orders Rear-Admiral Drury was to take command of the naval force. The home government also recommended that the armaments from the Cape and India should assemble at Rodriguez, 'not earlier than the first weeks in May' 1811, and that the first direct attack should be made on Mauritius as Bourbon was expected to follow the fate of the main island. If that attack failed, only then might it be advisable to occupy Bourbon.[104]

Minto had followed a different course of action. He was however relieved to receive the sanction of the home government to the policy of conquest. The arrangements already made could not be modified to fulfil the home government's orders. The composition of the expeditionary force, the place of rendezvous and the time of attack remained as arranged. As Major-General Abercromby was already in command, he could not be superseded by Sir Samuel Auchmuty, and the naval command was retained by Rear-Admiral Bertie of the Cape. Prior to the arrival of reinforcements, Farquhar and Keating busied themselves in issuing proclamations to the inhabitants of L'Ile de France in order to undermine opposition. They were promised 'justice, commerce and plenty' non-interference in their religion, customs and rights

[102] NLS M 38. Minto to Lady Minto, Calcutta, 9 September 1810.
[103] Ibid.
[104] NLS M 172. R. Dundas to Minto, Whitehall, 13 June 1810 (Most Secret). Ibid. Enclosure. Lord Liverpool to Sir S. Auchmuty, Downing Street, 8 June 1810.

if they did not oppose the British conquest. These pamphlets were distributed by the ships of the blockading squadron along the coast.[105]

The French navy at L'Ile de France, however, proved to be more than a match for the British navy in the same waters. On 13 August 1810, a squadron of three ships under Captain Pym captured the small island of Ile de la Passe situated about three miles from the main island and commanding the entrance to the harbour of Grand Port on the south-eastern coast of L'Ile de France. On 20 August, three French frigates under Duperre – the *Bellone*, *Minerve* and *Victor* with two previously captured British ships, the *Windham* and *Ceylon* – returned from their cruise from the Bay of Bengal and made for the Grand Port. They were fired upon by the British, but Duperre managed to enter the harbour of Grand Port leaving behind the *Windham*. Captains Pym and Willoughby decided to destroy Duperre's squadron before the three other French frigates *Venus*, *Astree* and *Manche*, could come from Port Louis to join battle. The four British frigates *Sirius*, *Nereide*, *Iphigenia* and *Magicienne* under Captains Pym, Willoughby, Lambert and Curtis respectively, made a joint attack on the French ships at anchor. The main difficulty encountered by them was of course that they were operating in an area which had not previously been charted by the British. As a result of the combat, *Sirius* and *Magicienne* were destroyed and *Iphigenia* and *Neriede* surrendered to the French after being nearly destroyed in battle. The British garrison at Isle de la Passe surrendered to the French on 23 August 1810, on the arrival of Hamelin's squadron from Port Louis.[106]

The British naval disaster at Isle de la Passe certainly gave the French a temporary naval superiority in the French Islands. A French merchantman which arrived off Port Louis in May 1811 brought the news of great rejoicing in Paris over the loss of the British at Isle de la Passe, and that Napoleon had decreed that no duties were to be imposed on the produce of L'Ile de France.[107] Prentout believed that the French naval victory at Grand Port might have been a turning point in the fortunes of Decaen.[108] Decaen actually sent *L'Iphigenie* and *L'Astree* with the corvette *L'Entreprenant* under the command of Captain Bouvet to cruise off Bourbon. Commodore Rowley of the *Boadicea* quickly responded with the *Otter*, *Staunch* and *Africaine*

---

[105] BL, IOR Secret Letters Received, Vol. 1. R.T. Farquhar to the Court of Directors, Bourbon, 30 July 1810. BL, IOR Home Misc. Series 701, pp. 393–400. Proclamation aux Habitants de L'Ile de France, by R.T. Farquhar.

[106] BL, IOR Ben. Sec. & Sep. Cons. 231. Cons. of 19 October 1810. Nos 10, 34–42. Correspondence on the naval operations at Isle de la Passe. TNA Adm. 1/63. Bertie to J.W. Croker, *Africaine*, St Paul's, 13 October 1810. A detailed account is given in Parkinson, *War in the Eastern Seas*, pp. 383–96; James, W., *Naval History of Great Britain* (London, 1902), Vol. V, pp. 147–70.

[107] NLS M 342, Barlow to Minto, Fort St George, 16 June 1811. Enclosure, Intelligence from the Captain of the *Hermes*.

[108] Prentout, *L'Ile de France sous Decaen*, pp. 561–68.

and came to the aid of the British ships at Grand Port. Bouvet's squadron therefore was forced to turn back. On being engaged by the *Africaine* on 12 September, Bouvet managed to take it; however, Rowley in turn retook the shattered *Africaine* the following day. In a naval action on 18 September, the French Commodore Hamelin captured the *Ceylon* with General Abercromby on board, but Rowley's immediate recovery of the *Ceylon* and following capture of the largest French frigate *La Venus* turned the tide of the battle in favour of the British.[109] The momentary naval superiority gained by the French was halted by Rowley and much of the credit for the ultimate success of the operations against Mauritius rightly belongs to him. Although the French naval successes were temporary, yet with Abercromby, Willoughby and Lambert taken prisoner and Captain Corbett dead prior to the action taken by Rowley, the success of the expedition appeared doubtful. Both sides suffered heavy casualties and many of the frigates on both sides were put out of action. Parkinson's comment on the defeat of the British at Grand Port is caustic: '… the defeat at Grand Port and the capture of the *Africaine* had revealed the weaknesses in the Navy which the Americans rediscovered in 1812; the neglect of gunnery and the over-confidence in innate national superiority'.[110]

On 19 October, Rear-Admiral Bertie arrived to conduct the operations against L'Ile de France in person. He found the French ships in the harbour and left Rowley with the *Boadicea*, *Nisus* and *Nereide* to watch them. Bertie joined Abercromby at the anchorage off Mauritius and were joined by Rear-Admiral Drury on 24 October who brought the *Russel*, *Clorinde*, *Doris*, *Phaeton*, *Bucephalus*, *Cornelia* and *Hesper*. Detaching *Cornelia* and *Hesper* to strengthen the blockade, Bertie sailed with the rest for Rodriguez. The division of troops from Bombay were already there. On 6 November, the Madras division arrived at Rodriguez, followed on the 12th by the division from Bourbon.[111] The presence of the Admirals of the Cape and the Indian station in the same scene at the same time presented problems of its own. Bertie would not share his command with Drury, who in turn was ordered to return to Madras immediately as Bertie declared that he had no business to quit his station.[112]

The obstacles to an attack on Mauritius with a considerable force were the difficulty of landing due to the coral reefs which surrounded every part

---

[109] BL, IOR Ben. Sec. & Sep. Cons. 231, Cons. of 7 December 1810. Nos 6, 8, 9, 15. BL, IOR Secret Letters Received, Vol. 1. R.T. Farquhar to the Earl of Liverpool, Bourbon, 11 October 1810. TNA Adm. 1/63. Bertie to J.W. Croker, *Africaine*, St Paul's, Bourbon, 13 October 1810.

[110] Parkinson, *War in the Eastern Seas*, p. 396.

[111] TNA Adm. 1/63. Vice Admiral Bertie to J.W. Croker, *Africaine*, Port Louis, 6 December 1810.

[112] Ibid., Bertie to Drury, *Africaine*, Rodriguez Roads, 4 November 1810.

of the coast, and finding a safe anchorage for a fleet of transports. These difficulties were alleviated significantly by Rowley who was able to outline a strategy after conducting a comprehensive reconnaissance of the coastline assisted by Lieutenants Street of the Staunch and Blakiston of the Madras Engineers. Every portion of the leeward side of the island was minutely examined, and a breach found in its natural defence. It was discovered that a fleet might anchor in the narrow passage formed by the little island of Coin de Mire and the main island and that in this spot, there were openings through the reefs which would admit several boats to enter abreast. The whole passage and the Mapon Bay within it were undefended.[113] Decaen evidently relied on the natural defences of the north coast to prevent enemy landings.

On 29 November most of the troops with artillery, stores and ammunition were safely landed at Mapon Bay about twelve miles from Port Louis.[114] The French blew up the magazines at Fort Malartic at the head of Grand Bay and retreated in order to take a stand nearer Port Louis. On 30 November the main body of the British army took up position about four miles from Port Louis. The French force between Port Louis and the British line numbered about 3,500 men with four guns and a howitzer under the command of General Vandermaesen, Decaen's second in command. Decaen himself, after a rapid reconnaissance under heavy fire, retired to Port Louis presumably to prepare for defence against an attack from the sea. On 1 December, a short engagement took place, as a result of which the French militia broke and fled. The British troops advanced and took up positions in front of Port Louis. In the meantime, the coastal batteries were taken and Admiral Bertie anchored off the harbour of Port Louis. Abercromby appeared to be in no hurry to deliver the final assault on Port Louis. Decaen, on his part, must have realised the impossibility of a successful opposition to such a large and powerful attack with an insufficient force at his command and no hope of immediate reinforcements. He therefore focused on planning his tactics in such a way as to gain favourable terms of capitulation.

On 3 December 1810, L'Ile de France surrendered. According to the negotiated terms, the French troops and officers, the officers of the navy, crews of the ships of war, as well as the civil authorities were not to be taken prisoners of war. The French troops were allowed to retain their arms and colours, without ammunition and were to be sent with their families to a port in France at the expense of the British. Decaen's demand that the French frigates were not to be surrendered and to be used as troop transports for restitution back to France was not accepted. All public property was taken over by the British and all private property respected. The colonists were given

113 BL, IOR Home Misc. Series 701. Abercromby to Minto, Port Louis, 7 December 1810.
114 TNA Adm. 1/63. Bertie to J.W. Croker, *Africaine*, Port Louis, 6 December 1810.

the option to quit their colony within two years with all movable property or remain under British occupation. The inhabitants were promised that the British would preserve their 'religion, laws and customs'.[115]

The Aftermath

The news of the surrender of L'Ile de France reached Calcutta on 25 January 1811. Minto believed it was a service 'the most important as it is universally considered here, and as in truth I believe it to be, that could be rendered to the East India Company and the nation in the East'.[116]

The Governor-General-in-Council congratulated the British community in India on the conquest of the French Islands:

> ... which by extinguishing the power so long possessed and so successfully exercised by the Enemy of maintaining a predatory warfare in the Indian Seas, has given security to navigation and commerce and augmented the sources of external strength and internal prosperity in this quarter of the British dominions; while it has added a territory not less valuable in a political than in a commercial point of view to the colonial possessions of the Crown.[117]

The Calcutta merchants presented an address to Minto, dated 31 January 1811, expressing joy and relief at the capture of the islands, 'which has for so many years past been the source of devastation to the commerce of India, to a magnitude almost exceeding belief'. In order to commemorate the conquest, they had a portrait of Minto hung in the Council Chamber.[118]

The capture of the French Islands was certainly a feather in the governor-general's cap. It destroyed the French naval force which had been so successful in their commerce-raiding exploits in the Indian Ocean for the past two decades. It deprived France of the last of their old colonies in the East, lamented by Prentout over the loss of 'little France' in the east.[119] Although the French emperor feigned to be happy to get rid of the bankrupt colonies,[120] in actual fact he had only recently ordered five frigates to the East carrying reinforcements to L'Ile de France and Java.

---

[115] BL, IOR Home Misc. Series 701. Articles of Capitulation for the Isle of France, 3 December 1810, pp. 83–92. The Capitulation was signed by General Vandermaesen and Captain Duperre on behalf of Decaen, and by Major-General Warde, Commodore Rowley and Major-General Abercromby.

[116] NLS M 377. Minto to Robert Dundas, Fort William, 25 January 1811.

[117] BL, IOR Ben. Sec. & Sep. Cons. 236. Cons. of 9 February 1811. No. 39. General Orders by the Governor-General-in-Council, Fort William, 7 February 1811.

[118] NLS Minto Papers, Box 67. Newspaper cutting, 9 February 1811.

[119] Prentout, *L'Ile de France sous Decaen*, p. 610.

[120] Ibid., p. 617.

The fall of Mauritius did not however mean the total expulsion of the French from the Eastern seas as many authors have stated.[121] The annexation of Holland had placed the Dutch overseas possessions in the power of France. Under stricter French control, Java could take the place of Mauritius, and Napoleon had indeed intended to strengthen Java by sending two French frigates, the *Meduse* and the *Nymphe*, transporting General Janssens who was to succeed Daendels as the Governor-General of Java. Hence it was clear that Minto's attention would now be centred on Java as a potential new stronghold of the French in the Eastern seas. Minto anticipated the French move regarding Java. He had contemplated its conquest even before sending the expedition against the French Islands. 'I have still,' Minto wrote, 'one object more… which will fill up the whole scheme of my warlike purposes, and which will purge the Eastern side of the globe of every hostile or rival European establishment.'[122]

---

[121] Sen, *The French in India*, p. 596. Also Field, A.G., 'The Expedition to Mauritius in 1810' (unpublished MA thesis, University of London, 1933).
[122] NLS M 38. No. 13. Minto to Lady Minto, Calcutta, 9 September 1810.

Five

PRE-EMPTING FRENCH INFLUENCE IN JAVA

Minto and the Dutch East Indies

Java became a French colony in July 1810. After the fall of L'Ile de France (Mauritius) it was the only colony where the Tricolour flag was still flying. Everywhere else in the world French sovereignty had been eliminated, except in Europe where Napoleonic influence was all encompassing. The frontiers of France stretched from the outskirts of Hamburg in the north to Naples in the south. Austria and Prussia were allies. Only Britain, Portugal, the islands of Sardinia and Sicily, tiny Montenegro on the Adriatic and disillusioned Russia were at odds with the French emperor. However, there was no fighting anywhere except in Spain. Java had become French after Holland was annexed to France after the abdication of King Louis. As the lone outpost among the Indonesian islands not occupied by the British, it was clearly threatened.[1]

In order to continue the global battle against Napoleon, British policy was compelled to examine specific areas of Europe as well. The most sensitive areas in British eyes were the Low Countries in general and the Scheldt estuary in particular. French control of Holland meant a permanent threat to George III's Hanoverian electorate, a danger that materialised in 1803 and expanded Napoleon's influence over northern Germany. It also gave the French access to the Dutch colonial empire, particularly the East Indies and at the Cape of Good Hope from where France could challenge British dominance in India and damage trade links with the East.[2]

Despite the strong interest in the regions mentioned, Britain's main strategic effort in 1808 onward was centred on the Iberian Peninsula. Supporting the Peninsular revolt meant that the French emperor lost the use of Spain's navy and the refuge, repair and building facilities provided by the assorted Spanish

---

[1] Fregosi, P., *Dreams of Empire: Napoleon and the First World War 1792–1815* (New York, 1990), Chap. 22, p. 319.

[2] Hall, C.D., *British Strategy in the Napoleonic War 1803–15* (Manchester University Press, 1992), Chap. 4, pp. 83–85.

ports. A further bonus was the elimination of five French ships of the line that had been sheltering in Cadiz since Trafalgar and another one in the port of Vigo; these in turn surrendered to the Spaniards in June 1808.[3] After the isolated French troops in Portugal had been removed, Britain liberated those Portuguese warships not secured in 1807 and also could secure eight Russian ships of the line sheltering in the Tagus while on their voyage from the Mediterranean to the Baltic and could gain the use of important Atlantic ports such as Lisbon and Oporto.[4]

As long as the revolt in Spain continued, Napoleon could make no credible claim to control that country's New World colonies. This nightmare prospect had haunted ministers' minds for many years and when the French first flooded into Spain in 1808, initially facing no Spanish resistance, the Cabinet was very alarmed. With the King of Spain as Napoleon's puppet, 'the Interval may be short between the seizure by France of the Spanish Government at Home, and the Occupation by the same Power of its Colonies abroad ...'[5] The eventual Spanish revolt relieved ministers from this and spared them from any necessity for direct military action of their own in the New World. During the course of 1808 British policy moved rapidly from encouraging independence among Spain's colonies to encouraging them to remain quiescent and supportive of the mother country against the French invader. Francophobic propaganda was disseminated in these territories and they were further guarded from any attempts at French influence by British naval power.[6] Fighting Napoleon in the Peninsula also provided a large measure of relief from fears of French attack elsewhere in the world. Castlereagh was concerned at the end of 1807 about the possibility of French operations against India, but could reflect by 1809 that any such schemes would have been shelved with the commitment of so many French troops to Spain.[7]

The Southern Ocean approach to India via the Dutch colony of Cape of Good Hope had undergone fluctuations in its considered strategic importance. In 1781, the directors of the British East India Company had called it the 'Gibraltar of India', a view prompting its capture in 1795. However by 1801, it had cost £1 million to hold and its potential as a source of danger seemed to have diminished. Further, Napoleon's Egyptian campaign in 1798–1801 seemed to suggest that future threats to India would come via the Middle East rather than the South Atlantic.[8] The Cape's only value lay in its

3   Ibid., p. 90.
4   Glover, M., *Britannia Sickens* (London, 1970), pp. 40–41. P.D., X, p. 144.
5   Nottingham University Library, Portland Papers, PwF 4117.
6   *Castlereagh Correspondence*, VI, pp. 364–67 and 374–75.
7   Hall, *British Strategy in the Napoleonic War*, Chap. 4, pp. 90–91.
8   Graham, G.S., *Britain in the Indian Ocean. A Study of Maritime Enterprise, 1810–50* (Oxford, 1967), pp. 24–27.

position as an Indian outpost astride the sea route to the East, providing as it did a forward defensive position and depriving the enemy of a base for the invasion of the subcontinent. British control permitted its use as a support for vessels in the Indian and China trades and removed another potential source of enemy privateering. It also served as a position from where troops could be drawn to India in the event of any emergency.[9]

The capture of the French Islands as detailed earlier left only the Dutch East Indies possessions as a source of danger. They had been largely quiescent until the arrival of the energetic Daendels as governor. His energy and boasting caused some alarm in Calcutta and there were fears that the numerous Arab trading vessels based in the Moluccas might be used to stage attacks on India. In June 1809, a French officer captured on Sumatra spoke of the anticipated arrival of a squadron of seven frigates, and papers in his possession detailed French influence in Burma and also mentioned an attack on Bengal. Minto therefore concluded that the danger from the Dutch islands was an immediate threat.[10]

Additional considerations included the protection of the trade route with China. Exports included cotton goods, pepper, sandalwood and the most lucrative of all, opium. Tea, porcelain, silks and satins came on the return passages with additional cargoes being loaded and discharged at Malacca. The value of the China trade to the British East India Company amounted to £10 million between the years 1806–08.[11]

1807–10

Until the end of the seventeenth century the Dutch East Indies, with its capital at Batavia, included all the Dutch colonies in the East. In the next century however, the Cape, Ceylon and the Dutch settlements in India enjoyed a considerable degree of independence from the Batavian government. The Dutch East Indies in the nineteenth century consisted of a group of islands including Borneo, the Celebes, Sumatra, Java, and the Moluccas or the Spice Islands – Amboyna, Banda, Ceram, Ternate and others. To the Dutch, the most important were Java and Moluccas to which they confined the cultivation of coffee, sugar and spices. The Dutch established numerous fortified posts on the islands with a view to enforce the prohibition of the cultivation of spices outside the allocated areas and to exclude all other European merchants from the eastern islands.

9   Hall, *British Strategy in the Napoleonic War*, Chap. 5, pp. 124–25.
10 Ibid., Chap. 8, p. 189.
11 Woodman, R., *The Victory of Seapower. Winning the Napoleonic War 1806–1814* (London, 2005), Part II: Exploiting Seapower – Overseas, p. 102.

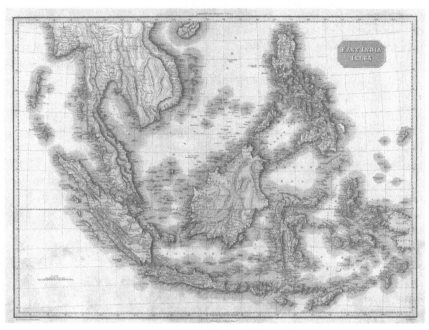

4 East India Isles (from J. Pinkerton, *A Modern Atlas, from the Latest and Best Authorities, Exhibiting the Various Divisions of the World with its chief Empires, Kingdoms, and States; in Sixty Maps, carefully reduced from the Largest and Most Authentic Sources*, Philadelphia, 1818)

The Dutch East Indies commanded the passage to China through either the Straits of Malacca or Sunda.[12] All of the British trade with China had to necessarily pass through either of these straits. Ships proceeding from China to Britain left between November and March in order to avoid the south-east monsoon which prevailed in the Eastern seas during May to August, and passing through the Straits of Malacca to Ceylon and Bombay en route to Britain. For the security of trade, the British established one or two posts on the two straits: one of these was the fortified settlement of Bencoolen, founded in 1685 and officially known as Fort Marlborough on the west coast of Sumatra. In 1786, the British purchased the little island of Pulu Penang off the Malayan coast from the Sultan of Kedah, and built Fort Cornwallis. Pulu Penang was renamed Prince of Wales' Island. In 1800, the British acquired a foothold on the Malay Peninsula, which was named Province Wellesley. The importance of the other settlements declined as that of Penang increased. In view of the strategic value of Penang and the facilities it appeared to hold out for ship-building, it was made a fourth presidency of the government of India in 1805.

[12] The Strait of Malacca is situated between Sumatra and the Malay peninsula, and the Strait of Sunda is between Sumatra and Java.

The relations between the British and the Dutch during the Revolutionary and Napoleonic Wars between 1793 and 1814 depended on the relations between Holland and France. At the outbreak of war in 1793, Holland joined Britian in declaring war against France. In 1795 however, in consequence of a bloodless revolution in Amsterdam, the Stadtholder fled and the new Dutch Republic, through its alliance with France, became involved in war with Britain. The Dutch colonies had to choose between the Stadtholder and the mother country. The Prince of Orange, residing at Kew near London, issued a circular letter dated 7 February 1795, ordering all the Dutch colonial governors to admit British troops and accept British protection. The Government of Batavia refused to surrender Java to the British, although Malacca and the Moluccas both surrendered in 1795.[13] In 1795–96, Trincomalee and the other Dutch settlements in Ceylon were occupied. The total extinction of Dutch power in the East Indies by the capture of Java was considered desirable by Henry Dundas, the Secretary of State for War. Orders were sent to Wellesley to that effect, and parallel orders were received by Admiral Rainier of the India station from the Admiralty, dated 21 October 1799. Rainier decided to blockade Batavia as a preliminary measure while preparations were being made by the Government of India for the military expedition. The naval operations against Batavia were very successful, and several Dutch and Malay vessels were taken or destroyed. The Dutch Governor did not offer to fight or surrender, but waited for the climate and disease to do their work. The sickness and mortality among the troops and seamen were so great that the British squadron was forced to withdraw in November 1800.[14] In the meantime, Wellesley decided to send an expedition to conquer the French Islands, as in his opinion 'neither the local position, actual state, genius and character of the people or peculiar resources of either Batavia, or Manilla' rendered their conquest as important as that of L'Ile de France.[15] Admiral Rainier, whose heart was set on the conquest of those places, refused to cooperate in the expedition against the French Islands on the pretext that he could not offer any assistance without the orders of the Admiralty.[16] The clash of authority between the naval commander-in-chief and the governor-general of India was chronic during the years of war. The admirals of the East India station considered themselves under the distinct authority of the Admiralty and not bound to comply with the orders or suggestions of the governor-general. Minto met with the same kind of attitude from Rear-Admiral Drury and Commodore Broughton. As it happened, no

---

[13] Vlekke, B.H., *Nusantara, A History of the East Indian Achipelago* (Cambridge, MA, 1945), Chap. XI, p. 220.

[14] Parkinson, *War in the Eastern Seas*, Chap. VII, pp. 163, 170–72. Only three were killed in action, but the loss from disease amounted to 151 men.

[15] Martin, *The Despatches of the Marquess Wellesley*, Vol. 2, p. 755.

[16] Ibid., pp. 753–58.

expeditions could be undertaken by Wellesley either against Mauritius or Batavia. On receipt of orders from Dundas, dated 6 October 1800, that an army should be dispatched from India to the Red Sea and Egypt,[17] Wellesley abandoned the idea of attacking the French Islands. The troops assembled at Trincomalee and Point de Galle were increased and dispatched under Major-General Baird to Egypt with Arthur Wellesley as second in command.[18] Wellesley expressed a hope that should the army return to India after a short and successful campaign, the projected expeditions against the French Islands and even Batavia might be revived.[19] Rainier gave orders for the raising of the blockade of Batavia and rallied his ships at Trincomalee for service in the Red Sea. For the rest of the war, Java enjoyed immunity from attack.

At the peace of Amiens in March 1802, the British restored all the occupied Dutch territories, except Ceylon, to Holland. The Dutch ambassador in London, Schimmelpennick, was told that as long as French influence was excluded from Java, the British had no desire to occupy it.[20] The Dutch Government in Batavia was so weak and non-aggressive in character that no alarm was felt and as a measure of economy, the British greatly reduced their fortified settlements in the East Indies. In November 1805, the post at Balambangan, an island a few miles north of Borneo, was abandoned and the evacuation of Malacca was considered by Sir George Barlow's government. Although Malacca was retained, its fortifications were destroyed at considerable expense and the garrison eventually withdrawn in 1808. Only a small civil population remained at Malacca.[21] Penang and Bencoolen badly needed reinforcements, which the Government of Bengal declared its inability to provide. The entire burden of protection the trade and the British settlements in the East Indies rested with the navy.

Java on the other hand, received reinforcements from Europe after 1803. Troops and a squadron of ships arrived under the command of Hartsinck, consisting of four ships of the line, three frigates and a number of armed vessels.[22] The Dutch ships did not offer to join the French in their game of piracy and the Batavian Government felt that so long as it refrained from actual hostilities against the British, Java would not be attacked.

An attack on Batavia and the resultant destruction of the Dutch navy was a favourite project of Rear-Admiral Edward Pellew, who succeeded Rainier.

---

[17] Ibid., pp. 436–37.

[18] Martin, *Despatches*, Vol. 2, pp. 440–52.

[19] Ibid., pp. 584–87.

[20] Renier, G.J., *Great Britain and the Establishment of the Kingdom of the Netherlands, 1813–15* (The Hague, 1930), p. 319.

[21] NLS M 39, No. 10. Minto to Lady Minto, Malacca, 31 May 1811.

[22] Hartsinck's squadron consisted of the *Revolutie, Pluto, Schrikerrwekker, Kontenaar, Pallas, Maria Riggerbergen, Phoenix, Aventurion, William, Maria Wilhelmina, Zee Ploeg* and other armed vessels. Parkinson, *War in the Eastern Seas*, p. 296.

In November 1806, Pellew with HMS *Culloden, Powerful, Russel, Belliqueux, Terpsichore, Seaflower* and the *Sir Francis Drake*, entered the Batavia roads and destroyed all the Dutch ships and merchantmen in the harbour, the dockyard and the establishment on the island of Onroost.[23] The Dutch navy was reduced to the few ships that were then in the harbour of Gressie.

Pellew sent a lengthy memorandum, dated 28 January 1807, to Barlow on the necessity of conquering Java as the best means of guaranteeing the security of the China trade. The establishment of French sovereignty over Holland in the person of King Louis Bonaparte in 1806 placed the Dutch colonies under stricter French control and direction. Under such circumstances, the system of military inactivity so long pursued by the Batavian Government from considerations of political expediency was likely to be replaced by a policy of active hostility against the British. The China trade and the Company's ships employed in that trade were liable to be greatly harassed by the French operating from Java. The Java seas, with their numerous islands and uncharted areas, made pursuit difficult and consequently were highly advantageous to piracy and privateering. Pellew wrote:

> An active force even of frigates only employed in that quarter would give serious uneasiness to our commerce in the China Seas, from the facility with which they might elude our pursuit, receiving shelter in the numerous Islands of those Seas, with the convenient resort of the Porte of Java and the Philippines.[24]

Pellew recommended that the Dutch should be dispossessed of Batavia before the French could effectively establish their authority there, and before any hostile operations against the Company's trade should actually commence from Java. Pellew wanted to dispense with the burden of providing strong convoys for the China trade. In his last cruise, Pellew had collected information about the weak state of the fortifications of Batavia, the aversion of the Dutch colonists toward the French and the Javanese insurrections in the subordinate settlements. This was therefore an opportune time to attack Batavia, and in Pellew's opinion a force consisting of 1,000 Europeans and an equal number of sepoys would be able to capture Batavia without a siege. The general unhealthiness of the city could be avoided by stationing the main body of the garrison after the conquest outside the city and frequently changing the garrison in the citadel. However, Pellew probably realised that he was being too sanguine in his expectations. He therefore added an alternative proposal that the

---

[23] TNA Adm. 1/179. Pellew to Admiralty, 1 January 1807.
[24] NLS M 180. Sir E. Pellew to G. Barlow, Madras Roads, 28 January 1807. Also TNA Adm. 1/179.

two remaining Dutch ships of the line, the *Pluto* and the *Revolutie* and the batteries at Gressie should be destroyed.[25]

Barlow rejected Pellew's proposal for an attack on Batavia and questioned the reality of the dangers from the French as outlined by him. Conditions in Europe, according to Barlow would not permit Bonaparte to send a naval force to the East and even if such an attempt were made the home government should be trusted to counteract any such exertions on the part of the enemy. The more practical objections to the proposed undertaking arose from the Indian Government's financial and political interests in India. Barlow repeated the same arguments that he had used in declining to undertake any expedition against the French Islands. He had no wish to increase the expenditure of his government, unless he was forced to do so by a matter of 'extreme necessity and emergency'.[26] Moreover, Barlow felt that the internal security and tranquillity of the Company's territories in India would be exposed to 'local agitation' if large numbers of European troops were absent from India for a long period of time. The number of European troops in India was less than what was needed. On political grounds therefore, the absence of a large number of European troops from India was considered undesirable, especially after the recent occurrence of the Vellore mutiny in the summer of 1806. Barlow was therefore willing to cooperate only in limited operations against Gressie.[27] Prior to any action being taken, Barlow left office. Java was to be conquered under the aegis of Minto, but not before it had been granted a respite for four years.

Shortly after Minto's arrival in Calcutta, in a minute dated 26 August 1807, he recalled Pellew's proposal for an attack on Batavia or Gressie. Minto's views concurred entirely with those of Barlow who was then senior member of the Council. It was decided that the operations against Gressie should be carried out immediately by Pellew with the assistance of 500 European troops and artillery to be fitted out from Fort St George, but Gressie was not to be permanently occupied. Pellew had recommended the occupation of Gressie, which he declared would facilitate future operations against Batavia and the Spice Islands. In the Supreme Government's opinion however, the expense of such an undertaking, the lack of adequate number of European troops in India, the hazard of multiplying the objectives of defence without an increase in the naval force, the state of the Company's finances, and 'the positive terms of the orders of the Court of Directors against any extensive system of offensive measures against the enemy in the eastern islands', compelled it to

---

25 NLS M 180. Sir E. Pellew to G. Barlow, Madras Roads, 28 January 1807. Also TNA Adm. 1/179.

26 NLS M 180. G. Barlow and Council to Pellew, Fort William, 14 February 1807.

27 Ibid. Also TNA Adm. 1/179. G. Barlow-in-Council to Pellew, Fort William, 16 February 1807.

limit its objectives to the destruction of the enemy's ships and works at Gressie without attempting to form an establishment on the island of Java.[28]

Minto has been criticised for postponing the proposed attack on Batavia in 1807, allowing the Dutch Governor-General Daendels time to improve the defences of Batavia so that a larger expedition had to be fitted out at a greater expense in 1811 than would have been necessary in 1807.[29] This criticism has been based on the imperfect estimation of obstacles that stood in the way of undertaking any foreign expedition from India, either against the French Islands or Java, in 1807–08. The Government's anxiety over the security of the north-west frontier, the lack of adequate numbers of European troops to maintain security at home as well as to attack the enemy's territories abroad precluded such an attempt. Moreover, Java did not have priority over Mauritius, which was the centre of the French naval activities in the Indian seas. If an expedition could at all be fitted out from India in 1807–08, it would in all probability have been directed against Mauritius rather than Batavia. Consequently, in 1807, Minto refused to undertake any large-scale operations against Java or any other Dutch or Spanish colonies in the Eastern seas for the primary reason that it was not felt to be an urgent necessity. Additionally, he tried to avoid measures which involved considerable expense and was afraid that the slightest relaxation of the system of rigid economy pursued by the Government would create an immediate speculation in the money market and drive the interest on the public debt back from eight to ten per cent. The economic consideration was not the only one which restrained Minto from adopting 'plans... which although useful and desirable in themselves are however not absolutely and obviously necessary'.[30] In 1807, Minto did not feel comfortable in undertaking such an expedition without the previous sanction of the home authorities. When Minto's friends, the Grenvillites were in office, plans for the extirpation of all the European enemies of Britain from their military and commercial posts east of the Cape had been discussed favourably by them. However, the new ministers, particularly Castlereagh, the Secretary of State for War and Colonies, were known to be opposed to such projects. When Castlereagh was President of the Board of Control (1804–06) orders had been sent to the Government of India prohibiting any expedition against Batavia or any other place in the Eastern seas and until new directions arrived from home, those were considered standing orders. The attention of the Indian Government was focused on the western part of India. Minto wrote to Pellew that although no actual invasion of British territories by a

28 TNA Adm. 1/179. Minto and Council (Barlow and Lumsden) to Pellew, Fort William 4 October 1807. TNA Adm. 1/179. Minto-in-Council to W. Petrie, Governor of Madras, Fort William, 2 October 1807. NLS M 159. Minto to Pellew, Calcutta, 6 October 1807.

29 Rainbow, S.G., 'English Expeditions to the Dutch East Indies during the Revolutionary and Napoleonic Wars', (MA thesis, London University, 1933), pp. 161–62.

30 NLS M 159. Minto to Pellew, Calcutta, 6 October 1807.

French army was yet to be feared, it was necessary to keep a watchful eye on the activities of the French between Mauritius, the western coast of India and the Persian Gulf, instead of undertaking a distant expedition to the eastward. Minto regretted however, that the military operations against Java couldn't be immediately undertaken for he realised that Java might in the near future be used by the enemy as a military and naval base.

'The impossibility,' Minto wrote, 'of embarking in these important designs is the more to be regretted as a very moderate effort could hardly at the present moment fail of success; and a future period the difficulty may be much greater.'[31]

It is interesting to note that at this time Minto believed that operations against Java should not only be authorised, but in a great measure be carried out by the home government.[32] Minto wrote to Pellew as well as to Robert Dundas, that the Government of India was not only financially and militarily unable to undertake such a large-scale operation on its own, but also that he felt 'the want of due authority to engage in such an enterprise, and our incompetence to adjust many points of the highest political importance which it must involve', for instance whether the Crown or Company would be represented and take responsibility for the captured territories and settlements, who was to bear the expenses or if shared, a description of the proportionate burden. These decisions could only be resolved after due consultation between HM Government and the Court of Directors.[33] In 1811 however, Minto went ahead with the expedition and settled the political arrangements without waiting for the previous sanction of the home authorities. In fact, even in 1807, Minto wrote to Robert Dundas that if the resources of the Government and the circumstances had permitted the undertaking he would not have allowed any 'formal incompetence' to stand in his way.[34]

The operations against Java in 1807–08 were confined to the destruction of the Dutch navy, which was already severely weakened. After Pellew's successful raid on the harbour of Batavia in January 1807, Captain Rainier of the *Caroline* and Captain Fleetwood Pellew of the *Psyche* carried on operations off Samarang. The *Caroline* captured seven vessels including one armed brig; and the *Psyche* entered the Samarang roads and captured the merchantman *Resolutie*, the brig *Ceres* and the corvette *Scipio*.[35] In October 1807, Pellew sailed with a powerful squadron including 500 European troops

[31] NLS M 159. Minto to Pellew, 6 October 1807.
[32] NLS M 193. Governor-General-in-Council to the Secret Committee, Fort William, 26 October 1807. Also BL, IOR Ben. Sec. Letters, Vol. 10.
[33] NLS M 193. Governor-General-in-Council to the Secret Committee, Fort William, 26 October 1807. Also BL, IOR Ben. Sec. Letters, Vol. 10.
[34] Ibid.
[35] TNA Adm. 1/179. Captain Fleetwood Pellew to Sir Edward Pellew, 3 September 1807. Also NLS M 210.

and sixty artillery under Colonel Lockhart of the Madras establishment for Gressie.[36] The Dutch commandant at Gressie refused to surrender at the first summons, although the two ships of war *Pluto* and *Revolutie* were in a dismantled state with their guns on shore. Pellew then sailed up the River Sourabaya and destroyed the batteries at Gressie. The terms of truce were arranged on 9 December 1807. The Dutch commandant had already scuttled the ships in the harbour and Pellew completed their destruction by burning them.[37] After 1807 therefore, the Dutch naval force in the East was practically non-existent. Before Pellew left the East India station in February 1808, he stated to the Admiralty that of the seven enemy ships in the Eastern seas at that time, six were French and the other, the *Mandarin*, was a small American vessel purchased by the Dutch and commanded by a Scotsman, Commodore Cowell.[38]

The year Minto arrived in India, French authority and control was more directly established over the Batavian Government. In June 1806, Napoleon had converted the Dutch Republic into a kingdom under this brother Louis Bonaparte. 'A Bonaparte had come to power in the Netherlands, and from now on military considerations took the first place in the colonial plans of The Hague.'[39] In the East Indies every Dutch settlement became equivalent to a French post where French frigates could find shelter and from where attacks might be directed against British trade and territory. In January 1807, on the orders of the emperor, Louis Bonaparte appointed Marshall Herman Willem Deandels, a Dutch Jacobin and a general in the French army as the governor-general of Java. As early as 1797, Daendels had suggested an attack on the British territories in India from Java.[40] Daendel's appointment therefore signified that Java might be used by Bonaparte in his war against Britain. Daendels had orders to improve the defences and the military strength of the colony and its finances.[41] After a difficult voyage from Holland via Lisbon and Morocco, Daendels arrived at Java on 1 February 1808. Daendels was as active a promoter of French interests as General Decaen in Mauritius. Under the mismanagement and corruption of his immediate predecessors, Siberg and Wiese, the Dutch power and authority in Java had declined. The interruption of trade with Europe greatly affected the prosperity of the colony. The Batavian Government sold coffee and spices to neutral traders, American,

---

36 BL, IOR Ben. Sec. & Pol. Cons. 202. Cons. of 28 December 1807. No. 5. Sir E. Pellew to Minto, Malacca Roads, 19 November 1807.

37 TNA Adm. 1/179. Pellew to Admiralty, HMS *Culloden* off Gressie, 14 December 1807. BL, IOR Ben. Sec. Cons. 204. Pellew to Minto, HMS *Culloden*, 15 December 1807.

38 TNA Adm. 1/181. Statement of the enemy force in the Indian seas. Pellew to Admiralty, 11 November 1807.

39 Vlekke, B.M., *The Story of the Dutch East Indies* (Cambridge, MA, 1946), p. 133.

40 Egerton, H.E., *Sir Stamford Raffles* (London, 1900), p. 34.

41 Vlekke, *Nusantara*, p. 233.

Danish and Arab, who came to buy and ship the products at their own risk. As long as the British blockade of Batavia was not strictly maintained, the profits of the trade filled the Batavian government's treasury. When Daendels came to office there were two million guilders in the treasury.[42] The passing of the Embargo Act in 1807–08, and the stringency of the British blockade, negatively impacted the prosperity of Batavia. By 1810, the treasury was exhausted and the value of paper money depreciated to the extent of 5 paper rix-dollars equal to 1 silver Spanish dollar.[43] Daendels resorted to the sale of government lands to stabilise the finances of his government.

Despite the financial embarrassments of his government, Daendels adopted a vigorous policy in Java. Taking advantage of the weakness of the Batavian Government, the Javanese princes had shaken off practically all control by the Dutch. Immediately after Daendels's arrival, hostilities commenced between his government and the rulers of Cheribon, Mataram and Bantam, as a result of which Dutch authority was once again firmly established. Daendels's first objective was the improvement of the military strength and fortifications of Batavia, which were in a state of disrepair and decline. The conscripted Javanese regiments and a handful of European troops of poor quality did not form an effective fighting force. Daendels raised a large army, recruited mainly from the island of Madura. Due to the lack of an adequate number of European officers however, these troops were inefficiently disciplined. Daendels began building roads, forts and coastal batteries and a highway was constructed from Bantam in the west to Pasuruan in the east, which linked the ports of the northern coast and enabled the Dutch to concentrate troops at any point within one-tenth of the time that would have been possible before. However, the road construction accomplished by forced peasant labour resulted in the loss of life of several workers and alienated the people of Java. At Bantam, Daendels built a series of forts using forced labour which caused a local revolt. The garrison and residential quarters of the governor-general were removed from Batavia to the healthier district of Weltervreden. A strong fortified citadel was built at Meester Cornelis, which was to be the main point of concentration in case of a British invasion. Daendels introduced many administrative and judicial reforms which were needed for societal order, but he succeeded in alienating virtually all of the population of Java. 'The Thundering Marshal' disregarded every law and consideration of humanity, 'but that which enjoined the preservation of the colony',[44] and set up an arbitrary rule. The Dutch inhabitants were as much alienated as the Javanese peasants and princes.

[42] Ibid., p. 229.
[43] BL, IOR Ben. Sec. Cons. 234. Cons. of 6 December 1811, No. 4. Proclamation No. 3 by Minto, dated 11 September 1811.
[44] Raffles, T.S., *The History of Java*, Vol. I (London, 1817), p. xlv.

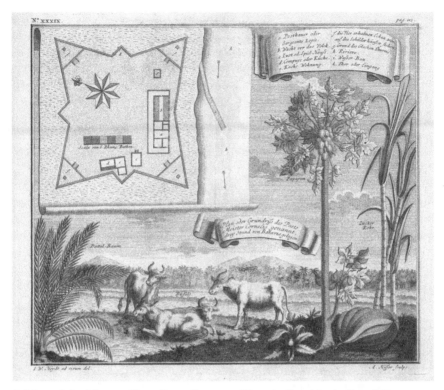

5 Map of the Meester Cornelis trading post (*Plan oder Grundriss des Posts Meister Cornelis genannt, drey Stund von Batavia gelegen, I. W. Heydt ad vivum del. / a. hoffer sculp.*, c. 1744).

Janssens reported that both natives and Europeans longed for the arrival of the British, 'not from any detestable Anglomania, but to escape a terror that desolated all the world'.[45]

Minto was acutely aware of Daendels's activities in Java and in October 1808 wrote to Dundas:

> Java is becoming every day more interesting. There has been a change of men & the greatest exertions are now making to strengthen the Dutch, that is to say the French possessions in that Island... We might yet deprive the Enemy of this settlement without great effort; but a little more time will increase the difficulty extremely. Nothing can be undertaken from hence without orders, at the same time I confess I do not feel quite easy in letting one of those seasons for an important service pass, which do not return.[46]

[45] Furnivall, J.S., *Netherlands India* (Cambridge, 1939), Chap. 3, p. 67.
[46] NLS M 160, Minto to R. Dundas, Fort William, 2 October, 1808.

Reports poured into Calcutta from the governments of Penang, Malacca and Bencoolen about the latest move of the enemy in the east. The government of Bencoolen reported the insurrection of some of the Javanese chiefs. The commandant at Malacca stated that Java could be taken by a force of 3,000 to 5,000 men and that perhaps a lesser force might be adequate for the undertaking if the disaffected chiefs could be persuaded to join. The Dutch force at this time was estimated at about 1,000 Europeans and about 10,000 native troops divided between Batavia, Samarang and Gressie.[47] Although no reinforcements from Europe had yet arrived at Batavia and the vigilance of the British navy in Europe largely precluded that possibility, the Government of India suspected that 'the French had a future design of augmenting strength of it [Java] and rendering it a centre of operations against our own Establishments to the Eastward and probably extrapolated to China'. In January 1809, therefore, Minto again placed before the Secret Committee his view that it would be a measure of prudent policy to undertake an expedition against the Dutch East Indies, a measure which would become indispensably necessary and at the same time more arduous, if the French were allowed to strengthen and consolidate their position in Java.[48]

The resident at Bencoolen expressed anxiety over the safety of his settlement, for the extraordinary activity of Marshal Daendels, the large force raised by him and the expected arrival of reinforcements from Europe which aroused a suspicion that the enemy might attack the ill-defended British settlements and destroy the spice cultivation belonging to individuals and the Company.[49] In October 1809, the French corvette *Creole* of eighteen guns belonging to Hamelin's squadron, attacked and destroyed the British settlement at Tappanooly on the west coast of Sumatra. The loss to the Company was estimated at 6,000 Spanish dollars exclusive of the military stores taken.[50] The plunder of Tappanooly showed that the navy could not be solely depended upon to protect the settlements from attack by the enemy. The naval force employed by Drury on the west coast of Sumatra for the protection of trade during these months was considerable. The *Blanche*, *Rattlesnake*, *Sir Francis Drake*, *Diomede* and the cutter *Sylvia* were in that area and the *Belliquieu* off Acheen head. Drury therefore complained to Minto that

[47] BL, IOR Ben. Sec. & Sep. Cons. 213. Cons. of 20 May 1809, No. 44. R. Parry to Minto, Fort Marlborough, 17 March 1809.
[48] BL, IOR Ben. Sec. Letters, Vol. 11, Governor-General-in-Council to the Secret Committee, Fort William, 10 January 1809.
[49] BL, IOR Fac. Rec. Java 12. R. Parry to Edmonstone, Fort Marlborough, 25 June 1809.
[50] BL, IOR Java 12. Parry to Edmonstone, 31 October 1809. BL, IOR Java 12. Parry to Edmonstone, 7 November 1809. BL, IOR Java 12. John Prince to R. Parry, 27 October 1809. At the time of attack the resident at Tappanooly, John Prince was away and the settlement was in charge of his assistant Mr Hayes, who had another Englishman, a Mr Watts, and twelve sepoys with him. Hayes and Watts were taken prisoner of war.

'unless settlements are in some degree capable of making resistance, they must expect to suffer from these kinds of depredations'.[51]

Tappanooly was recovered and reinforcements were hurried to Bencoolen. Minto sought Drury's cooperation in the measures to be adopted against the French Islands, which was the centre from which the French carried on their attacks against the British settlements and commerce in the Eastern seas.[52] In the meantime, the blockade of Dutch ports was continued.

In June 1809, Colonel de la Houssaye, a French officer belonging to Daendels's army and an aide-de-camp to Daendels, was seized by the British on board a native prow off Sumatra. The colonel stated that he was travelling for reasons of health; but one or two false statements made by him and the large amount of cash in his pocket created suspicion.[53] The resident at Bencoolen sent him as a prisoner to Penang.[54] When Houssaye arrived at Penang, his papers were seized and letters from the Government of Batavia to the King of Ava and to various persons at Calcutta and other parts of India were found.[55] Houssaye was on a special mission from Daendels to the King of Acheen, and to the Burmese Government to establish some sort of connection between those governments and Batavia inimical to the British. The names of two British-born subjects in India were found among his papers. Of these, Montgomery was immediately transported to Britain; Meyer, who resided at Serampore, was allowed to return to Java. The names of Mr Brunel at Tranquebar and Mr Kock at Malacca were also found and they were placed under close observation. Houssaye died in Chandernagore, where he was kept a prisoner, before his transport to Britain could be arranged.[56]

The Government of Bengal dispatched a political agent, David Campbell, to Acheen in Sumatra to detect and counteract any French intrigues in that quarter. Campbell was to propose to the King of Acheen that all Europeans other than the British should be excluded from his kingdom. He was also to

---

51 BL, IOR Java 12. Drury to Minto, HMS *Russel*, Bombay Harbour, 3 December 1809.

52 BL, IOR Fac. Rec. Java 12. Minto to Drury, Fort St George, 5 December 1809 and 7 December 1809.

53 BL, IOR Ben. Sec. & Sep. Cons. 222. Cons. of 26 September 1809, No. 2. R. Parry to Col. Macalister-in-Council, Fort Marlborough, 15 June 1809. Houssaye stated that seven French frigates with troops were shortly expected at L'Ile de France. He was most probably trying to cause alarm. He also showed Parry a copy of a letter from Decaen to Daendels recounting French successes in Spain.

54 BL, IOR Ben. Sec. & Sep. Cons. 222. Cons. of 26 September 1809, No. 2. Parry to Macalister, 20 June 1809.

55 BL, IOR Ben. Sec. & Sep. Cons. 222. Cons. of 26 September 1809, No. 2. Fort William, Letters & enclosures from Prince of Wales Island.

56 BL, IOR Ben. Sec. & Sep. Cons. 223. Cons. of 21 November 1809. Nos 36, 37, 38. Ibid. Cons. of 9 December 1809, Nos 1–4. BL, IOR Ben. Sec. & Sep. Cons. 222. Cons. of 26 September 1809. No. 4. Lumsden & Colebrooke to Minto (then in Madras), 26 September 1809.

ascertain the possibilities of establishing a British settlement in Acheen.[57] Campbell found a few Frenchmen[58] and Portuguese in Acheen, but the king was favourably disposed toward the British. The King of Acheen denied any connection with the French or Dutch hostile to British interests, and explained that his uncle, in an attempt to usurp the throne, had applied to Batavia for aid, and that Houssaye's mission probably had some reference to it. The king requested British aid to consolidate his position in Acheen. Campbell reported that if the Government wanted it, an establishment could easily be formed in Acheen, by taking a grant of territory from the king and establishing a resident with political and commercial duties.[59]

In July 1809, Captain John Canning[60] was deputed to Burma (Myanmar). He carried letters from Minto to the Viceroy of Pegu and to the King of Ava.[61] Canning was to proceed to Rangoon and eventually to the capital, Amarapura, to explain to the king the nature of the British blockade of the French Islands, which was supposed to adversely affect the Burmese trade, and also to find out the extent of the French influence in the Burmese court.[62] The latter fear had its roots in the past and was stirred up by the abortive mission of Houssaye. Both John Shore and Wellesley had sent diplomatic agents to the court of Ava because of the suspected connection between Mauritius and Burma.[63]

Canning reached Rangoon on 2 October 1809. He found that the trade of Burma was almost wholly with the British territories and that the king derived a large part of his income from the port dues and trade taxes paid by the British merchants trading with Rangoon. The Burmese trade with Mauritius was practically non-existent, and Canning reported that no merchant would risk sending a ship to the French Islands now that notice of the blockade was given. Canning left Rangoon on 23 December 1809 and arrived at Amarapura on 10 February 1810. He found the Burmese court seething with

57   BL, IOR Ben. Sec. Letters, Vol. 12. Vice-President-in-Council to the Secret Committee, Fort William, 6 January 1810. BL, IOR Ben. Pol. & Sec. Cons. 225. Cons. of 16 June 1801. No. 3. Edmonstone to D. Campbell, 13 June 1810.

58   A Frenchman, L'Etoille was the young King of Acheen's most influential counsellor, but L'Etoille was an adventurer, not a French agent.

59   BL, IOR Ben. Pol. Cons., R. 119, Vol. 17. Cons. of 29 October 1810, Nos 3 & 4. Campbell to Edmonstone, *Modeste* at Sea, 14 July 1810 and 24 July 1810. Acheen was weak and poor, the king's army did not exceed 400–500 men. The chief source of revenue was the duties levied at the ports on exports and imports. At the king's request, Campbell gave him thirty muskets and a few barrels of gunpowder.

60   Canning had accompanied Colonel Michael Symes to Burma in 1802. In May 1803, Wellesley sent him to Rangoon in the capacity of agent of Colonel Symes, but Canning was forced to leave Rangoon due to the unfriendliness of the Governor of Rangoon. Diplomatic relations with Burma were severed after that incident.

61   BL, IOR Ben. Pol. Cons. R. 118. Vol. 43. Cons. of 20 July 1809, Nos 9 & 10.

62   Ibid., No. 11. Edmonstone to Canning, 20 July 1809.

63   Hall, D.G.E., *Europe and Burma* (Oxford, 1945), pp. 86–97.

intrigues and jealousies regarding the succession to the throne and found no trace of the French. The Burmese minister enquired about the principles and justification of the blockade and appeared to be satisfied with Canning's explanation. He was granted an interview by the king on 28 February 1810. The King of Ava refused to accept the governor-general as his equal, and declared that he would only deal on equal terms with the King of England. The Burmese king's letter to the governor-general was written in an objectionable style, which, according to Canning, surpassed 'the usual bounds of even Burmese insolence'. The heir-apparent was given a vague hope of assistance in the coming struggle for the throne by Canning, although he was not authorised to do so. The former issued an order that the lieutenant-governor of Rangoon should not in future grant passports or protection to ships bound for the French Islands.[64] Canning's report satisfied Minto that there was no pernicious French influence in Burma and that the Houssaye affair had aroused a false alarm. Minto did not wish to establish a British influence on the court of Amarapura, although Canning had made an opening by holding out a hope of assistance to the heir-apparent. Minto disapproved of this part of Canning's conduct because 'it never could be in the contemplation of the Government to interpose its power for that purpose'.[65] Minto was unwilling to extend the liabilities of the Government, unless it was unavoidable for the sake of the security of the Company's territories in India. He had no further interest in Burma once he was satisfied that there was no hostile European influence in the Burmese court.[66]

The blockade of Java and the Moluccas by Rear-Admiral Drury was established in June 1809 on the orders of the Admiralty.[67] One of the objectives of the blockade was to prevent interactions between Batavia and L'Ile de France, and to prevent the Arab vessels from acting as an intermediary between the two. Certain political and commercial considerations relating to India caused Minto to object to the blockade. From the trade of the Arab vessels between Java, the Moluccas, the French Islands and the Red Sea, the Government of India did not expect any grave or unexpected evil as the trade of the Arabs between the Dutch and the French Islands was inconsiderable and stopping it was not likely to affect the interests of either of those states or that of the Company in a material degree. 'But', Minto wrote to Drury,

---

64 BL, IOR Ben. Pol. Cons. R.119, Vol. 4. Cons. of 29 May 1810, Paper No. 1. Canning's Report, 8 May 1810.

65 Ibid., No. 2. Edmonstone to Canning, Fort William, 29 May 1810.

66 In 1811, the Government of India became involved in a dispute with the Burmese king in connection with the Mag refugees and their depradations on the Arakan frontier under their leader Nga Chin Pyan or Kingbering. Canning was sent to Burma again in October 1811. The dispute with the Burmese king over the Mag refugees and Kingbering was not settled before the end of Minto's term in office. Banerjee, A.C., *The Eastern Frontier of British India, 1784–1826* (Calcutta, 1946), pp. 232–51.

67 BL, IOR Ben. Pol. Cons. R. 118, Vol. 42. Drury to Minto, 10 June 1809.

'As it comprehends the Trade of every Eastern State without exception, we apprehend that the effect of it must be to annihilate the Trade and to place us in a condition of hostility with all the Malay States of the Eastern Archipelago.'[68]

The Malay states carried on trade with the British as well as the Dutch. Being unacquainted with the European Law of Nations, the enforcement of the blockade, causing the interruption of their trade and capture of their ships, would be regarded by them as acts of hostility on the part of the British, and invite reciprocal hostility against all British subjects trading with their ports. The cessation of trade between the company and the Malay states would also adversely affect the opium trade, which was one of the principal sources of the Company's revenue. As the blockade of the Dutch East Indies was principally related to that of the French Islands, and as the stoppage of the trade of the Malay states with Java was essentially independent, Minto asked Drury not to enforce the blockade too rigorously as far as the Malay prows were concerned. The Governor-General-in-Council wrote to Drury:

> The practical introduction of the Maritime Laws of Europe into this Country is indeed an innovation in the System of our foreign relations of such magnitude and so entirely unsuited to the habits prejudices conceptions and imperfect Civilisation of the Maritime States of Asia, that in our opinion great caution should be used in carrying them into effect, and their operation should be limited to those cases in which the national advantage is certain, at least to counterbalance the local evils from which perhaps it is inseparable.[69]

The Government directed Drury, if not to relinquish altogether the measure of blockading the Dutch ports, at least to limit it to the ships actually trading between those ports and the French Islands. Drury refused to believe there was any real ground for the Supreme Government's apprehensions regarding the unfavourable consequences of the blockade. He assured Minto that he would interfere as little as possible with the Malay prows, which he said were in any case hostile toward all foreign vessels and attacked them whenever they were sure of success.[70] To the Admiralty, however, Drury complained against 'that propensity which is met throughout this Country to direct the navy as a machine, which never can be permitted'.[71] Drury therefore went ahead with the blockade without any modification.

68 BL, IOR Fac. Rec. Java 12. Governor-General-in-Council to Drury, Fort William, 26 June 1809. TNA Adm. 1/182, Fort William, 26 June 1809.
69 BL, IOR Fac. Rec. Java 12. Governor-General-in-Council to Drury, Fort William, 26 June 1809. Also TNA Adm. 1/182.
70 BL, IOR Fac. Rec. Java 12. Drury to Minto, HMS *Russel*, Madras Roads, 18 July 1809. TNA Adm. 1/182. HMS *Russel*, Madras Roads, 18 July 1809.
71 TNA Adm. 1/182. Drury to W. Pole, HMS *Russel*, Madras Roads, 17 July 1809.

The fears of the Government were soon confirmed. The interference of the British ships with the Malay prows, whether for the purpose of examining papers or otherwise, were bound to give rise to misunderstandings from the want of a proper medium of communication and the difference in naval customs. Few of the Malay vessels had regular papers and their crews were entirely ignorant of the language in which they were spoken to. Consequently, it was not long before hostilities took place. The annual fleet of the Bugguese prows from Borneo bound eastward to Malacca and Prince of Wales Island fell in with HMS *La Piedmontaise*. A severe action took place which arose from a mutual misunderstanding of motives.[72] The Supreme Government, being anxious for the continuance of trade with the Malay states, again requested Drury that a modification of the blockade should be announced to the Malay states in order to encourage them to renew commercial interactions with the British.[73] To the King of Boni, with whose merchant fleet the action had taken place, Minto sent an apology and an explanation in order to restore his confidence so that his ships should continue to freely trade with British ports. A present of cloth and military goods accompanied the explanation as a peace offering.[74] The government of Prince of Wales Island also found it necessary to explain to the different Malay states the nature and principles of the blockade.[75]

Drury, although he refused to relinquish the blockade of Java and the Moluccas, which had been made 'the watchword for a universal outcry... lest the Political, and Commercial Interests of India should suffer',[76] found it impossible to maintain the blockade effectively. He had an extensive coast to cover and failed to interrupt the Dutch trade to any considerable extent even after the most vigorous cruising. In the course of six months the British took or destroyed only seven French corvettes in the Java and Molucca Seas. In order to lessen the number of ports to be blockaded and at the same time to add the valuable spice trade to the Company's opium trade, Drury decided to occupy the Spice Islands.[77] He applied to Minto who was then in Madras, to provide about 200 Europeans for the service. In October 1809, Captains Tucker, Montague and Spencer of the *Dover*, *Cornwallis* and *Samarang* were commissioned to occupy Amboyna. The Government of Fort St George

---

[72] BL, IOR Fac. Rec. Java 12. The Government of Prince of Wales Island to the Vice-President-in-Council, 2 November 1809, Fort Cornwallis.

[73] BL, IOR Fac. Rec. Java 12. Minto to Drury, Fort St George, 18 January 1810.

[74] BL, IOR Fac. Rec. Java 12. Minto to the King of Boni, Fort St George, 22 January 1810.

[75] BL, IOR Fac. Rec. Java 12. The Government of Prince of Wales Island to the Vice-President-in-Council, 2 November 1809.

[76] TNA Adm. 1/182. Drury to J.W. Croker, HMS *Caroline*, Madras Roads, 22 April 1810.

[77] The Spice Islands, Amboyna, Banda, Ceram, Ternate and their dependencies were occupied during the war of 1793–1802 and restored to the Dutch at the peace of Amiens, 1802.

provided 130 men of the Madras 2nd European Regiment and forty-six European artillery under Captain Court.[78]

On 9 December 1809, Captain Tucker in *Dover* along with *Cornwallis* and *Samarang* anchored off Amboyna in the Moluccas. Amboyna was heavily fortified with Victoria Castle mounting over 200 guns. More artillery lay in the Wagoo battery, an offshore piled outwork, and the elevated works at Wannetoo and Batto-Gautong. Tucker anchored in Laetitia Bay for several days making his preparations, while the Dutch scuttled three ships in the harbour and added their crews to the defenders. On the 16th, having lowered boats on the offshore side of this ships and filled them with seamen, marines and a detachment of the Madras European regiment, Tucker's squadron weighed as if to depart. By keeping their sails aflutter, the ships edged obliquely across the bay towards a selected landing place under fire from the batteries. At the appropriate moment, the ships bore round, engaged the batteries and put 400 men ashore. They stormed the Wannetoo battery and scrambled across difficult terrain to force the Dutch and native gunners to abandon Batto-Gautong.[79]

Commander Spencer of the *Samarang* now landed with a party of seamen and marines with two field guns that he brought to bear on Wagoo and the pile battery driving out their garrisons. Similarly, the captured guns on Batto-Gautong opened fire on Victoria Castle and the governor surrendered. One of the three vessels scuttled in the harbour; the twelve-gun brig *Mandarin* was raised.[80]

On 19 February 1810, Amboyna surrendered to the British. The Dutch garrison numbered over 1,300 men of which 130 were Europeans and there were over 1,000 Javanese and Madurese soldiers.[81] Colonel Filz[82] declared that he could offer no effective resistance to the British due to the desertion of the Amboynese. The European garrison was also largely composed of Polish and Hungarian prisoners of war sent to Amboyna in 1803.[83] The island dependencies of Amboyna-Saperoua, Harouka, Nasso-Laut, Bouro, Manippa and Gorontello were occupied soon after.[84] Captain Court took over

---

[78] BL, IOR Ben. Pol. Cons. R. 119. Vol. 14, No.4. A. Falconer, Chief Secretary to the Government of Fort St George to Capt. Court, 13 October 1809. NLS M 201. Governor-General-in-Council to the Court of Directors, Fort William, 15 December 1810.

[79] Woodman, *The Victory of Seapower*, Part II: Exploiting Seapower – Overseas, p. 104.

[80] Ibid.

[81] BL, IOR Ben. Pol. Cons. R. 119, Vol. 14, No. 23. Captain Court to the Government of Fort St George, 16 April 1810. Ibid., No. 3. Articles of Capitulation signed by Filz, Tucker and Court, 18 February 1810.

[82] Colonel Filz was court-martialled and shot by the order of Daendels on his return to Batavia.

[83] BL, IOR Ben. Pol. Cons. R. 119, Vol. 4, no. 46. Court to the Chief Secretary of the Government of Fort St George, 6 March 1810.

[84] *Asiatic Annual Register*, 1810–11, pp. 21–27.

the government of Amboyna until further orders were received from Bengal. Many of the former officers who were willing to take an oath of allegiance to the King of England were retained in their offices. The paper money, which was in circulation at a deflated rate, was guaranteed by the British, but not the public debt. The Dutch garrison was conveyed by the end of April to Java on British transports, according to the terms of the capitulation.[85] On 10 August 1810, the island of Banda was taken by HMS *Caroline*, *Piedmontaise* and *Baracouta* under Captain Cole with a company of European troops under Captain Nixon.[86] On 31 August, the island of Ternate was taken by the joint efforts of Captain Tucker of the *Dover* and Captain Forbes of the Madras European regiment.[87] With the Moluccas in British hands, there remained only Java to complete Minto's grand design.[88]

The Spice Islands were dependencies of Batavia and tributaries to its commerce. After their capture, the question arose whether they should be occupied till at least the end of the war in Europe or be abandoned after rendering them militarily innocuous. Drury asked the Supreme Government whether it wanted to retain possession of the Moluccas until a decision was taken by the Crown or the Court of Directors and proposed to hand them over to the management of the Company on behalf of the king. Otherwise he proposed to destroy the fortifications and remove all the ships, troops and the Dutch inhabitants from the islands and leave them to the natives.[89]

Minto was then at Madras, and Robert Farquhar, who was special commissioner at the Moluccas during the former occupation, was also there preparing to leave with the expedition against Bourbon. On the basis of the information supplied by Farquhar, Minto decided to retain the Moluccas on behalf of the East India Company. The primary consideration was of course the commercial advantages to be gained by occupying the islands. The occupation of the Moluccas meant not only a curtailment of the Dutch trade and power in the East Indies but also an equivalent gain to the Company of the rich trade in spice. According to the estimate given by Farquhar, after the disbursement of the civil and military expenses of the government of the islands, a profit of £200,000 per annum could be made if the spices were sold in India and twice that sum if they were sold in Europe.[90] In the

---

[85] BL, IOR Ben. Pol. Cons. R. 119, Vol. 4, No. 46. Court to the Government of Fort St George, 6 March 1810. BL, IOR Ben. Pol. Cons. R.119, Vol. 14, No. 6. Court to the Government of Fort St George, 15 April 1810.

[86] TNA Adm. 1/183. Captain Cole to Drury, 10 August 1810. BL, IOR Ben. Pol. Cons. R.119. Vol. 19, Nixon to Fort St George, 12 August 1810.

[87] *Asiatic Annual Register*, 1810–11, pp. 27–32.

[88] Woodman, *The Victory of Seapower*, Part II: Exploiting Seapower – Overseas, p. 106.

[89] NLS Minto Papers BOX 67. Minto to Charles Grant, Chairman to the East India Company, Madras, 30 April 1810. TNA Adm. 1/182. Drury to Admiralty, Madras Roads, 22 April 1810.

[90] BL, IOR Ben. Pol. Cons. R.119, Vol. 4. No. 42. R.T. Farquhar's memorandum, 25 April

first year an advance had to be made from Bengal because the spices found in the storehouses of Amboyna and the other islands were claimed by the navy and the troops as a prize. However, from the second year the Company could profitably engage in the spice trade by bringing in the produce annually to Calcutta and Madras and selling it in the public market at those places. Politically and strategically too, the occupation of the Moluccas was considered advantageous to the British. These islands were suitable places of refuge, repairs and supplies to the Company's ships engaged in the China trade at a time when these seas were infested with pirates and privateers. Moreover, Minto had in mind the expulsion of the Dutch from Java and the establishment of British authority and influence in the East Indies, and he felt that 'nothing could be more unfavourable to the promotion of such views than an example of indifference to Native Interests as opposed to the Dutch and a sudden and instant abandonment of the former to the destructive vengeance of the latter'.[91]

It was extremely unlikely that if the Spice Islands were abandoned, Daendels would immediately take steps to recover possession, and the inhabitants of the Spice Islands would have to pay dearly for their disaffection to the Dutch at the time of the British attack. On these 'united grounds', commercial, political and human, Minto sealed his decision.[92] Captain Court was confirmed in his office and the Moluccas were placed under the direct control of the Government of Bengal.[93] He was later replaced by Mr Marten, former assistant to the resident at Bencoolen. Major Kelly was sent with reinforcements to take charge of the garrison at Amboyna, which consisted of about 360 Europeans and 600 to 1,000 Amboynese corps raised by Captain Court.[94] Minto actually wanted to keep the Moluccas under the Company as a part of the Company's territories in India. He wrote to the Chairman of the Court of Directors, 'There can be little doubt, that the French Islands will be placed more advantageously & conveniently under the King's immediate Government than under that of the Company. I am disposed to think otherwise respecting the Moluccas, both from their local situation & from their connexion with trade.'[95] Minto later expressed the same opinion with regard to Java.

1810.
[91] NLS M 201. Governor-General-in-Council to the Court of Directors, Fort William, 15 December 1810.
[92] BL, IOR Ben. Pol. Cons. R. 119, Vol. 4, No. 41. Governor-General's minute, Fort St George, 25 April 1810.
[93] Ibid. No. 59. A. Falconer to Captain Court, 2 May 1810.
[94] Ibid., Vol. 19, No. 105. Edmonstone to Marten, 23 November 1810. NLS M 201, Governor-General-in-Council to the Court of Directors, Fort William, 15 December 1810.
[95] NLS Minto Papers, Box 67. Minto to Charles Grant, 30 April 1810.

The Conquest of Java

At the time the operations against the French Islands were undertaken, the Governor-General-in-Council wrote to the Secret Committee:

> It is on the Island of Java alone that the power of the Enemy can ever become formidable. The small extent of the Territory of the French Islands, their distance from India and deficient resource impose a limit on the aggrandizement of the strength of the French and on their means of injury in that quarter. But no such limitation attends the possessions of the Dutch in the Eastern Islands.[96]

The appointment of an officer of Daendels's celebrity and the military measures adopted by him indicated the importance the French attached to Java. Daendels's attachment to the French and hostility toward the British was well known. Although he had not received any reinforcements from Europe, Daendels was busy raising a local army in Java, whose number was estimated to be between 15,000 and 20,000 men. His aims were most probably defensive rather than aggressive, but a powerful European neighbour was always a source of discomfort to the British in India. Unlike the French Islands, Java was self-sufficient and therefore a large number of troops could be raised and maintained on the island notwithstanding the inconvenience of a blockade. The geographical situation of Java gave it a particular importance in the eyes of the British. It was situated closer to the Bay of Bengal than the French Islands were and it was also dangerously close to the route through which the China trade operated. The Government's anxiety for the safety of the China trade is quite understandable, as between the years 1793 and 1810 the East India Company's trade with India yielded an average annual profit of £309,561, whereas the trade with China yielded an annual profit of £981,932.[97] The Dutch had caused no trouble so far, but if after the loss of the French Islands the French frigates used Java as a base of operations, the security of the China trade would be seriously threatened. It was not improbable that after the loss of the French Islands, all attention of the French would be focused on Java, which would then be their only foothold east of the Cape. Holland was annexed by France in 1810, and therefore its colonial policy was more directly under the control of the French Government than ever before. Minto wrote to the Secret Committee on 26 October 1810:

> Indeed from the first establishment of the French authority and even influence in Holland, we have been accustomed to regard the exclusion of the Dutch

[96] BL, IOR Ben. Sec. Letters, Vol. 12. Governor-General-in-Council to the Secret Committee, Fort William, 23 January 1810.

[97] Parliament Papers, House of Commons, 1812, VI, East India Affairs, 4th Report, p. 431.

power from Java and the Eastern seas generally as one of those essential objects of national policy to which the British Arms might perhaps be more beneficially directed than to any other and it requires no argument to prove that the recent events in Europe as they have affected the United Provinces alone increase in a high degree both the importance and the urgency of extinguishing in the Island of Java, a power which is now formally as well as substantially directed by French Counsel and the Seat of which is in fact a province of the French Empire.[98]

The capture of the French Islands was undertaken prior to Java as it was a direct base of French operations in the East and allowed routine raids on British shipping in the Arabian Sea as well as the Bay of Bengal. It was decided that action would be taken against Java immediately after the conquest of Mauritius as successive steps of Minto's project for the expulsion of the French from all their footholds in the Eastern seas. The essential unity of the two expeditions is best described in Minto's own words to Abercromby:

> It is superfluous to advert to the extreme importance of the complete expulsion of the Enemy's power from the Indian Seas. This object will be but imperfectly accomplished by the conquest of the French Islands... I have all along, however, combined the expulsion of the Dutch from their Eastern Establishments with the conquest of the French Islands as an essential part of the same plan, recommended by the same principles of policy & rendered at once more urgent and more easy of execution by success in the former enterprise.[99]

The expedition against Java was to follow closely on the heels of the conquest of the French Islands so as to deprive the French of an opportunity of reinforcing Java. The occupation of the Spice Islands must have warned Daendels that Batavia would be attacked next. It is extremely doubtful if Daendels had any hopes of reinforcements from Europe. That possibility however could not be entirely overlooked, as Minto observed, 'no degree of vigilance on the part of the Government in England or of the Navy in India could with certainty prevent the arrival of such reinforcements at Java'.[100] It was necessary to subvert the French power in the East Indies before it entrenched itself too firmly to be dislodged easily by the British. In 1810–11, conditions in Java were favourable to a successful attack because of the general disaffection of the inhabitants to Daendels's government and the alienation of the Javanese princes. Besides, the political situation in India might not always remain so tranquil as to permit the Government to undertake a foreign expedition at a future date. For all these reasons, Minto

---

[98] NLS M 196. Governor-General-in-Council to the Secret Committee, 26 October 1810.

[99] BL, IOR Ben. Sec. & Sep. Cons. 236. Cons. of 7 January 1811, No. 1. Minto to Major-General Abercromby, Fort William, 3 September 1810.

[100] NLS M 196. Governor-General-in-Council to the Secret Committee, 26 October 1810.

decided to send an expedition against Java as soon as the European troops returned from Mauritius. Farquhar and Abercromby were requested to return the European troops to India immediately after the conclusion of operations against Mauritius, leaving a garrison of Cape troops at Port Louis. A force of 4,000 Europeans and an equal number of sepoys with a due proportion of artillery and pioneers was considered adequate for a successful attack on Batavia. Drury's cooperation was sought in the undertaking.[101]

At the time the expedition against Mauritius was about to sail from India in September 1810, Minto adopted certain preliminary measures for a successful attack on Java. It was necessary to collect complete and accurate information about Daendels's army and fortifications than had been received so far from various sources, and to find out if the Javanese and the Malay princes of the neighbouring islands were disposed to cooperate with the British against the Dutch, or at least remain neutral in the coming contest. For this purpose, Minto employed Thomas Stamford Raffles, who was then on a visit to Calcutta.[102]

Raffles came to Calcutta from Malacca toward the end of June 1810 specifically to visit Minto and they immediately struck up a partnership. Minto found in Raffles an expert and enthusiast about the affairs of the eastern island and whose services would be extremely useful. Raffles found in Minto the patron who offered him the opening he sought. John Leyden and Robert Farquhar were among others whom Minto consulted with regard to Malay affairs. Leyden's interest in the East was academic, but Farquhar could have been a prospective rival of Raffles. From Bourbon and Mauritius, Farquhar wrote to Minto about the necessity of occupying Java, and the ease with which the French–Dutch power in Java might be overthrown in conjunction with the Javanese chiefs and by winning over the people 'by a little address and negociation'. He enumerated the resources of Java, and offered to give up his office as governor of Mauritius if he was offered Java.[103] Raffles's memorandum to Minto, written in 1810, was along similar lines.[104]

[101] BL, IOR Fac. Rec. Java 12. Minto to Abercromby, 5 October 1810. Ibid., Minto to the Earl of Caledon, 19 October 1810. Ibid., Minto to Drury, 5 October 1810.

[102] Raffles was then assistant secretary to the Government of Prince of Wales Island. When it was decided that the Moluccas should be retained, Drury recommended to Minto that Raffles might be appointed resident at Amboyna. Raffles was not interested in that appointment as he believed such an office would be very temporary. He was not happy with the prospect of a post at Penang, and 'with the expectation of still further advance in my interest with Lord Minto', he came to Calcutta toward the end of June 1810. Lady Raffles, *Memoir of the Life and Public Services of Sir Thomas Stamford Raffles* (London, 1830), p. 88.

[103] BL, IOR Ben. Sec. & Sep. Cons. 231. Cons. of 19 October 1810, No. 11. R.T. Farquhar to Minto, Bourbon, 21 August 1810. BL, IOR Ben. Sec. & Sep. Cons. 233. Cons. of 3 May 1811, No. 1. Farquhar to the Governor-General-in-Council, Port Louis, Isle of France, 18 January 1811.

[104] BL, IOR MSS. Eur. E.104. Raff. Col. II, pp. 1–21. Memorandum proposing the capture of Java from the French, 1810, by Raffles. Incomplete manuscript.

Lady Raffles writes in her memoir: 'Mr. Raffles... communicated to Lord Minto information of so important a nature, that his Lordship was induced to undertake without delay, the reduction of Java and its dependencies.'[105]

Such a statement has naturally been criticised by historians in possession of the facts of the case as misleading and motivated by the desire to claim all the honours for Raffles.[106] Wurtzburg apologises for Lady Raffles's blunder and, according to him, the words 'without delay' are significant here, meaning that although Minto had decided to undertake an expedition against Java before Raffles saw him or presented his memorandum, 'yet it was the arrival of Raffles with authentic information and the means to supplement it to the maximum degree that alone enabled Minto to proceed with his project "without delay"'.[107] Minto had already decided however that the operations against Java would be undertaken as soon as possible after the return of the European troops on the successful completion of the operations against L'Ile de France.

On 19 October 1810, Raffles was appointed agent to the governor-general with the Malay states. He was to proceed to the Prince of Wales Island, then to Malacca and as far eastward as necessary for the purpose of obtaining the most accurate information of the nature and extent of the Dutch force and other local information advantageous for the attack, as well as to prepare the Malay chiefs for the planned assault on Java. He was to collect by means of charts, plans and reports information regarding Daendels's military establishments, facilities of landing, the nature of the country in general, and particularly the enemy's position, the primary points at which the attack should be directed, and the facilities of communication from point to point. He was to select Malay and European guides and interpreters to assist in the operation. Captain William Farquhar, the resident at Malacca, was to assist Raffles in all military matters. The disaffected Javanese chiefs were to be encouraged and an expectation of British help held out to them and Raffles's suggestions respecting the relations to be maintained with Palambang, Bantam, Lampong and Bali were sanctioned by the Government. After collecting the necessary information and ascertaining the disposition of the Javanese rulers, Raffles was to return to Bengal by the end of February or the beginning of March for another personal consultation with Minto. If however his return was likely to hamper proceedings, he was to await the arrival of the expedition in Malacca.[108]

Minto had not yet come to any decision about the policy to be pursued after the conquest with regard to the Dutch settlements in Java and the

[105] Lady Raffles, *Memoir*, p. 22.
[106] Vlekke, *Nusantara*, pp. 239, footnote.
[107] Wurtzburg, C.E., *Raffles of the Eastern Isles* (London, 1954), p. 103.
[108] BL, IOR Fac. Rec. Java 12. Edmonstone to Raffles, Fort William, 19 October 1810. BL, IOR Ben. Sec. Letters, Vol. 12. Minto to the Secret Committee, Fort William, 26 October 1810.

neighbouring islands, which were dependent on the Dutch. In October 1810, therefore, while conveying their decision to send an expedition against Java to the Secret Committee, the Governor-General-in-Council wrote:

> It is proper however generally to observe that we contemplate rather the extinction of the Enemy's power than the establishment of our own on the same basis and to the same extent, rather to emancipate the Chiefs of the Island and its dependencies than to reduce them under a similar authority of our own. To form in short, an establishment which while it afforded to the British Government all the commercial advantages of the Island, shall restore to the several chiefs the exercise of their independent authority, and bestow upon the Inhabitants the beneficial use of their own soil and labour.[109]

According to Minto, the future policy regarding Java ought to be determined by a consideration of the means of the Company for maintaining it and must also secure the main objective in view, that is, the permanent exclusion of the French from the Eastern seas.[110] The Secret Committee recommended that after destroying all the forts, batteries and works of defence, and taking possession of all arms, ammunition and military stores, the island should be left to the Javanese, distributing among them if advisable the arms and ammunition taken from the Dutch. The home authorities regarded the expulsion of the French and the Dutch from Java as a purely a war-measure and entertained no thoughts of either temporary or permanent occupation of Java.

Minto was relieved at the sanction of the home authorities for the Java expedition, but he decided to ignore their orders about the abandonment of the island after conquest. In his opinion, the Secret Committee's orders were based on a miscalculation of Java's importance. It was not a little island in the Pacific which could be safely abandoned after dismantling its fortifications. It was an ancient Dutch colony where there were numerous European, Chinese and other non-Javanese settlers, who owned property and had taken roots in the country. They could not be left exposed to 'the vindictive power of the Malay Princes and natives' all of whom had so long been the underdogs. It was also feared that if all European control was withdrawn from Java, the island would quickly become a centre of piracy which was already a menace in those seas as the Malay prows considered acts of piracy quite legitimate. On the advice of Leyden and Raffles, Minto had come to the conclusion that the Malays could not yet be trusted with total independence, but that 'the benevolent supervision' of a European power was essential for the peace and prosperity of the island. He decided

---

[109] BL, IOR Ben. Sec. Letters, Vol. 12. Governor-General-in-Council to the Secret Committee, 26 October 1810.
[110] Ibid.

that British authority was to be substituted for the Dutch, 'with such modifi-
cations as shall appear adapted at once to our moderate and unambitious
views to the protection of the old Colonists and to the care and benefit of
the Native States and people'.[111]

The Company's commercial interests in the East Indies were a critical
consideration. Minto believed that a commercial connection with Java could
be profitably maintained only by the presence of British supervision and
authority on the spot. The two principal objectives in his view were: first,
to secure the freedom of British trade on the coast as well as in the interior
of Java, with the guarantee of protection to British agents; and second,
the exclusion of all other European traders from the East Indies without a
licence from the British. Minto also considered entering into arrangements
with the Malay chiefs, which would secure to the British a monopoly of the
purchase of the produce of the country. The exports from Java were mainly
coffee, sugar, arrack grain and tobacco. Its imports were opium, piece goods
and other sundry articles. Minto visualised an expansion of the Company's
markets in the East Indies. The transference of the Dutch trade with Japan to
the Company was also an important point of consideration.[112]

Minto suggested to Dundas that should the Company decline to occupy
any part of Java, whether HM Government might not retain the Dutch settlements in Java as a royal government. In any case, he decided to retain the
conquered territories provisionally and to succeed to the established relations
between the Dutch and the native states.[113] Minto wrote to Sir Samuel
Auchmuty:

> I do not regard the short and general instructions of the Secret Committee as
> binding in a strict and literal acceptation of that document. Such orders, issued
> from a distance, always involve a certain latitude of discretion in their execution
> by those, who may be enabled by vicinity to the scene of action, and by a closer
> view of the subject to discern all the practical consequences of the measure....
> I conceived that our protecting Government must for a time supply the place
> of that which we are to abolish.[114]

At the same time the Secret Committee's orders were received, Drury
received parallel orders from the Lords Commissioners of the Admiralty
directing him to withdraw the blockade of Java and to cooperate with the
Government of Bengal in the operations against Java. Drury decided to send
as many ships as he could spare to the Straits of Sunda in order to intercept

---

[111] NLS M 196. Secret & Separate General Letter. Minto to the Secret Committee, 22 January
1811.
[112] BL, IOR Eur. MSS. C. 34. Raff. Col. I. Minto to Raffles, Calcutta, 8 February 1811
(Private). NLS M 377. Minto to R. Dundas, Fort William, 25 January 1811.
[113] NLS M 377. Minto to R. Dundas, Fort William, 24 January 1811.
[114] NLS M 372. Minto to Sir Samuel Auchmuty, Fort William, 31 January 1811.

any reinforcements which the French might send to Java and to afford protection to the homeward bound China fleet, which usually left China about the middle of January.

As it was necessary to embark on the expedition prior to the onset of the south-west monsoon the latest possible date of departure was established to be 1 March. The Madras Government started making preparations on its own for the departure of the expedition from Madras without waiting for the orders of the Government of Bengal. As the troops returning from Mauritius were likely to be unfit for immediate departure for another service abroad, Barlow and Auchmuty decided not to employ them at all in the Java expedition. According to their arrangement, troops were to be drawn from the different stations in southern India, from Goa, Cannanore, Hyderabad, Masulipatam, Trichnopoly and a corps of artillery and 1,500 Europeans from Ceylon. In this way Barlow expected to raise a total force of 4,000 Europeans and 3,000 sepoys – altogether 7,000 troops exclusive of cavalry and pioneers. Bombay and Bengal were approached to provide tonnage. Drury of course offered his utmost cooperation in ships and salt provisions, and agreed to receive on board his squadron 1,500 to 2,000 Europeans.[115]

Minto was thoroughly disgruntled at the attempt of the Government of Madras to pursue an independent course of action. He suspected Drury was behind it all and requested that Barlow and Auchmuty be guided solely by the orders sent to them by the Supreme Government. Military preparations were already underway in Bengal. The sepoy troops were assembling at Fort William from distant parts and nothing but the lack of adequate tonnage would delay their departure for Malacca later than the middle of March. Moreover, in view of the distance of the various stations from which Barlow proposed to draw troops and the lack of tonnage until some of the transports returned from Mauritius, it was unlikely that the entire force could sail together from Madras by 1 March. Hence, this fact, in Minto's opinion cancelled the only justification of the Madras Government's separate arrangements. He regretted having to reject Barlow's arrangements totally, but he regarded it as a case 'entirely at variance with the habits as well as the legal constitution of the Government of India' that one of the subordinate governments should without reference to the Supreme Government adopt plans in the execution of measures originating with the latter and committed to its care by the authorities at home. The Governor-General-in-Council reaffirmed his original plan that the European troops should be drawn partly from the troops returning from Mauritius, partly from Fort St George and Ceylon and the sepoys entirely from Bengal. According to his calculations,

---

[115] BL, IOR Fac. Rec. Java 12. Sir G. Barlow to Minto, Fort St George, 13 January 1811. Ibid., S. Auchmuty to Minto, Fort St George, 13 January 1811. Ibid., Barlow-in-Council to T. Maitland, 13 January 1811. Ibid., Barlow-in-Council to J. Duncan, 13 January 1811.

the troops would reach the point of attack in Java by the end of June and that approximately a month would be needed to close the campaign successfully.[116]

The Supreme Government wrote to Bombay, Ceylon and Goa cancelling the arrangements made with them by the Government of Fort St George. Bombay was to provide transports and a stock of provisions and water, and also to transport the salt provisions which Drury had consented to provide from the king's stores at Bombay.[117] Captain Courtland Schuyler, the British resident at Goa, was directed to provide only the 78th European Regiment, and not also the sepoy troops as suggested by the Madras Government.[118] The aid from Ceylon was limited to a detachment of Royal Artillery and a detachment of 600 Europeans if it could be spared in order to make up the deficiency in the regiments returning from the French Islands.[119] The European troops were to embark from Madras and the sepoys and a part of the artillery from Calcutta not later than the middle of March to rendezvous at Malacca. The exact plan of action to be followed thereafter was to be decided on the receipt of information from Raffles about the passage to Java and the disposition of Javanese and Malay chiefs.[120]

In the beginning of February 1811, two of the three divisions of troops sent back from Mauritius returned to Fort St George.[121] Drury, although frustrated in his attempt to assume the initiative, agreed to cooperate with the ships at his disposal and to supply salt provisions sufficient to feed 6,000 men for about four months.[122]

The most remarkable feature of the Java expedition was the presence of the governor-general. On the eve of the departure of the expedition, Minto surprised everybody by announcing his decision to accompany it in person.[123]

---

[116] BL, IOR Fac. Rec. Java 11. Governor-General-in-Council to Barlow-in-Council, Fort William, 8 February 1811. Ibid., Governor-General-in-Council to Drury, 8 February 1811. NLS M 372. Minto to S. Auchmuty, Fort William, 31 January 1811. BL, IOR Ben. Sec. Letters, Vol. 13. Governor-General-in-Council to the Secret Committee, 28 February 1811.

[117] BL, IOR Java 11. Governor-General-in-Council to J. Duncan-in-Council, 6 February 1811.

[118] BL, IOR Java 11. Governor-General-in-Council to Captain C. Schuyler, 6 February 1811.

[119] Ibid., Governor-General-in-Council to T. Maitland, 17 January 1811.

[120] BL, IOR Java 12. Governor-General-in-Council to Drury, 19 January 1811.

[121] BL, IOR Java 12. Barlow-in-Council to the Governor-General-in-Council, 11 February 1811.

[122] Ibid., Drury to Minto, Madras Roads, 2 February 1811. Drury's hurry to push on the Java expedition is quite understandable, not only because Batavia was expected to provide a rich plunder, but also because his term of office was about to close. A new naval commander-in-chief had been promised some time previously, and his arrival was eagerly awaited by Minto. Drury naturally wanted the operations against Java to be completed or at least well underway before that happened. Admiral Bertie had turned him away from Mauritius, and it is sad that Drury died just on the eve of the sailing of the Java expedition, on 6 March 1811, at Madras.

[123] The impact of Minto's decision on the Government circle at Calcutta is best described in Captain Taylor's (Military Secretary to the Governor-General) words. 'His Lordship gave the bigwigs at the seat of government a terrible shock. They threw up their hands in horror

Curzon's comment on it later was that it was 'a most undesirable proceeding, undertaken on his own responsibility and without orders'.[124] The absence of the governor-general from India for however short a period, in this case it was for seven months, was a measure which could only be justified by considerations of extreme importance and necessity. Minto's decision to go to Java therefore indicates not only the importance he attached to Java as a valuable acquisition to the Company, but also the personal responsibility he felt for the success of the military operations against the island. He had decided to push on the expedition to Java via Malacca after May, despite Drury's warning about the hazards of the south-west monsoon in the Java seas, mainly in the hope that the more experienced seamen in Malacca would be able to hit upon a safe route for the fleet to Java. Raffles had been instructed to devote his particular attention to this and to communicate to the Government the result of his enquiries. Since much of the desired information from Malacca remained to be obtained and the departure of the army from India could no longer be delayed, Minto decided to go at least to Malacca. He wrote to Raffles on 8 February 1811:

> The improbability of your returning to Bengal in time, with the information which can alone enable me to frame instructions for the conduct of the expedition and for settling the consequent arrangements has been very obvious for some time. The expediency not to say the necessity of my approaching the scene and bringing the authority of Government at least within reach of reference is evident. That resolution is therefore taken.[125]

His plan was to meet Raffles at Malacca, and there in conference with him and Auchmuty to draw up the final plans, military and political. He did not intend to interfere with Auchmuty's command or conduct of the expedition, but he felt that by his presence he would be able to prevent the king's navy from assuming too authoritative a role or pursuing any separate or independent course of action which would throw his plans out of gear.[126]

---

at the Governor-General demeaning himself over a paltry place like Java;... Lord M... said "let them think what they please, it makes no odds to me'." Extract from Captain Taylor's diary. Printed in Wurzburg, *Raffles*, p. 131.
John Leyden wrote to Raffles, 'All are utterly confounded by his Lordship's resolution, of which nobody had the slightest suspicion... Indeed, more than half are as yet thunderstruck and are very far from believing that he has any real intention of visiting Java. "No," say they, "to go and take such a little paltry place would not be decorous, no, no."' Leyden to Raffles, undated. Probable date February/March 1811. Printed in Lady Raffles, *Memoir*, p. 26.

[124] Curzon, G.N., Marquis of Kedleston, *British Government in India: The Story of the Viceroys and Government Houses*, 2 Vols (London, 1925), Vol. 2, p. 184.

[125] BL, IOR Eur. MSS. C.34. Raff. Col. I. Minto to Raffles, Calcutta, 8 February 1811.

[126] NLS M 372. Minto to S. Auchmuty, Fort William, 31 January 1811. NLS M 377. Minto to R. Dundas, 25 January 1811. NLS M 39. No. 5. Minto to Lady Minto, Calcutta, 25 February 1811. Minto Papers, Box 67. Minto to Gilbert Elliot, 14 March 1811.

Minto's other objective in going to Java was to make the political and administrative arrangements after the conquest himself, instead of delegating that function to Raffles or anyone else by providing broad and general directions as to the system to be adopted there. He felt he would be better able to offer advice to the Court of Directors and HM Government on questions that were awaiting their final decision if he collected personal experience and first-hand information about Java. It was provisionally decided that after the overthrow of the Dutch power, an interim government would be established in Batavia for the protection of the Dutch, Javanese and Chinese inhabitants from the consequences of anarchy. The Dutch themselves were to be largely employed in the new government. Batavia, Samarang and Gressie were to be retained. The commercial arrangements and political relations with the Malay chiefs would also have to be determined. It was impossible to provide adequate instructions on all these points from Calcutta because of the insufficient information and data at the disposal of the Government. Although certain general directions could be given, it was not possible to provide for all future exigencies. In a minute dated 25 February 1811, Minto wrote:

> It would certainly be impracticable to provide definitely, by instructions framed before the commencement of operations, for the nature and extent of the establishment to be maintained on the Island of Java and its dependencies; for the engagements to be concluded with the native Chiefs of the Islands; for the adjustment of the various interests involved in the result of the Enterprize, and for the decision of the numerous questions which may be expected to arise, both during its progress and after its successfull termination.[127]

Java was to crown the system he had adopted to remove the French from the Indian seas, and it also opened a prospect of a wider and more permanent establishment of British influence in the Malayan world. 'The object we have in view,' wrote Minto, 'is of the greatest national importance and value, and it is of infinite consequence that the first political arrangements should be made on right principles.'[128] He would have been equally responsible for these arrangements had he remained at Calcutta but clearly wouldn't have the ability to make these decisions to his satisfaction as he would if he was physically present. Apart from matters of state, Minto looked forward to enjoying his trip to Java. He wrote to Lady Minto:

> It is not a matter of taste or choice... but of duty, that is to say of necessity, that I am going to friskify in this manner, although I confess,... I never engaged

---

[127] BL, IOR Ben. Sec. & Sep. Cons. 236. Cons. of 9 March 1811, No.1. Governor-General's minute, Fort William, 25 February 1811.

[128] NLS M 39, No. 6. Minto to Lady Minto, 20 March 1811. Printed in Countess of Minto, *Lord Minto in India*, pp. 251–52, as part of a letter from Minto to Lady Minto, dated 25 February 1811.

in any affair with greater interest or with more pleasure; and you will easily conceive what a gratifying break this kind of adventure must make in the monotony of my not less laborious life at Fort William.[129]

Minto's decision to go to Java was regarded with varying sentiments by his colleagues, the public and the Court of Directors. After the first moment of surprise, his colleagues in the Calcutta Council agreed with him that it was the best course to follow under the circumstances, especially as there were no pressing problems at home which required his personal attention. Among the public, who did not know what his real intentions were, various speculations went around, for example, that Minto was either going home after touching at Madras, or that he was going on a tour of Mauritius, Bencoolen and other outlying settlements, and some even thought that serious trouble had broken out in Madras and Minto was going there to settle it.[130] The home authorities, when they heard of it, did not think it at all satisfactory that Minto should have absented himself from India.[131] In the opinion of the Directors, instead of giving his whole attention to Java he should have attended to the more important matters of his office, namely the financial remittances to the Company, which were overdue. It was alleged by his enemies that he went to Java to get a share in the prize.[132]

On the other hand, those who regarded Java as a valuable acquisition to the Company regarded Minto's going to Java as setting the seal on the annexation of Java. An idealist like John Leyden, who was an expert on Malay history and customs, had extravagant ideas of reviving the ancient confederacy of the Malay states under the governor-general. He wrote to Raffles that some of the councillors, naming Lumsden and Colebrooke, were in favour of 'accustoming the Malays to independence', that Raffles and he should exert all their influence with Minto in order to prevent such a course of action. The oppressed people of Java were to be told that the 'Good Maharaja of Bengal' was coming to deliver them from Dutch oppression and to establish a benevolent government.[133] Raffles was less of a visionary than Leyden, and with him the political and commercial considerations cut more ice. He wanted to retain in the hands of the British as many of the commercial advantages then

[129] Ibid.

[130] NLS M 39. Minto to Lady Minto, Calcutta, 25 February 1811.

[131] NLS Minto Papers, Box 72. Robert Dundas to Minto, 10 July 1811. Also BL, IOR Home Misc. Series 831(c). 4.

[132] NLS M 83. Gilbert Elliot to Minto, London, 2 April 1812. Gilbert Elliot, Minto's eldest son, writes of an interview with Bosanquet, Chairman of the East India Company, that Bosanquet, 'carefully avoided the most distant insinuation of his satisfaction with anything you have done', that although he did not openly blame Minto for going to Java, he regretted that Minto was not at Calcutta when his letters arrived there.

[133] Lady Raffles, *Memoir*, p. 25. Leyden to Raffles, undated, probable date February/March 1811.

enjoyed by the Dutch as possible. An entirely new field of lucrative commerce would be opened to the East India Company by the extension of its authority over the Dutch East Indies.

So far, the British had been interlopers in the East Indies trade, as smugglers and contraband traders, with the help of native traders. They had now the opportunity of taking over the whole of the Dutch trade and maintaining the monopolies established by the Dutch in the trade in opium, tin and spices. Raffles proposed that Java should become the centre of British power in the East Indies, and Malacca, Penang and Bencoolen were to follow its direction.[134] Raffles wrote to Minto, 'The Eastern trade... was the foundation of the Dutch prosperity in Europe, and... they derived greater resources from the Eastern part of India [the East Indies], than the English have ever done from the Western [India proper]. We have now the opportunity of uniting both.'[135]

Evidently the idea of Greater India was not totally forgotten. Java and the eastern islands had once been closely connected with India. The eastern islands were ancient Hindu colonies. The temptation to draw an analogy between Minto's expedition to Java and the ancient Hindu attempts at expansion over the eastern islands is irresistible and the legitimate objectives of overseas expansion from India.

Minto had a specifically chosen group of experts to accompany him to Java, some of whom were to hold the key positions in the new Java administration. John Leyden, whom Minto described as 'a perfect Malay' for his knowledge of the language, literature and history of the Malays, went as assistant to the governor-general.[136] Hugh Hope,[137] described by Minto as 'a tolerable Dutchman' because of his mastery of the Dutch tongue and family connections went with him as deputy-secretary; Archibald Seton, the resident at Delhi, who was appointed Governor of Prince of Wales Island; Rochonnet, an ex-Dutch officer who supplied information about the military forces in Java and other local information and Stubenvolt, an ex-Prussian officer formerly brigade-major of the Dutch troops at Ternate. Rochonnet's local knowledge was useful and Stubenvolt's fluency in English, Dutch and Malay languages rendered him useful as an interpreter and translator.

---

[134] BL, IOR Eur. MSS. C.34. Raff. Col. I: Raffles to Minto, Malacca, 18 February 1811.

[135] BL, IOR Eur. MSS. C.34. Raff. Col. I. Raffles to Minto, Malacca, 18 February 1811.

[136] Dr John Casper Leyden, born on 8 September 1775 at Denholm on the Teviot. In 1803, came out to India as assistant surgeon and naturalist attached to the Commission of Survey in Mysore. He was later appointed teacher of Hindustani language in the College at Fort William. Went to Malacca in 1808 to recover his health, struck up a close friendship with Raffles, and became deeply interested in the language and history of the Malays. Leyden's opinion in all matters connected with the Malays was considered weighty by both Minto and Raffles. Unfortunately he died a few days after the fall of Cornelis.

[137] Hugh Hope was brother of Sir John Hope, one of Wellington's Peninsular Generals. Hope had recently arrived from Mauritius and held a post in the export warehouse.

Minto and his party left Calcutta on board the Company's cruiser *Mornington* on 9 March 1811 for Madras in order to change to a swifter vessel, the *Modeste*, for Java.[138] The expedition sailed in different divisions from Calcutta and Madras during the course of March and April. The Bengal quota consisted of 4,000 sepoy volunteers formed into four battalions and drawn from all parts of northern India, and also the governor-general's bodyguard for service in the field numbering 1,000 men then at Barrackpore, was to form a reserve battalion at Prince of Wales Island or Malacca. The whole force from Bengal exceeded 5,000 men. The European force from Madras, consisting of 4,000 infantry, a corps of cavalry and a detachment of artillery from Ceylon, sailed in two divisions from Madras in April.[139] The first division from Madras sailed on 15 April under Colonel Gillespie; and the second on the 29th under Major-General Wetherall. The delay in the sailing of troops from Madras was mainly due to the late arrival of the transports from Bombay, all of which were not in an equally good condition.[140] By sailing on the 29th, the last division from Madras luckily escaped disaster, for a violent hurricane came ashore at Madras on 2 May which destroyed all the ships in the harbour including the *Chichester* store ship, HMS *Dover* and a number of merchantmen. A large amount of the stores and many horses belonging to the expedition were lost.[141] If the last division of European troops had been caught in the hurricane and destroyed, it is doubtful if the attack on Java could have been carried out that year. The whole force assembled at Malacca by the middle of June. It consisted of 11,028 men of whom 5,472 were Europeans.[142]

Since December 1810, Raffles had stationed himself at Malacca and opened communications with some of the Javanese and Malay chiefs through Indonesian merchants and princes, and sent British officers in certain cases. Bantam was in revolt, and although Daendels had sent a punitive expedition to Bantam, the rebels had taken shelter in the hills and woods. The chiefs of Cheribon were alienated by Daendels's interference in the succession and banishment of some of the chiefs and the destruction of the coffee planta-tions by the Dutch. The sultans of Palembang and Mataram were also hostile to the Dutch. Raffles was particularly interested in the Sultan of Palembang, whom he believed to be one of the richest Malay chieftains and was said to have 'Godowns [warehouses] stored with Dollars and Gold hoarded by his ancestors'. Hearing that Daendels had sent some Dutch ships to Palembang

[138] BL, IOR Ben. Sec. Letters, Vol. 13. Minto to Secret Committee, *Mornington* at sea, 15 March 1811.
[139] NLS M 209. Minto to the Chairman of the Court of Directors, *Mornington* at sea, 15 March 1811. BL, IOR Ben. Sec. Letters, Vol. 13. Minto to the Secret Committee, 15 March 1811.
[140] BL, IOR Ben. Sec. Letters, Vol. 13. Minto to the Secret Committee, Malacca, 14 June 1811.
[141] NLS M 174. Minto to General Hewitt, Malacca, 14 June 1811. BL, IOR Ben. Sec. Letters, Vol. 13. Vice-President-in-Council to the Secret Committee, Fort William, 4 July 1811.
[142] BL, IOR Fac. Rec. Java 13. Return of troops at Malacca, 13 June 1811.

to enforce payment of some arrears and Raffles wrote immediately to the Sultan of Palembang urging him to be on his guard against the Dutch and assuring help if he should want to get rid of them. Raffles sent Tunku Mahomed a relation of the sultan, as his confidential agent to Palembang.[143] The Sultan of Palembang used this letter as an excuse to massacre the entire Dutch population in his kingdom soon after the Dutch were defeated. To Lingen, Bantam and Cheribon, Raffles sent his 'best assistant' Tunku Pangeran of Siak. Tunku Pangeran and his men were to go first to Lingen and with the permission of the sultan examine the harbours at Bangka and Lampong for the presence of any Dutch vessels. After secretly landing the banished Cheribon princes at Cheribon, the Tunku was to go to the rebels at Bantam with Raffles's letter and from there open communications with the Susuhonan or the emperor at Solo. Another agent was to carry Raffles's letter to Madura and to the Sultan of Mataram.[144]

The underlying statement of Raffles's communications to the Javanese and Malay chiefs was that the British were thinking of relieving them from the authority of the Dutch and the French and wished to find out their feelings about it. He assured them, with apparent sincerity, that the British had no desire for more territories, and that their only wish was to 'expel their European Enemies and to act as true friends to all Rajahs and legal authorities'. If the Malay rajas were willing to become friends of the British, they were to give to his agents a written paper to that effect, but to be careful not to appear as open enemies of the Dutch before the British began their operations in Java.[145] The Sultan of Madura, Raffles heard, had refused to furnish any more troops to Daendels, and he was sure that this was brought about by the communications he had sent to the sultan earlier.[146] Captain Greig of the *Minto* brig and Lieutenant Smith of the *Arethusa* cutter, who had carried letters to Bali, had been warmly received. The Raja of Bali Baliling had assisted in sending letters to the Susuhonan, the Sultan of Mataram, the Sultan of Madura and the Panambuhan of Samanap. According to Raffles, the Sultan of Carang Asam and Lombok offered his services to the British as soon as he heard of the expedition.[147]

The most serious problem facing the expedition was the difficulties and risks involved in making a passage from Malacca to Java with a large

---

[143] BL, IOR MSS. Eur. C.35. Raff. Col. I. Raffles to Minto, Malacca, 15 December 1810 (Private).

[144] BL, IOR MSS. Eur. C.35. Raff. Col. Raffles to Minto, Malacca, 15 December 1810 (Private).

[145] BL, IOR MSS. Eur. C.34. Raff. Col. I. pp. 83–87. Raffles's instructions to Tunku Pangeran of Siak. Ibid., pp. 67–98. Translations of Malay letters written to Native Princes etc., Previous to the expedition.

[146] BL, IOR MSS. Eur. C.35. Raff. Col. Raffles to Minto, 6 May 1811.

[147] BL, IOR MSS. Eur. E.105. Raff. Col. III. Raffles to Minto, Undated. Probable date January/May 1811, Malacca.

fleet of transports during the monsoon. Although Raffles had previously reported that Daendels was concentrating his forces near Buitenzorg on the west coast of Java,[148] it was now known that the Dutch forces were concentrated at Weltevreeden and Meester Cornelis near Batavia on the east coast. Consequently, a landing had to be made near Batavia for a swift and successful attack. The usual direct route from Malacca to the north-east coast of Java would be obstructed by the south-west monsoon. In order to find a safe passage for the fleet, Raffles consulted several experienced eastern traders both at Malacca and at Penang and asked the opinion of naval officers who were experienced in those seas, particularly Captains Carnegy, Greig, Tait, Stewart, Scott and Smith. According to Captains Carnegy and Tait, the northern route around Borneo was perhaps the only feasible one under the circumstances. However, they could suggest no way of avoiding the dangers of either the narrow Balabac passage or the Soolo Archipelago, of which very little was known, nor how the Straits of Macasar could be passed where the winds were proverbially variable and the currents strong. Borneo's east coast was covered with shoals and the Macasar coast entirely devoid of soundings. Five weeks was the shortest time in which this passage could be made, but it was just as likely to take eight if conditions were unfavourable in the Straits of Macasar.[149] Hence this proposal of the northern route was not particularly acceptable.

The only alternative was to take the route through the Straits of Durion in preference to any other. Captains Scott and Steward, who knew this passage well, thought there was a good chance of making it, although slight delays might occur. It was known that Dutch Indiamen were in the habit of making this passage at any time from May till September by the following route: Malacca–the Straits of Durion–Pulu Vaccla–Succadana–Batavia. It was proposed that the British fleet should adopt this route. Doubts about the channel between the Karimata Islands and the mainland of Borneo were removed by the exertions of Captain Greig who had made an actual survey of the channel. He was assisted by Mr Burns who had long been a resident at Pontianak, on the west coast of Borneo and had once brought a fleet through this passage without difficulty.[150] Captain Greig[151] was actually making the survey when Minto reached Malacca.

[148] BL, IOR Fac. Rec. Java 13. Raffles to Edmonstone, Malacca, 31 January 1810.

[149] BL, IOR MSS. Eur. C.34. Raff. Col. I. Memorandum respecting passage from Malacca to Java, 22 May 1811, Malacca.

[150] BL, IOR Eur. MSS. C.34. Raff. Col. I, pp. 111–18. Memorandum respecting the passage from Malacca to Java, presented by Raffles to Minto, Malacca, 22 May 1811.

[151] Captain Greig was a country ship-master who had a wide knowledge of the Eastern seas. He was given charge of the schooner *Minto* during the Java expedition; and was largely responsible for ascertaining the passage from Malacca to Java which was actually followed. Minto had the highest opinion of his abilities as a seaman. About Greig he wrote, 'Greig is

On Greig's return, it was decided that the fleet, which consisted of nearly a hundred ships, should sail in small divisions in order to avoid mishap in the narrow parts of the passage, first through the Straits of Singapore, a common passage to China, and then make the west coast of Borneo not further north than Pontianak, at a point near where the fleet was to assemble. Following this, the ships were to sail southward along the coast of Borneo with the help of favourable land breeze and tide, and meet at Tangoong Samba, an island on the south-western extremity of Borneo. From there, the north-eastern cost of Java could be made in three or four days.

On 22 July news was received from a prize vessel taken at Gressie that three French frigates had entered the port of Surabaya. These were the ships that brought General Janssens to Java on 27 April 1811. The British only heard of his arrival when they were actually off Java. The *Modeste* immediately left for Java and Minto had the first glimpse of 'the land of promise' on 25 July 1811. The rest of the fleet crossed over to Java, making the Bumkin Island off Indramaya point near Cheribon by 30 July. The passage from Malacca to Java was therefore completed in forty-two days without a single mishap regardless of the monsoon or the unfamiliarity of the route to the British sailors[152] and this was regarded by Minto as a cause for self-congratulation. He wrote to Lady Minto:

> This voyage is made interesting by the very positive opinions which Admiral Drury had given himself, & had managed to obtain a countenance to from several quarters of authority on such question that it was impracticable to make a passage to Java with a fleet of transports, if it should sail from Madras later than the 1st of March. It was with this opinion that I had to contend in pushing forward the expedition in the present season… the result has furnished another testimony in favour of the virtue called obstinacy, which is entitled by success to the more polite name of firmness.[153]

The British armada off Java consisted of nearly a hundred sail, including four men of war, fourteen frigates and seven sloops of war, eight Company's cruisers, fifty-seven transports and numerous gunboats and auxiliaries.[154]

---

a plain, modest, unassuming Fife man, with excellent natural parts and character.' NLS M 39, Minto to Lady Minto, ended 3 August 1811.

[152] NLS M 174. Minto to Hewitt, Weltevreeden, 18 August 1811. NLS M 39. No. 11. Minto to Lady Minto, *Modeste* off Java, ended 3 August 1811. BL, IOR Ben. Sec. Letters Vol.13. Minto to the Secret Committee, Weltevreeden, 29 August 1811. Ibid. Vice-President-in-Council to the Secret Committee, 23 August 1811, Fort William.

[153] NLS M 39. No. 11. Minto to Lady Minto, *Modeste* off Java, ended 3 August 1811.

[154] The British fleet off Java consisted of the *Illustrious, Minden, Lion* and *Scipion,* men of war; *Modeste, Akbar, Caroline, Leda, Bucephalus, Doris, Psyche, Phaeton, Cornelia, Drake, Hussar, President, Phoebe, Nisus,* frigates; *Hecate, Hesper, Harpy, Baracouta, Samarang, Dasher, Procris,* sloops of war; *Malabar, Mornington, Aurora, Nautilus, Vestal, Ariel, Thetis, Psyche,* Company's cruisers; fifty-seven transports and several gunboats. BL, IOR Ben. Sec. Letters, Vol. 13.

Rear-Admiral Stopford of the Cape station, hearing of Drury's death, joined the expedition off Java in order to assume the naval command.[155] The army consisted of more than 10,000 well equipped and highly disciplined men and if the seamen and marines were added, the total force exceeded 12,000 men. Numerically, the army raised by Daendels was supposed to be stronger. The exact number and composition of the Dutch army was not known. According to Raffles's estimate, Daendels had an army of 30,000 men.[156] However, the effective strength of the Dutch force was not nearly half as formidable as its number. Only about a thousand were Europeans belonging to the artillery and cavalry regiments, and their efficiency was impaired by a lack of discipline and the climate. The army was officered principally by foreigners, scarcely one-fourth were Dutch and the rest were Germans, Russians, French, Italians or mixed race Dutch. Most of them were promoted from the ranks and few had any qualifications for commissions. Consequently, although a large number of native infantry were raised, they were not efficiently trained or disciplined. Daendels did not trust the Javanese. His army was drawn from the adjacent islands and the dependencies of Java, mainly from Madura, Bali, Sumatra, Celebes, Borneo and the Moluccas, the native chiefs being compelled to furnish quotas of recruits.[157] The state of this army was described by Minto to the Secret Committee: 'These are partly slaves, partly vassal subjects, disliking... the restraints of European discipline; all forced into ranks, all hating the Dutch, ill found, paid in paper at 75 p.cent discount, by the latest accounts, deserting habitually in considerable numbers.'[158]

Such an army was unlikely to offer a strong and determined resistance to an invading force, especially if inducements such as better pay and a prospect of freedom from oppression were held out to them. In an open war or guerrilla tactics, such an army was likely to desert immediately; the only way to make them fight was in a strongly fortified post. This was exactly the tactic adopted by Daendels and by his successor Janssens in resisting the British invasion. No opposition was to be made to the landing of the British army, but every impediment was to be thrown to their advance by destroying bridges, withdrawing all supplies, contaminating water and leaving disease and climate to sap the energy of the invaders. The main stand was to be made at the fortified citadel at Meester Cornelis, six miles from Batavia.

Vice-President-in-Council to the Secret Committee, Fort William, 23 August 1811. Thorn, Major W., *Memoir of the Conquest of Java* (London, 1815), p. 16.

[155] NLS M 496. Rear-Admiral Stopford to Minto, HMS *Scipion* off Responde Island, 17 July 1811.

[156] BL, IOR Eur. MSS. E.105. Raff. Col. III, pp. 81–124. Raffles to Minto, undated. Probable date Malacca, between January and May 1811, because Raffles's similar reports to Minto on Java before the conquest were dated about this period.

[157] BL, IOR Fac. Rec. Java 13. Raffles to Edmonstone, Malacca, 31 January 1811.

[158] BL, IOR Ben. Sec. Letters Vol. 13. Minto to the Secret Committee, 15 March 1811.

General Janssens had arrived in Java on 27 April 1811, with three French frigates and a few European troops.[159] Daendels was recalled because his enemies reported to Bonaparte that he intended assuming independence in Java. Daendels left Java toward the end of June in one of the frigates that brought Janssens. It is doubtful if Janssens believed the British invasion could be successfully resisted with the resources at his disposal. However, he had once before surrendered a Dutch colony (the Cape of Good Hope) to the British, and at the time of his appointment to Java, Bonaparte had warned him against a second surrender.[160] Janssens therefore prepared to defend Java at Cornelis, although the colony was bankrupt, the army inefficient and disloyal and the inhabitants quite indifferent. On the eve of the British landing, Janssens appealed to the allegiance of the inhabitants in a Proclamation. Batavia was abandoned and all movable public and private property were ordered to be removed to Cornelis. Anything likely to be of assistance to the invaders, for example, horses, buffaloes, boats, were ordered to be removed to the interior of the country. The public storehouses and magazines which could not be protected were burned. All civil and military officers were called up to attend Janssens at Cornelis, leaving their families and slaves unprotected in Batavia. The inhabitants of Java were urged to prove their loyalty to the emperor and to do everything in their power to oppose the invaders.[161]

The landing of the British troops on 4 August 1811 near the village of Chillingehing about nine miles east of Batavia was safe and uneventful.[162] Minto issued Proclamations to the Dutch and native inhabitants of Java, assuring them that the British had no quarrels with them and invited their cooperation with regard to the objective in view, 'to expel the recently established power of the French and to receive the Island under British protection'.[163] Cornelis was about fourteen miles from Chillingehing, but because of the heat and especially as no horses, cattle or labour could be procured to carry the stores and provisions, it was decided to take the shorter road to Batavia.

Janssens withdrew his troops from Batavia on 6 August after setting fire to the public stores. All European civilians were compelled to report to Cornelis and the remaining population, mostly women and children were in an unprotected state, while the town was looted by Malays. On the first summons,

---

[159] Ibid., Vice-President-in-Council to the Secret Committee, Fort William, 24 September 1811.
[160] Thorn, *Memoir*, p. 103.
[161] BL, IOR Eur. MSS. E.105. Raff. Col. III., pp. 293–98. General J.W. Janssens's proclamation previous to the landing of the British army in Java, dated 2 August 1811. A translation.
[162] NLS Box 59. Captain Taylor's journal, 28 February–10 December 1811. NLS M 39. No. 13. Minto to Lady Minto, Chillingehing, Java, 6 August 1811.
[163] BL, IOR Fac. Rec. Java 13. Proclamation to the Dutch inhabitants of Java, 4 August 1811, p. 213. Ibid., p. 225. Proclamation to the Native inhabitants (translated into Malay and Javanese languages).

Batavia surrendered on 8 August. The inhabitants appeared glad to receive some level of protection and Batavia was placed under martial law.[164]

Although it was apparent that neither the Dutch nor the Javanese had any love for the French Government, they showed no desire to assist the British in overthrowing it. The Malays probably thought it prudent to wait for the result of the combat before declaring in favour of any party. Notwithstanding Raffles's assurances that the native princes and peoples were eagerly awaiting the British to overthrow the French–Dutch government, no active help was forthcoming. Indeed during the long interval between the occupation of Batavia on 8 August and the storming of Cornelis on 26 August, the Batavians were doubtful of British victory and enquired when they would re-embark.[165]

From Batavia, Minto sent summonses to Janssens which were refused. On 10 August, the advance under Gillespie marched to Weltevreeden, which was a large but unfortified cantonment built by Daendels between Batavia and Cornelis. The first major action took place on the road to Cornelis and from 10 August, British troops took up quarters at Weltevreeden. Minto established his headquarters there in preference to Batavia.

Cornelis presented a problem. In Minto's words, 'Cornelis is a military post of great strength, on which all the art of French engineering has been long bestowed. It is considered the citadel of Java, in which the colony itself is to be defended.'[166] Janssens had gathered all available force, except a few hundred at Samarang and Gressie, behind the walls of Cornelis. According to Major Thorn, the army at Cornelis could not have been less than 13,000 men on the morning of 26 August, although Janssens in his report to the Minister of Marine and Colonies stated that his army was weakened by disease and that he could not muster more than 8,000 men.[167] The total number of the British army was about 12,000 including sailors and marines, but the number of sick, wounded and dead steadily increased so on 26 August also stood at around 7,000 active servicemen. The two armies were nearly equal in number on the eve of the physical storming of the citadel. This was delayed by Auchmuty's desire to try the batteries first, although Gillespie maintained that Cornelius could only be taken by storm. The batteries proved a failure and

[164] NLS M 39. Minto to Lady Minto, 9 August 1811. Ibid., Box 59. Captain Taylor's journal, 28 February–10 December 1811. Thorn, *Memoir*, p. 29.

[165] NLS Minto Papers Box 59. Captain Taylor's journal kept during the Java expedition, begun 28 February 1811 and ended on 10 December 1811. Taylor writes 'we knew next to nothing of the nature of their works [forts], nor had we received the slightest information or assistance unless compelled from either Dutch or Malay or Chinese inhabitant, who were to have received us we were told with open arms'.

[166] NLS M 39. No. 13. Minto to Lady Minto, 12 August 1811. Cornelis was surrounded on one side by the River Jakarta and on the other by an artificial waterway. It had seven redoubts and several batteries mounted with heavy guns. On its capture, 250 guns were taken. NLS Minto Papers Box 59. Captain Taylor's journal, 28 February–10 December 1811.

[167] Thorn, *Memoir*, pp. 90–91.

it appeared that Janssens could hold out long enough to create a stalemate. Luckily a German deserter arrived from Janssens's camp with information about the inner fortifications.[168] This crucial information showed Auchmuty that storming Cornelius was the only way to capture the fortress and on the morning of 26 August, Gillespie led the advance and in Minto's words 'stood first in the roll of that day's fame'.[169] All accounts of the battle agree that it was difficult struggle under heavy fire.[170] Five thousand prisoners were taken. Janssens and Jumelle escaped with barely three hundred horsemen to Buitenzorg. Janssens was summoned to capitulate, which he refused as he was thinking of the fate promised to him by Napoleon if he did surrender. He had to therefore make a show of determined resistance. The total number of men he hoped to gather at Samarang could not have been more than 100 Europeans and 2,000 Malays and additionally he had no money and no other resources. Indeed, he later admitted that even if he won the campaign, he would not have been able to carry on the administration of Java for the lack of finance.[171] Janssens and Jumelle took separate roads to the east in order to make a final stand at Samarang. Jumelle was taken prisoner at Cheribon, The detachment under Major Le Blanc which followed Jumelle, surrendered to Robison without realising how small Robison's force actually was. The two French frigates *Meduse* and *Nymphe* which had so long been blockaded at Surabaya by the British frigate *Bucephalus* and sloop of war *Baracouta* managed to escape through the narrow passage between Gressie and Madura. They took the British ships with them. Janssens reached Samarang on 2 September and called the native troops that remained at Surabaya and Gressie to join him. The Susuhonan sent a body of troops under one of his generals to assist Janssens. However, with the native troops deserting in large numbers, and left with a handful of officers in the end, Janssens finally agreed to surrender. He demanded a consultation with Auchmuty to determine the terms, but Auchmuty insisted on unconditional surrender and on 18 September 1811, at Oenarang, the final documents of capitulation were signed by Janssens.[172] Minto wrote to Hewitt, 'It has been an arduous and even anxious, but throughout, a most prosperous enterprize.'[173]

The capitulation embraced not only Java but all its dependencies and stipulated that all military men were to be made prisoners of war and that

---

[168] NLS Minto Papers, Box 59. Captain Taylor's journal.

[169] NLS M 39. No.13. Minto to Lady Minto, 28 August 1811.

[170] Ibid. BL, IOR Fac. Rec. Java 9. Sir S. Auchmuty to Minto, Weltevreeden, 31 August 1811. Printed in Thorn, *Memoir*, pp. 80–87. NLS Minto Papers, Box 59. Captain Taylor's journal.

[171] Day, Clive, *The Policy and Administration of the Dutch in Java* (London, 1904), p. 165.

[172] NLS Minto Papers Box 59, Captain Taylor's journal. BL, IOR Fac. Rec. Java 9. S. Auchmuty to Minto, *Modeste* off Samarang, 21 September 1811. NLS M 174. Minto to Hewitt, Weltevreeden, 17 September 1811; Ibid., 30 September 1811. NLS M 204. Governor-General-in-Council to the Court of Directors, Fort William, 20 January 1812.

[173] NLS M 174. Minto to Hewitt, Kedgeree Roads, 17 November 1811.

the British were to have their hands free on three essential points: the future administration of the island, the guarantee of the public debt and the liquidation of the paper money.[174]

During the operations against Java, the navy did not always cooperate with Minto and Auchmuty in terms of the generally approved course of action. After Batavia was occupied on 8 August 1811, Minto asked Stopford to depute one of his captains to carry his letters to the chiefs of Madura inviting them to trade with Batavia and also to occupy the Dutch factory at Samanap on that island.[175] Operations against Samanap were successfully carried out by Captain Harris of the *Sir Francis Drake* and Captain Pellew of the *Phaeton*. All the Dutch settlers were made prisoners of war and public property confiscated. Captain Harris set himself up as the Governor of Madura.[176] He appointed Captain Pellew Commandant of Samanap and also made several other appointments on that island and the expense accounts he sent amounted to almost £9,000 per year.[177] Minto strongly protested against such extraordinary steps. Captain Harris due to depart for Britain, carried a letter of recommendation from Stopford to the Admiralty to confirm him in his office as Governor of Madura which was regarded as a splendid naval base.[178] This plan to make Madura an independent naval station did not however, materialise. Again when Admiral Stopford occupied Gressie and Surabaya, soon after Janssen's capitulation, he made appointments of a port captain and a harbour master at Surabaya without first conferring with Minto, who later revoked them.[179]

There was also dispute over the prize. Stopford objected to the right of the Company's men to the prize money. Shortly after landing in Java, Minto had with the approval of Auchmuty and Commodore Broughton, appointed a prize-agent, Captain Flint to supervise the sale and distribution of prizes. Stopford on his arrival protested against the appointment of the prize-agent, and notified Captain Flint that if he interfered in any way with the sale of prize-property he would be liable to criminal prosecution. Stopford wanted to appropriate all the plunder to the navy and he cited the Naval Prize Act

174 BL, IOR Fac. Rec. Java 9. S. Auchmuty to Minto, *Modeste* off Samarang, 21 September 1811. Ibid. Articles of Capitulation, 18 September 1811.

175 NLS M 496. Minto to Stopford, HMS *Modeste*, Batavia Roads, 10 August 1811.

176 Ibid. Captain Harris to Stopford, Samanap, 1 September 1811. Ibid. Stopford to Minto, HMS *Scipion* off Sedaya, 20 September 1811.

177 NLS M 209. Minto to Bosanquet (Chairman of the East India Company), Java, 5 October 1811. NLS Minto Papers Box 59. Captain Taylor's journal.

178 NLS M 209. Minto to Bosanquet, Java, 5 October 1811. Ibid. M 204. Governor-General-in-Council to the Court of Directors, Fort William, 20 January 1812. Ibid. M 496. Minto to Stopford, 23 March 1812.

179 NLS M 209. Minto to Bosanquet, Java, 5 October 1811. Ibid. M 204. Governor-General-in-Council to the Court of Directors, Fort William, 20 January 1812.

214 Defending British India against Napoleon

of 1805 in support of his claim.[180] Minto pointed out that the Act of 1805 could not be said to be applicable in a case in which the king's navy and army had acted conjointly with the Company's troops and marines for that Act had made no provision for such cases. On the other hand, the Company's Charter vested in the East India Company a right to all prizes captured under circumstances similar to the Java expedition with the reservation that in the event of the king's ships and troops cooperating with the Company's forces in such expeditions, the king reserved the prerogative of distributing the prize property. Hence, there could be no objection, Minto told Stopford, to the appointment of a prize-agent on behalf of the Company to take charge of the custody and management of the captured property, until the orders of HM Government should be known. Besides, he claimed that since the Company was bearing all the expenses of the expedition, except those of the king's navy, it had a substantial right to the prize-property. Stopford did not press his exclusive claims and left Java before he received Minto's reply. The management and distribution of the captured property was therefore carried out as agreed between Minto, Auchmuty and Broughton.[181]

The conquest of Java and the French Islands gave the British a unique position in the Eastern seas. For the first time for many years, the British were without a European rival in this area. Minto's one great ambition was to eliminate the French flag from the East and on its accomplishment he wrote with elation to the Earl of Liverpool:

> An Empire, which for two centuries has contributed greatly to the power, prosperity and grandeur of one of the principal and most respected States of Europe, has thus been wrested from the short usurpation of the French Government, added to the dominion of the British Crown; and converted from a seat of hostile machination and commercial competition, into an augmentation of British power and prosperity... by the successive reduction of the French Islands and Java, the British nation has neither an enemy nor a rival left from the Cape of Good Hope to Cape Horn.[182]

The expulsion of the French from Java and the consequent relief of the Company's possessions and trade in the east from 'the prospective dangers... and expected aggrandizement'[183] of the French was the first part of Minto's plans regarding Java. The second part of his plan was to add Java to the British Empire. He regarded it as a valuable acquisition in view of Britain's

[180] NLS M 496. Stopford to Minto, 2 September 1811.
[181] NLS M 496. Minto to Stopford. Undated draft of reply to Stopford's letter of 2 September 1811. NLS M 204. Governor-General-in-Council to the Court of Directors, Fort William, 20 January 1812.
[182] NLS M 206. Minto to Lord Liverpool, Batavia, 2 September 1811.
[183] NLS M 202. Governor-General-in-Council to the Court of Directors, Fort William, 9 December 1811.

commercial and geopolitical interests not only in the region, but in the fact that it also secured the critically important trade route to China. After the conquest, Java and its dependencies were annexed provisionally to the East India Company and the country was administered under the direct super-vision of the Government of Bengal.

The British conquest if not followed by occupation would merely unchain the forces of destruction and massacre on the island and Minto believed that if it was known that the British intended on granting independence to the Javanese, the opposition of the Dutch colonists to the British invasion would have been much more determined that it actually was. The Dutch colonists did not seem to mind passing under British authority in preference to that of the French. They probably expected from past experience that the Dutch possessions in the East Indies would be restored to Holland at the end of the war in Europe, as actually happened, although Minto and Raffles hoped to persuade the home authorities to retain Java permanently.

In making the necessary arrangements, civil and military, for the admin-istration of Java, Minto's main focus was to define as clearly as possible the extent of powers attached to the these two branches of public authority. The civil authority was to be supreme in Java and he requested to the Secret Committee that Java should not be placed under a military governor.[184] A large force, however, consisting of 3,697 Europeans and 4,654 sepoys was left on the island to carry on the work of pacification, to establish British authority more firmly and also to guard against the possible future arrival of a French force in Java if Napoleon were so inclined. The island was divided into three principal military districts: Batavia, Samarang and Surabaya and small garrisons were sent to Fort Angier in Bantam and Madura. The military force in Java was to be reduced eventually and the establishment formed on the most economical scale.[185] The military was to be subordinate to the civil authority, and the Commander of the Forces was at the same time to enjoy exclusively 'the Military Command properly so-called of the army'. Minto emphasised that 'the public force or army of any country is not a separate or independent body, but an instrument of the State, to be employed in its service, directed by those who guide its Counsels, and in a word entirely subordinate to Government'.[186] The relation between the

---

[184] BL, IOR Ben. Sec. Letters, Vol. 13. Minto to the Secret Committee, Batavia, 18 October 1811.

[185] BL, IOR Ben. Sec. Cons. 234. Cons. of 13 December 1811, No. 4. Minute of the Governor-General relative to the military arrangements in Java, 29 November 1811. Ibid. No. 7. Orders by the Governor-General on military appointments and allowances in Java. BL, IOR Ben. Sec. Letters, Vol. 13. Minto to the Secret Committee, 3 September 1811.

[186] BL, IOR Fac. Rec. Java 14. BL, IOR Ben. Sec. Cons. 234. Cons. of 13 December 1811, No. 9. Instructions of Minto to Raffles and Gillespie concerning the respective powers of the Lt Governor and the Commander of the Forces.

lieutenant-governor and the commander of the forces was to be analogous to that of the Supreme Government and the commander-in-chief in Bengal. All military operations of any kind and every order with regard to supplies, rations, allowances and any act of the army involving expense or affecting policy were to have the prior sanction of the lieutenant-governor alone or in council.[187]

The Dutch held a large proportion of the public offices under the new administration. It was Minto's policy to employ the Dutch in the civil administration not only because it was a way of reconciling them to the change of authority, but also because the necessary qualifications for these offices a knowledge of Dutch and Malay languages and local experience could not immediately be acquired by the Company's junior civil servants. The Dutch president, vice-president, members and officers of the Supreme Court of Justice, and those of the Sheriff's Court and the Chamber of Accounts were continued. The commissioners and officers for the superintendence of marriages and settling of small debts and the Dutch interpreters and translators were confirmed in their offices.

The problem of slavery attracted Minto's attention from the beginning of his tenure in all corners of the empire. To the Secret Committee he wrote:

> The state of Slavery has attracted my serious and anxious attention. That monstrous system prevails to a calamitous extent throughout these Eastern Regions of India, and produces... in all cases most of the miseries incident to that mode of procuring the Service of men. But it is too general to be suddenly suppressed by any one power in so many separate and independent Countries.[188]

Slavery was recognised by both Dutch and Mohammedan law and was too closely involved in the system of economy throughout the Eastern islands to be interfered with immediately by the British Government. Minto decided that the British Government should at least not be owners of slaves. During his short visit to Malacca he liberated the Government slaves, altogether nineteen men, women and children and arranged for their employment as free labourers.[189] In Java he left instructions with Raffles that no purchase of

---

[187] BL, IOR Fac. Rec. Java 14. Ben. Sec. Cons. 234, Cons. of 13 December 1811, No. 9. Instructions of Minto to Raffles and Gillespie concerning the respective powers of the Lt Governor and the Commander of the Forces. NLS M 498. Minto to Gillespie, HMS *Modeste*, 28 October 1811.

[188] BL, IOR Ben. Sec. Letters Vol. 13. Minto to the Secret Committee, Weltevreeden, 5 October 1811.

[189] NLS M 39, No. 10. Minto to Lady Minto, Malacca, 31 May 1811. NLS M 497. Minto to Gilbert Elliot, 1 September 1812. At Malacca, Minto received a present of seven slaves, five boys and two girls from one of the Rajas of Bali. They were emancipated but remained in his charge as orphans.

slaves was to be made by the Government and the importation of slaves into Java was to be restricted although it could not be totally abolished.

At the time of the British conquest, the Dutch settlements in Java were in the grip of a severe inflation. As the trade with Europe, and later on that with America, stopped during the war in Europe, the colony was on its last legs as far as finance was concerned. The currency consisted of two types of paper, one issued by the Government and the other by the Orphan Chamber under authority given by the Government, but the credit of the Government was not pledged to the latter. The excess of paper rix-dollars for one Spanish silver dollar was about five to one. It presented a serious problem to the new government. If the paper money was cancelled immediately it would have caused general distress to the people, while on the other hand, it was important not to burden the new administration with the large unpaid debt of a former enemy government. It was therefore declared by Minto that an amount not exceeding 4.5 million rix-dollars in Government paper and 4 million of the Orphan paper would be recognised as legal tender at the rate of 6.5 paper rix-dollars to one Spanish silver dollar. In order to provide a fund for the gradual liquidation of this debt, the paper money was to be charged an annual duty of 5 per cent on the value fixed, and the money raised from the duty was to be invested in government securities bearing interest so that the fund might accumulate speedily.[190] The relation between the sicca rupee and the Spanish dollar was fixed on the intrinsic value of each, and the relative value of the sicca rupee to all other coins was regulated according to the exchange already established by the Dutch Government and by usage between the Spanish dollar and other coins.[191] The resources of Java were extensive and would, Minto hoped, not only cover but exceed the expenditure of the Government. Although a surplus could not be expected in the first year due to the extraordinary charges of the war, a surplus was expected in the following years under the new and improved system of administration. The chief source of revenue of Java was commercial, not territorial. The finances of the Government of Java might have been stabilised by the proceeds of trade in opium, spice and timber, but the Government of Bengal proposed to throw open the trade in opium to the Calcutta merchants. Minto expected that the Company would gain more by the Calcutta merchants opening markets for opium in Java than by the Java Government's monopoly of opium sales in Java. Regardless, the experiment was to be made and during the years of trial, the Bengal Government agreed to compensate the Java Government for the loss of its revenue from opium.[192] Another potential source of revenue

---

[190] BL, IOR Ben. Sec. Cons. 234. Cons. of 6 December 1811. No. 4. Proclamation (No. 3), Done at Molenvliet by Lord Minto, 11 September 1811.

[191] Ibid. Proclamation (No. 4) Done at Molenvliet by Lord Minto, 11 September 1811.

[192] BL, IOR Eur. MSS. C.34. Raff. Col. I. Minto to Raffles, 28 February 1812.

for Java was also unavailable to the Government of Java, as the spices from the Moluccas continued to be sent directly to the markets in Calcutta and Madras. The result was an increase in the export of spices from the island and the consequent acute depression of the value of paper money which fell to 90–100 per cent of the exchange rates fixed by Minto in 1811.[193] The Government of Bengal asked Raffles not to draw any more bills on Bengal.[194] Acute financial distress was primary challenge of the new Government in Java and Minto wrote to the Secret Committee:

> … the value of the Island the face of prosperity which every part of the Country wears even weighed down as it has been by a most oppressive system and often a most iniquitous and grinding administration of Government, very far exceeds any notion which had ever been conceived by Strangers… Yet every acknowledged principle of Good Government is unheard of in Java, and all the mischievous deteriorating and grievous maxims of a narrow monopolising harsh and malignant policy are in full force and vigour in every department of affairs.[195]

Under the Dutch, land was the property of the Government, and large tracts were cultivated and managed on behalf of the Government by public officers known as regents. The Dutch Government also exacted at an arbitrary price the produce of land under individual cultivators. Java was similar to a large government plantation in which no individual interest in land exceeded the term of a year at a time. Minto found the whole system of property ownership, or lack thereof, 'vicious and adverse alike to the Interest of Government and people'.[196] He proposed that the systems of forced coffee cultivation, of contingent and forced deliveries were to be abolished and the land system reformed in order to stimulate the industry of the Javanese and to bring greater revenue to the Government. The revenues and monopolies were all in farms and the farmers were almost universally Chinese. Although these farms had to be renewed for the remaining months of the year, Minto recommended the abolition of all revenue farms in the hands of the Chinese who were regarded as interlopers.[197] Prior to his departure from Java, Minto discussed the proposed changes in land reform with Raffles, but cautioned that 'the system is too extensive to be suddenly or ignorantly attempted'.[198]

---

[193] Bastin, J., *The Native Policies of Sir Stamford Raffles in Java and Sumatra* (Oxford, 1957), p. 19.

[194] NLS Minto Papers Box 76. Raffles to Minto, Ryswick, 30 October 1812.

[195] BL, IOR Ben. Sec. Letters, Vol. 13. Minto to the Secret Committee, Weltevreeden, 5 October 1811.

[196] Ibid.

[197] BL, IOR Ben. Sec. Letters, Vol. 13. Minto to the Secret Committee, Weltevreeden, 5 October 1811.

[198] BL, IOR Eur. MSS. C.34. Raff. Col. I. Minto to Raffles, 26 February 1812. Minto mentions certain notes on land reform that he left with Raffles, which contained his suggestions and ideas, which had also been developed in personal conferences in Java. Lady Raffles,

Minto's objective in Java was to combine the interests of the state with the happiness and prosperity of the people. He wrote to R. Dundas, that although Java might have to be restored to Holland at the end of the war:

> ... this ought not surely to prevent us from beginning to perform the first duty of Governments, in improving the condition of mankind, and of a people that has become subject to our authority, and tributary to our prosperity... our policy should lead to the improvement of the country, & if not our policy, the eternal & fundamental law by which Governments and subjects are united.[199]

He revealed himself as an exponent of the Burkean doctrine of trusteeship and declared to the people of Java that although the establishment of British authority in Java was unconditional as a result of the conquest, yet:

> An English Government does not require the Articles of Capitulation to impose those duties which are prompted by a Sense of Justice and beneficient disposition. The people of Java are exhorted to consider their new Connexion with England as founded on principles of mutual advantage, and to be conducted in a spirit of Kindness and Affection. Providence has brought to them a protecting and benevolent Government they will cheerfully perform the reciprocal duties of allegiance and attachment.[200]

Furnivall writes that the Dutch themselves regarded the British occupation as a turning point in their colonial administration.[201] The medieval structure of the Dutch rule in Java with its system of contingent and forced deliveries, torture and mutilation as forms of punishment, non-recognition of rights of its subjects or of its duties toward them was abolished during the five years of British occupation. Minto was anxious that Java should be permanently annexed to the Company's possessions. He wrote to Liverpool, Secretary of State for War and the Colonies in June 1812, '... all the concerns of Java and the Moluccas... are too intimately connected with the Company's privileges & affairs to admit of their being withdrawn from its superintendence, & being placed under a totally different power, with opposite interests in many respects, & with rival pretentions, feelings and habits'.[202]

His views however found no support from the Directors. The Duke of Buckinghamshire, who became the President of the Board of Control after R. Dundas, informed him in March 1813 that although nothing was as yet finally

---

Memoir, p. 212. *Substance of a Minute recorded by the Honourable Thomas Stamford Raffles*, on the 11 February 1814... (London, 1814), p. 4.

199 NLS M 377. Minto to R. Dundas, Weltevreeden, 6 October 1811.

200 BL, IOR Ben. Sec. Cons. BEN 234. Cons. of 6 December 1811, No. 4. Proclamation (No. 2) Done at Molenvliet, 11 September 1811 by Lord Minto.

201 Furnivall, *Netherlands India*, pp. 67, 78.

202 NLS M 497. Minto to Liverpool, 9 June 1812 (Copy).

settled regarding Java, there was no doubt of its being ultimately constituted into a Crown Colony. General Maitland, former Governor of Ceylon who was then in England, was tipped for the office of head of Government of Java.[203] In October 1813, Lord Bathurst, Secretary for War and the Colonies in Liverpool's administration, wrote to Buckinghamshire that the Government had decided to place Java and its dependencies on the footing of a royal government similar to Ceylon and requested him to make the necessary arrangements to carry these orders into effect.[204] However, before these new arrangements could be made, negotiations for peace began in Europe and Java was one of the colonial conquests that Castlereagh, now Foreign Secretary, was willing to barter in order to gain a better bargain elsewhere.

Napoleon's Continental System was a serious threat to Britain, but only so long as it could be imposed on the whole of Europe. The revolt of Spain and Portugal and the defection of Sweden and Turkey caused direct setbacks. Tsar Alexander I, tiring of a policy that served French interests, opened his ports to neutral shipping and relations with the French deteriorated to the point that Napoleon prepared to invade Russia in the spring of 1812. The strategic motive for this attack arose directly from the Continental System, that is, had there been no economic warfare against Britain, there would be no need to make an enemy of Russia.[205] The French army crossed the Russian frontier on 24 June and on 7 September won a costly and limited victory at Borodino before entering Moscow. However, the Russians did not allow Napoleon the luxury of a decisive battle and the supply chain to the French army was becoming increasingly tenuous and difficult as a result of the onset of winter. In mid-October, Napoleon began his retreat. The French armies were not equipped for retreat, either psychologically or practically, and between 500,000 to 570,000 men out of an original strength of 650,000 died or were captured.[206] The tsar sent his Baltic fleet to winter in British ports, a powerful gesture of confidence which encouraged the ministry in London where Lord Liverpool had established the strongest government since the fall of Pitt in 1801.[207] In June 1813, Wellington's decisive victory at Vitoria effectively ended French presence in Spain with the exception of Catalonia and re-established the reputation of the British army.[208]

Britain spent most of 1814 negotiating peace settlements with European allies from a position of strength having contributed an army of 150,000 men

---

[203] NLS Minto Papers Box 76. Buckinghamshire to Minto, Hamilton Place, 16 March 1813.

[204] BL, IOR Fac. Rec. Java 65. Lord Bathurst to the Earl of Buckinghamshire, Downing Street, 26 October 1813.

[205] Rodger, N.A.M., *The Command of the Ocean: A Naval History of Britain 1649–1815* (New York, 2005), Chap. 36, p. 563.

[206] Ibid.

[207] Ibid.

[208] Ibid., p. 564.

to the final campaigns against Napoleon and having paid for 425,000 more. It was certainly possible to retain the French and Dutch colonial empires, but Britain chose not to do so. The small Dutch territory of Guyana, which was an important cotton producer, was the only colony retained on economic grounds. The other places retained by Britain – Malta, the Cape of Good Hope, Ceylon and Mauritius – were all of strategic, not economic importance.[209] They were critical locations in terms of safeguarding global trade. Trade not territory was the key to Britain's prosperity: seaborne trade secured by naval power which was a fundamental difference compared to that taken by Napoleon, and perhaps in the long term contributed to the eventuality and sustainability of Britain's victory.

The mortal danger to Britain had come from a dominant European power controlling the Low Countries and able to build a powerful fleet in the Channel. The primary aim was therefore to ensure that no future Napoleon or Louis XIV could conquer Flanders and build a fleet at Antwerp. A powerful new Kingdom of the Netherlands was created, ruled by the House of Orange, covering the former Dutch Republic, the Austrian Netherlands, Liege and Luxembourg. In order to bolster their economic foundation and resources, the East Indies were returned to safeguard Britain's position and situation in Europe.[210] 'The establishment of a balance of power in Europe', a secret article of the peace treaty declared, 'requires that Holland should be established on a scale to make her capable of preserving her independence by her own resources'.[211]

Stamford Raffles complained at the loss of Java, but the British Government wanted trade and security and were convinced that a restored Dutch empire was no danger to either. In the words of a cabinet memorandum, 'the Dutch are dependent on British support and could never in the long run constitute a serious threat to British commercial interests in South-East Asia'.[212] Martinique and Guadeloupe were returned to France for similar reasons, to give the restored Bourbon monarchy dignity and consequence, but not enough power to be dangerous – to make France 'commercial and pacific' rather than 'military and conquering' as Castlereagh told the House of Commons.[213] Having achieved Dundas's earlier aim of destroying French sea power, Britain could afford to be generous. Fundamentally, the 'Jewel in the

---

[209] Ibid., p. 572.

[210] Ibid., p. 573.

[211] 'L'etablissment d'un juste equilibre en Europe exigeant que la Hollande soit constituee dans les proportions qui la mettent a meme de soutenir son independence par ses propres moyens...' Lutun, 'Les Clauses navales', p. 51, quoting Secret Art. 3.

[212] De Moor, J.A., 'A Very Unpleasant Relationship. Trade and Strategy in the Eastern Seas: Anglo-Dutch Relations in the Nineteenth Century from a Colonial Perspective', in Raven, J.G.A. and Rodger, N.A.M. (eds), *Anglo-Dutch Relationship in War and Peace, 1688–1988* (Edinburgh, 1990), p. 59.

[213] Lutun, B., *Les Clauses navales* (Paris, 2005), p. 54.

Crown' (India) was protected and contributed (by 1818) tax revenues of £18 million (a third of Britain's GDP) and an army of 180,000 men. This portion of the empire was entirely self-supporting, although its trade and connection with Britain depended on command of the sea.[214]

Napoleon's final defeats in 1814 and 1815 were the result of a coalition of powers who were rivals as well as allies in that they had the same interest in the balance of naval and colonial power as the British had in the balance of power in Europe. It was the essential uncompromising nature of Napoleon and his overwhelming ambition to be all conquering in an era of increasing mutual cooperation and trade that led to his downfall.[215]

[214] Rodger, *Command of the Ocean*, Chap. 36, p. 573.
[215] Ibid., p. 574.

Six

LEGACY OF LORD MINTO

End of an Era

No politician can make a situation. His skill consists in his well-playing the game dealt to him by fortune, and following the indications given him by nature, times, and circumstances.[1]

These words, written by Burke to Minto during the years of their close association, could easily be regarded as Minto's guiding motto during his career in India. Minto left India with no regrets. During the six years he held office, he was conscious of performing the duties of his office rigorously, without sparing himself in any way. The three main factors that determined his foreign policy were the Napoleonic War, a broader conception of Indian defence, and the glimpse of a possible eastward expansion of British power from India, thus changing an emergency into an advantage. The European war greatly influenced the direction of his administration in India. The counteraction of Britain's European enemies in India, in the neighbouring states of Asia and in the Indian Ocean became the basis of his foreign policy. The foreign policy of the British Government in India was throughout its history closely related to Britain's relations with other European powers who also had interests in Asia. Minto's foreign policy was perceptively influenced by the exigencies of the European situation. The treaty of Tilsit (July 1807) left Britain in a critical state of isolation in Europe. This situation, coupled with the presence of the French in Turkey and Persia during 1807–09, caused gravest anxiety for the security of the British possessions in India, which amounted to a 'Gallophobia'. The political missions to Persia, Afghanistan, Lahore and Sind originated from this feeling of insecurity. Minto's policy was to counteract the French threat as far away from the actual frontiers of the Company's territories as possible, and also to neutralise the intervening states between the Sutlej and Persia. The Spanish resistance in 1808 finally enabled

---

[1]   Countess of Minto, *Life and Letters*, Vol. 2, p. 172. Burke to Sir Gilbert Elliot, 22 September 1793.

the British to come to grips with the enemy in Europe. The improvement in the European situation, combined with Persia's coolness toward their French ally, caused a shifting of emphasis in Minto's foreign policy. As the panic created by the French threat in the north-west disappeared, intrinsic British interests, either political or commercial, exercised the predominant influence in the shaping of future policy with regard to each of these states. The disappearance of the French threat also gave a new direction to Minto's foreign policy. Instead of being on the defensive, he could assume the offensive against the French in the Eastern seas. The conquest of the French Islands and the Dutch East Indies gave the finishing touches to his anti-French foreign policy.

The main aim of Minto's foreign policy was the security of the Company's trade and territories in India. His diplomatic preparation had in view the building up of two lines of defence, the first in Persia, the other in Afghanistan, Sind and the Punjab. The security of British interests in India was achieved by securing allies, weakening enemies, or at least by ensuring their neutrality. The French threat from the north-west was a vague and uncertain danger, but from it emerged a conception of Indian defence based on Persia and the Persian Gulf. In Minto's view, Persia and the Gulf were of primary strategic importance. In 1807, the alarm for the safety of India caused both the Foreign Office and the Governor-General of India to adopt measures to counteract the French position in the Middle East by means of diplomacy. This created the further problem of a dispute between Minto and the home government as to who should conduct the diplomatic relations with Persia. In view of Persia's relations with France and Russia, the Foreign Office decided to open direct diplomatic relations with the shah. In fact it was suggested by the Court of Directors to Canning that the British envoy to Persia should bear royal credentials, so that he would enjoy greater prestige than if he was solely accredited by the Company. Harford Jones was the representative of both the Crown and the Company in Persia, and was placed under Minto's orders. The controversy that arose from the interactions of the three major characters – Minto, Malcolm and Harford Jones – were a result of deliberate miscommunication and assumption of rights and responsibilities. It may certainly be speculated that Malcolm's persistent interference and misrepresentation of facts to Minto directly caused the confusion and dispute between Minto and Harford Jones, and that the dispute between Minto and the home authorities over his treatment of HM envoy to Persia would not ordinarily have arisen. The appointment of Sir Gore Ouseley as the British Ambassador to Persia meant the temporary exclusion of the voice of the Company's Government in India from the conduct of Anglo-Persian relations. The payment of subsidy to Persia and also part of the expense of Ouseley's establishment were allotted to India revenues. Minto did not demand that the conduct of relations with Persia should be the monopoly of the Indian Government. He claimed for it a share in the direction of the policy due to the close connection between Indian defence and Persian politics. In the final arrangement of this issue in 1860, although the Foreign Office was given full responsibility for the conduct of diplomatic relations with Persia, the Indian Government received a consultative status. This was the principle that Minto had tried to establish at the beginning of the century.

Minto's dispute with Harford Jones brings out clearly his ideas about the powers and prerogatives of the Company's Government in India. In his opinion, the Company's Government in India was vested by Parliament with certain inalienable powers which were comparable to 'the powers attached to sovereignty'. One of his main contentions was that Harford Jones misrepresented the powers and functions of the Company's Government to the Persian Court by comparing its relation to the Crown with that of a Persian province to the shah. The Company's Government owed allegiance to the Crown, but its authority was based on Parliamentary statutes which even the Crown could not dispute. Minto's opinion was that all arrangements affecting the measures and resources of the British Government in India should be in the hands of the supreme authority in India, for 'an opposite arrangement would indeed involve the annihilation of the powers and the responsibility vested in the Supreme Government of India by a formal act of the legislature and by the constitution of the East India Company'.[2]

Minto's views about the status and powers of the Company's Government in India were very similar to those of Wellesley, and in fact of other imperial pro-consuls who ruled India. Wellesley wrote to Castlereagh in a letter dated 15 December 1803, 'The Company with relation to its territory in India, must be viewed in the capacity of a sovereign power.'[3] Minto could not easily forgive Sir Harford Jones for representing the Company's Government in India as a subordinate agency of the Crown and for disregarding its statutory character.[4]

Minto sought to establish the right of the Company to deal with the sovereign independent states of Asia on an equal footing. It was a claim however that these states refused to recognise. The independent monarchs with whom Minto opened diplomatic relations would only admit the King

---

2 TNA FO 60/3. Minto to Malcolm, 26 October 1809.

3 Martin, *Despatches of Wellesley*, Vol. 3, p. 529.

4 C.F. Ilbert: 'British authority in India may be traced, historically to a twofold source. It is derived partly from the British Crown and Parliament, partly from the Great Mogul and other native rules of India. In England, the powers and privileges granted by royal charter to the East India Company were confirmed, supplemented, regulated and curtailed by successive Acts of Parliament, and were finally transferred to the Crown.'

'In India, concessions granted by, or wrested from, native rulers gradually established the Company and the Crown as territorial sovereigns, in rivalry with other country powers; and finally left the British Crown exercising undivided sovereignty throughout British India, and paramount authority over the subordinate native States.' Ilbert, Sir C.F., *The Government of India* (Oxford, 1922, 3rd edn), p. 1.

of England as their equal. The powers and constitution of the Company's Government in India were not very clear to these states, but the Company was rapidly becoming a power that exercised the powers, and claimed the dignity, of a sovereign authority.

The project of establishing a naval and military post in the Gulf, which Minto adopted on the strong recommendation of Malcolm, was not actually carried out. However, it is significant that the occupation of a post in the Gulf was considered an effective strategy to intimidate Persia, and to establish British influence in the countries bordering the Gulf.[5] Throughout the later history of British-Indian foreign policy, Persia remained one of the primary considerations in the policy of defence, although its importance varied greatly according to the circumstances of the moment.

Minto's Afghan policy was not striking in its results, but it was the first attempt made by the British Government to open diplomatic relations with the Amir of Kabul. The political mission to Afghanistan was sent not only with a view to secure an additional defensive prop against a probable French attempt to infiltrate into that country, but also to collect geographical and other information about the countries beyond the Indus of which very little was known before Elphinstone's mission. The connection formed with Shah Shuja was unfortunate in view of later events, but the responsibility for Lord Auckland's ill-advised aggressive policy and the Afghan war of 1840–42 cannot be ascribed to Minto. It is remarkable that the implications of Russian aggression on Georgia during the early part of the nineteenth century were not properly grasped by the British. They were extremely reluctant to grant any aid to Persia to resist the Russian advance. Toward the middle of the century, Britain's relations with Russia and the Russian pressure on Central Asia became the determining factors in British relations with Persia and Afghanistan. The bogey of the Russian menace caused the British to think seriously of the defence of India in Afghanistan, a phase that ended only with the conclusion of the Anglo-Russian Convention of 1907.

It is a usual practice with historians interested in this subject to label Minto's policies toward Persia, Afghanistan, Lahore and Sind as a 'grand diplomatic offensive' against the Bonapartist menace, and to describe the objective in view as the formation of defensive alliances with these states against the French. However, it is perhaps a fallacy to generalise this quite so broadly. Although an anti-French bias was the originating and recurring factor, Minto's policies with regard to each of these states followed their separate courses. In Sind for instance, Minto's objective was not the conclusion of any

[5]   The island of Kharak was occupied by the British in June 1838 as a countermove to the siege of Herat by the Persians, and the British residency was moved from Bushire to Kharak. Kharak was evacuated in 1842, but occupied again in 1856, and finally restored to Persia at the end of the war between Britain and Persia in 1857. Curzon, G.N., *Persia and the Persian Question* (London, 1892), Vol. 2, p. 405.

specific alliance, but the establishment of a commercial factory or political residency as a preliminary to the establishment of British influence in Lower Sind. Again, diplomatic relations with Ranjit Singh of Lahore, begun as a counterpoise to the French, ended in the delimitation of mutual frontiers. Minto's diplomatic missions to Afghanistan, Sind and the Punjab may be regarded as feelers to judge the attitude of these powers toward the British. Such stern critics of Minto as the home authorities acknowledged that his diplomatic missions could not be regarded as a waste of money and effort even if no specific defensive engagements were formed with these states. In their opinion, the collection of information about these regions, a knowledge of the character and attitudes of the different ruling powers and of their military strength and resources would be useful for future reference. These advantages were regarded as ample compensation and justification for the expenditure incurred in these missions.[6]

As a result of Minto's settlement with the Sikhs, the north-west frontier of the Company's territories was extended from the Jamuna to the Sutlej, and a British military cantonment was established at Ludhiana. The cis-Sutlej states were taken under British protection and Ranjit Singh's ambition to bring the petty principalities between the Sutlej and Jamuna under his rule was thwarted. The union of the Sikhs under a single strong ruler was regarded by Minto as detrimental to the peace and tranquillity of the Company's territories. The mission to Ranjit Singh was dispatched with the objective of forming a defensive alliance against the French. However, even before the favourable turn of events in Europe rendered that alliance redundant, Minto was determined to oppose the extension of Ranjit Singh's authority over the cis-Sutlej states and regard the total subversion of his power as a desirable outcome. The extension of British protection to the cis-Sutlej states was certainly a departure from the policy of non-interference and withdrawal pursued by Barlow in his settlement with the Marathas in 1806. It was rather, a reiteration of the policy of Lord Lake and Wellesley. Minto's settlement with Ranjit Singh and the cis-Sutlej states remained the basis of British relations with the Sikhs for almost three decades. In 1831, Bentinck renewed the treaty of 1809 with Ranjit Singh. Minto checked the extension of Ranjit Singh's authority south of the Sutlej when his power was still comparatively weak. Despite the increase and consolidation of Ranjit Singh's power after 1809, he followed a cautious policy regarding the British. He extended his dominion at the cost of the Afghans without alarming the British by violating the treaty of 1809 in any way. The perspicacity of the Sikh ruler, who realised early his inability to offer successful resistance to British arms, was responsible for the maintenance of peace between the British and the Sikhs during his lifetime.

---

6 BL, IOR Board's Secret Drafts, Vol. 3, No. 56. Secret Committee to the Governor-General-in-Council, 2 October 1809 (Secret).

The Anglo-Sikh war broke out shortly after his death in 1839. The policy of non-interference was therefore greatly modified by Minto. A strict adherence to that policy he found was contrary to the Company's interests. Malcolm, even if one discounts his abhorrence for the policy of withdrawal, probably expressed a general feeling when he wrote to Wellesley in 1809:

> The Evils of the non-Interference system have been severely felt during the late preparations, on the northwestern frontier of Hindostan. We have at last been obliged to take the Sikh Chiefs to the southward of the Sutledge, under our protection, a cantonment has been formed... at Lodhana a Post on the banks of that River. Scindiah keeps moving about Malwah deriving his chief subsistence from the occasional plunder of the Jypore Territories. Holkar is still Insane, the Chief management of his military Concerns has devolved on Meer Khan, but the Power of all the Marhatta Chiefs is Extinct, & Lord Minto is... too well convinced of the admirable wisdom of the policy which led to their reduction ever to allow them to revive their strength.[7]

The period of nearly a decade (1805–13) between Wellesley and the Marquess of Hastings has been described as period of non-interference and withdrawal. That thesis is evidently based on the policy pursued by Cornwallis during his very short second governor-generalship and by Barlow after him, rather than on a close examination of Minto's policies. The absence of any major war with any of the Indian powers during Minto's administration is probably one of the reasons for the popular belief that it was a period of peace, economy and non-interference. However, the active external policies adopted by Minto were more reminiscent of Wellesley than of either Cornwallis or Barlow. Many of the measures Minto adopted had been earlier considered and rejected by Barlow on the ground that they were not so urgently necessary as to justify a departure from the system of economy and non-interference. Wellesley's wars had left the Company supreme in the subcontinent. There was thus no immediate need for a forward policy within India. This was heavily emphasised by the Court of Directors' insistence on economy and their reluctance to pursue the policy of expansion that had characterised the Wellesley regime. While in retrospect the danger of a French invasion from the north-west was certainly not very acute or imminent, it is doubtful if either Cornwallis or Barlow would have been prompted to adopt a similar active external policy as Minto under similar circumstances. Minto's attitude toward the French threat to India was noticeably different from that of men like Barlow who had been in India for a longer time and were more used to these occasional alarms about the safety of the Company's possessions. Minto, with his fresh experience of European power-politics and his own active participation in the plans to build up resistance to Bonaparte in

---

[7]   BL Add. MSS 37285, ff. 169–70. Malcolm to Wellesley, Bombay, 18 April 1809 (Private).

his earlier diplomatic career in Europe, was in a way pre-dedicated to the policy of counteracting the French in the East. His foreign policy has to be understood as a reflection of this preconception. In a letter dated 7 October 1812, to Lady Minto, he wrote:

> I perceive with great concern & sometimes with a little dismay, the tone of whimpering after peace arising gradually in England & growing too much into a fashion – a desire for peace, because we are tired of war, not because its object is attained, which in the present war is mere security against subjugation, is little better than to call Craven, & submit to all the consequences of defeat.[8]

He regarded the opposition to the French in India as an assistance to Britain's war effort in Europe. This necessarily meant the adoption of a more active policy than was enjoined on him by the Directors, and a departure from the policy of peace and economy. His plans for establishing a post in the Gulf, a factory in Sind, communications with the Afghan court, the extension of the Company's frontiers from the Jamuna to the Sutlej, the conquest of the French Islands and Java can hardly be regarded as manifestations of a policy of withdrawal or of maintaining the status quo.

The men who were chiefly instrumental in carrying out his diplomatic policies would probably have welcomed a bolder departure from the policy of non-interference. Neither the Company's civil service nor the army were well paid. Naturally the ambitious young men in the Company's service sought wider fields for their activities, which were likely to bring them greater fame and fortune. These men were impatient under Barlow's rule, and their repressed energies found an outlet under Minto's patronage. Malcolm, Metcalfe and Elphinstone belonged to the forward school of diplomacy. Each of them advocated a more aggressive policy than Minto was willing to undertake. The moderating influence exercised by Minto prevented the adoption of policies of gross aggression. According to the testimony of Malcolm, an inveterate critic of the policy of non-interference:

> The government of Lord Minto had no result more important than the impression it conveyed to the authorities at home of the utter impracticability of perseverance in that neutral policy they had desired to pursue. It was a progressive return to a course of action more suited to the extent, the character, and the condition of the British power; but when compelled to depart from the line prescribed, the measures adopted by this nobleman were so moderate, and the sentiments he recorded so just, that it was impossible to refuse assent to their expediency and wisdom.[9]

---

8 NLS M 40. Minto to Lady Minto, Calcutta, 7 October 1812.
9 Malcolm, Sir J., *The Political History of India from 1784 to 1823* (London, 1826), Vol. 1, pp. 440–41.

Wellesley had driven the French out of the subcontinent, but Minto sought to ensure their total exclusion from the peripheries of India. His policy was at first defensive, but as the European situation began to change in favour of Britain, a policy that had been admittedly defensive could undergo a subtle transformation into a forward and expansionist one, directed toward the prevention of not merely French, but also of Dutch rivalry being ever again a serious threat to the British presence in South and South-East Asia. The conquest of the French Islands and the Dutch East Indies had the effect of rendering the Indian Ocean a preserve of the British for the rest of the war, as Britain's naval superiority or a blockade of the French Islands alone could not prevent French privateers operating from Bourbon and Mauritius from carrying out raids on British commerce-carriers in the Indian Ocean with impunity. The extremely successful activities of the French privateers in the Indian Ocean have been compared to the German U-boat campaign during the Second World War. The expulsion of the French from their colonies in the Eastern seas was an objective of the British from the beginning of the war in 1793. Wellesley's wars in India and the Egyptian campaign prevented the execution of the plans for overseas conquests. Minto, on the other hand, was unencumbered by any major internal war which enabled him to adopt and execute such plans.

It is generally believed that the French Islands were occupied in consequence of orders from home, but Minto pre-emptively decided to undertake the expeditions against Bourbon, Mauritius and Java before such orders were received by him. The fact that Mauritius became a Crown colony immediately after its conquest has also contributed to obliterate Minto's name in connection with it. Mauritius became a permanent British acquisition. At the Congress of Vienna (1814), Castlereagh was instructed to use Britain's colonial conquests for bargaining with Talleyrand. Britain wanted to retain only those recent conquests which were of strategic value. Castlereagh claimed Malta, the Cape of Good Hope, Mauritius, Tobago and St Lucia as the sine qua non conditions of peace and in these, Britain gained the necessary strategic control over the Mediterranean and the routes to India and the West Indies. By the Treaty of Paris (30 May 1814), the French were restored to all the territories they possessed in India on 1 January 1792. Bourbon was restored to France, but Mauritius was retained as a Crown colony.[10] It afforded an additional safety valve in the sea route to India.

Minto's views with regard to the Dutch East Indies were certainly expansionist. When he came to office, the British had only a few scattered and weakly defended settlements in the East Indies. The rest of the Malayan archipelago was a Dutch monopoly. Minto's policy with regard to the Dutch East Indies originated from a desire to expel all European enemies of the British from the Indian Ocean, but it gradually widened in scope. Instead of

[10] Webster, C.K., *The Foreign Policy of Castlereagh, 1812–1815* (London, 1931), pp. 195–96, 270.

abandoning the Dutch settlements in the eastern archipelago after destroying their military defences and forces according to the recommendation of the home authorities, Minto decided to occupy them in order to secure to the Company the rich trade in spices. His Malayan policy assumed a wider scope under the influence of Stamford Raffles and John Leyden. This broader policy aimed at establishing relations with the independent Malay chiefs in the eastern archipelago, so that Britain could retain commercial and political agreements with these chiefs even if the Dutch settlements were restored to Holland after the war. Much of this policy remained on paper, but whatever part of it was actually accomplished by Raffles had the sanction and support of Minto. Between 1810 and 1813, the British not only held the Dutch settlements in the East Indies, but established relations with the Malay chiefs of Borneo, Sumatra, Bali and Java. For a period of five years from 1811 to 1816, the Malayan archipelago remained a preserve of the British.

Minto's earlier association with Burke had considerable influence on his understanding of and attitude toward the problems of the Company's rule in India. Burke was a defender of the established order. He stood for the preservation of the laws, customs and traditions of India as he had defended the French monarchy against the disruptive principles of the French Revolution. His attack on Warren Hastings has been interpreted as a crusade 'designed to protect the Indian constitution from the disastrous meddling of the West'.[11] Burke was undoubtedly one of the formative influences on the shaping of British policy toward India. Minto, also a Whig and one of Burke's lieutenants in the impeachment of Hastings, imbibed his ideas of trusteeship and conservatism. He refrained from interfering with the established order, which probably partly explains the absence of any urge for social reform on his part although he was aware of the leading social problems of the day, especially related to sati, slavery and a lack of educational opportunities in the Company's territories in India. His understanding of the people whom he governed was not very great. In his opinion any attempt on his part to enter the spirit of a different culture was bound to be superficial and unsatisfactory. An illustration of this attitude is given in a letter to Lady Minto:

> I had made a firm resolution when I came to India that I would not attempt to learn any oriental language whatever and my reason was that I knew the utmost it was possible to accomplish was a very poor smattering which might perhaps make me conceited, but could do me no other good; and for this I must have neglected many real duties.[12]

Minto was cautious about interfering with the existing order in Bengal. He felt more at liberty to act in the newly conquered Dutch settlements in Java.

---

11 Bearce, G.D., *British Attitudes towards India, 1784–1858* (Oxford, 1961).
12 NLS M 40. Minto to Lady Minto, Calcutta, 7 October 1812.

Here, in the Dutch East Indies, he sought to make the British Government synonymous with good government and the happiness of the people. His humanitarian actions in Malacca and Batavia evoked the following sentimental ebullition from Archibald Seton:

> How strangely and how unexpectedly events are brought about! Who could have foreseen, while you were urging a British senate to extend a protecting arm to the victims of the oppression of a British judge… that You were destined to visit the Chersonesus Aurea, and there to become, not remotely or indirectly, not coldly or by proxy, but personally and immediately 'The prisoners guardian, and the mourner's friend.'… if a Burke or a Howard, while in a state of bliss can have the means of knowing what is passing on our earth, their happiness may be still increased by witnessing such conduct in him who was once their friend.[13]

Minto had the ability, so important in the head of a state, to recognise and utilise talents in others. In Java, he laid down the principles of a humanitarian government and left his able lieutenant Raffles in charge of the administration.

Minto made a bid to break down the Dutch monopoly of the East Indies, but his policy of expansion was not supported by the home authorities. Conquest was a recognised method of colonial expansion, but although Britain had a legal right to the conquered Dutch colonies, the ministers did not regard it expedient to retain possession of so many Dutch colonies. Britain's reputation in Europe was more important than making large colonial acquisitions. The main motive of the ministers was of course the creation of a strong state on the borders of France, and it was particularly necessary to keep up the popular feeling in the Netherlands, not only in favour of Britain, but also for the restored Prince of Orange.[14] The Cape was retained, for which an indemnity was paid to Holland. Java and the Spice Islands were restored, as the ministers did not wish to retain any of the recently conquered colonies for their commercial value alone. Minto died before the negotiations for peace began. Had he lived he would probably have tried to move the ministers and the Court of Directors to reconsider the case of Java. However, Java had not yet yielded any commercial profits. The Directors naturally regarded it as a source of financial embarrassment to the Company, although Raffles gave assurances of a surplus in normal times. By a Convention signed on 13 August 1814, Castlereagh agreed to restore all the Dutch possessions in the East Indies within six months of ratification.[15] The actual transfer was delayed and it was not until 19 August 1816 that the Dutch flag was again hoisted in

[13] NLS M 339. A Seton to Minto, Penang, 3 February 1812.
[14] Webster, *Foreign Policy of Castlereagh*, pp. 194–96, 272–73, 305, 491. Webster, C.K., *British Diplomacy, 1813–1815* (London, 1921), pp. 126, 178.
[15] Renier, *Great Britain and the Netherlands*, pp. 319–36.

Batavia.[16] The Spice Islands were restored in 1817, and Malacca and Padang in 1818.[17] By tacit agreement, the treaties concluded by the British with the Malay chiefs were also relinquished. Consequently, the whole eastern archipelago again became a Dutch 'sphere of influence'. The British retained their outposts at Penang and Bencoolen. However, it was not until the founding of Singapore in 1818 that the British were able to establish themselves at a vantage point within the Malayan archipelago and challenge the Dutch political and commercial monopoly of the East Indies.

The eighteenth century can be described as an era when British policy in India concentrated primarily on survival. Aggression was undertaken to ensure survival, but in Minto's administration, and the policy he adopted in external relations, can be regarded as the ushering in of the nineteenth-century phase, when India was to become a base for the expansion of British power in other parts of the world. Some traces of this development are found in Wellesley's imperial policy, but the outlines became more clearly etched in Minto's external policies. While it is true that parts of his policy did not secure final approval of the home authorities, whose European preoccupations forced them to abandon some of the gains of Minto's achievements, from his diplomatic missions to the north-west of India and the conquests of Mauritius and Java in the east emerges the basis of an idea of India being the base around which a protective buffer should be built. K.M. Panikkar writes, 'An integrated conception of the defence of India, and a doctrine of Indian defence supported by a consistent foreign policy are among the two major contributions of Britain to the Indian people.'[18]

The major result of European conflicts in the age of the balance of power was the intertwining concept of foreign policy and national and colonial defence. Foreign policy, defensive as well as offensive, was often shaped in consequence of a threat to security, and depended for its success essentially on the military power of the state. The defence of British possessions in India was the consistent aim of the foreign policy of the British Indian Government. The essential difference in the defensive policy of the British and the earlier rulers of northern India was that the British sought to meet the threat to the security of their possessions at a distance from their actual frontiers, whereas earlier rulers had offered the first resistance to a foreign invader on the Indo-Gangetic plain. With the expansion of British power in India the area encircling the subcontinent assumed extreme strategic importance for Indian defence. The British Indian Government built a network of neutrals, buffer states and spheres of influence. In the latter part of the nineteenth century, the empire was thought of 'as consisting of a kernel which the rich lands

---

16 Raffles, *History of Java*, Vol. 1, p. xxvii.
17 Renier, *Great Britain and the Netherlands*, p. 338.
18 Panikkar, K.M., *Problems of Indian Defence* (London, 1960), p. 23.

directly administered, and of a protective rind'.[19] Clearly the nucleus of this idea may be traced to the beginning of the century as expressed in Minto's foreign policy.

Postscript

On 10 January 1812, a vote of thanks was passed in Parliament in favour of Minto for the conquest of Bourbon, Mauritius and Java. It suited the ministers at the beginning of a session of Parliament and possibly near the close of their administration to extol all their achievements and Java could not possibly be mentioned without referring to the governor-general. The vote of thanks was passed unanimously in the House of Lords, where it was introduced by Lord Liverpool and supported by Lords Moira, Buckinghamshire and Grenville.[20] In the House of Commons, it met with unexpected opposition from Sheridan, Whitbread and Sir Henry Montgomery. Montgomery remarked that Minto had liberated all the slaves in Java who were 'the most blood-thirsty fellows'.[21] This allegation was unsupported by facts. Sheridan's speech was particularly cutting. He declared that Minto's accompanying the expedition to Java 'savoured too much of the French revolution, where a deputy from the convention always accompanied the troops – not to share the danger, but to participate in the glory'.[22] Charles Grant, the only Director present, William Fremantle, Grenville's representative Elliot of Wells and several others spoke in favour of Minto.[23]

In June 1812, Minto wrote to his son Gilbert Elliot directing him to inform the Chairman of the Company of his intention of leaving office on 1 January 1814 so that his successor might be appointed in time to arrive at Calcutta to take charge at that time.[24] He wrote to Lady Minto:

> I cannot retain the same conciliatory views of the conduct which is now held towards me, if I am superceded in India before the time I have fixed for my return. As there can be no public ground for my removal, & that affront must be put upon me merely to make room for another man, I cannot admit that I stand upon such low ground in my present office, or in the public estimation in England, as to be turned to the right about whenever it may suit another person's convenience, or arrangements of patronage at home… I cannot help feeling that I have been rather lightly dealt with already upon this point, in the very public discussions & speculations which have taken place, on a sort of

19   Wint, G., *The British in Asia* (London, 1954), p. 21.
20   Hansard, *The Parliamentary Debates, Vol. XXI* (London, 1812), pp. 126–31.
21   Ibid., p. 141.
22   Ibid., p. 138.
23   Ibid., pp. 131–46. NLS M 497. Elliot of Wells to Minto, 15 January 1812.
24   NLS M 497. Minto to Gilbert Elliot, 10 June 1812.

presumption that I was to give way whenever a choice among the competitors for my office should be amicably adjusted, without any reference or regard to me. If this principle should be acted upon, & I am recalled otherwise than upon my own resignation, I shall feel no satisfaction is now offer'd & shall think I am stroked with one hand only because I am buffeted with the other. ... However I do not much apprehend that this will happen.[25]

The Directors were disappointed at not receiving the financial surplus which Minto had so confidently promised them. They had expected a large remittance and had depended on it to meet the financial liabilities of the Company. In May 1809 Minto had promised to send 1 million pounds sterling annually for the next four years. On that expectation, the Directors had accepted more than four million pounds sterling of Indian debt. However, with the failure of Minto to keep his side of the bargain, the Company's financial burden increased.[26] Elphinstone wrote to Minto in April 1812 that the lack of financial remittances from India could not have taken place at a worse time, for the Company had just begun to negotiate with the Government for the renewal of the Charter, and had asked for financial assistance from it to meet the Company's outstanding liabilities. A sizeable remittance from India would have given them substantial ground to stand upon.[27] Bosanquet criticised Minto for going to Java when he should have been attending to the important matter of financial remittances to the Company.[28] Parry wrote to Minto that the Court was mortified to find the fleet from Bengal had arrived without the Company's silk for which the Court had sent to Bengal bullion worth £300,000. Silk was received by the manufacturers privately to the detriment of the Company. Parry wrote that the Company's loss was prodigious and the traders, the Agency Houses and the Company's shareholders raised a terrific clamour. He wrote, 'They assert that your financial arrangement had disappointed the Bengal Government & put everything in Confusion at Home & abroad, so that no party is satisfied.'[29]

On 14 November 1812, the Directors received the intimation of Minto's wish to resign office early in 1814.[30] However, on 7 November 1812 the Duke of Buckinghamshire, the new President of the Board of Control, wrote to Minto that the Prince Regent had communicated to Liverpool that Lord Moira had consented to go to India, and had ordered Liverpool to take steps for Moira's immediate appointment as Governor-General of Bengal. Buckinghamshire added that Moira's standing with the regent and

25 NLS M 40. Minto to Lady Minto, Barrackpore, 10 June 1812.
26 Tripathi, A., *Trade and Finance in Bengal Presidency* (Calcutta, 1956), pp. 123–24. In all, Minto sent back about £1,858,719 to the Company. Ibid., footnote, p. 124.
27 NLS M 192. W.F. Elphinstone to Minto, London, 4 April 1812.
28 NLS M 83. Gilbert Elliot to Minto, London, 2 April 1812.
29 NLS M 192. Parry to Minto, 18 September 1812.
30 NLS Minto Papers Box 73. Hugh Inglis to Gilbert Elliot, 14 November 1812.

the ministers made it impossible to postpone the measure. In order to spare Minto any discredit or dishonour, he proposed to Liverpool that Minto should be given an earldom instead of a viscountcy which had been awarded earlier. Liverpool agreed to this proposal.[31]

Minto's recall therefore cannot be said to have been the act of either the Directors or the ministers. It was purely a measure of royal patronage. The regent obviously thought more of Moira's pecuniary embarrassments in Britain than the merits or demerits of Minto's administration in India. This also clearly established the fact that there was no connection between the recall of Minto and Barlow. On 7 November 1812, the ministers demanded Minto's recall and soon afterward on 2 December 1812, the Court of Directors recalled Barlow, both on substantively different grounds.[32]

Minto in the meantime had started making his own preparations for return. He sent a more formal letter of resignation to the Court of Directors, dated 24 November 1812.[33] When the orders of his recall reached him in April 1813, he was taken aback. He wrote:

> Lord Moira's appointment… was determined upon without any consideration of my wishes with regard to the period of my return to Europe. In other words, the intention was to remove & supercede me, and if Lord Moira had sailed at the time first proposed that is say in December, it is not unlikely that he would himself have brought me the first account of a change entirely unexpected & which I had indeed every reason to think impossible.[34]

He'd first heard of Moira's appointment through unofficial channels. Afterwards he received the letters from Buckinghamshire, Parry and Grant. Minto tried to convince himself that 'this measure implies no imputation on me… it is simply an exertion of favour towards another person, too powerful & too impatient, to be stopped by the weaker considerations of justice or delicacy'.[35]

Minto could have justly protested against the injustice of his recall but the fact that sweetened the bitter pill was the offer of an earldom. The temptation of an earldom he found difficult to resist, although its acceptance deprived him of the basis of protest. His mind worked in two ways. He felt:

---

[31] NLS M 497. Lord Buckinghamshire to Minto, 7 November 1812.

[32] NLS M 497. Edward Parry to Minto, India House, 18 December 1812 (Received at Calcutta on 28 May 1813). Edward Parry, William Astell, George Smith and John Bebb signed a protest against the recall of either Minto or Barlow. Grant was away in Scotland at the time. He recorded his dissent afterwards. Ibid., Charles Grant to Minto, London, 21 December 1812.

[33] NLS M 209. Minto to the Chairman of the East India Company, Fort William, 24 November 1812.

[34] NLS M 210. Minto to Sir Samuel Hood, Calcutta, 24 April 1813.

[35] Ibid.

I should place myself on higher ground by rejecting this compromise, than by a change of title,… it may perhaps be a public duty,… to abstain from everything that can be construed or is likely to be misconstrued into any degree of countenance on my part to a measure which involves, besides a slight to myself, no inconsiderable violation of public principles. On the other hand… the slight to me is an incidental consequence & not a primary object of the measure, & regretted… certainly by those who have carried the measure into effect, &… an atonement is offer'd as a public testimony of those sentiments.[36]

He felt he had earned the earldom by his services and was unwilling to relinquish that long-sought honour on the ground of offended dignity. He therefore accepted the arrangement, with a protest.[37] Clearly he was also eager to get back to Minto. According to his own calculations he'd saved £80,000 during his years in India with which he hoped to resuscitate the fortunes of the Minto family.[38]

Although Moira was first expected to sail from England in December 1812, it was postponed to a later date. Minto decided not to sail until November 1813 due to family reasons and the monsoon.[39] It meant that he would remain at Calcutta, after Moira assumed office. Such a situation was likely to be embarrassing, but Minto regarded it with characteristic calmness and even amusement. He wrote to Lady Minto, 'Lord Moira is naturally disposed to act handsomely on all occasions, & I shall have no disposition to give him offence or umbrage. So that I think the rising & the setting sun may drive their chariots very peaceably & amicably round the Calcutta course.'[40]

Yet he must have left India with the disappointment of a man whose efforts and services were not fully appreciated by his countrymen. His services were only reluctantly acknowledged by the home authorities. The lack of powerful friends either in the Court of Directors or in the Government was the root cause of the indifference shown toward him.[41] Minto reached London in May 1814, but died shortly afterwards on 21 June 1814 on his way from London to Minto.[42] He was interred in Westminster Abbey, an honour shared with him by only Canning and Lawrence. In Curzon's opinion, the compliment was 'due less to personal claims, than to the tragic circumstances of his death'.[43]

---

[36] NLS M 497. Minto to Gilbert Elliot, 27 June 1813.

[37] Ibid., Minto to Buckinghamshire, Calcutta, 28 June 1813.

[38] NLS Minto Papers, Box 64, Minto to Lady Minto, Calcutta, 23 December 1812.

[39] NLS M 210. Minto to Sir Samuel Hood, Calcutta, 24 April 1813. Minto's two daughters-in-law, wives of John Elliot and Captain George Elliot, were expecting to be confined in August and October 1813.

[40] NLS M 40. Minto to Lady Minto, Calcutta, 25 June 1813.

[41] *Lord Minto in India*, pp. 385, 392.

[42] Ibid.

[43] Curzon, *British Government in India*, Vol. 2, p. 139. Curzon writes, 'The sole representation of the first Lord Minto in Calcutta was a bust in St. John's Church, which had been presented

The conflict in Europe turned decisively in 1812 following Napoleon's disastrous invasion of Russia. His forces were severely depleted and during the period 1812–14, the Sixth Coalition finally defeated him at the Battle of Leipzig. Napoleon was forced to abdicate and was exiled to Elba. Following his escape and return, he reorganised his forces for a final showdown at Waterloo in June 1815 where on his ultimate defeat, the Congress of Vienna in 1815 redrew the political contours of Europe including the European empires in India and South-East Asia. The events of the war proved that the foreign European possessions in India offered little threat to British India. Therefore as a means of encouraging international trade, the French were readmitted to their old settlements on the Indian mainland and both they and the Dutch recognised for the first time, British sovereignty over the Company's possessions.[44] The French also agreed to maintain no troops and to erect no fortresses and the Company was entirely freed of the European menace in India.[45] Britain returned the island of Bourbon to France, but retained Mauritius. Similarly the Dutch could also be treated generously as they no longer posed a serious threat to British interests and all of the occupied colonies, namely Java, Malacca and the Spice Islands of the Moluccas were all returned to the Netherlands. While this made perfect sense to Castlereagh and the Foreign Office, the interests of the East India Company in terms of being able to control trade in South-East Asia were adversely affected, and a possible opportunity to advance British commerce in the region, and also to continue the land and revenue collection reforms initiated by Minto in Java, were surrendered. Within India, Lord Moira was able to subdue the Ghurkhas on the border with Nepal and signed the Treaty of Sagauli in 1816 establishing a permanent peace between Nepal and British India, and with the final defeat of the Marathas following the third Anglo-Maratha War in 1818, the British Indian Empire was secure.

On 22 March 1813, Lord Castlereagh introduced a discussion on the renewal of the charter into a committee of the House of Commons. He declared that the Government did not wish to interfere with the Company's political powers, but that it was ready to consider a relaxation of its commercial privileges.[46] The Directors obtained permission to call witnesses and for the rest of March and April fifty-one witnesses gave evidence focused on the political danger of admitting 'trade speculators' to India and the majority also opposed a movement to introduce unrestricted dispatch of mission-aries. Neither the ministers nor Parliament took the slightest notice of the

by himself at the request of the Vestry, who were much gratified at his regular attendance in Church, and at this restoration of the building.'

[44] Dodwell, *Cambridge History of India*, V, p. 596.
[45] Board's Secret Drafts, Vol. 4, 4 November 1814.
[46] Philips, *The East India Company*, pp. 188–93.

large body of evidence that the Company had presented.[47] On 31 May the
House of Commons agreed to proceed by the resolution and throughout the
proceedings there were rarely more than 100 members present of whom the
Government had a comfortable majority. The Company was again entrusted
for a period of twenty years with the administration of the Indian territories.
The second resolution continued the monopoly of the China trade with the
Company and the third critical resolution proposed to open the Indian trade
to all licensed British merchants.[48] The bill reflected the efforts of Wilberforce
and his party of twenty Evangelicals in the House of Commons who had
insisted on incorporating the moral obligations of the British in administering
the Company's possessions.[49] Clause 33 declared that the Government's duty
was 'to promote the interest and happiness of the native inhabitants of India'.

The Directors gained more by the Charter Act of 1813 than they had
expected by retaining their political functions, the profitable part of their trade
and patronage. The introduction of private traders soon proved that they could
conduct trade with India far more profitably and on a more extensive scale
than the Company.[50] The ending of the East India Company's monopoly
of trade with India has been viewed by historians as a significant event in
the emergence of British commitment to free trade. The act opened trade
between Britain, India and South-East Asia to merchants outside London and
the East India Company, provided that such trade was conducted by ships of
350 tonnes and above. Trade was restricted to the main East India Company
settlements, and the Company China trade monopoly was preserved. In order
to defend northern textile manufacturers from competition, the produce of
Indian cotton manufacturers was restricted from import; this allowed British
manufacturers to export cheap cotton and resulted in the elimination of the
Indian cotton industry.[51] For the first time, independent British traders could
hire their own vessels and trade freely with the main presidencies of India.
They could ship out British manufactured goods on speculation and purchase
Indian made goods for the UK and European markets. Indian firms were also
free to engage in their own speculative commercial ventures with Britain.[52]

The single most profitable part of Company commercial activity was
the trade with China involving the export of Indian and South-East Asian
produce in exchange for tea and other Chinese manufactured goods for sale
in Britain and Europe. Raw cotton and the illegal opium trade were the

[47] Add. MSS. 29188, f.105, 5 June 1813.
[48] *East India House Debates*, II, Series 3. 11.
[49] Add. MSS. 29188, F.136, 23 June 1813, Papers of Warren Hastings.
[50] Value of private trade goods sold at London, 1812–13, £2,553,627; 1814–15, £4,607,152; 1818–19, £4,352,857. *Lords' Select Committee, Appendix*, 1174.
[51] Webster, A., 'The Political Economy of Trade Liberalization: The East India Company Charter Act of 1813', *The Economic History Review*, 43, 3 (August 1990), pp. 404–19.
[52] Webster, *Twilight of the East India Company* (Woodbridge, 2009), p. 65.

most lucrative. The Company commandeered the production of opium in India under its monopoly and was in turn distributed to agency houses who smuggled the product into China. Receipts were paid into the Company's treasury at Canton in exchange for bills of exchange payable in India or London.[53] The increase in the revenues from this trade in opium were doubled in a period of five years between 1800 and 1805 in the region of Rs 4–5 million per annum, rising to a high of Rs 7 million in 1814–15. In volume, this trade amounted to 3–4,000 chests of opium annually.[54]

As Webster has indicated, the return of the Dutch colonies in the region following the end of the Napoleonic Wars was part of the British strategy of bolstering the Netherlands against the threat of future French expansionism, but it was also a source of great concern for the East India Company, the India agency houses and their allies in London. During the war, the British had built substantial commercial interests in occupied Dutch possessions such as Java, including coffee and spice plantations as well as trading interests.[55] They feared a revival of Dutch power and pre-war practices such as establishing exclusive trading treaties with local states of the Malay archipelago. In February 1819, Lord Castlereagh brought to Baron Fagel (the Dutch Ambassador in London) a specific complaint about recent increases in trade duties in Java.[56]

In November 1818, the British Governor-General Lord Moira (the Marquis of Hastings) met with Raffles (Governor of Bencoolen) in Calcutta. Hastings, in the tradition of Minto, gave Raffles instructions for a mission to several locations in the Malay archipelago.[57] Raffles orders were to establish a new British port at the southern tip of the Malay Peninsula and to explore a diplomatic solution to the civil war in northern Sumatra. The most famous outcome of this mission was the British acquisition of Singapore in February 1819 as a result of Raffles's agreement with a senior minister of the Malay state of Johore. British ownership was confirmed by the Treaty of London agreed between the Dutch and the British in 1824. Minto's earlier vision with regard to the importance of Java both strategically and commercially were brought sharply into focus and the need to protect both the China trade route as well as the establishment of new markets in the Malay Peninsula were crucial to both the agency houses and the Company administration in Bengal.

Free trade with India during the 1820s brought a series of challenges as newly arrived merchants had to compete with the older trading houses, which

---

[53] Greenberg, M., *British Trade and the Opening of China 1800–1842* (Cambridge, 1951), pp. 8–13.

[54] Ibid., p. 221.

[55] Knight, G.R., 'John Palmer and Plantation Development in Western Java in the Early Nineteenth Century', *Bijdragen*, 131, 2/3 (1975), pp. 309–37.

[56] TNA, FO 37/109, Castlereagh to Fagel, 10 February 1819.

[57] BL, OIOC, Dutch Records I/2/29. Minute by Governor General Hastings, November 1818.

had established profitability and held ancillary businesses such as shipbuilding and plantation agriculture. As a result, there was an increase in highly speculative pursuits such as new construction and new crop ventures which added to financial stresses.[58] Additionally, the outbreak of war between British India and Burma in 1824 due to the expansionist tendencies of the Konbaung dynasty led to an expenditure (over two years) of almost £4.8 million, proving to be the sixth-most expensive of the British imperial conflicts in the nineteenth century.[59] Third, the British domestic market was also affected when a sudden rise in the price of bullion in Britain in 1818. For three years after the signing of the Treaty of Paris in 1815 the Government acquiesced to the Bank of England's various arguments that resumption of cash payments should be delayed whether the exchanges had stabilised, or the bond market had strengthened, or foreign trade had picked up or its gold reserves were increased. Finally in 1819, the Government initiated a bill to force the Bank to resume convertibility after initial experiments in 1817 at limited convertibility had succeeded without any harmful consequences. Even so, the Bank managed to make the transition as difficult as possible, first by amassing a large stock of gold, which helped keep up the price of gold in the markets and then by withdrawing the notes from circulation that the Government used to repay £10 million of exchequer bills that had been held by the Bank. Further, it refused to lower its rate of discount on bills and notes even as its loan business to the private sector declined. The resulting price deflation intensified both agricultural and manufacturing distress.[60] This led in turn to the progressive curtailments of bullion exports to Bengal and contributed to a fall in the amount of money in circulation in India, exacerbating the shortage of capital available for increasing demands of government and the agency houses. Clearly increasing competition for a commodity product (indigo) which was the mainstay of the Company's revenue to Britain caused the resulting increased supply to result in a collapse of the market price and as a result the Company had to ship bullion to Britain in turn to meet its debt. Asiya Siddiqi argues that export performance in terms of value was severely undermined by a drain of gold from India by the Company as tribute, which exacerbated a decline in the value of the silver rupee against gold-based currencies such as sterling.[61] The terms of trade were such that Britain was

---

[58] Crawfurd, J., 'A Sketch of the Commercial Resources and Monetary and Mercantile System of British India, with Suggestions for their Improvement by means of Banking Establishments' (1837), in K.N. Chaudhuri (ed.), *The Economic Development of India under the East India Company 1814–1858* (Cambridge, 1971), pp. 217–316.

[59] Peers, D.M., 'War and Public Finance in Early Nineteenth Century British India: The First Burma War', *The International History Review*, 9,4 (1989), pp. 628–647 (p. 639).

[60] Neal, L., 'The Financial Crisis of 1825 and the Restructuring of the British Financial System', *Review, Federal Reserve Bank of St. Louis* (1998), p. 58.

[61] Siddiqi, A. (ed.), *Trade and Finance in Colonial India 1750–1860* (Delhi, 1995), pp. 17–27.

furnished with cheaper primary produce to fuel its industrial revolution while suppressing earnings and living standards in India.[62]

The growing discontent between the handling of European creditors of failed agency houses versus their Indian counterparts under British colonial law severely undermined Anglo-Indian trust and there was a tendency toward a creation of separate European and Indian financial and mercantile spheres as outlined by Bagchi.[63] At the same time that the financial crisis in Calcutta was unfolding, the latest round of discussions about the renewal of the East India Company's charter was underway in Britain. The privatisation of Indian trade resulted in a domino effect on the Company in terms of it being unable to support its China trade as the Company found it extremely difficult to increase the volume of its exports of Indian goods to China. Bowen estimates that after 1814 the Company needed to generate £1 million in profits each year in order to meet its heavy debt, charges and other obligations in Britain.[64] There were also increasing doubts about the efficiency of retaining a China trade monopoly as American traders could circumvent this by purchasing British-made goods from merchant houses such as Barings, William Brown of Liverpool and Charles Everett.[65] Thus there was a growing trend indicating that only through the introduction of free trade under which British private traders could compete on equal terms with others would Britain's share of the lucrative Chinese market be preserved.

The Charter Act of 1833 was successfully steered through the House of Commons by Macaulay in the summer of that year with the effective compromise outlined in the bill of ending the Company's commercial life, while retaining its political, governing function. This meant that basically the Company's institutions covering all aspects of bureaucracy and expertise would continue to influence imperial policy in India. The direct result of the Company becoming an organ of government and releasing its final and most closely held monopoly (that of the China trade) resulted in the creation of new chambers of commerce where the founding merchants realised that they had to be directly responsible for the fiscal health of their organisation and members resulting in a network to provide mutual political support and commercial intelligence to continue to improve business performance. Returning briefly to the importance of China, in 1834–35, China received 36.6 per cent of Indian exports by value, and 37.8 per cent in 1837–38.[66]

[62] Siddiqi, A., 'Money and Prices in the Earlier Stages of Empire: India and Britain 1760–1840', *Indian Economic and Social History Review*, 18, 3–4 (1981), pp. 231–62.

[63] Bagchi, A.K., 'Transition from Indian to British Indian Systems of Money and Banking 1800–1850', *Modern Asian Studies*, 19, 3 (1985), pp. 501–19 (p. 516).

[64] Bowen, H.V., *Business of Empire*, pp. 258–59.

[65] Ibid., p. 256.

[66] Chaudhuri, K.N., 'Foreign Trade and Balance of Payments (1757–1947)', in D. Kumar (ed.), *The Cambridge History of Modern India Volume 2: 1757–2003* (Hyderabad, 2005), p. 861.

Opium was the major product and the Qing Administration initially allowed the trade in the narcotic as it received an indirect tax from users, they also benefitted from the increased tea exports to Britain, a monopoly held by the Qing imperial treasury and its agents.[67] However, as addiction to opium spread, the Chinese Government wished to put a forcible halt to the trade and seized and destroyed 20,000 chests of opium (approximately 1.2 million kg).[68] The British Government, though not objecting to China's control of the drug, objected to the seizure and initiated the First Opium War (1839–42) resulting in the Treaty of Nanjing in 1842 that ceded the port of Hong Kong to the British and provided free access to five treaty ports of Shanghai, Guangzhou, Ningbo, Fuzhou and Amoy.[69]

One can argue that Minto's role was particularly visionary in terms of his being able to anticipate and direct the creation of these regional spheres of influence and recognising the importance of free trade and land reform, while advocating the role of the Company as being advisory rather than subsidiary to the Crown. In a sense, after the aggressive campaigns of Wellesley, his administration provided a diplomatic foil to create a stable operating base in India while expanding the trading interests of the company by first ensuring a buffer against all hostile challenges. Clearly, if Java were allowed to develop its land reforms and revenue collection systems it could have become a very profitable outpost for the British. Unfortunately due to circumstances outside his control, notwithstanding his tremendous effort Java was returned to the Dutch. This basic issue (the strategic geopolitical importance of a position in the Malay Peninsula) was the later acquisition of Singapore and the creation of the Straits Settlements under Raffles, a selected protégé of Minto, clearly vindicating his original plan. Mauritius as a settlement while being retained by the British could have also benefitted from the identical land and labour reforms as proposed by Minto for Java. Mismanagement of resources, an underestimation of costs and logistics (of labour and freight) and the Sugar Duties Act of 1846, coupled with unrestricted speculation on the sugar trade, led to enormous losses of the trading houses. At least four of the failing London houses had plantations on Mauritius worth £1.5 million.[70]

Further, the three primary methods of repatriating funds for the Company are worth examining. The first involved the sale by the Company in London of bills payable in India to British traders wishing to import Indian and Asian

---

67 Peyrefitte, A., *The Immobile Empire: The First Great Collision of East and West – The Astonishing History of Britain's Grand, Ill-Fated Expedition to Open China to Western Trade, 1792–94* (New York, 1992), p. 520.

68 Farooqui, A., *Smuggling as Subversion: Colonialism, Indian Merchants, and the Politics of Opium, 1790–1843* (Lanham, MD, 2005).

69 Tsang, S., *A Modern History of Hong Kong* (London, 2007), pp. 3–13, 29.

70 Hugh Hunter's testimony, Select Committee of the Commons on Sugar and Coffee Planting, Vol. 23 part 1 (first report), 21 February 1848, p. 214.

produce. The second method involved the Company authorities at Canton (Guangzhou) in China receiving Spanish dollars from traders exporting opium and other goods from India to China in return for bills payable in India. These dollars would then be issued by the Company in Canton to other British private traders purchasing Chinese tea and other goods in return for bills payable to the Company in London. This practice ended with the first Opium War.[71] The third and most controversial method was the 'hypothecation system'. This involved firms in India buying products and paying for them with bills drawn on (payable by) the London East India agency houses. The recipients of these bills would sell them to the East India Company, which would then transmit them to London for payment by the London houses. This encouraged unnecessary speculation as the Company's purchases would vary unpredictably from year to year, exacerbating the problem of the falling price of Indian goods in Britain and resulting in widely fluctuating exchange rates between the sterling and the rupee, resulting eventually in the commercial crisis of 1847–48.

British imperial strategy in Asia in the first half of the nineteenth century was initially related to individuals and their independent vision, followed by a gradual decentralisation of power and control leading to an informal and formal network of private trading houses. However, this decentralisation should in itself have ideally been controlled in terms of first establishing areas of specialisation and function where each participant whether an acquired territory or trading house worked according to their specific skill set and devoted their resources to optimising production while others could focus on the logistics of transport and supply. The seeds of these ideas were outlined by the First Earl of Minto.

[71] Tripathi, A., 'Indo-British Trade between 1833 and 1847', p. 278.

APPENDIX: GOVERNMENT OF THE EAST INDIA COMPANY

Court of Proprietors / Directors[1]

Until 1784, the home government of the East India Company had consisted of the Proprietors of India Stock and twenty-four Directors.[2] Any person who purchased shares in the capital stock of the East India Company was denominated a Proprietor and was permitted to attend the meetings of the Central Court of Proprietors. A purchase of £500 stock entitled the holder to vote 'in a show of hands'; possession of £1,000, £3,000, £6,000 and more than £10,000 stock gave the Proprietor single, double, triple and quadruple votes respectively in a ballot. Four votes was the maximum possible.[3] The Investors of the Company included the banking, shipping and commercial interests of the City of London[4] and the returned Anglo-Indians or 'Nabobs' who acquired India Stock either as a convenient investment yielding an annual return of 8 per cent[5] or as a means by which they could gain influence, a Directorship, power and patronage in the Company.[6]

The meetings of the Proprietors were held quarterly (in March, June, September and December) but could be called at any time by the Directors or a quorum of nine of the Proprietors. Prior to 1784, the Court of Proprietors had the power to reverse the decisions of the Directors and on several occasions resulted in prolonged and bitter struggle and deadlock on critical issues, but Pitt's India Act of 1784 which created a Board of Control to manage the proceedings of India House, decreed that the Court of Proprietors could not veto a proposal made by the Directors and approved

---

[1] Philips, *The East India Company*, pp. 2–9.
[2] There were 2,163 Proprietors in 1800; 2,140 in 1831; Wisset, *East India Affairs*. Alexander, *E.I. Magazine*, p. 348.
[3] Auber, *Constitution of the East India Company*, p. 349.
[4] Forty-six of the forty-nine Proprietors who held over £10,000 stock in 1799 lived in London or the immediate vicinity. Parkinson, C.N., *Trade in the Eastern Seas, 1793–1813* (Cambridge, 1937), p. 11.
[5] Dividend payouts were fixed at 8 per cent in 1784 and at 10.5 per cent in 1793. 24 George III, c.34, 33 George III, c.31.
[6] See Malcolm, *Political History of India*, II, p. 122.

by the Board. This greatly weakened the power of the Proprietors, but in the period from 1784 to 1834 still represented an expression of public opinion on the response to the Company's government and policies both in India and Britain. The form of proceedings at these meetings was based on the House of Commons, but all important questions were referred for final decision to a ballot which usually took place a fortnight after the meeting.

The most important function of the Proprietors was to elect the twenty-four Directors who formed the executive body of the Company in Britain. Since 1709, the Court of Directors comprised twenty-four members and Pitt in 1784 maintained that number indicating that the presence of a large number of Directors facilitated independence and allowed a level of security against the prejudice of political interests so that patronage in the Company was diffused.

The election of the Directors by ballot took place annually on the second Wednesday in April. A necessary minimum requirement for formal qualification included the possession of £2,000 of India stock. Anyone falling below this minimum threshold was automatically disqualified.

The Regulating Act of 1773 had instituted a system of election (which lasted until 1853), whereby six Directors were chosen in each year to replace six retiring Directors, the latter not being eligible for re-election until the following April.[7] Each Director therefore held office for four years and then 'went out by rotation' for a year. The Court became co-optive and by 1784, it was customary for the Directors in office to unite to ensure the return of the six Directors 'out by rotation'. In 1822, out of thirty Directors, ten had been in office for at least ten years, six had served for over twenty years and two for thirty years. The only available chance of gaining admission to this select 'House List' of recommended Directors drawn up by the Chairman in March each year, was by the death or disqualification of a Director.[8]

Throughout the period 1784–1834 there existed a well-organised City and Shipping interest and also a large but unstructured Indian interest. Later in the period between the years 1824 and 1830, the Private Trade interest exerted considerable influence in the elections through the East India agency houses in London. Competition for vacancies in the Directorship was so fierce that Proprietors regularly announced their candidature four or five years before they expected to gain election. An attempt was made to maintain representatives of each of the major branches of the Company including those experienced in field service covering military and naval operations.

[7]   Add. MSS. 29177, f.52, Jul 1799, Toone to Hastings.
[8]   The Directors zealously retained their position. In 1829 they decreed that one of their number, John Benn, should resign because he had lost both sight and hearing. Benn indignantly opposed the Court's verdict because, 'he hoped to be restored to useful vision and his hearing is liable to variation being sometimes worse, sometimes better'. Minutes, Secret Committee, 4 February 1829.

Between 1784 and 1834, 110 different Directors held office of whom well over half had resided in India. Following the release of the monopoly on trade with India during the renewal of the charter in 1813, the Private Trade and City interests steadily increased their influence at the expense of the Indian interest.[9] This was in a sense detrimental as opinions on India and associated foreign policy were not always expressed by those possessing actual knowledge of field experience in the respective regions. All letters from India and appeals from their servants were read in Court and final decisions were taken on reports of sub-committees. Summary Policies for India were read and signed by a quorum of thirteen Directors. All points at issue were decided by a ballot, usually by a show of hands for convenience. Controversial topics were decided by a secret ballot taken by a sub-group whose opinions were revealed by previous debate in India House, but most of the important business was decided by the thirteen separate committees covering different business interest groups.

Secret Committee[10]

The most important Committee of the Directors with regard to the political government of India was the Secret Committee. The official statutory origin in 1784 was actually preceded by several decades of informal existence and was an essential part of the Company's home organisation. Peter Auber, who served the Company as Assistant Secretary and Secretary from 1818 to 1836, listed the year of inception as 1748, though it is quite probable that the Committee originated in the resolution of the Court of Committees of 23 April 1683: 'The Court taking into consideration that in transacting the affairs relating to Bantam it is necessary that the same be managed with all privacy: they were pleased to nominate the Governor, Deputy and Sir Josia Child to be a secret committee for the carrying on that business.'[11]

Henceforth, the Directors often appointed a Secret Committee consisting of three or four members to deal with emergency political situations and provide foreign policy leadership and recommendations in an efficient and rapid manner, for example, the course that the Company's ships were to take on the voyage between India and China. The powers of the committee were renewed annually and in April 1741 the Secret Committee appeared on the list of the Court's subcommittees.[12] During the War of Austrian Succession, the Secret Committee was empowered to give orders 'for the security of the

9   *E.I. Debates*, 17 December 1794. Alexander, op. cit. (1832), p. 477.
10 Dodwell, *Cambridge History of India*, V, pp. 201, 315. Philips, *The East India Company*, pp. 9–19.
11 Court Book, 33, f.135. 6 March 1694.
12 Court Book, 59, f.270. 6 March 1694.

Company's shipping and settlements' and in the execution of its duties, corresponded regularly with the ministers.[13]

Between 1754 and 1781, the Secret Committee exercised various powers in directing the Company's military and naval operations, conducted negotiations with Indian powers and represented the Court of Directors in its dealings with the ministers, for example, taking charge of the negotiations with regard to the Company's involvement for the Treaty of Paris in 1763. The precedent of rapid decision-making with regard to crucial issues allowed Pitt and Dundas the pathway to establish a permanent statutory Secret Committee in 1784, consisting of not more than three Directors through which the Ministry could send secret advisory messages to India. Although the primary role was to pass these advisory bulletins between the Board of Control and the Governments in India, in practice, the Secret Committee often originated statements of policy and strategic approach through both renewals of the Charter Act in 1813 and 1833, exerting considerable influence in the determination of the home government's external policy, for example, Minto's Consultation and request for Secret Committee feedback with regard to his proposed attack on the Dutch East Indies. Consisting as it did of the Chairman, Deputy Chairman and one other (usually a senior Director), the Secret Committee became the 'cabinet council' of the Company and enjoyed frequent consultation on all important India business with the President of the Board and the ministers.[14]

---

13 Court Book, 61, f.10, 10 April 1744.
14 See Home Misc. 456e, f.365. Philips, *The East India Company*, p. 11.

BIBLIOGRAPHY

Primary Sources

Manuscripts

Bodleian Library, Oxford
No. 2. Dissertation on the Invasion of India, 1814, by J. Macdonald
No. 3. Copy of a letter from John Malcolm to Lord Minto on the state of Persia, 6 October 1810
Miscellaneous Indian Papers. MSS. Eng. Misc. C 325
Papers of the Russells of Swallowfield, Berkshire, 19th century

British Library, London
1. Additional Manuscripts:
Add. MSS. 35918. Report on Malcolm's mission to Persia, 1810
Add. MSS. 37285. Papers related to Malcolm's Persian mission, 1808–09 and other letters of Malcolm
Add. MSS. 37292. Letters to Robert Farquhar, 1810
Add. MSS. 38323. Letters to and from the Earl of Liverpool, 1811
Add. MSS. 38578. Minto to Robert Dundas, 1810
Add. MSS. 41768. Correspondence related to Malcolm's mission to Persia, 1808
Copies of some of these letters are also included in the official records and private papers of the first Earl of Minto

2. India Office Records:
Bengal Political Consultations: Range 118, Vols 42–43; Range 119, Vols. 4, 14, 17, 19
Bengal Secret Consultations (1808): Vol. 204
Bengal Secret and Political Consultations (1807–12): Vols 202, 205–18, 225, 226, 233, 234
Bengal Secret and Separate Consultations (1807–12): Vols 219–23, 228–31, 236
Board's Drafts of Secret Letters and Despatches to India (Bengal): Vol. 3 (March 1804–December 1810); Vol. 4 (January 1811–November 1814)
The Factory Records Series, of which two series entitled Persia and Java have been referenced: Java Series: Vols 9–14, 65; Persia Series: Vols 25–31
The French in India series: Vols 1, 12, 14
The Home Miscellaneous Series, a miscellaneous collection of papers covering the entire period of the East India Company's Government in India: Vol. 24, Vol. 506, Vol. 511, Vols 592–95, Vols 657–59, Vol. 701, Vols 733, 736–37, Vol. 817, Vol. 831
Personal Records: Vol. 4.
Secret Letters received from Bengal: First Series, Vols 10–14 (1807–13) (5 Vols)

Secret Letters Received (various): Vol.1 Letters from Bourbon and Mauritius (24 July 1810 to 2 April 1811); Vol. 6 Letters from Harford Jones (11 July 1798 to 11 June 1809); Vol. 7 Letters from Harford Jones (7 November 1807 to 31 May 1811)

3. India Office Private Collections:

Elphinstone Collection: MSS. Eur. F. 88, Box 13 G (vol. m), 13 H (vols n and o), 13 J (vol. q), 13 I (vols l and i), 13 F (vol. h)

Acquired by the British Library (India Office Records) (formerly Commonwealth Relations Office Library) in 1961. Stored in Boxes.

Raffles Collection: Minor Collections, Eur, MSS. 232–35, 244

A detailed description of the documents in each volume is given in Kaye, G.B. and Johnstone, E.H., *Catalogue of Manuscripts in European Languages, India Office Library, Minor Collections and Manuscripts* (London, 1937), Vol. ii, part ii, pp. 774–93, 814–16.

The National Archives, Kew
The Foreign Office Records relating to Persia
FO 60/1 (January 1807 to December 1808)
FO 60/2 (January to December 1809)
FO 60/3 (January to November 1810)
FO 60/4 (February to July 1810)
FO 60/5 (January 1811 to December 1812)
FO 60/6 (cont.)

The Admiralty Records
Admiralty in-letters from the Commanders-in-Chief at the Cape of Good Hope and East Indies Station
Adm. 1/63 Cape of Good Hope 1810–11
Adm. 1/177 East Indies 1806
Adm. 1/178 East Indies 1806
Adm. 1/179 East Indies 1807
Adm. 1/180 East Indies 1808
Adm. 1/181 East Indies 1809
Adm. 1/182 East Indies 1809–10
Adm. 1/183 East Indies 1811
Adm. 1/184 East Indies 1812

Admiralty out-letters
Adm. 2/1366

National Library of Scotland, Edinburgh
Minto Papers. Private papers of the first Earl of Minto, 1807–13
The Minto Collection acquired by the National Library of Scotland by purchase in 1958 is an untapped and unique source. It represents a large collection, of which the papers of the first Earl of Minto form an extensive section. The inventory consists of the title of each volume or series, with the year and manuscript number. The references to the Minto Papers provided in this book are according to the records of the inventory.

Official
Political General Letters (1807–12) (M.199 to M.204) (6 vols)
Proceedings of the Persian Department (1807–13) (M.211 to M.235 in serial order)
Proceedings of the Political Department (1807–13) (M.378 to M.483 in serial order)
Proceedings of the Secret Department (1807–13) (M.236 to M.332 in serial order)
Secret and Separate General Letters (1807–12) (M.193 to M.198) (6 vols)
Copies of these official records are in the British Library (India Office Records), London.

Private
The Minto Collection consists of private correspondence between the first Earl of Minto and his family, friends, associates and assistants in Britain and in India. These are like a diary or logbook, containing not only personal or domestic news, but also his views and impressions about political events, people and sometimes an exposition or defence of any particular action or policy, some written over a period of a week or longer.

Copies of Minto's letters and despatches (1807–13) M.206
Copy letter-book of Minto (1806–12) M.157 to M.162 (6 vols)
Correspondence between Gillespie and Minto (1811–13) M.498
Correspondence between Minto and Barlow (1808–13) M.335, M.342, M.345, M.346 (4 vols)
Correspondence between Minto and General Hewitt (1807–11) M.173 to M.174 (2 vols)
Correspondence with Sir Edward Pellew (1807–12) M.180, M.210
Dispatch from Bengal to Fort St George, 27 May 1809 M.351
Dispatches from Robert Farquhar (1811–12) M.487, M.494 (2 vols)
Gilbert and Mary Elliot to Lord Minto, M.83 to M.84 (2 vols)
Elliot of Wells to Lord Minto, M.68
Hopkin's Memoir on the Defence of India (1808) M.333
Letters between Minto and Edmonstone (1809–13) M.358
Letters from Major-General Abercromby and Major-General Warde M.371
Letters from Sir Samuel Auchmuty (1810–12) M.372
Letters from Commodore Broughton and other naval officers regarding Java (1811–12), M.496
Letters from the Earl of Buckinghamshire (1809–13) M.359
Letters from Rear-Admiral Drury (1808–10) M.336
Letters from Jonathan Duncan M.337 (1808–10), M.490 (1811), M.499 (1811–13)
Letters from Robert Dundas to Minto (1807–10) M.172
Letters from Brigadier-General Malcolm (1807–11) M.181 to M.190 (10 vols)
Letters from Archibald Seton to Minto, M.339 (1808–12) and M.504 (1813)
Letters to Minto from the East India Company (1807–12) M.192
Letters to Minto from England (1808–14) M.87
Letters to Minto from Europe (1806–13) M.90 to M.91 (2 vols)
Lady Minto to Lord Minto (1806–13) M.58 to M.61 (4 vols)
Lord Minto to Lady Minto (1806–13) M.33 to M.40 (8 vols)
Minto to the East India Company (1807–13) M.209
Minto to Gilbert Elliot, M.93
Minto to Melville (Robert Dundas) and Buckinghamshire (1810–13) M.377
Minto's Correspondence with England on recall (1811–13) M.497
Miscellaneous letters and reports on Java M.138

Reports and Correspondence about the French Islands (1810) M.365, M.368, M.369 (3 vols)

Boxes

33 boxes of miscellaneous uncatalogued letters, reports, bills and papers

BOX numbers 51–53 (1806); 54–58 (1807); 59–61 (1808); 62–63 (1809); 64–67 (1810); 68–71 (1811); 72–75 (1812); 76–78 (1813); 79–80 (1814); 81–83 (various)

Printed

Bibliographical

A Guide to the Reports on collections of manuscripts of private families, corporations and institutions in Great Britain and Ireland issued by the Historical Manuscript Commission. Part I. Topographical (London, 1914). Part II. Index of Persons (London, 1935)

Foster, W., *A Guide to the India Office Records, 1600–1858* (London, 1919)

Hill S.C., *Catalogue of the Home Miscellaneous Series of the India Office Records* (London, 1927)

Kaye, G.B. and Johnstone, E.H., *Catalogue of Manuscripts in European Languages, India Office Library, Minor Collections and Miscellaneous Manuscripts* (London, 1937), Vol. II, part ii

Contemporary Official Publications, Letters, Memoirs, Periodicals, Histories

Aitchison, C.U., *A Collection of Treaties, Engagements and Sanads Relating to India and Neighbouring Countries* (Calcutta, 1929, 5th edn), Vols I, VII, XIII

Ambrose, R.L., Letter to Edward Parry on the present Crisis of Affairs in India (London, 1807). Tracts, Vol. 69

Asiatic Annual Register 1799–1811 (15 vols)

Brydges, Sir Harford Jones, *An Account of the transactions of His Majesty's Mission to the Court of Persia in the years 1807–11* (London, 1834)

Brydges, Sir Harford Jones, A letter on the present state of British interests and affairs in Persia, addressed to Marquis Wellesley (London, 1838)

Brydges, Sir Harford Jones, The dynasty of the Kajars translated from the original Persian manuscript (London, 1833)

Buckingham and Chandos, Duke of, *Courts and Cabinets of George III*, Vol. IV (London, 1855)

Buckingham and Chandos, Duke of, *Courts and Cabinets under Regency*, 2 vols (London, 1856)

Elphinstone, M., *An Account of the Kingdom of Caubul, and its dependencies in Persia, Tartars, and India* (London, 1839, 3rd edn)

Forster, G., *A journey from Bengal to England through the northern part of India, Kashmire, Afghanistan and Persia, and into Russia by the Caspian Sea* (London, 1798)

Gardane, Alfred de, *Mission du General Gardane en Perse sous le premier empire* (Paris, 1865)

Grant, Charles, Viscount de Vaux, *The History of Mauritius* (London, 1801)

Hansard, Parliamentary Debates, Vols VII and XXI (London, 1812)

Hickey, W., *Memoirs of William Hickey*, Vol. IV, ed. A. Spencer (London, 1925)

Historical Manuscripts Commission, Fortescue V, VIII

Hopkins, D., *The Dangers of British India, from French Invasion and Missionary Establishments* (London, 1809)

Kaye, Sir J.W., *History of the War in Afghanistan*, 2 Vols (London, 1851)

Kaye, Sir J.W., *The Life and Correspondence of Charles, Lord Metcalfe* (London, 1854)

Kaye, Sir J.W., *The Life and Correspondence of Sir John Malcolm*, 2 Vols (London, 1856)

Kaye, Sir J.W., *Selections from the Papers of Lord Metcalfe* (London, 1855)

Malcolm, Sir J., *Sketches of Persia* (London, 1828)

Malcolm, Sir J., *The History of Persia*, 2 Vols (London, 1829)

Malcolm, Sir J., *The Political History of India from 1784 to 1823* (London, 1826)

Martin, R.M., *The Despatches, Minutes and Correspondence of the Marquess Wellesley during his administration in India*, 5 Vols (London, 1836–37)

Minto, the Countess of, *Life and Letters of Sir Gilbert Elliot, 1751 to 1806*, 3 Vols (London, 1874)

Minto, the Countess of, *Lord Minto in India* (London, 1880)

Moorcroft, W. and Trebeck, G., *Travels in the Himalayan provinces of Hindustan and the Punjab from 1819 to 1825*, 2 Vols (London, 1841)

Morier, J., *The Adventures of Hajji Baba of Ispahan in England*, 2 Vols (London, 1828)

Owen, S.J., *A selection from the despatches, treaties and other papers of the marquess Wellesley* (Oxford, 1877)

Parliamentary Papers, House of Commons, 1812, Vol. 6

Punjab Government Records, Vol. II The Ludhiana Agency Records (1808–1815) (Lahore, 1911)

Raffles, Lady Sophia, *Memoir of the Life and Public Services of Sir Thomas Stamford Raffles* (London, 1830)

Raffles, T.S., Substance of a Minute recorded by the Honourable Thomas Stamford Raffles, Lieutenant-Governor of Java and its Dependencies, on the 11th February 1814; on the Introduction of an Improved System of Internal Management and the Establishment of a Land Rental on the Island of Java (London, 1814)

Raffles, T.S., *The History of Java*, 2 Vols (London, 1817)

Reynolds, Rev. J., *Memoir of Sir Gore Ouseley* (London, 1846)

Stockdale, J.J., *Sketches, civil and military; of the Island of Java and its immediate dependencies* (London, 1811)

Sutherland, Captain J., *Sketches of the Relations subsisting between the British Government and the Different Native States* (Calcutta, 1837)

Thompson, J.T., *Translations from the "Hakayit Abdulla"* (London, 1874)

Thorn, Major W., *Memoir of the Conquest of Java* (London, 1815)

Tracts, Vol. 66, Remarks on the Extension of Territory in India subsequent to the Acts of Parliament passed in 1784 and 1793 (London, 1812)

Tracts, Vol. 69, Inquiry into the Feasibility of the supposed Expedition of Buonaparte to the East, by Eyles Irwin (London, 1798)

Tracts, Vol. 109, Review of the Affairs of India from 1798 to 1806 (London, 1807, 2nd edn)

Tracts, Vol. 109, A Dissertation on the Defence of the British Territorial Possessions in Hindostan (London, 1812)

Secondary Sources

Books, Articles and Theses

Allardyce, A., *Scotland and Scotsmen in the 18th Century*, Vol. I (Edinburgh and London, 1838)

Amini, Iradj, *Napoleon and Persia: Franco-Persian Relations under the First Empire* (Washington, DC, 1999)

Auber, F., *Rise and Progress of the British Power in India*, 2 Vols (London, 1837)

Bagchi, A.K., 'Transition from Indian to British Indian Systems of Money and Banking 1800–1850', *Modern Asian Studies*, 19, 3 (1985)

Banerjee, A.C., *The Eastern Frontier of British India, 1784–1826* (Calcutta, 1946, 2nd edn)

Banerjee, A.C., *Anglo-Sikh Relations* (Calcutta, 1949)

Bastin, J., *The Native Policies of Sir Stamford Raffles in Java and Sumatra* (Oxford, 1957)

Bearce, G.D., *British Attitudes towards India 1784–1858* (Oxford, 1961)

Boulger, D.C., *The Life of Sir Stamford Raffles* (London, 1899)

Bowen, H.V., *The Business of Empire: The East India Company and Imperial Britain, 1756–1833* (Cambridge, 2006)

Buckland, C.E., *Dictionary of Indian Biography* (London, 1906)

Bullard, Sir R., *Britain and the Middle East* (London, 1951)

Butterfield, H., *Napoleon* (Great Lives Series) (London, 1939)

Cain, P.J. and Hopkins, A.G., *British Imperialism 1688–2000* (Edinburgh, 2001)

Cambridge History of British Empire, Vol. 2 (Cambridge, 1929–39)

V Cambridge History of India, Vol. V, edited by Dodwell, H.H. (Cambridge, 1929)

vCharles-Roux, F.J.Les origins de l'Expedition d'Egypte (Paris, 1910)

vChaudhuri, K.N. 'Foreign Trade and Balance of Payments (1757-1947)' in D. Kumar (ed) *The Cambridge History of Modern India Volume 2:1757-2003* (Hyderabad, 2005)

Chevalier, E.Histoire de la marine francaise sous le Consulat et l'Empire (Paris, 1886)

V Colebrooke, Sir T.E.Life of Mountstuart Elphinstone, 2 Vols. (London, 1884)

Coupland, R., *Britain and India, 1600–1941* (London, 1942) (pamphlet)

Coupland, R., *Raffles, 1781–1826* (Oxford, 1934, 2nd edn)

Crawfurd, J., 'A Sketch of the Commercial Resources and Monetary and Mercantile System of British India, with Suggestions for their Improvement by means of Banking Establishments' (1837), in K.N. Chaudhuri (ed.), *The Economic Development of India under the East India Company 1814–1858* (Cambridge, 1971)

Crowhurst, P., *The French War on Trade: Privateering 1793–1815* (Aldershot, 1989)

Cunningham, J.D.,*History of the Sikhs* (Calcutta, 1903, reprint of 1st edn)

Curzon, G.N., *Marquis of Kedleston, British Government in India: The Story of the Viceroys and Government Houses*, 2 Vols (London, 1925)

Curzon, G.N., *Persia and the Persian Question*, 2 Vols (London, 1892)

Curzon, G.N., *Frontiers* (Oxford, 1907)

Das Gupta, S.N., 'The Treaty with Banjer Massin, 1812', *Indian Historical Records Commission Proceedings*, XXVI, p. II

Das Gupta, S.N., 'Stamford Raffles and the Gillespie Calumnies', *Indian Historical Records Commission Proceedings*, XXVIII, p. II

Davies, C.C., *An Historical Atlas of the Indian Peninsula* (Oxford, 1959, 2nd edn)

Davies, C.C., *The Problem of the North-West Frontier, 1890–1908* (Cambridge, 1932)

Davis, H.C., 'The Great Game in Asia 1800–1844', *Proceedings of the British Academy*, XII (1926)

Day, C., *The Policy and Administration of the Dutch in Java* (London, 1904)

De Moor, J.A., 'A Very Unpleasant Relationship. Trade and Strategy in the Eastern Seas: Anglo Dutch Relations in the Nineteenth Century from a Colonial Perspective', in J.G.A. Raven and N.A.M. Rodger (eds), *Anglo-Dutch Relationship in War and Peace, 1688–1988* (Edinburgh, 1990)

Dictionary of National Biography (currently known as *Oxford Dictionary of National Biography* updated and republished in 2004)

Egerton, H.E., *Sir Stamford Raffles* (London, 1900)

Fabre, Eugene-Joseph, *La Guerre maritime dans l'Inde sous le Consulat et l'Empire* (Paris, 1883)

Farooqui, A., *Smuggling as Subversion: Colonialism, Indian Merchants, and the Politics of Opium, 1790–1843* (Lanham, MD, 2005)

Farooqui, M.B.A., *British Relations with the cis-Sutlej States, 1809–1823* (Punjab Government Record Office Publications 1941, Monograph 19)

Field, A.G., 'The Expedition to Mauritius in 1810' (MA thesis, London University, 1931)

Freemantle, A.F.,*England in the Nineteenth Century, 1806–1810* (London, 1930)

Fregosi, P., *Dreams of Empire: Napoleon and the First World War 1792–1815* (New York, 1990)

Furnivall, J.S., *Netherlands India: A Study of Plural Economy* (Cambridge, 1939)

Furnivall, J.S., *Colonial Policy and Practice* (Cambridge, 1948)

Glover, M., *Britannia Sickens* (London, 1970)

Gopal, S., *The Viceroyalty of Lord Ripon, 1880–1884* (Oxford, 1953)

Graham, G.S., *Britain in the Indian Ocean. A Study of Maritime Enterprise, 1810–50* (Oxford, 1967)

Greenberg, M., *British Trade and the Opening of China 1800–1842* (Cambridge, 1951)

Griffin, Sir L.H., *The Rajahs of the Punjab* (London, 1873, 2nd edn)

Griffin, Sir L.H., *Ranjit Singh* (Oxford, 1893)

Hall, C.D., *British Strategy in the Napoleonic War 1803–15* (Manchester, 1992)

Hall, D.G.E., *Europe and Burma* (Oxford, 1945)

Hall, D.G.E., *History of South East Asia* (London, 1956)

Harlow, V. and Hadden, F., *Documents on British Colonial Policy 1783–1833* (Oxford, 1953)

Hoskins, H.L., *British Routes to India* (Philadelphia, PA, 1928)

Huttenback, R.A., *British Relations with Sind, 1799–1843* (Berkeley, CA, 1962)

Ilbert, Sir C., *Government of India* (London, 1922)

James, W., *Naval History of Great Britain*, Vol. V (London, 1902)

Kaplan, J., *Elbeuf during the Revolutionary Period: History and Social Structure* (Baltimore, MD, 1964)

Kiernan, V., *Metcalfe's Mission to Lahore* (Punjab Government Record Office Publications 1941, Monograph 21)

Knight, G.R., 'John Palmer and Plantation Development in Western Java in the Early Nineteenth Century', *Bijdragen*, 131, 2/3 (1975), pp. 309–37

Lambrick, H.T., *Sir Charles Napier and Sind* (Oxford, 1952)

Lawrence, J., *Raj: The Making and Unmaking of British India* (New York, 1998)

Lawson, P., *The East India Company: A History* (London, 1993)

Lutun, B., *Les Clauses navales* (Paris, 2005)

Magnus, P., *Edmund Burke* (London, 1939)

Majumdar, R.C., Raychaudhuri, H.C. and Datta, K., *An Advanced History of India* (London, 1946)

Malleson, Colonel G.B., *Final French Struggles in India and on the Indian Seas* (London, 1878)

Marshman, J.C., *Abridgement of the History of India from the Earliest Period to the Present Time* (Edinburgh, 1901)

Mill, J. and Wilson, H.H., *The History of British India*, Vol. III (London, 1844)

Misra, B.B., *The Central Administration of the East India Company 1773–1834* (Manchester, 1959)

Morris, H., *The Life of Charles Grant* (London, 1904)

Neal, L., 'The Financial Crisis of 1825 and the Restructuring of the British Financial System', *Review Federal Reserve Bank of St. Louis Annual Review* (1998)

Norman, C.B., *The Corsairs of France* (London, 1887)

Norris, J.A., *The First Afghan War* (Cambridge, 1967)

Panikkar, K.M., *Asia and Western Dominance* (London, 1954)

Panikkar, K.M., *Problem of Indian Defence* (London, 1960)

Parkinson, C.N., *Trade in the Eastern Seas, 1793–1813* (Cambridge, 1937)

Parkinson, C.N., *War in the Eastern Seas, 1793–1815* (London, 1954)

Peyrefitte, A., *The Immobile Empire: The First Great Collision of East and West – The Astonishing History of Britain's Grand, Ill-fated Expedition to Open China to Western Trade, 1792–94* (New York, 1992)

Philips, C.H., *The East India Company, 1784–1834* (Manchester, 1961)

Prasad, B., *The Foundations of India's Foreign Policy, Vol. 1, 1860–1882* (Calcutta, 1955)

Prasad, B., 'The Trend of India's Foreign Policy in the 19th Century', *Enquiry* (New Delhi), 3 (April 1960)

Prentout, H., *L'Ile de France sous Decaen* (Paris, 1901)

Rainbow, S.G., 'English Expeditions to the Dutch East Indies during the Revolutionary and Napoleonic Wars' (MA thesis, London University, 1933)

Rawlinson, Sir H.,*England and Russia in the East* (London, 1875)

Renier, G.J., *Great Britain and the Establishment of the Kingdom of the Netherlands, 1813–15* (The Hague, 1930)

Richmond, Sir H.,*The Navy in India, 1763–1783* (London, 1931)

Richmond, Sir H.,*Statesmen and Sea Power* (Oxford, 1946)

Roberts, P.E., *India under Wellesley* (London, 1929)

Roberts, P.E., *History of British India under the Company and the Crown* (3rd edn, completed by T.G.P. Spear, London, 1952)

Rodger, N.A.M., *The Command of the Ocean: A Naval History of Britain 1649–1815* (New York, 2005)

Rose, Holland, *Life of Napoleon I* (London, 1934, 8th edn)

Rose, Holland, *The Revolutionary and Napoleonic Era, 1789–1815* (Cambridge, 1935)

Rose, J.H., *Cambridge History of the British Empire*, Vol. 2 (Cambridge, 1929–59).

Seeley, Sir J.H., *The Expansion of England* (London, 1885)

Sen, S.P., *The French in India* (Calcutta, 1958)

Shadman, F., 'The Relations between Britain and Persia, 1800–1815' (PhD thesis, London University, 1939)

Siddiqi, A., 'Money and Prices in the Earlier Stages of Empire: India and Britain 1760–1840', *Indian Economic and Social History Review*, 18, 3–4 (1981)

Siddiqi, A. (ed.), *Trade and Finance in Colonial India 1750–1860* (Delhi, 1995)

Singh, S.K., 'Minto and Goa', *Indian Historical Records Commission Proceedings*, XXIX, p. II

Singh, S.K., 'Minto and the East India Company's Turkish Arabia Affairs', *Indian Historical Records Commission Proceedings*, XXX

Sinha, N.K., *Ranjit Singh* (Calcutta, 1951, 3rd edn)

Smith, V.A., *The Oxford History of India from the Earliest Times to the End of 1911* (Oxford, 1919 and 1958 edns)

Steven-Watson, J.,*The Reign of George III* (Oxford, 1960)

Strachey, Sir J., *India: Its Administration and Progress* (London, 1903)

Swettenham, Sir F., *British Malaya* (London, 1948)

Sykes, Sir P.M., *History of Persia*, 2 Vols (London, 1921, 2nd edn)

Thompson, E., *The Life of Charles, Lord Metcalfe* (London, 1937)

Thompson, E. and Garratt, G.T., *Rise and Fulfilment of British Rule in India* (London, 1934)

Thornton, E., *The History of the British Empire in India*, Vol. IV (London, 1843)

Tolley, B.H., 'The Liverpool Campaign Against the Order in Council and the War of 1812', in J.R. Harris (ed.), *Liverpool and Merseyside Essays in the Economic and Social History of the Port and its Hinterland* (London, 1969), pp. 98–146.

Tregonning, K.G., 'Factors in the Foundation of Penang', *Journal of the Greater India Society*, XVII (1958)

Tripathi, A., *Trade and Finance in Bengal Presidency* (Calcutta, 1956)

Tsang, S., *A Modern History of Hong Kong* (London, 2007)

Vlekke, B.H.H., *Nusantara. A History of the East Indian Archipelago* (Cambridge, MA, 1945)

Vlekke, B.H.H., *The Story of the Dutch East Indies* (Cambridge, MA, 1946)

Ward, Sir A.W. and Gooch, G.F. (eds), *Cambridge History of British Foreign Policy*, Vol. 1 (Cambridge, 1922)

Ward, P., *British Naval Power in the East 1794–1805: The Command of Admiral Peter Rainier* (Woodbridge, 2013)

Watson, R.G., *A History of Persia from the Beginning of the Nineteenth Century to the Year 1858* (London, 1866)

Webster, A., 'The Political Economy of Trade Liberalization: The East India Company Charter Act of 1813', *The Economic History Review*, 43, 3 (1990)

Webster, A., *The Twilight of the East India Company: The Evolution of Anglo-Asian Commerce and Politics 1790–1860* (Woodbridge, 2009)

Webster, C.K., *British Diplomacy, 1813–1815* (London, 1921)

Webster, C.K., *The Foreign Policy of Castlereagh 1812–15* (London, 1931)

Wellington, D.C., *French East India Companies: A Historical Account and Record of Trade* (Lanham, MD, 2006)

Wilson, Sir A.T., *The Persian Gulf* (London, 1939, 3rd impression)

Wint, G., *The British in Asia* (London, 1954)

Wolpert, Stanley, *A New History of India* (Oxford, 2009)

Woodman, D., *The Making of Burma* (London, 1962)

Woodman, R., *The Victory of Seapower. Winning the Napoleonic War 1806–1814* (London, 2005)

Woodruff, P., *The Men Who Ruled India. The Founders* (London, 1953)

Wurtzburg, C.E., *Raffles of the Eastern Isles* (London, 1954)

INDEX

WORLDS OF THE EAST INDIA COMPANY

The Richest East India Merchant: The Life and Business of John Palmer of Calcutta, 1767–1836, Anthony Webster

The Great Uprising in India, 1857–58: Untold Stories, Indian and British, Rosie Llewellyn-Jones

The Twilight of the East India Company: The Evolution of Anglo-Asian Commerce and Politics, 1790–1860, Anthony Webster

Scottish Orientalists and India: The Muir Brothers, Religion, Education and Empire, Avril A. Powell

The East India Company's London Workers: Management of the Warehouse Labourers, 1800–1858, Margaret Makepeace

The East India Company's Maritime Service, 1746–1834: Masters of the Eastern Seas, Jean Sutton

The East India Company and Religion, 1698–1858, Penelope Carson

British Naval Power in the East, 1794–1805: The Command of Admiral Peter Rainier, Peter A. Ward

The Emergence of British Power in India, 1600–1784: A Grand Strategic Interpretation, G. J. Bryant

Naval Resistance to Britain's Growing Power in India, 1660–1800: The Saffron Banner and the Tiger of Mysore, Philip MacDougall

Trade and Empire in Early Nineteenth-Century Southeast Asia: Gillian Maclaine and his Business Network, G. Roger Knight

Lascars and Indian Ocean Seafaring, 1780–1860: Shipboard Life, Unrest and Mutiny, Aaron Jaffer